Julia – ex-Snowdon
with best wishes
Peter Susie Barrett

Wandering & Wondering in Wales

with artist & writer

PETER & SUSAN BARRETT

Wandering & Wondering in Wales

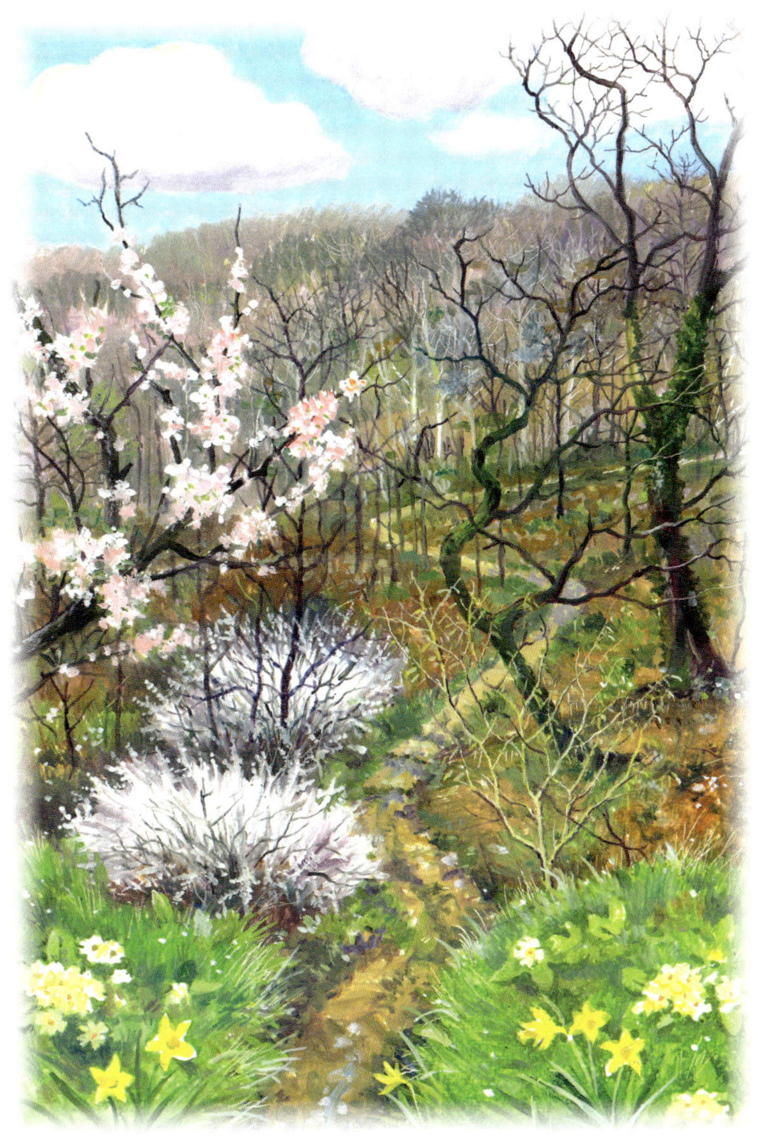

with artist & writer
PETER & SUSAN BARRETT

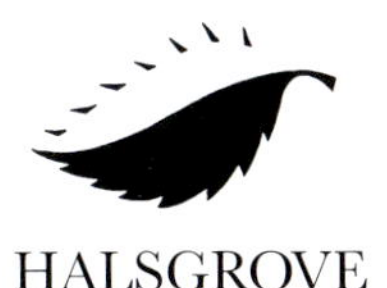

HALSGROVE

In memory of our friend Gareth Weekes

Published in 2024

A CIP catalogue record for this book is available from the British Library.

ISBN: 978 0 85704 374 0

Halsgrove
Halsgrove House,
Ryelands Business Park,
Bagley Road, Wellington,
Somerset TA21 9PZ
Tel: 01823 653777
Fax: 01823 216796
email: sales@halsgrove.com

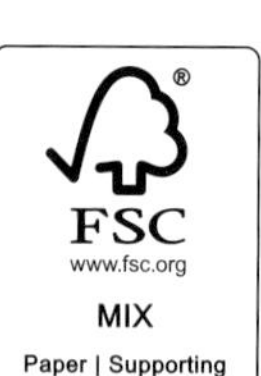

Part of the Halsgrove group of companies
Information on all Halsgrove titles is available at: www.halsgrove.com

Printed and bound in India by Nutech Print Services - India

Contents

The Start 6

1. February and March in the borderlands 8

2. March and April in the south 32

3. April and May in the southwest 58

4. June in the north 90

5. July and September in mid Wales 128

Homeward bound 158

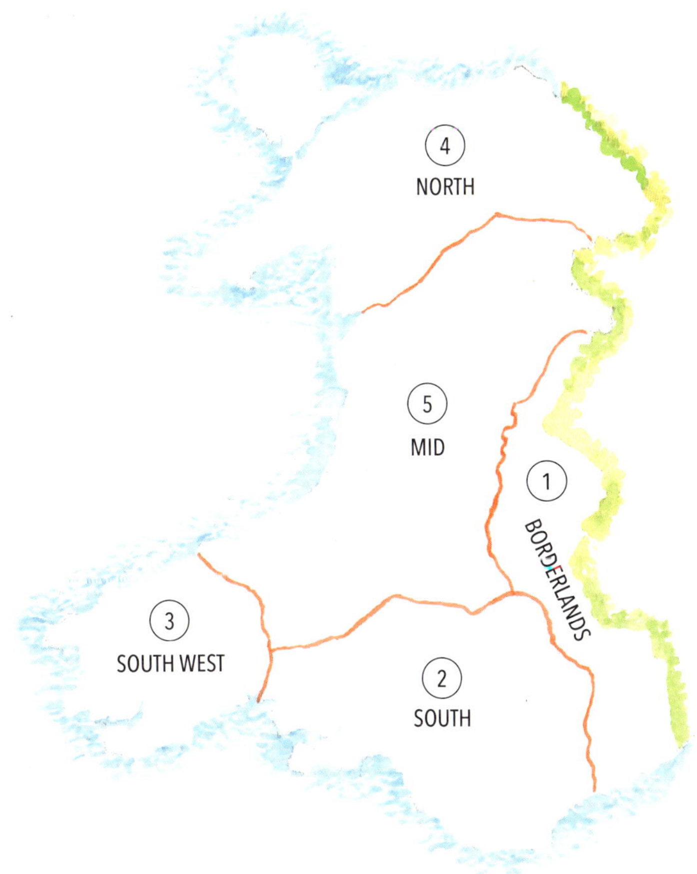

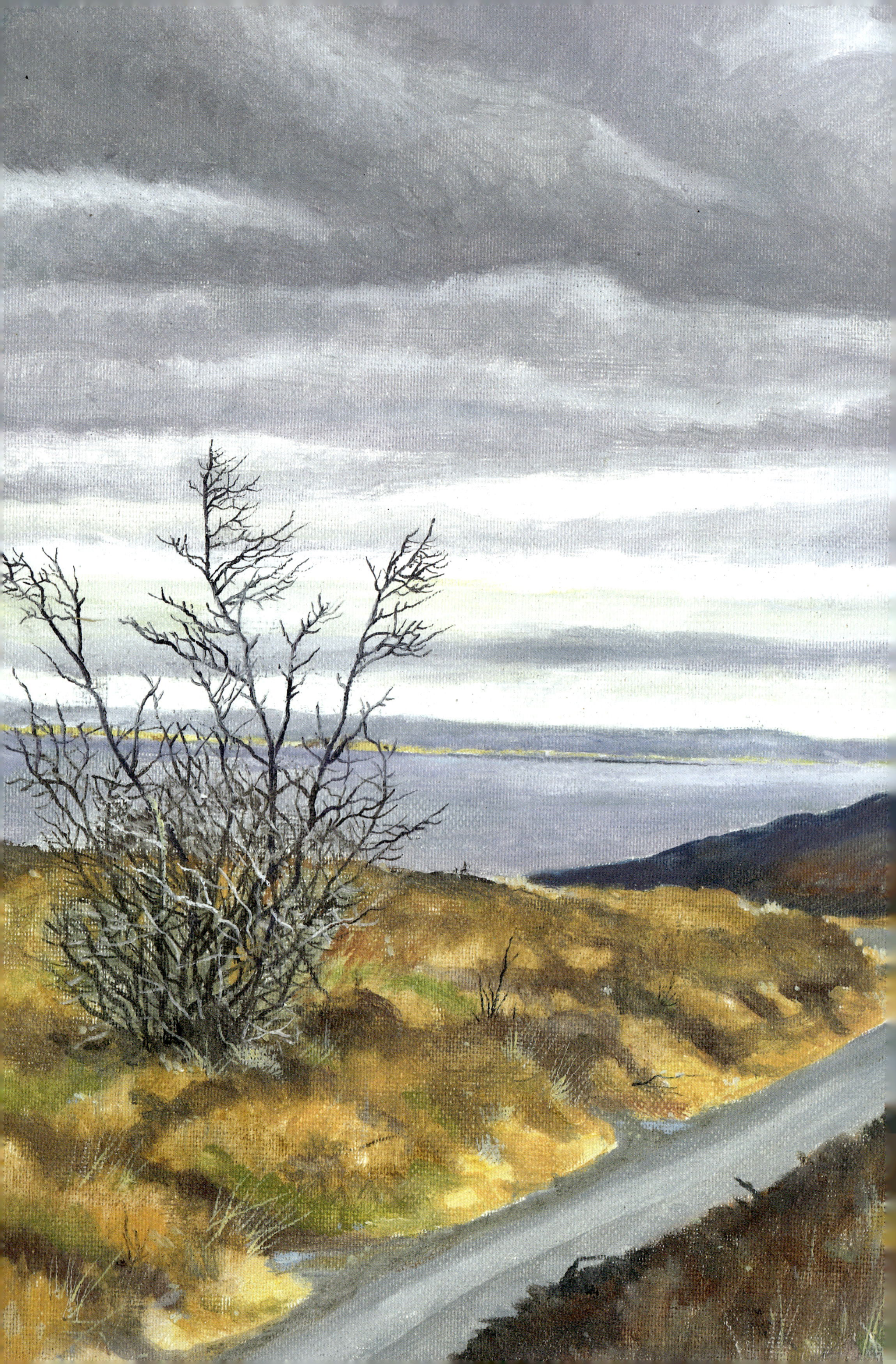

The Start

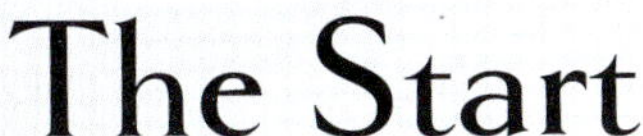

From a high point near our home on the borders of Devon and Somerset in the southwest of England, we can see Wales. Today, in the January sunshine, a shining band of white is visible on the far side of the grey Bristol Channel. We wonder what Welsh town this might be, so far away yet seeming so close. We plan to find out.

During the sixty-three years of our marriage, we've worked independently, Peter as an artist and I as a writer. We've also produced books together, the results of the notes and sketches we've made while spending time in various parts of the world, mainly America, Greece, and New Zealand. No longer do we want to go so far afield. We'll take our notebooks and sketchbooks to Wales, the country on our doorstep.

South Wales coast seen from Exmoor.

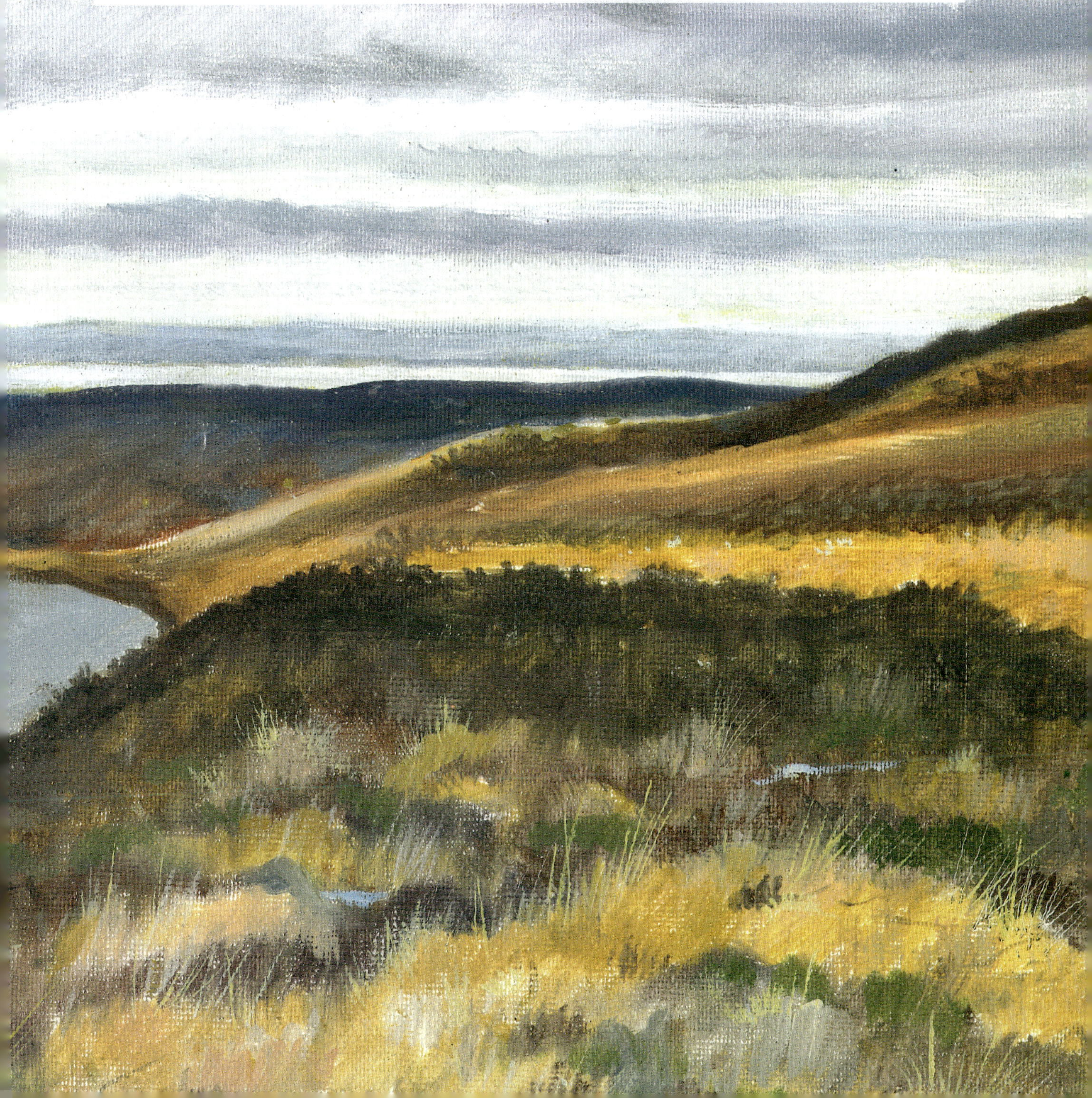

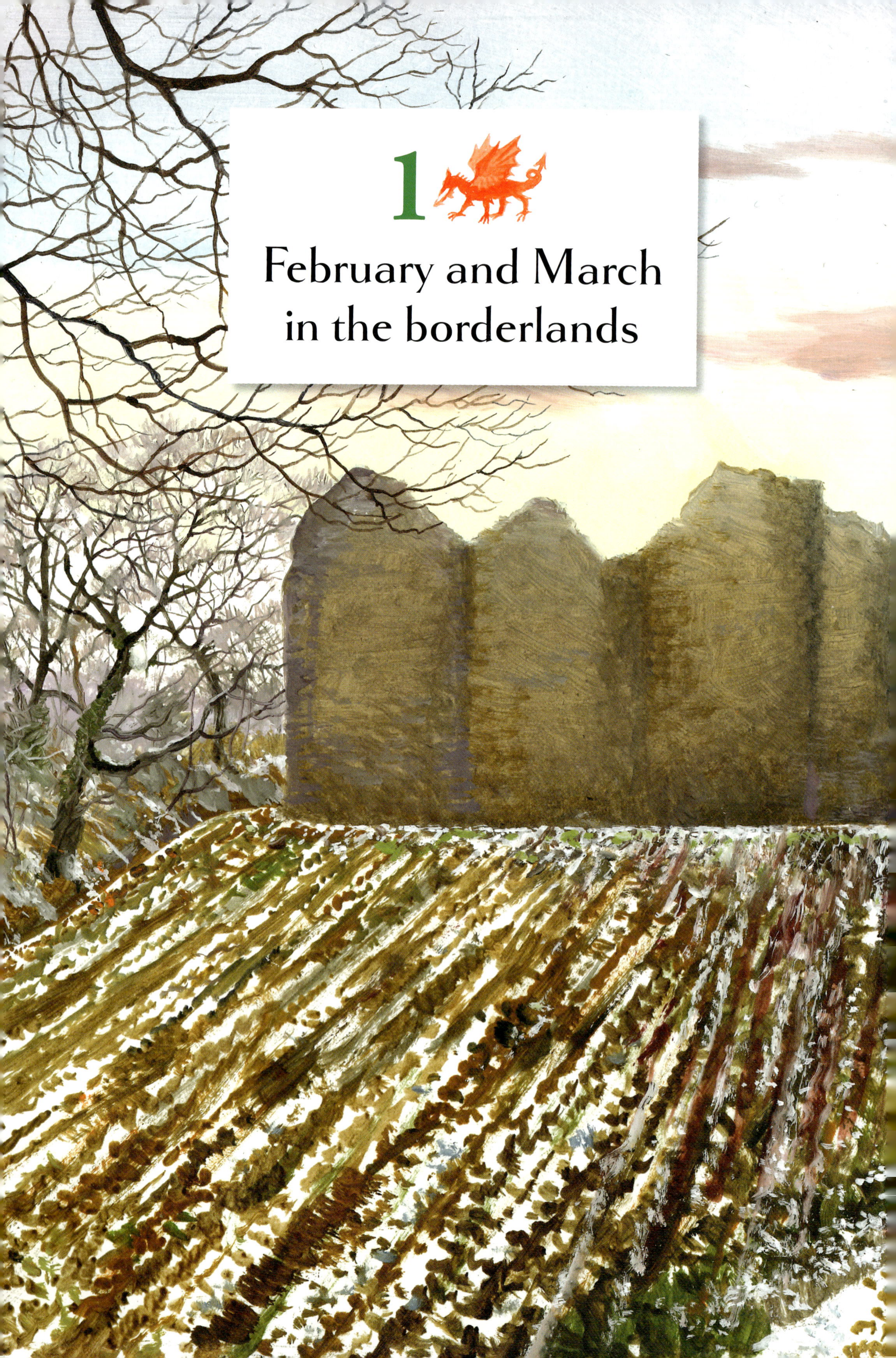

1 February and March in the borderlands

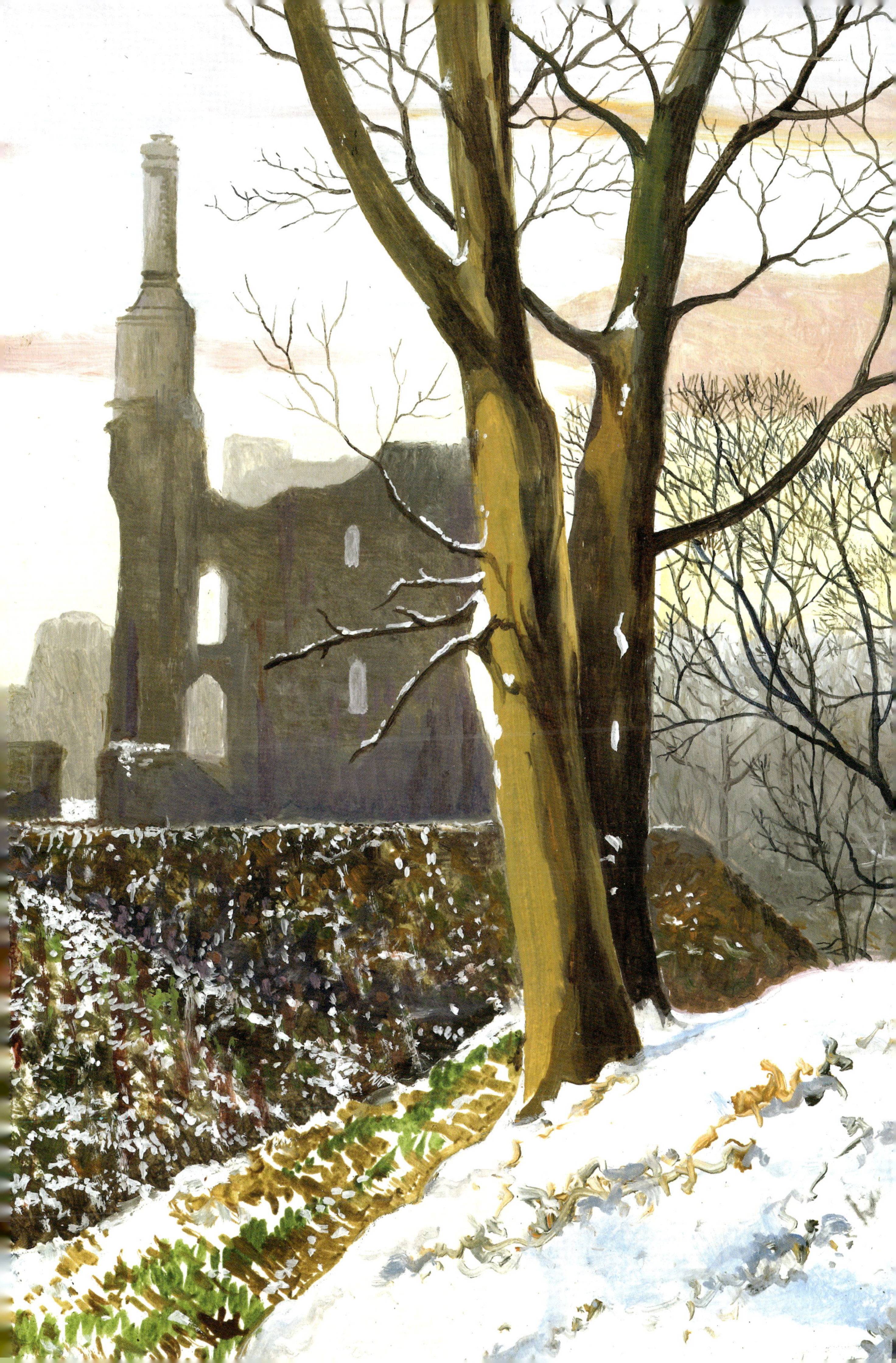

February and March in the borderlands

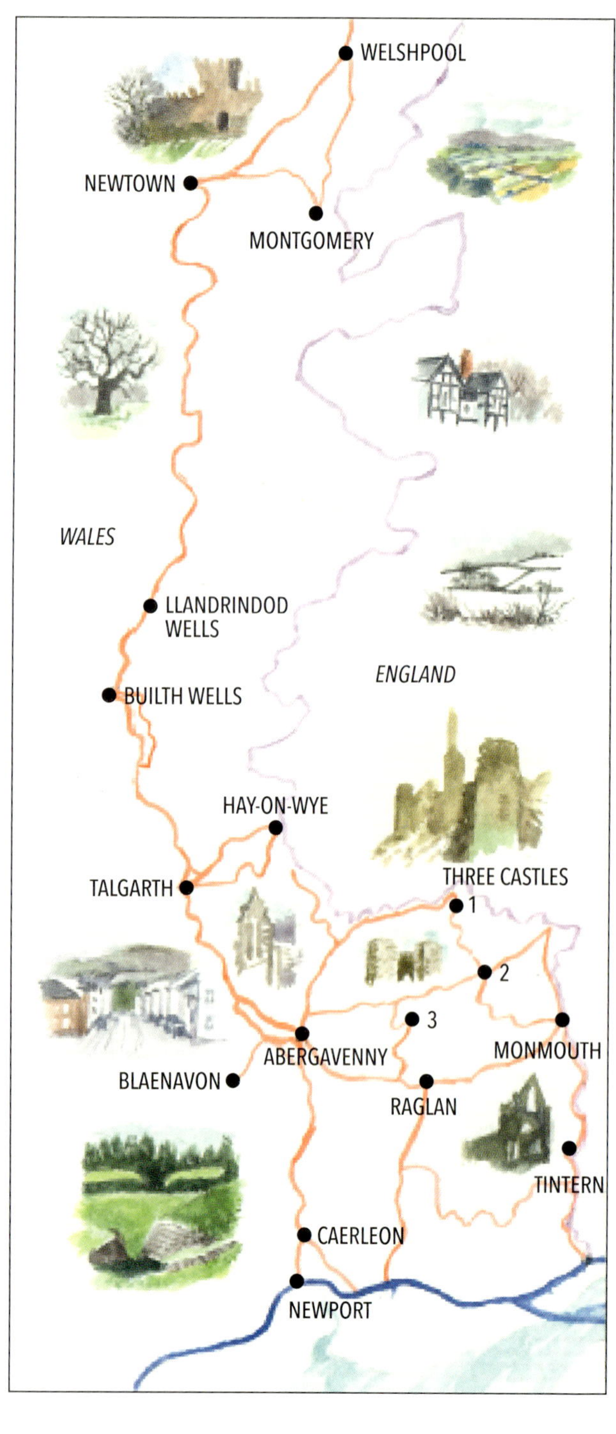

Caerleon

Musical chimes break the deep silence of Caerleon's Roman amphitheatre. Twelve o'clock is striking somewhere in the town. The steady toll emphasises the theatre's silence. Grass-covered mounds at intervals around the vast lawn of the stage mark the tiers of stone seats. The place is deserted. I lean on my stick and wonder. Who sat in this theatre? What did they watch? What were the plays and displays? Were the performances only for the occupying Romans or could the Welsh locals come to marvel at the actors, watch enactments of battles, witness gladiator fights, listen to the language of the occupiers, become indoctrinated in the Roman way of life?

In the distance, four people appear at the entrance from the town. They slowly make their way towards the theatre and then go down one of the entrances onto the stage. One of the four is acting as guide. She sounds like a patient, pleasant schoolteacher. As the group come to a halt in the centre of the stage, I'm reminded how actors' voices are clearly audible by everyone in an amphitheatre wherever they sit, something I learnt in the early 1960s in the ancient ruins of sunbaked Greece.

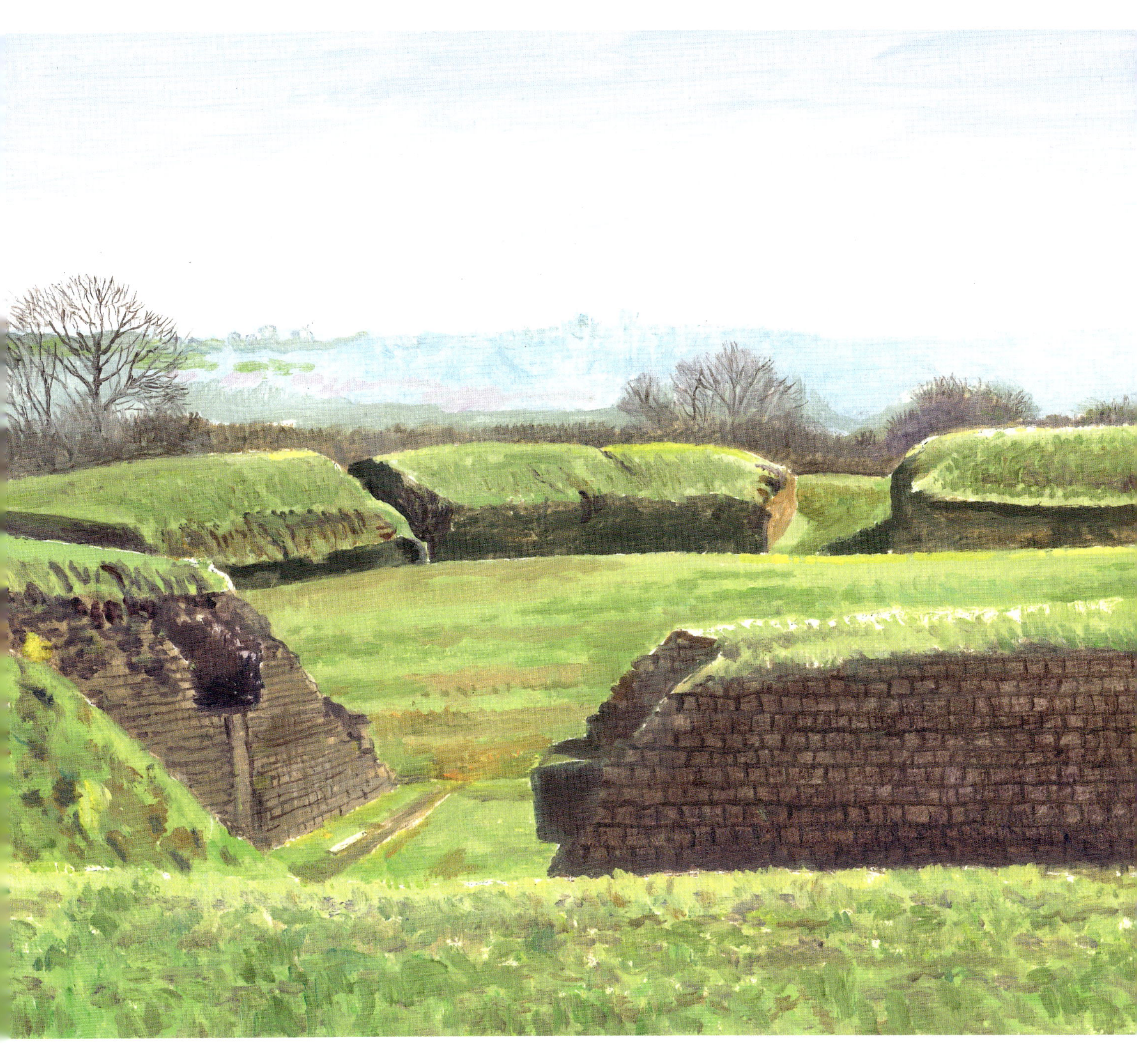

Amphitheatre, Caerleon

The tiers of stone seats in Caerleon's Roman amphitheatre slumber beneath a smooth, green blanket of grass. Only the audience is missing.

Past and present mingle. Peter spent part of his early boyhood in Wales. His father, an accountant with the Army and Navy Stores, had been drafted into the Ministry of Food which was moved to North Wales in 1940. Here Peter's preference for a quiet, rural life had its origin. Today he's found a ramshackle farmyard on the far side of the amphitheatre's boundary. He's engrossed in watching two calves who are, in turn, watching him. We are on our first exploratory trip, learning if our planned book on Wales is something we can still do.

We've already learnt our first lesson. If you ever see a small, blue car wandering around a major roundabout, think of us. We read signs very slowly if we can spot them at all. Unknown ways through unknown towns test us to and beyond our limits.

That first day we decided to delete Newport and its Transporter Bridge from our plan. Instead, we'd go north from Caerleon to find the next goal on our list: the Big Pit at Blaenavon.

We got hopelessly lost in the town, defeated by a number of closed roads. Our enthusiasm for The Book and our wish to find the museum, the Big Pit or whatever else Blaenavon has to offer was waning to the point of vanishing altogether. Food was the answer. We parked off a steep street of tightly-terraced houses in order to eat our picnic lunch. I wanted to gaze and wonder at the street's stacked houses, two at each step down, but the car park was bounded by a tall, grey stone wall and the side of a newish building. What about eating our picnic lunch at the nice place we passed on our way here? We'd find our way back eastwards across the end of the high ridge reminiscent of the moorland of Somerset's Quantock Hills and Exmoor. So, we put the picnic basket back in the boot and left Blaenavon, feeling a mixture of relief and remorse.

We ate our sandwiches by a pond which reflected the blue sky. The temperature on the high moor was close to freezing. From the warmth of the car, I could see a sign by the pond. I should get out and read it. But I didn't. I began planning quite a different sort of book about Wales, one that required only indoor research. Eating, Drinking and Sleeping in Wales would be the new title. You may hold images of places in your head, based on photographs and other people's descriptions. The reality can come as a surprise.

Being for the first time in a mining town and seeing the terraced houses of Blaenavon, I was struck by the generous size of the windows. The rooms inside could not possibly be as dark and pokey as I'd imagined. Later, Kate, a graduate with a degree in Politics, Philosophy and Economics, corrected my impression. "The ground floor windows may look large but in the old days no-one ever sat in the front room. All the life of the household took place in the tiny, dark, back room." Her uncle and aunt still live in one of the miners' houses now owned by the council. As a child she often visited them and still does. Out in the countryside, she has recently overseen the building of luxurious, ensuite rooms for the diners who enjoy her chef husband's five-star meals, leaving them so well wined and dined they are unfit to drive home.

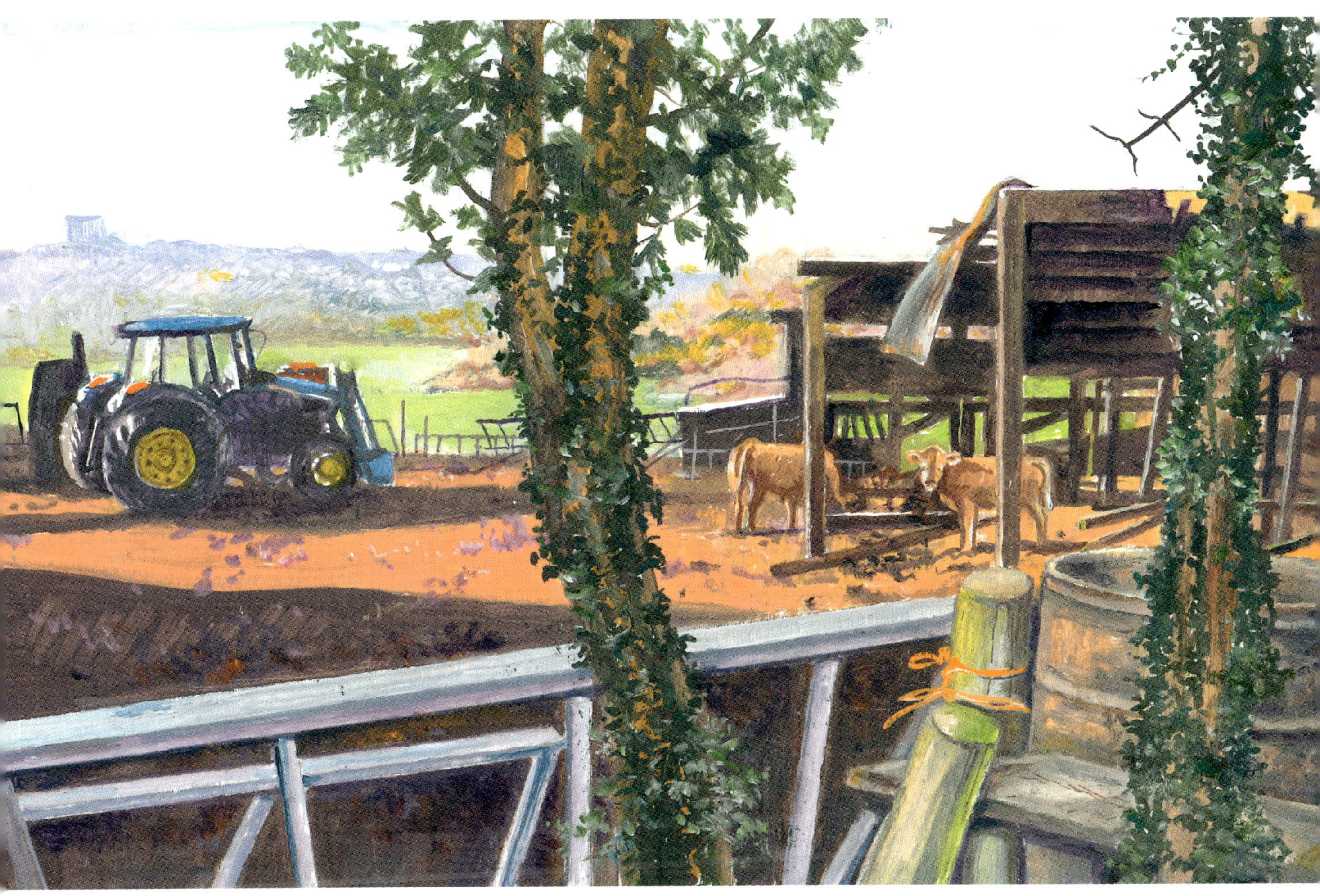

Farmyard beside Caerleon amphitheatre

From the far side of a fence, calves exchange appraising stares with present day visitors to Caerleon's ruined amphitheatre. In Roman times as many as 6000 legionnaires would watch the fights of gladiators in the arena.

The experience of comfort and good food sits alongside the recollection of a Welsh mining valley's disaster fifty-seven years ago. On October 21st, 1966, in the village of Aberfan, at the start of the school day and after a period of continuously heavy rain, waste tip Number 7 slid down the hillside to engulf Pantglas Junior School and 19 terraced houses in black slurry. 144 people died as a result of being buried alive. One hundred and sixteen of these were young children, eagerly awaiting half-term. Local people had long warned that the tip was sited dangerously close to the village.

On February 6th, 2023, earthquakes and aftershocks on the Turkish-Syrian border brought down a huge number of tall apartment blocks, which had been built with scant regard for regulations. The count of the dead was still continuing at the end of the month. The number had reached 49,495 people. "In the midst of life we are in death," says the Book of Common Prayer.

Tintern

Freezing fog has rimed the tops of trees, turning each twig into a frosted delicacy against the sky. The valley is wrapped in a grey blanket of silence. There is no-one around. A small rowing boat lies tipped sideways on the riverbank. It looks off-duty. We're in a peaceful haven, seemingly uninhabited. Calm, content.

"The world is too much with us.

Getting and spending we lay waste our powers"...

These lines from Wordsworth's "Recollections of Early Childhood" haunted me yesterday as we struggled in traffic. Today I am thinking of lines he'd composed a few years earlier. The date is recorded in the title of the poem: July 13th, 1798. He'd climbed to a point on the wooded hillside above the Abbey. This was his second visit to Tintern and in the poem he reflected on the difference between his past and present responses to the scene.

The first time I visited Tintern was with my parents. They'd driven me from Devon to stay with my school friend Sheena in Hereford. We were on our way home and I was in floods of tears at being torn away from my school friend's elder brother with whom I'd become hopelessly in love. He went around the house singing *"If you knew Susie like I know Susie."* I was just sixteen and pretending as hard as I could that the song had nothing to do with me while earnestly hoping it had everything to do with me. We hadn't even brushed hands. In 1954 I could barely see the Abbey through a veil of tears.

On February 8th, 2023, the sun is making its presence felt behind the fog. The ruined abbey stands out against the opalescent sky like a black stencil. A great tit sings lustily in a tree, insisting on its two-tone argument. A wood pigeon takes over, sounding like a gossiping villager.

"And then this happened and that happened, would you believe it? No, would you."

The pigeon is a Welsh storyteller, without a doubt. He tells an old story, true or maybe not. Fact and fiction, history and legend, merge in Wales like the present and the past. Even the boundary between England and Wales weaves in and out, unlike the ruler-straight lines the Victorians drew on maps of Africa. Here in Tintern, the boundary lies in the middle of the River Wye. You can't get more fluid than that.

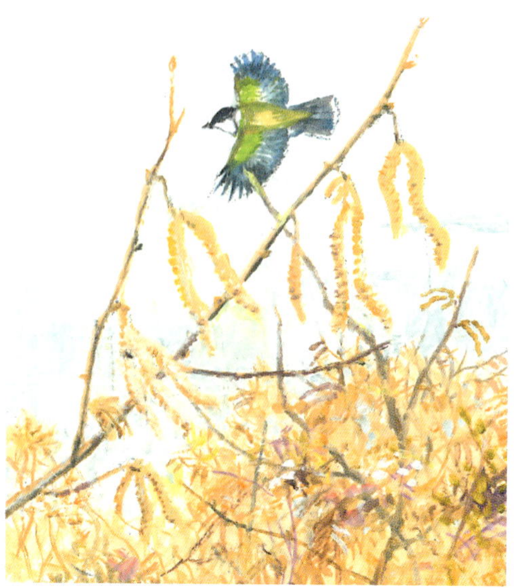

Great tit and catkins

Dangling clusters of hazel flowers form the backdrop to a great tit's two-tone insistence that spring has arrived.

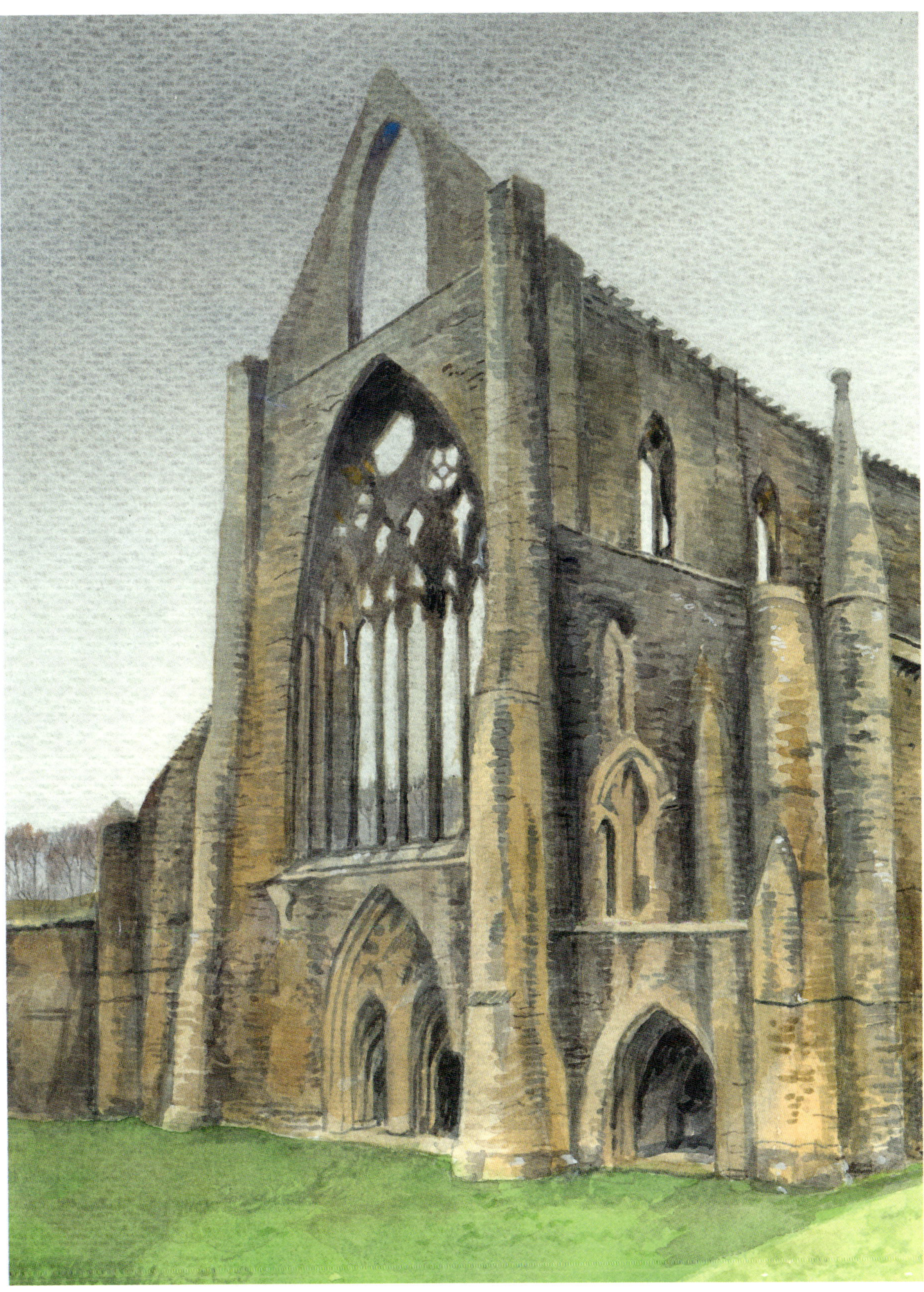

Tintern Abbey

A monastery was built on the Welsh bank of the River Wye at Tintern in the 12th century, It was founded by the Cistercians, an order which adopted the Rule of St Benedict. Their monasteries should be built "in places remote from the conversation of men." The monks would pray while lay brothers worked. Peace and quiet reigned for 400 years. After the Dissolution of the Monasteries, the abbey fell into ruin, creating a scene that has attracted poets and painters including Wordsworth and Turner, besides thousands of visitors from across the world – 70,000 a year by the twenty-first century. Yet still the peaceful atmosphere prevails.

A Cornish friend called David has lent us a small book: *Welsh Without Worry*. This is what we need. We certainly don't want to worry and yet we would like to learn a little everyday Welsh. We practise as we drive. David's book tells us how to pronounce a double 'll'. You lay your tongue behind your front teeth and send your breath out sharply. This sounds like a river flowing either side of a midstream boulder. Llandovery, we say to each other, Llandrindod, Llandegfedd. We've pretty well mastered the double l but now we remember that a 'w' makes an 'oo' sound. Or is it an 'uh'? Or is 'uh' the sound a 'y' makes? We tie ourselves in knots over long place names in much the same way as yesterday at a roundabout when we became the boulder in a stream of traffic.

To hear what Welsh sounds like, I've watched a video of a red-haired young woman reciting a poem. I've polished my description. The language is like a stream running through boggy moorland.

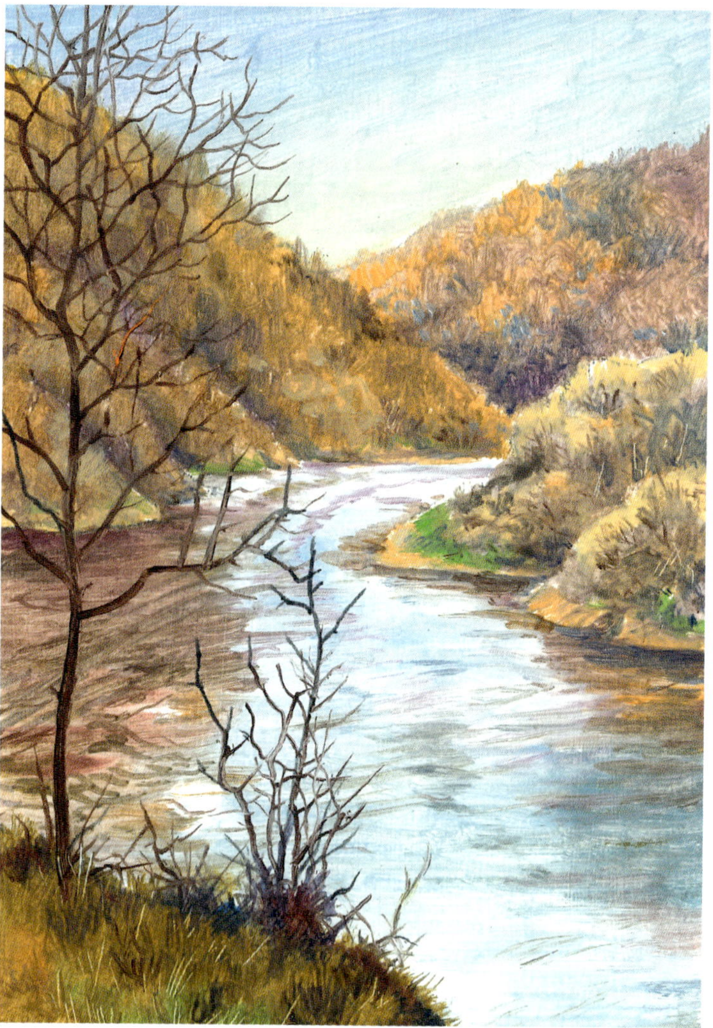

River Wye

The Wye runs for 165 miles from its source high in mid Wales to the Severn estuary, forming in its lower reaches the boundary between Wales and England. In medieval times the river was known by the Latin word for wandering, 'vaga'. In his poem written above Tintern Abbey, Wordsworth called the river "the wanderer through the woods". The Wye Valley has been designated an Area of Outstanding Natural Beauty while, to our generation's shame, the river has become one of the most polluted in the United Kingdom.

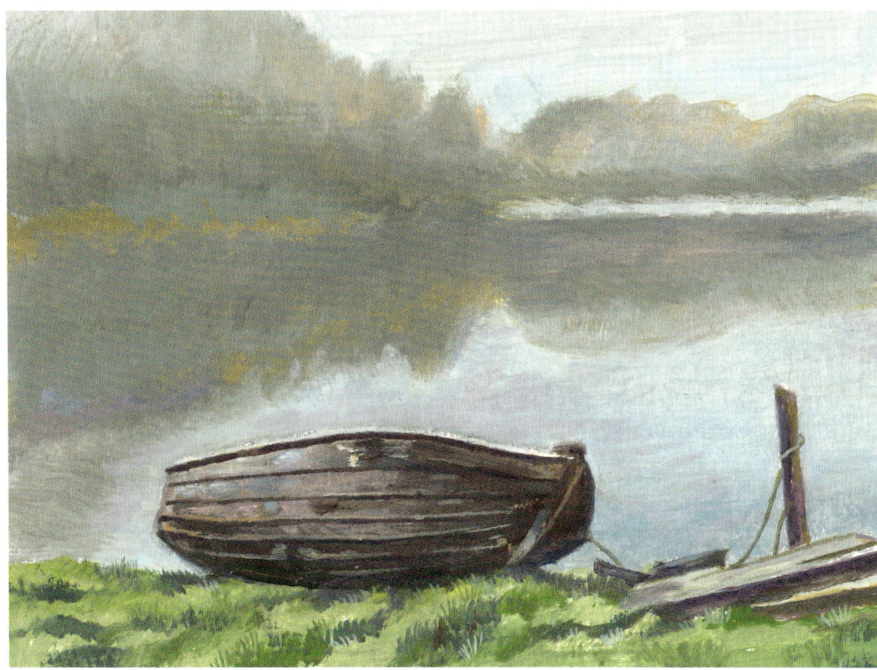

A rowing boat lies on its side on the Welsh bank of the River Wye.

A rowing boat lies upturned on the Welsh bank of the River Wye at Tintern. Early morning mist swathes the trees on the far English bank. The boundary between Wales and England lies in mid stream.

Skenfrith and The White Castle

The Normans, I've learnt, built 600 earth and timber castles in the first forty years after the Conquest, three of these in the region known as the Welsh Marches. The title derives from an ancient Celtic word, *mereg*, meaning boundary. It can also refer to the counties on the English side of the border: Cheshire, Shropshire, Herefordshire, Worcestershire, and Gloucestershire. We will keep our eye on the jagged line of the boundary and stay in Wales, for the sake of this book.

In Monmouth we look briefly at the tower on the Welsh side of the bridge across the Wye but yesterday's reluctance to tangle with towns returns. Instead, we'll find a few of the many castles built as strongholds by the incoming Normans against the wild Welsh. We have a castle known as the White Castle in our sights. We plunge off northwards from the town.

Out in the gentle countryside our spirits revive but we are soon flummoxed by signs – or lack of them. We are reminded of our wartime childhoods when all place signs in Britain were removed to mystify any invading Germans. Maybe the present-day Welsh wish to keep visitors similarly confused.

There are many compensations in being lost. In the middle of what seems like nowhere, we cross a stone bridge over a river. On our right we glimpse the earth-red ruins of a castle. We discover this is Skenfrith which with Grosmont and the White Castle are known, prosaically enough, as the Three Castles. We wander around the ruins and the village; in fact, we almost tiptoe, not wanting to disturb in any way the place's intense tranquility. The only sign of life comes from someone putting out her dustbin. "Yes," she says, "we're lucky to live here." As for us, we're lucky to be here in winter. In summer this would be a very different place. Were I a villager, I'd certainly be tempted to build a stronghold against modern-day invaders.

In the Iron Age they built forts with spiked wooden palisades against marauders. The Romans and, later, the Normans replaced Celtic wooden structures with stone. Skenfrith's ruined walls reveal the techniques of thirteenth-century builders. Will today's buildings last as long?

Determined to find the White Castle, we drive on along miles of narrow lanes through hilly, farmed landscape. Catkins dangle from hazel trees, promising spring and more visitors. A red mail van is the only other vehicle we meet in an hour. The postman knows his territory so well he is not at all sure how best to direct us. The daily negotiation of his round is so automatic that it takes him time and a wrinkled brow to work out the number of turnings we should take left or right. this way or that. In the end we drive three sides of a long oblong to reach the castle. Summer visitors will surely have Satnav and no trouble.

We eat our lunch in the small car park between the castle grounds and a path leading to Offa's Dyk**e.** A young woman with a baby in a sling on her back and a white dog scampering hither and thither at her feet are the only other visitors. She's a brisk, solitary walker from one of the few houses nearby.

The Dyke formed the boundary between England and Wales over many centuries. Although it is named after Offa, who was the Anglo-Saxon king of Mercia between AD 757 and 796, it had earlier origins. In AD 369 a Roman historian mentioned the emperor Septimus Severus "who built a wall for 133 miles from sea to sea." The present walk along Offa's Dyke is 82 miles long, 133 kilometres. I wonder if the Romans measured distance in miles or kilometres or another unit of measurement entirely. Shepherds in Greece used to talk of places being a number of cigarettes away.

The White Castle on its hilltop is greedy of space but, I'm relieved to see, it's close to the car park. It's spread over three fortified areas. With its tall, round towers pierced by narrow slits for shooting arrows, portcullises, and drawbridges over deep moats, it would have been extremely difficult to assault. I try to imagine how the Celts from the surrounding countryside might have gone about an attack. Their best course of action, I decided, was to lay siege. Even if the invaders had laid up great stocks of food, cereals, and meat, both live and salted, there would be a time limit to their supplies. As I ate my sandwich I tussled over the business of invasion and defence. Invaders have to be defenders, too. And vice versa. In Ukraine, Putin's army has to defend the territory it has invaded. Here in the border country the invaders had to defend themselves against the locals who got on with their lives while defending their land by attacking the invaders. I thought of the two fists of a boxer: attack and defence in swift succession.

From the White Castle, we continued to Raglan, a favourite castle from a previous visit. But we arrived within half an hour of closing time. The advantage of visiting Wales in the winter is the lack of crowds. The disadvantage: short days and the possibility of bad weather.

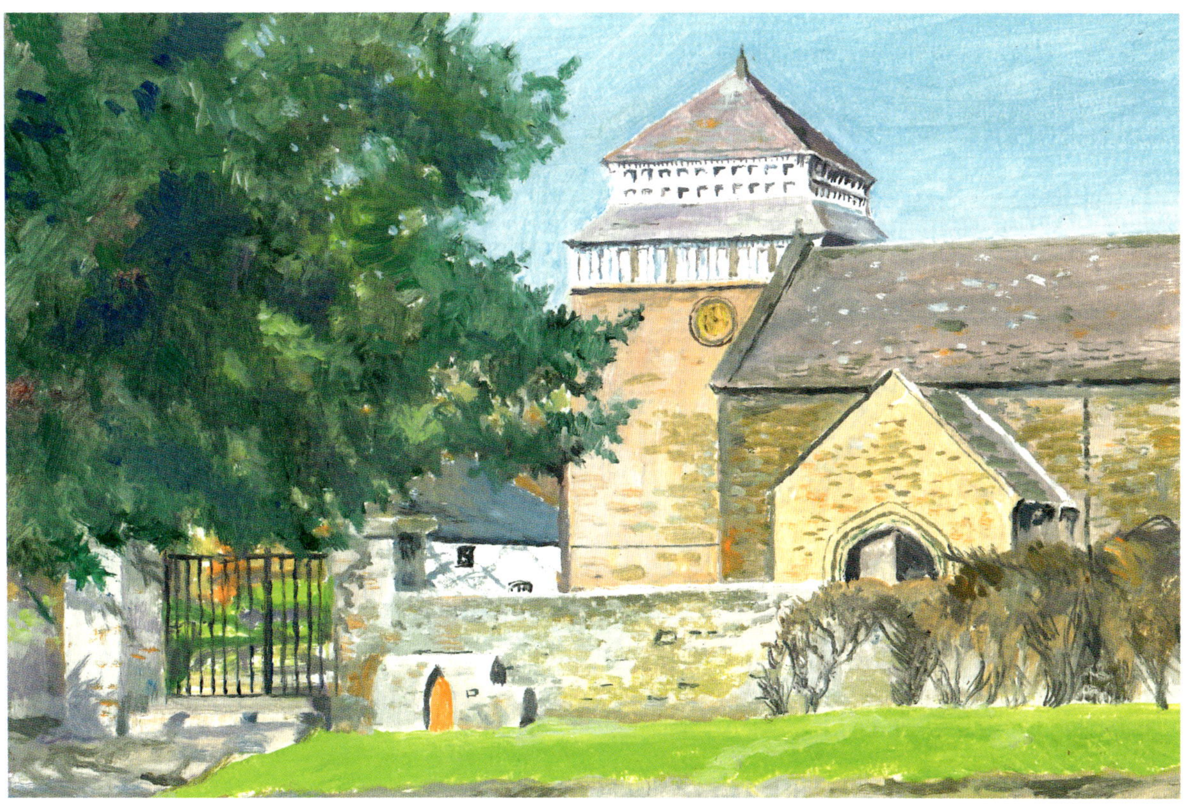

Skenfrith church

Skenfrith's church stands beside the ruins of the castle. Its unusual tower dominates the cluster of village houses as though keeping watch over the inhabitants. Birds chirping in the trees emphasise the intense quiet.

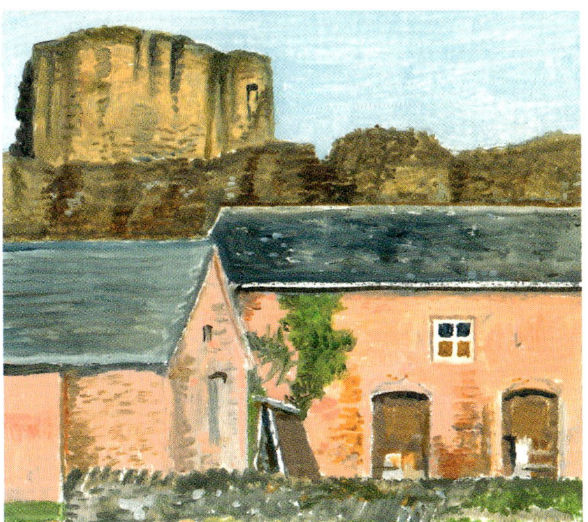

Skenfrith Castle walls

After a castle falls into ruin, it becomes useful building material, even providing ready-built walls for "lean-to" houses and store rooms as at Skenfrith.

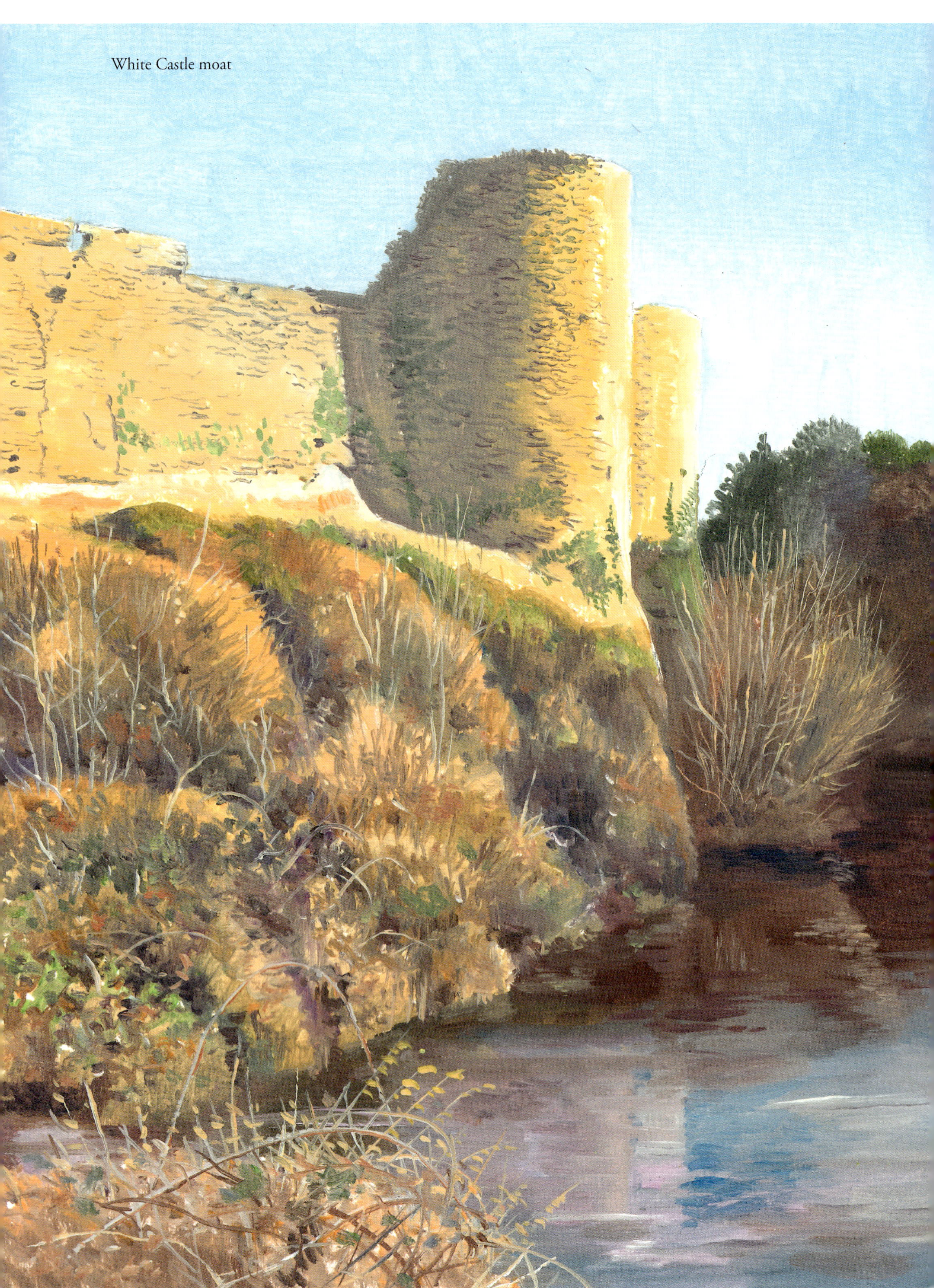

White Castle moat

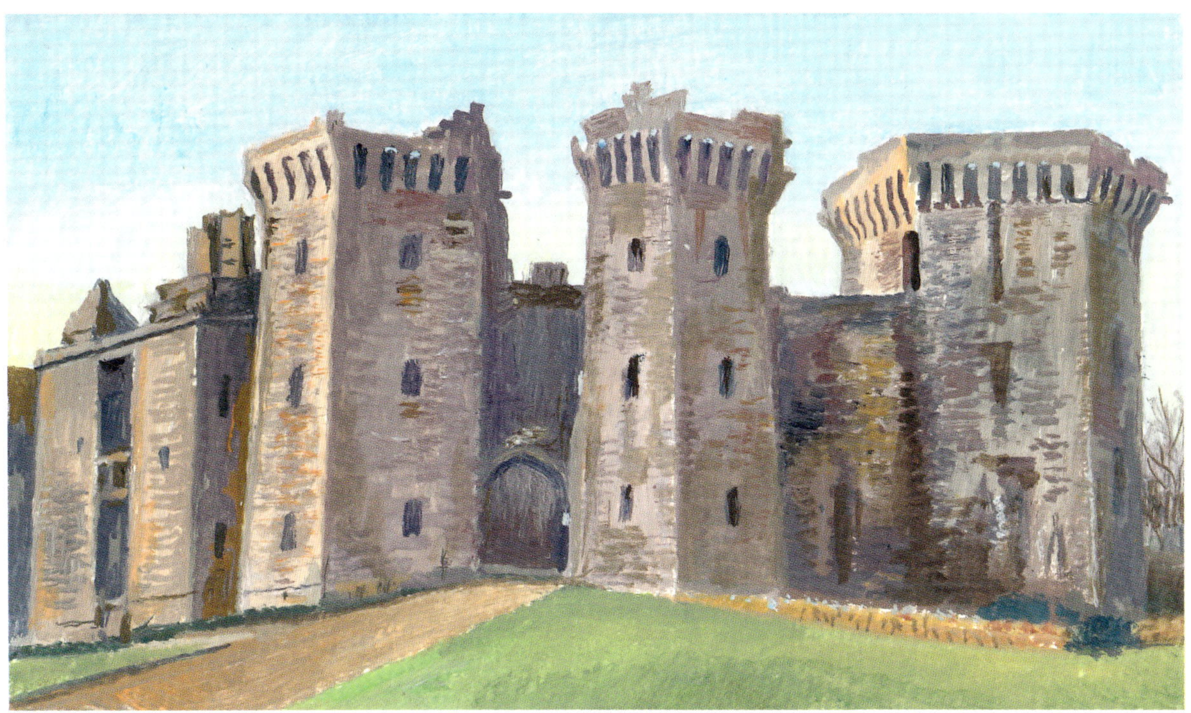

Raglan Castle

Today's ruins are the remains of the fifteenth century castle built on an earlier Norman fortification by Sir William ap Herbert, a Welshman. His descendants continued to extend and embellish the castle. Its heyday came to an end in the Civil War. In 1642 its Royalist-supporting owner. Henry Somerset, the 5th Earl of Worcester, held the castle against besieging Parliamentarians before finally capitulating. The long process of decay began.

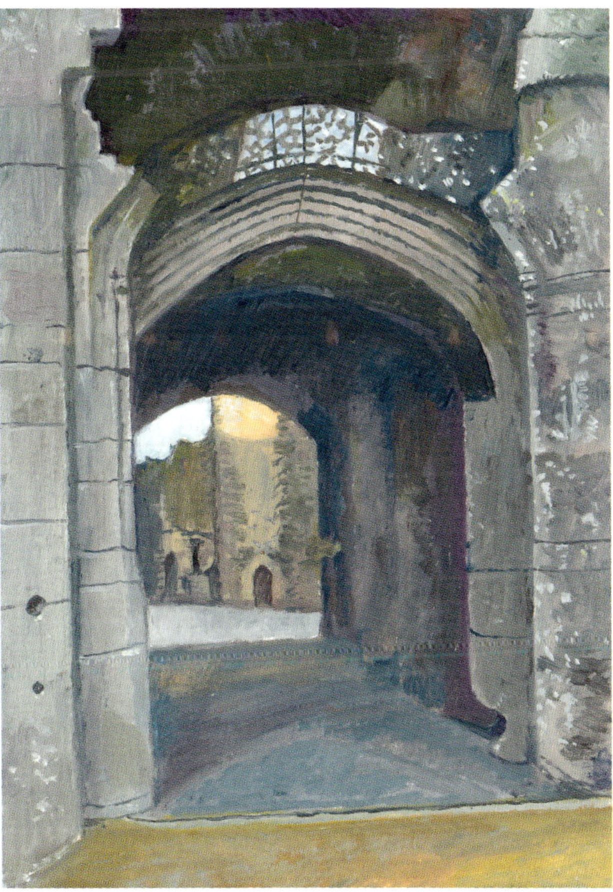

Raglan Castle archways

The Black Mountain

On another day in March there was snow lying on the Sugar Loaf, one of the higher points of the Black Mountain which is over 2300 feet high. Snowdon, which we'll visit later in the year, is 3560 ft above sea level. I think of Papingo, a village in the Pindos mountains of Greece where we lived for a while. It lies at a height of 3143 feet above sea level. Even there in the warmer south of Europe, the villagers used to leave for the winter before central heating made life more comfortable. My mind turns to our friend Jennie who lived with us on a Greek island and has read my work with a sharp eye open for mistyping. She did the same for Bruce Chatwin, a brilliant writer. His *On the Black Hill* was set in this area and I've just ordered it to re-read. Jennie lives in Talgarth in the summer months but in India in the winter, so we bypassed the town and took a detour to eat our picnic lunch on the banks of the Edw river. A footpath led across a field below a wooded hill, a lovely, tranquil scene but it was cold. Our collapsible chairs remained in the boot and we sat in the car.

In Llandrindod Wells we warmed up in the Aspidistra Café, a welcome find with a bright spark of a waitress called Karen, thin and tall as a telegraph pole. Originally from north London she didn't bother with the letters t and g. Everyone was *darlin'*. Net curtains covered the lower half of the cafe's windows. The back of each chair held a horseshoe of padded velvet in a dusky pink matching the paint on the wooden panelling waist-high on the walls. We might have been whisked back to the 1930s. What with the warmth of Karen and the food and drink, it was hard to leave. However, our appetite for discovery returned on the next stretch of road. The A483 north to Newtown is a pleasure to follow, a winding road through gentle countryside.

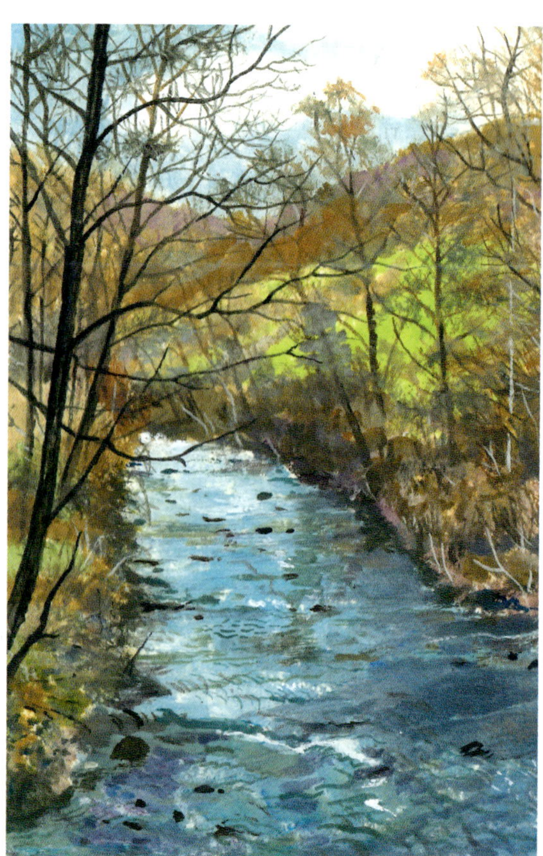

River Edw

The River Edw flows from Cregrina to join the Wye below Aberedw. Its 9-mile length provides homes for trout and the trout provide sport for fishermen.

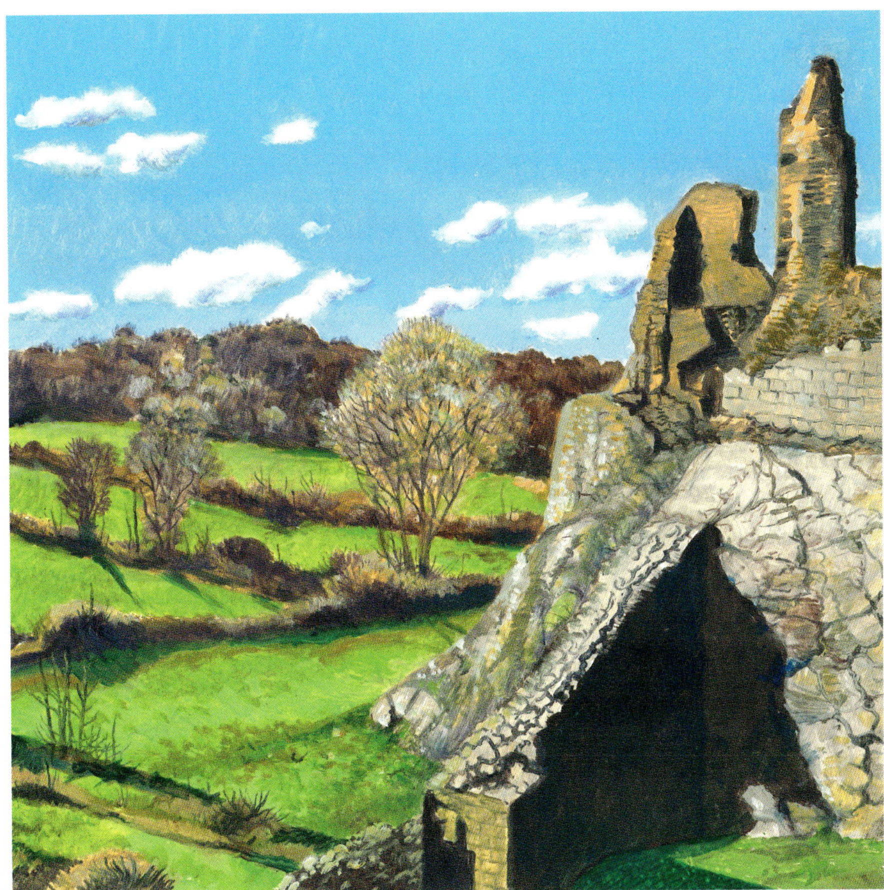

Montgomery Castle
The rocky hill rising behind the present village of Montgomery attracted the attention of one of Henry III's advisers. He considered it would make a suitable site for an impregnable castle to replace the nearby motte and bailey fortification built in the 1070s by Roger de Montgomery, the Earl of Shrewsbury. The stone castle was designed by Hubert de Burgh who also rebuilt the White Castle and the castles at Skenfrith and Grosmont in the same period of the thirteenth century.

Montgomery, Garthmyl and Powys Castle

Approaching the border village of Montgomery, we caught a glimpse of the ruins of the castle rising above the bare treetops on an outcrop of craggy rock. It is hard to imagine how the thirteenth-century stone masons managed to build its outer walls on the rim of the precipitous, rocky pinnacle. They did the job well. The lower portions of the massively thick walls still stand.

From inside the castle, it is possible to survey the expanse of surrounding countryside to the north, east and west. This is the borderland that the Norman defenders of the castle watched over while the Welsh prince, Llywelyn the Great, mustered his forces. He attacked the castle in 1223 and again in 1231. Fourteen years later his son Dafydd had a go. All efforts to dislodge the invaders of their country came to nothing for the next four hundred years. In 1649 – almost a midway point between Llywelyn's day and ours – the castle was demolished. It had fallen in the Civil War to the Parliamentarians, and the victorious Roundheads did not want rivals to regain a stronghold in Wales.

There are three other visitors to the castle beside ourselves: a couple in their sixties who tell us that they didn't want to return to work after Covid's restrictions, and a lone, local woman in a beret who is keen to act as our guide to the area. She recommends a number of places to visit; most of them are cafés. These snippets of conversation reinforce the picture of Welsh tourism at this time of year. We are part of a scattered army of grey and white-haired visitors, although I guess we are older than most and have not retired from the fray. Thankfully, we can still follow our lifetime's occupations.

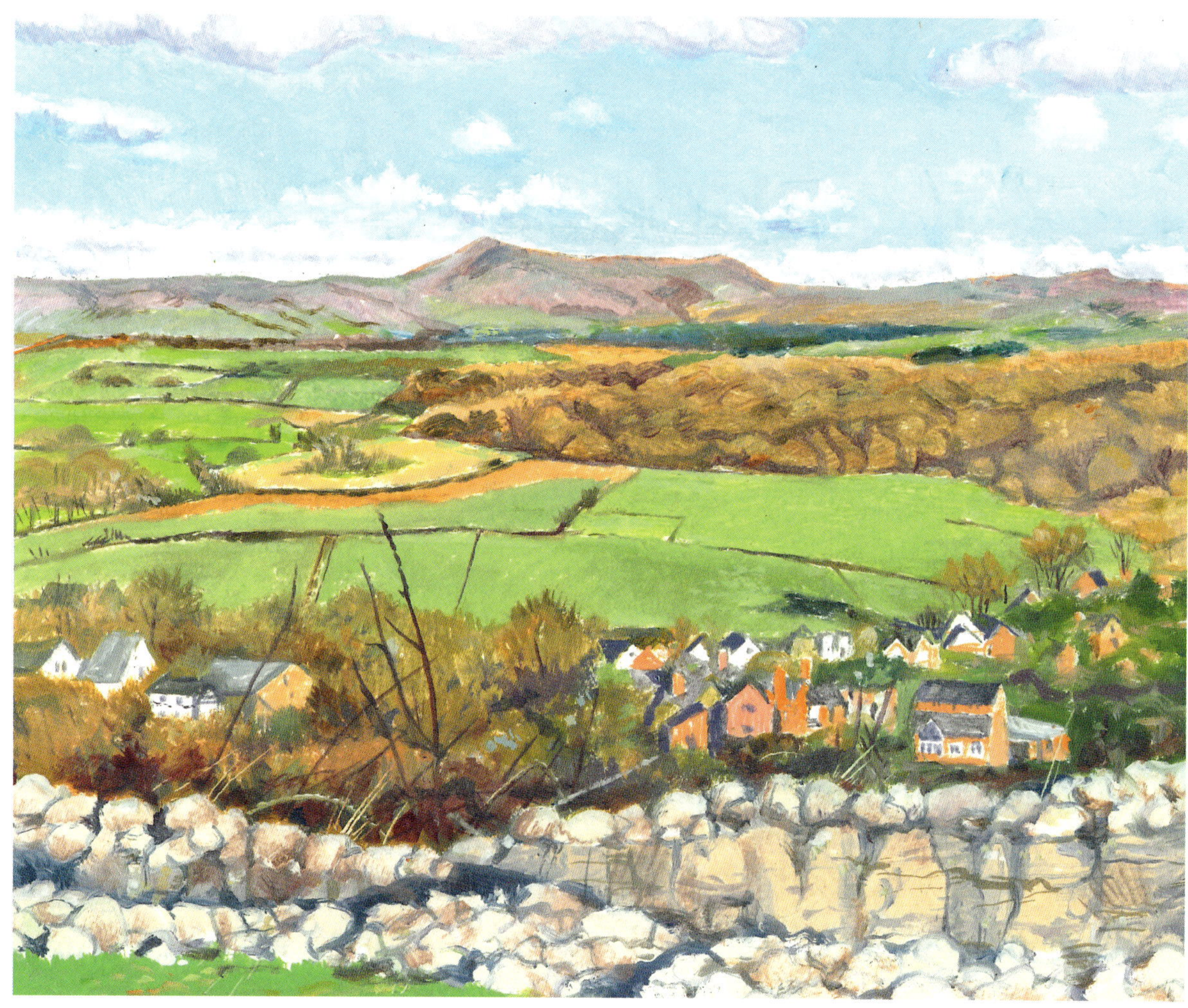

View from Montgomery Castle

Standing within the castle's ruined walls high above the village of Montgomery, the view stretches as far as Corndon Hill near Shrewsbury. Defenders would have excellent advance warning of any attack.

But what about the snow? Heavy falls are forecast. The sky is dark with it.

That night, lorries thunder past our room in the hotel near Garthmyl. There won't be any meal here tonight, it's announced by the manager, as they have a problem with the supply of gas. We can go a mile or two up the road to a pub. That night it became apparent that the A483 is a favoured route. Traffic continued all night with only the slightest lull around three or four in the morning. Snow fell around five, but the lorries continued. So, instead of staying a second night there, we decided to return to Montgomery. The Dragon Hotel beckoned. Before that and despite the snow, we would visit Powys Castle, a short distance up the road on the way to Welshpool.

A notice at the entrance announced that the castle was closed. However, the gates were open. Our Montgomery volunteer guide in her beret had enthused about the castle's park. So, in we drove. At once our spirits rose. Parkland stretched out before us. We were greeted by vistas of gaunt oak trees stretching twisted, snow-rimmed arms towards the dark sky; a few, lone waterfowl pottered about on a steel-grey lake; geometrically trimmed box hedges hid the castle's formal gardens; a pair of ornate gates, with a winged dragon proudly dominating the pillars on each side provided the appropriate setting for the battlements of the castle looming in the misty background. The decorative gates represent a pertinent question raised by all borderlands. On which side of the border would you rather be?

The little snow that had fallen overnight and during the day didn't interfere with our progress, but we were relieved to get to the Dragon Hotel. After only one visit, Montgomery with its black and white, half-timbered buildings and atmospheric castle on its rock had become a favourite place. I fully intended to find answers the next day to the various questions I had in mind with a visit to the town's museum and bookshop. But we drew the curtains in the morning to see our Blue Nissan Micra sitting under half a foot of snow. The town was silent. Being snowbound was not part of our plan.

Dragon gates, Powys Castle

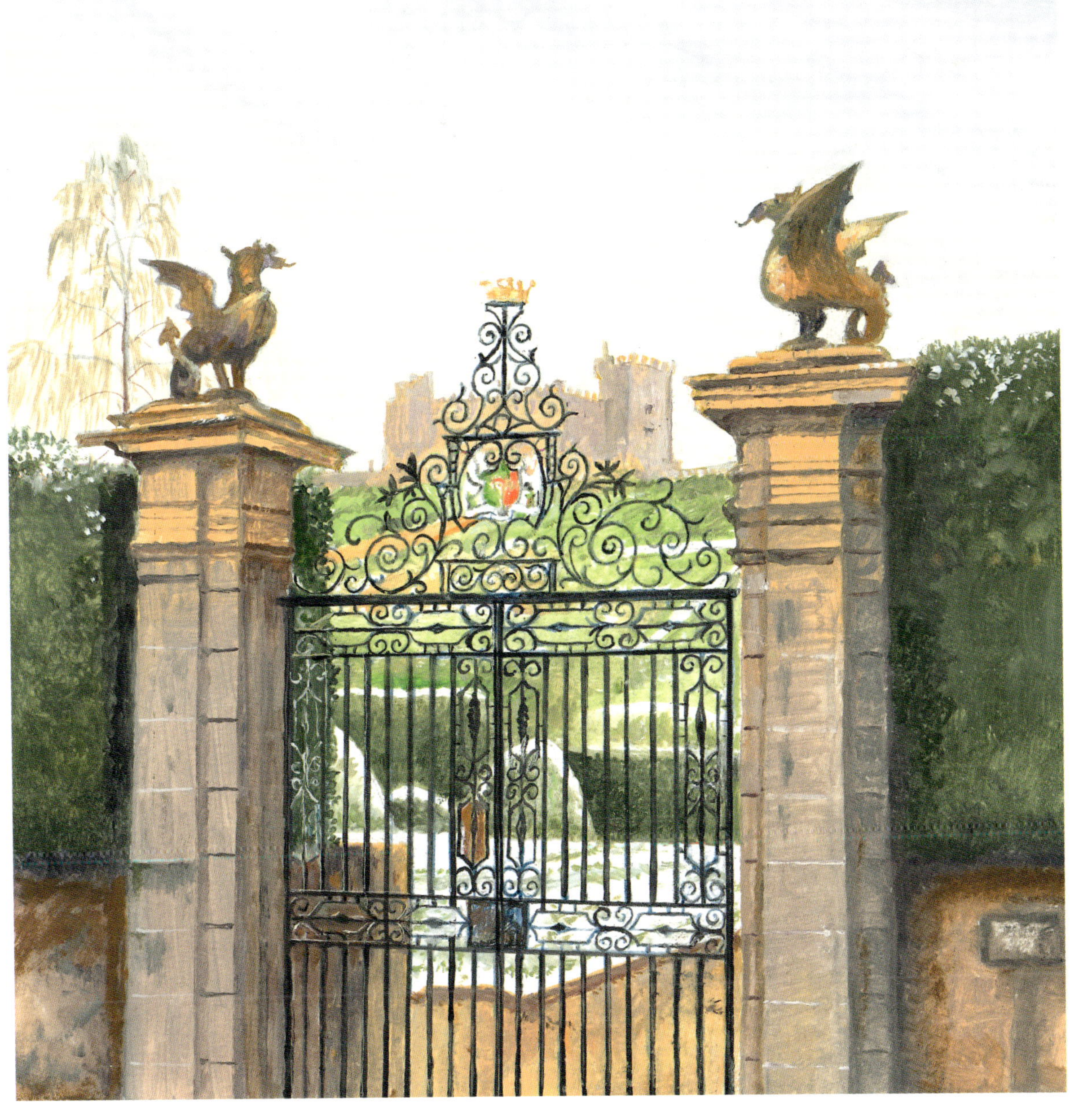

The only other couple in the dining room for breakfast came to our aid. Armed with large shovels borrowed from the hotel, they dug a path out for us and their own car. A fire-fighter and a police officer in the Missing Persons division, their compact strength, fiery energy and cheerful good will, made me think of the pair of dragons on the top of the pillars guarding the neat garden of Powys Castle. What better dragons to have around when you need them.

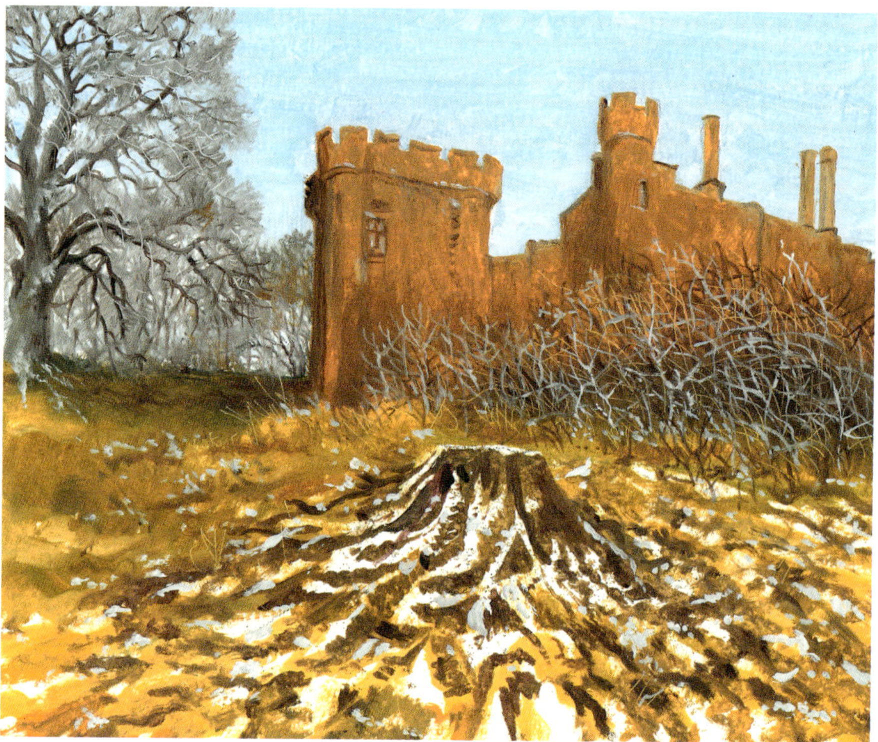

Powys Castle

Powys Castle is unusual in many ways. It was established in the thirteenth century by a Welsh prince and not a Norman baron. Unlike most Welsh castles that we can visit today, it is not a ruin. Now in the hands of the National Trust, a part of the castle is still home to the Herbert family who became owners in the sixteenth century. Standing high above its formal gardens in an extensive park and grounds, Powys Castle is an impressive monument to an aristocratic family's continuity and commitment.

Dragon Hotel

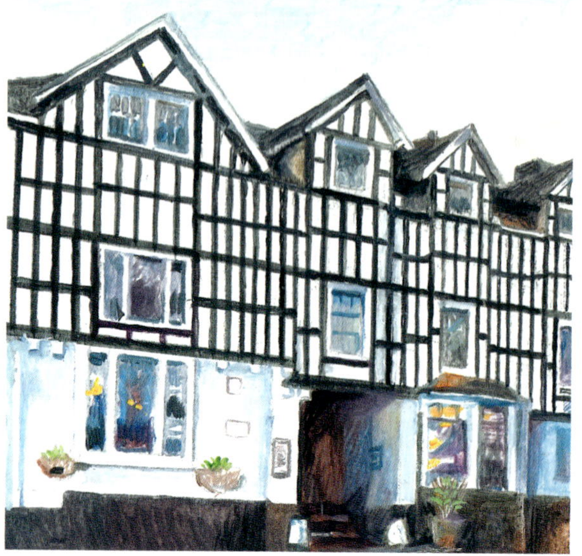

Blue Nissan in snow

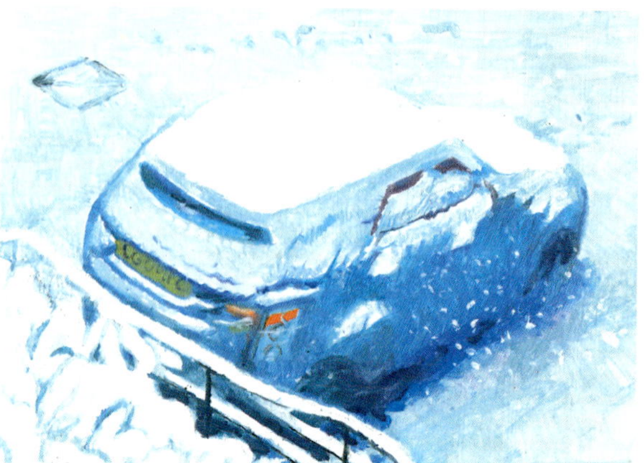

Grosmont Castle and Shop

In the window of the village Post Office and Stores there is everything you might need on a spring-cleaning expedition to a country cottage, from tea bags to wet wipes and disinfectant. The shop is run by the village community. Do they have a siege in mind? Today all that has happened is a peaceful visit by an elderly English couple (ourselves) and a cheerful charge by four local lads who have come to toboggan down the steep slopes of the castle's moat.

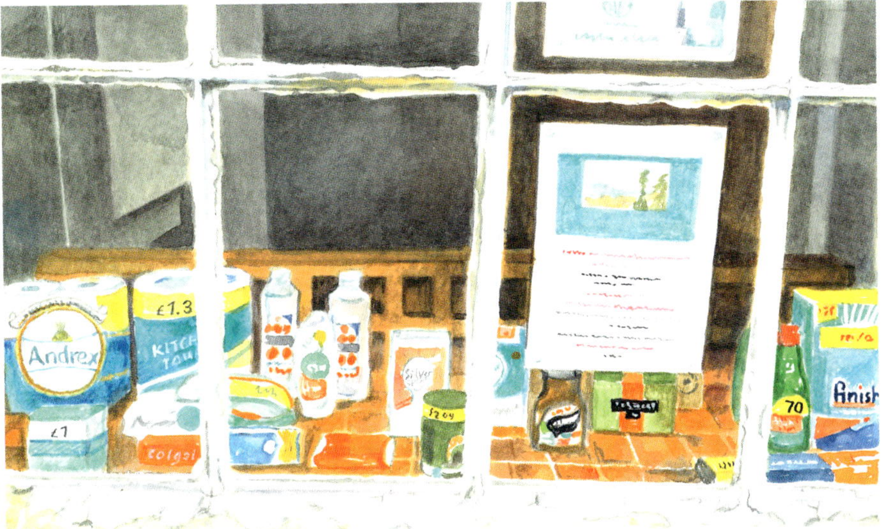

Grosmont village stores

The window display of Grosmont village stores exerts an irresistible fascination. I gaze at it for some time, sending silent praise to a group of locals who opted to make the village part of a charitable programme called Futures. The group vowed at their last meeting to support any plans to save the shop. The Town Hall is in their sights, too.

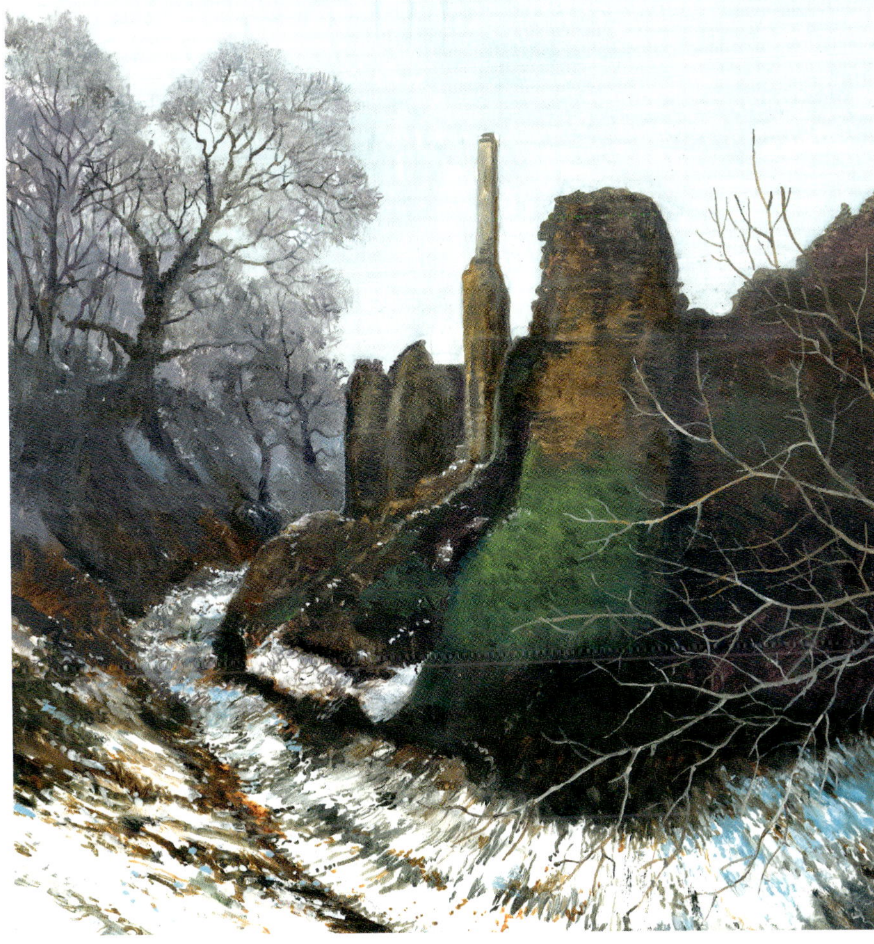

Grosmont Castle

On a cold winter's day the only other visitors to Grosmont Castle were four lads with tin trays preparing to toboggan down the sides of the moat.

The way home

South of Hay-on-Wye there's a road that climbs to Hay Bluff, a flat-topped hill with long views over the Wye Valley and the borderlands between Wales and England. Its Welsh name is Penbegwyb (pronounce that as best you can). This added to its attraction, as our home address includes *Pen,* the Celtic word for headland. I wanted to see the countryside that Bruce Chatwin wrote about so movingly in *On the Black Hill.* We stopped to ask a walker the way and she advised against risking the route. There would be snow on the high ground. In any case, we had booked supper at the restaurant 1861, Cross Ash, where we'd stopped briefly in February at the start of our explorations. Here's what I noted at the time.

We feel well-disposed towards Simon and Kate and worry for their future in providing gourmet meals with comfortable rooms in what is pretty well the middle of nowhere, even if it is located at the midpoint of The Three Castles. We are the only guests. We'd get a different picture if we were here in fine summer weather rather than a snowstorm in March.

Who knows? We may return.

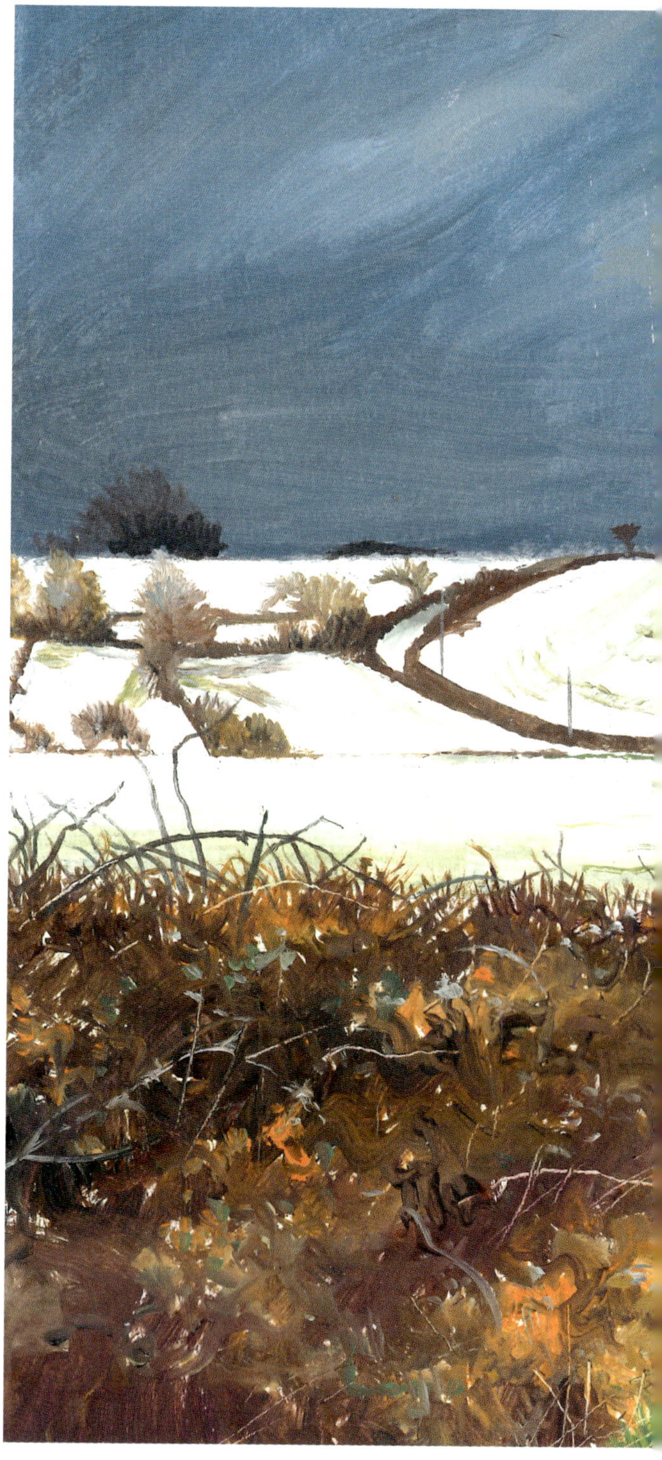

Winding road in the borderlands

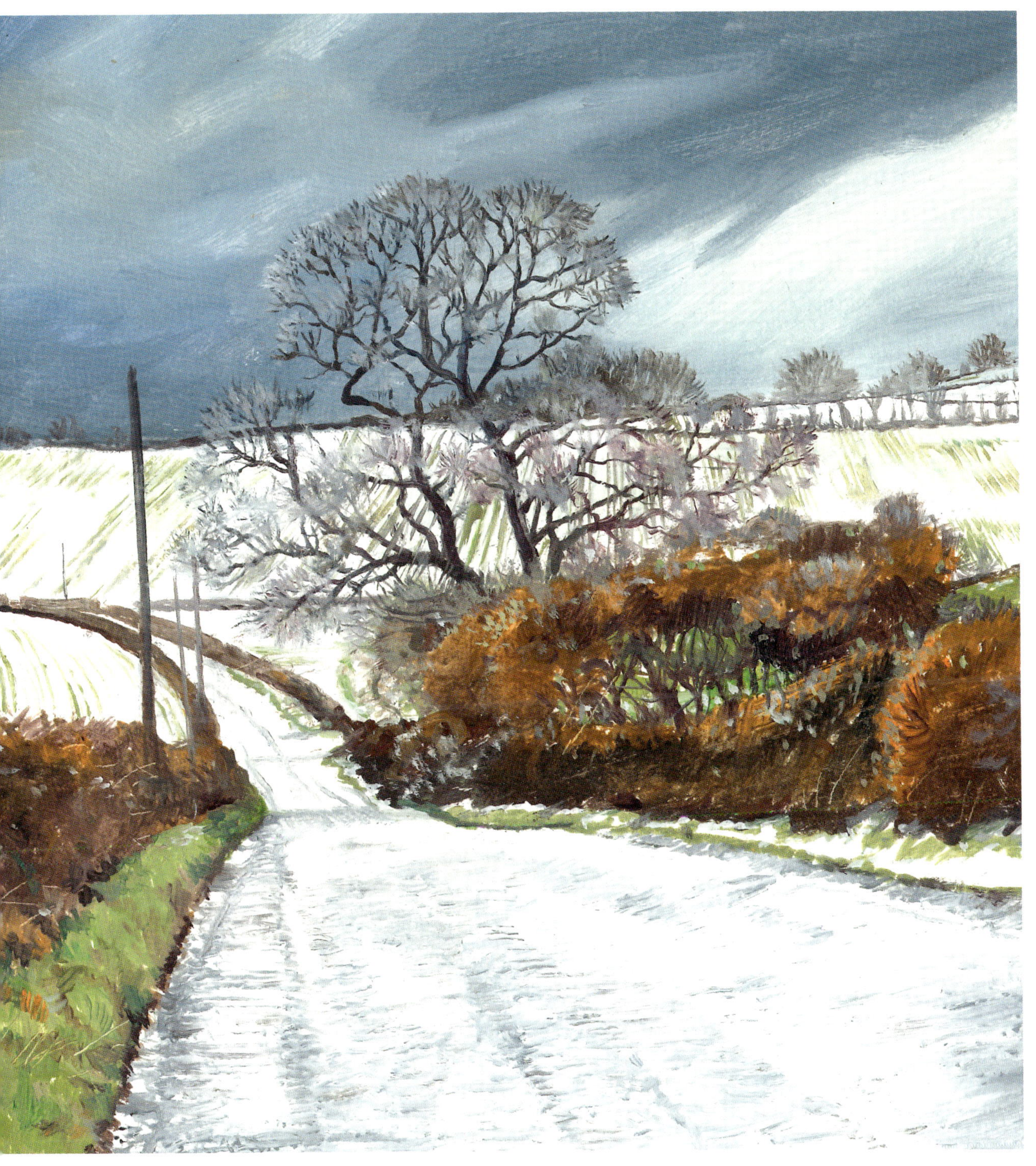

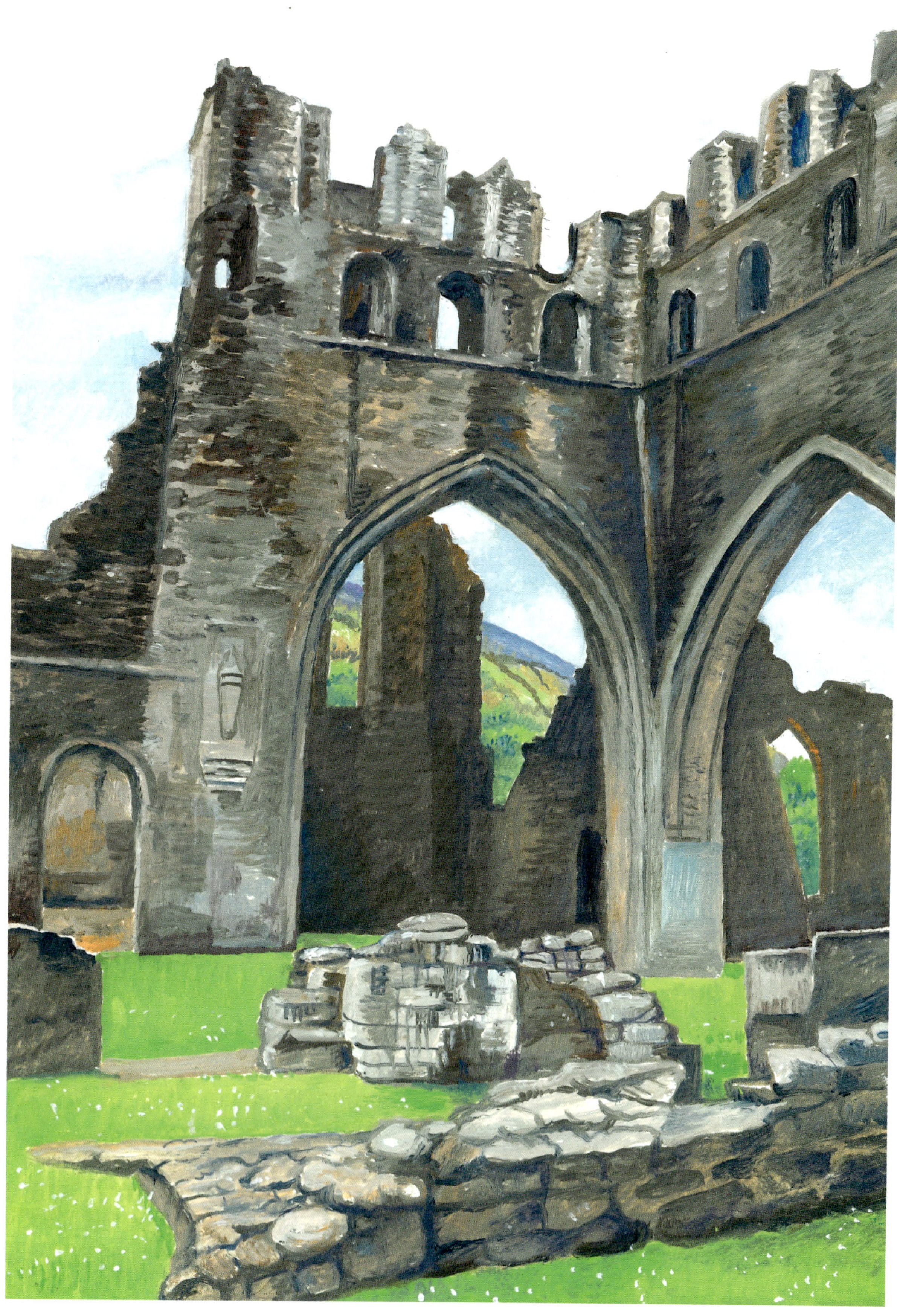

Llanthony

And return we did, in late spring, to catch up on things we'd missed earlier. This was Peter's second visit to Llanthony. He camped here as a Boy Scout in the early 1950s, one of the brighter interludes in his Dulwich teenage life. Now, in 2023, we want to include Llanthony Priory in this first section of our book. We join centuries of visitors, adding to the uncountable number who have breathed in the deep quiet and grandeur of the ruined priory in its river valley setting. The first visitor known to have recorded his impressions of the place was Giraldus Cambrensis, Gerald of Wales. In his twelfth-century exploration of his home country, he described Llanthony as being "fixed amongst a barbarous people." He obviously didn't consider himself a barbarian.

Nor are the inhabitants of the area any longer barbarous, as we've learnt during our time in the borderlands. They are welcoming and proud of their country. It was announced on the news that the Brecon Beacons are to be known by their Welsh name: Bannau Brycheiniog. This translates as the peaks of the kingdom of Brychan, who was a fifth-century king. Now we're in the twenty-first century and following in the footsteps of Gerald of Wales, recording our impressions of the place. The past is always present, especially in the ruins of castles and abbeys in the Welsh borderlands.

Llanthony Priory

As Peter remembers from boyhood, Llanthony was called an abbey when he camped in a nearby field as a boy scout. In fact, it was not an abbey but an Augustinian priory, originally founded in the twelfth century., By the time of Owain Glyndŵr's rebellion in the early fifteenth century, it was in dire straits, finally falling into ruin after Henry VIII's Dissolution of the Monasteries. A few miles down the valley, a monastic institution called Llanthony Abbey was founded in the nineteenth century. This later became the home of Eric Gill, a designer and graphic artist of dubious personal reputation. In July 2023 the abbey went on sale with an Abergavenny estate agency for £1,500,000.

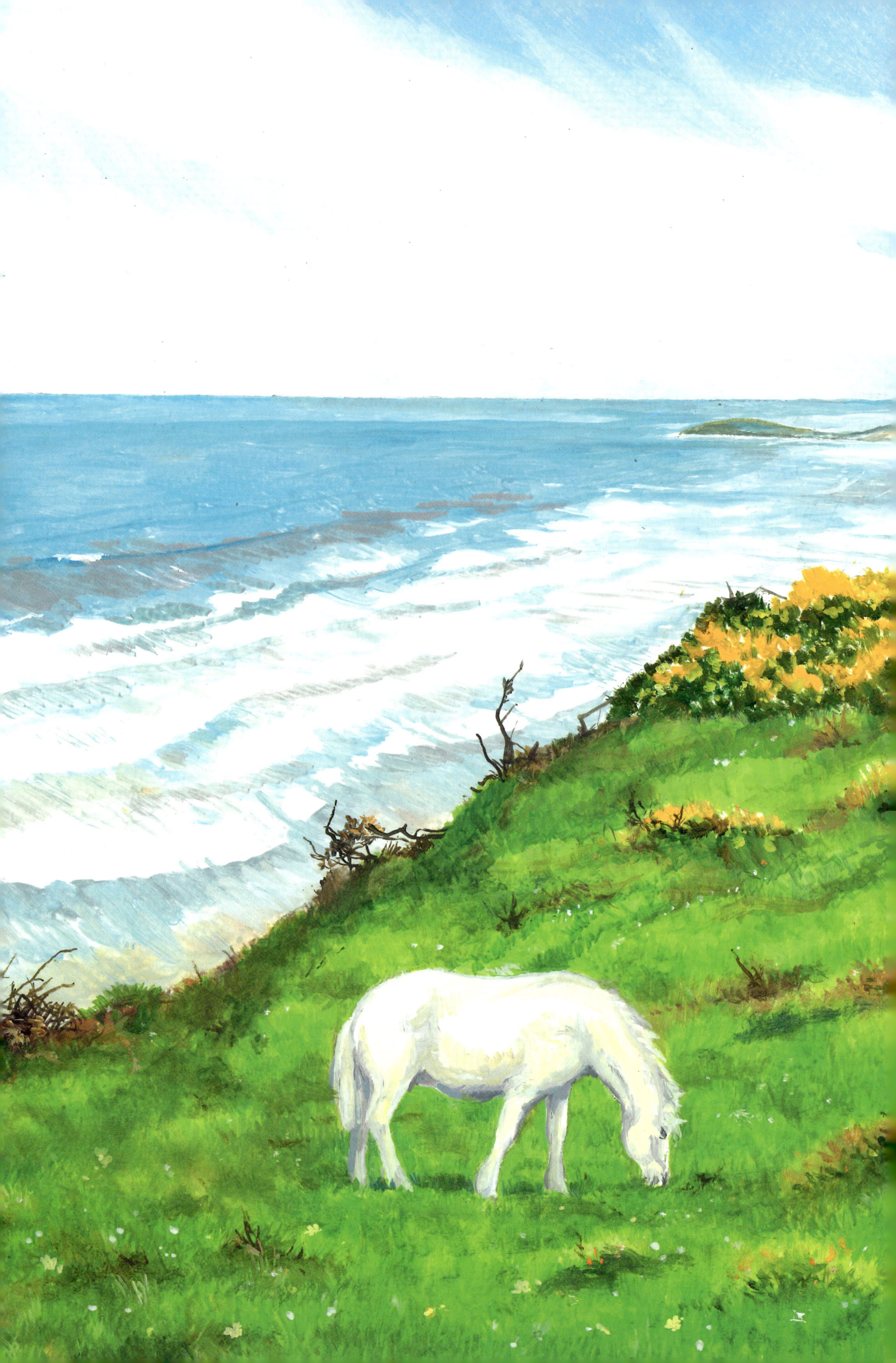

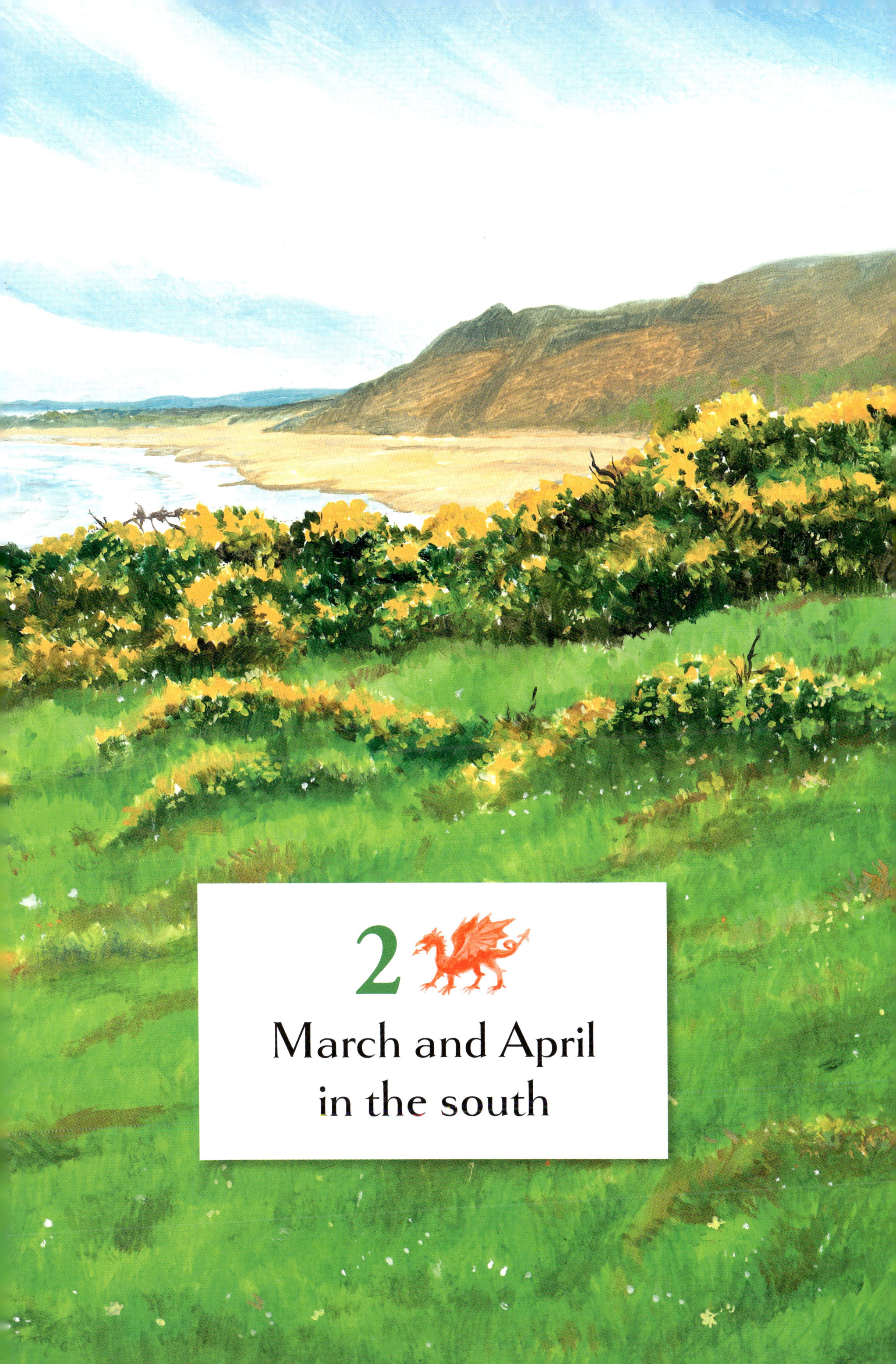

2 March and April in the south

March and April in the south

Port Talbot and Swansea

Sea, sun, and sand: the classic ingredients of a summer holiday. But it's March and here we are in Swansea on a fine spring day. The road curves around the city's wide bay. We park near a stall selling ice cream. The sun is warm. The sea lies the far side of a long wall bounding a beach. Sand eddies under the trestle table where we sit to eat our sandwiches. The way sand invades the town can be a problem, we learn from the stallholder while she learns, in turn, we're from Devon. "It's a shame," she says, "that we no longer have the ferry." It used to ply the channel between Swansea and Ilfracombe. Two months ago, we looked across at Wales from Exmoor, before the first of our explorations. Now we are looking at England from Wales. The coast is clearly visible, twenty or thirty miles away. On the view's eastern edge stand buildings that shine white against a greyish purple line of hills. I guess this is Hinkley C, the latest version of the nuclear power station built on the shores of the Bristol Channel in Bridgewater Bay. Model A was built in the late 1950s. Model B is in the process of being decommissioned. Nuclear energy, one of the solutions to the climate crisis,

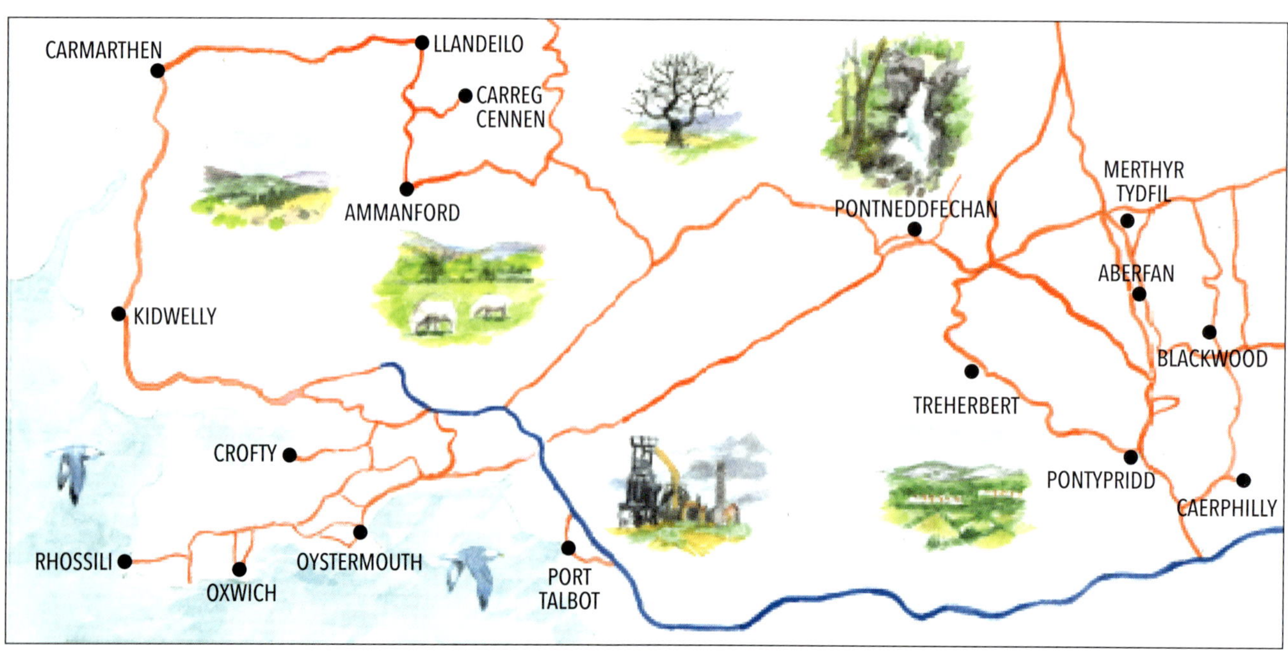

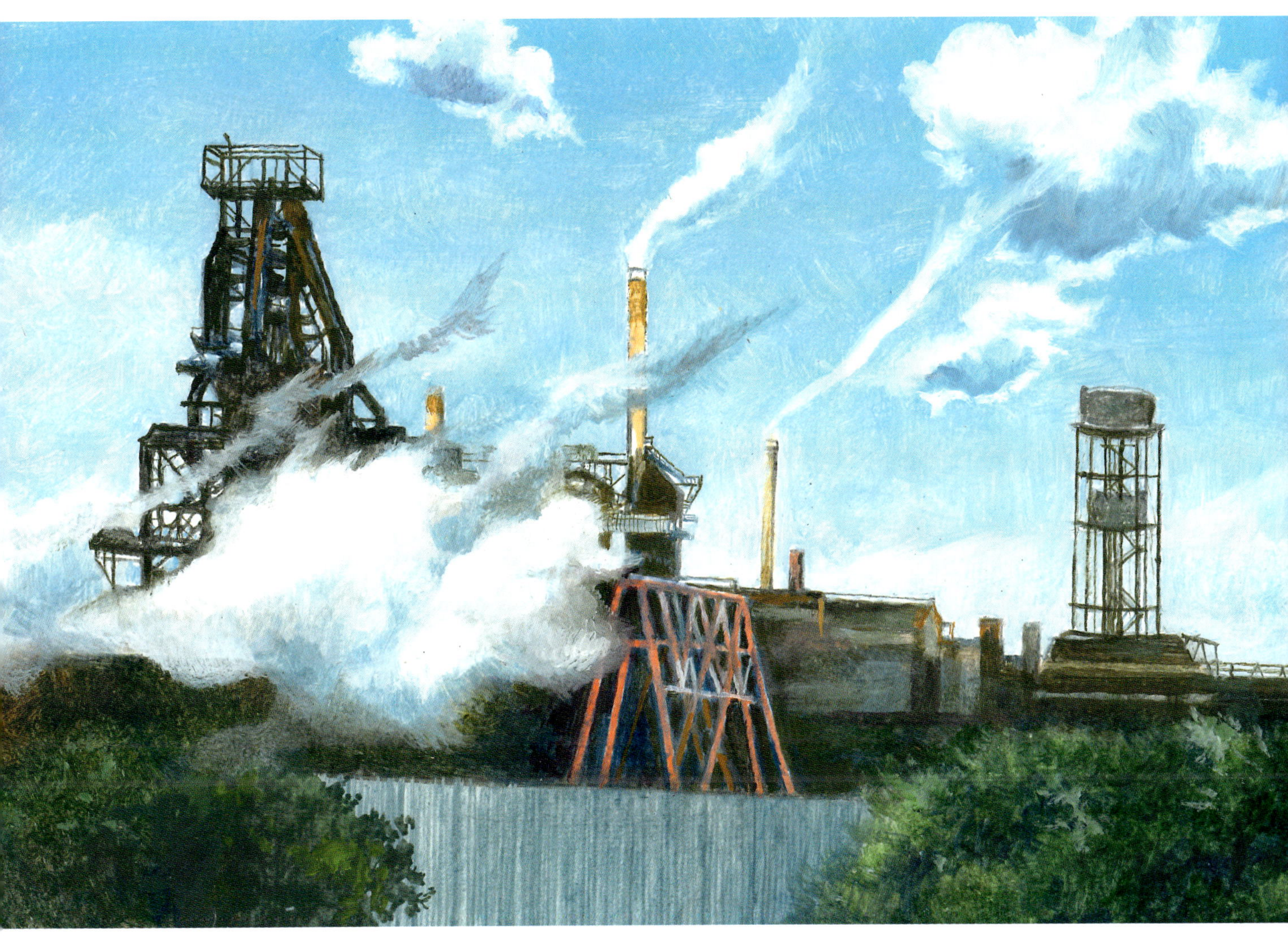

Port Talbot steelworks

A great many jobs will be lost as the Port Talbot steelworks change from coal-fired furnaces to electrically-powered methods. The environment benefits at the work force's expense, as do we all benefit as the world goes greener.

comes at the unattractively high costs involved in installation and long-term waste disposal. France and China are taking the lion's share of financing Hinkley C. They'll take the profits, too.

In similar fashion, an Indian conglomerate, TATA, bought the Port Talbot steelworks when the plant was in danger of closing. On our way this morning we turned off to see the site. Not far from the motorway a network of broad roads and roundabouts led us to a vast complex of chimneys and buildings divided into blocks and protected by high, spiked, iron railings. Billows of steam emanated from the works. The energy of the plant infected us with excitement. Power, whatever its source, can exert a powerful fascination. I could understand how James Watt, watching his mother's kettle boil, had the idea that led to steam engines and from there to Welsh coal mining. Now coal is being phased out as a source of energy. In the valleys slag heaps have become green hills.

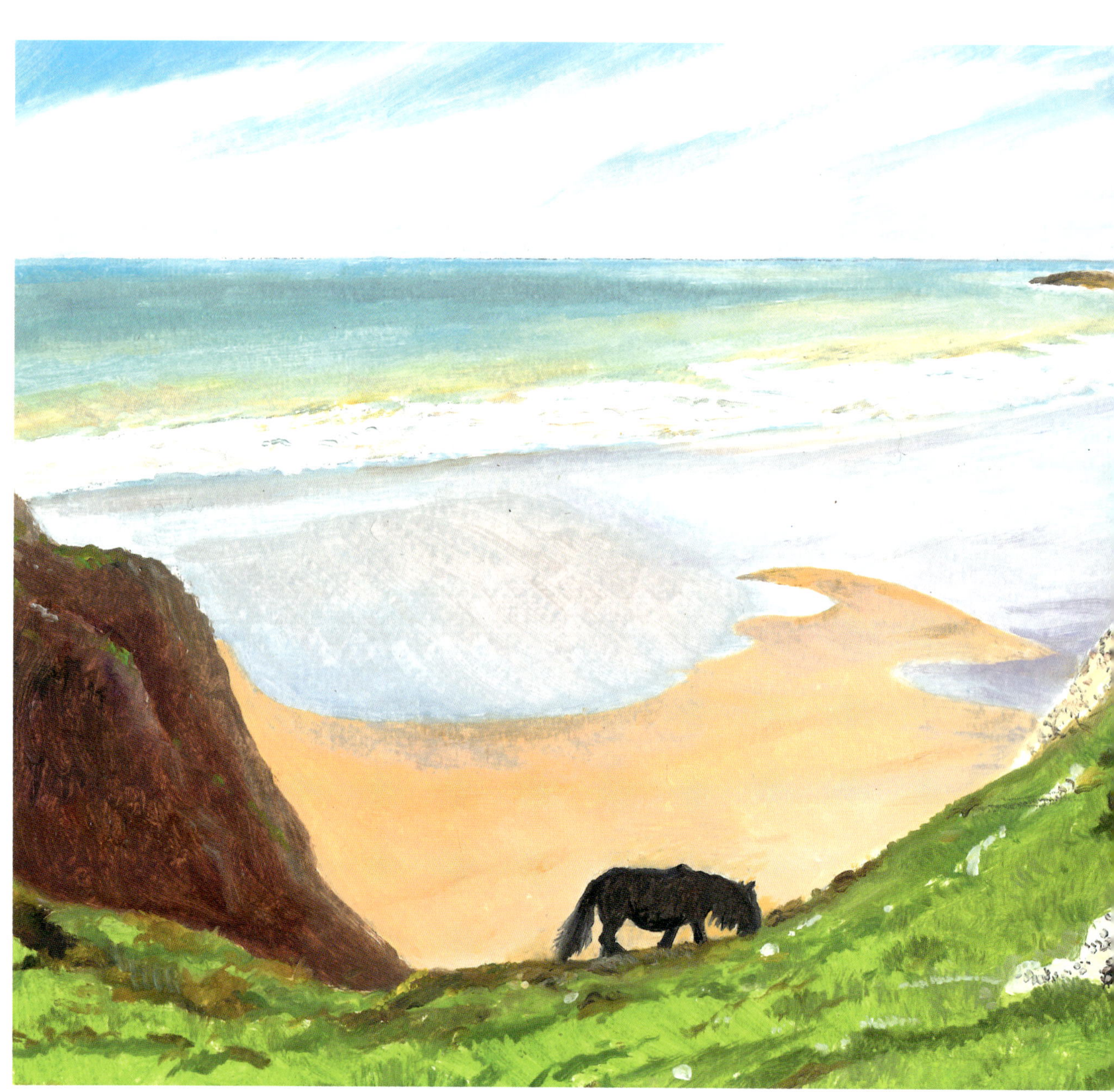

Welsh pony, Rhossili beach

The ponies that graze the grassy cliffs of Rhossili Bay lead free and healthy lives, unlike their predecessors who spent years pulling wagons full of coal in underground tunnels.

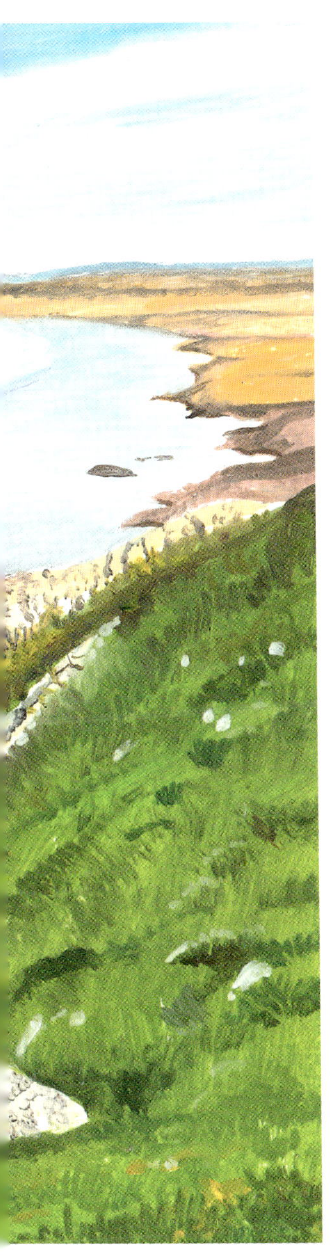

The Gower peninsula

So many people had told us we'd love the Gower that I was doubtful about it from the start. As it turned out, we liked its furthest point, the Worm's Head. Rocky bumps of land clearly inspired the headland's name, worm being an old word for dragon. The sea foams beneath its chin. This final headland forms one side of Rhossili beach, a splendid expanse of sand stretching away in a generous curve to the next promontory. Yes, we do like this bit of the Gower, but not the parts we were ensnared in earlier in the afternoon while making our way through the outskirts of Swansea. What do all the people who live in all the houses do for a living? That's the question that's perennially prompted by such places, raised as I was on the edges of Dartmoor. It took a long drive to emerge from the suburbs and we were in a network of winding lanes, losing our way in the countryside. We passed a few, tree-framed, sandy coves; pretty enough but we weren't tempted to explore them. We had Oxwich bay and a nature reserve further west in our sights. After a fair amount of hither and thithering we found ourselves turning down a lane guarded by a castle tower with a neatly white-painted and curtained window on its ground floor. The tower was, in fact, someone's home, a good example of recycling. Further on, we met a young couple on a long circular walk. They'd parked by a grey stone bridge over a rushing stream in a tangled wood. They talked about Rhossili beach. It sounded tempting. We replaced Oxwich with Rhossili as our afternoon's target.

The size of the car park at the head of the bay took us by surprise. It was full. Do we lead that sheltered a life? If there are this number of cars wanting to park in March, what can it be like in the summer? A little walk along the headland, I sat on a welcome bench with my eyes on the bay stretching away below and my ears tuned into the snatches of conversation as other visitors strode past. I was reminded of the pigeons of Tintern. "And this happened, then that happened, would you believe it? No, *would* you." But unlike the monotonous pigeons, the language and accents spoke of every part of the world, America, Germany, Japan …

Woodland stream

The permanently wet ground in woodlands encourages the growth of a variety of mosses and fungi.

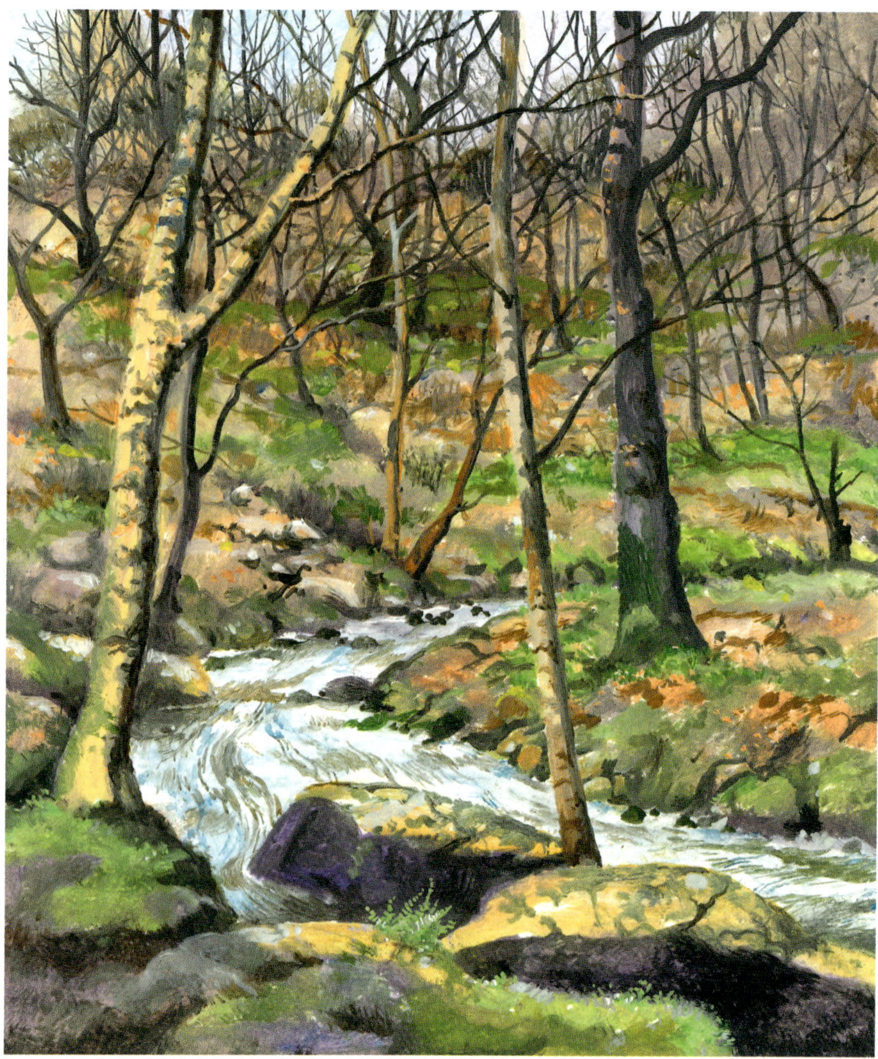

View to Worm's Head

The final lump of cliffs sheltering Rhossili Bay to the southeast is called Worm's Head. Dragons were sometimes called worms, perhaps as a way of making them less powerful and frightening.

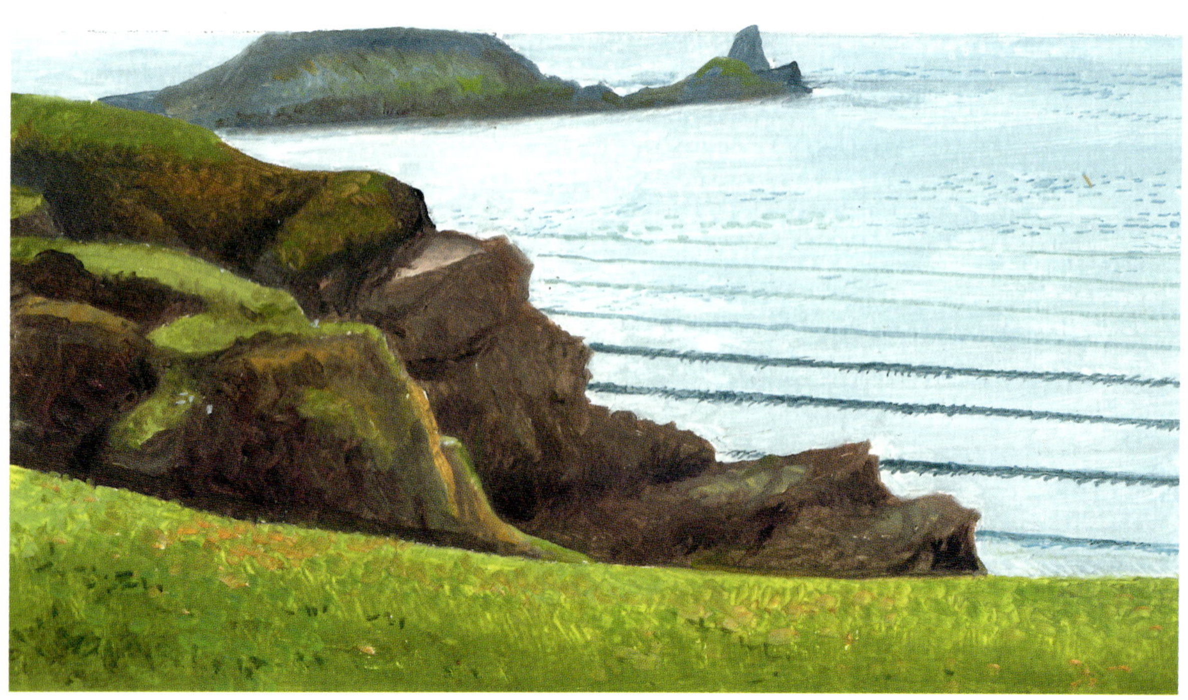

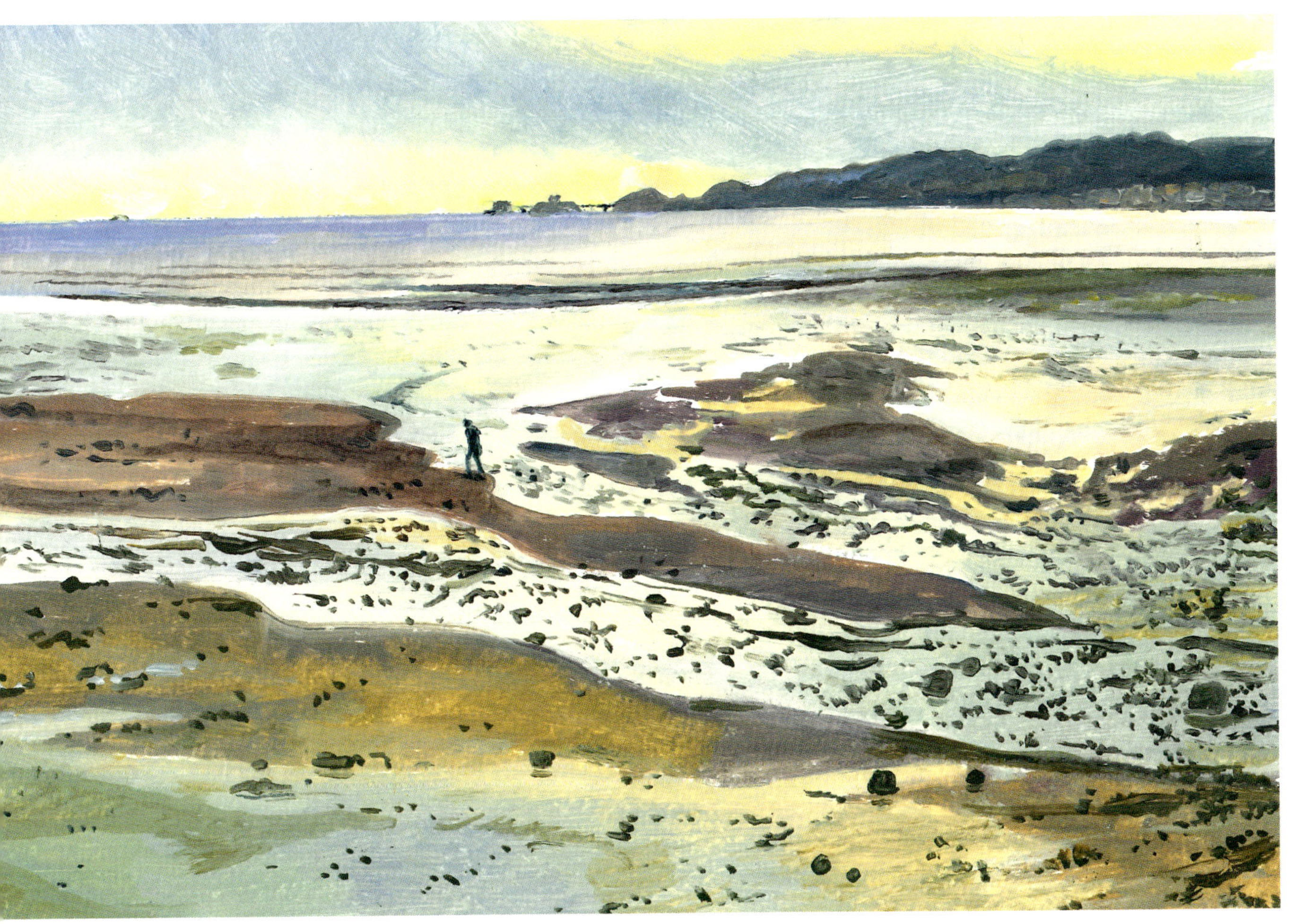

Gower coast at Oystermouth

Oystermouth is the name of the village in Swansea Bay in the district of the Mumbles. The two names are often used, one for the other.

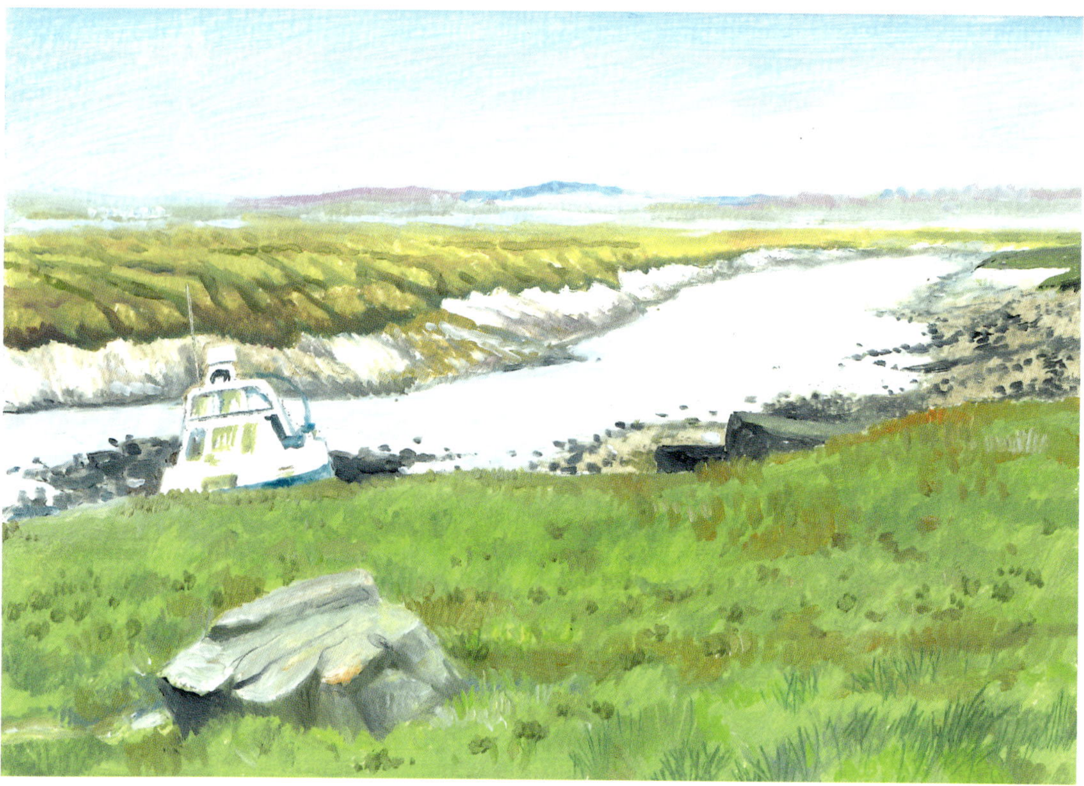

North Gower coast

The north coast of the Gower is marshy and mostly flat. As a result, it is less crowded than the south. This is one of its attractions.

My mind strayed to a beach in South Island, New Zealand, where the only other occupants of a 4-mile-long stretch of sand was a family group of sea lions: father, mother and pup, playing together with strands of kelp. Peter has the painting he did of this scene hanging in his studio. What a contrast to the present scene, busy with walkers heading off to the Worm's Head or back from it. To my left, the headland, the dragon's body, stretched away in decreasing heights towards the final humps and lumps, the dragon's head. Below me, the sea formed a steady succession of wrinkles towards the shore. The sand shone white in places where the last wave had curled over, turned, and retreated. In the foreground, four or five ponies cropped the grass between gorse bushes in flower, their butter-yellow blossom pinpricks of light against the blue of the sea a sheer cliff-drop below. *"Don't go too near the edge!"* I heard my great-grandmotherly warning. For the ponies, the warning is not needed. They know exactly how close they are to the familiar edge. How fortunate they are to be in the open air, high up on a cliff, and not pulling carts hundreds of feet underground as their forefathers did.

Yes, we do like the Gower and so do others from all over the world, all year round.

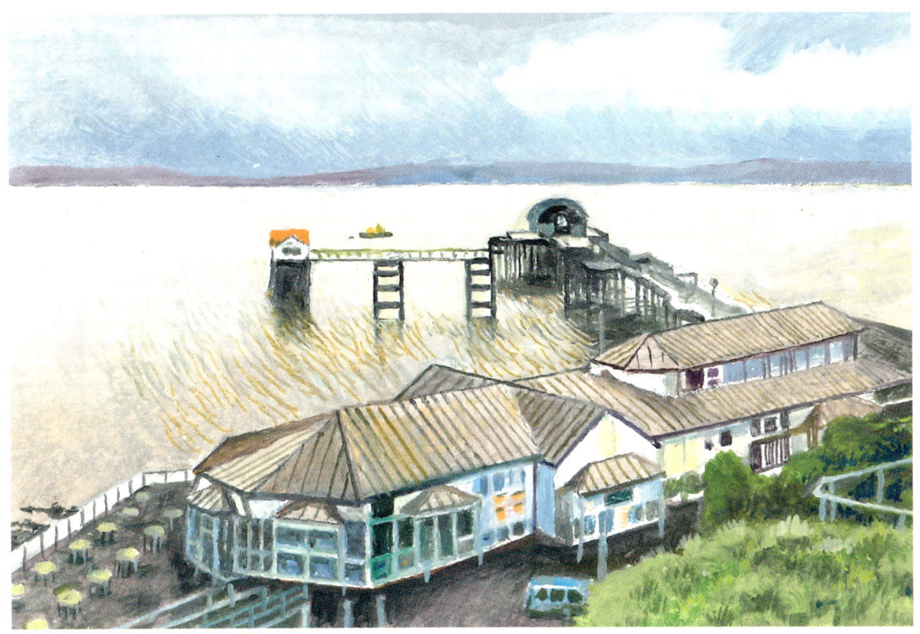

Oystermouth Pier

Oystermouth Pier makes an attractive focal point for a trip to the Gower.

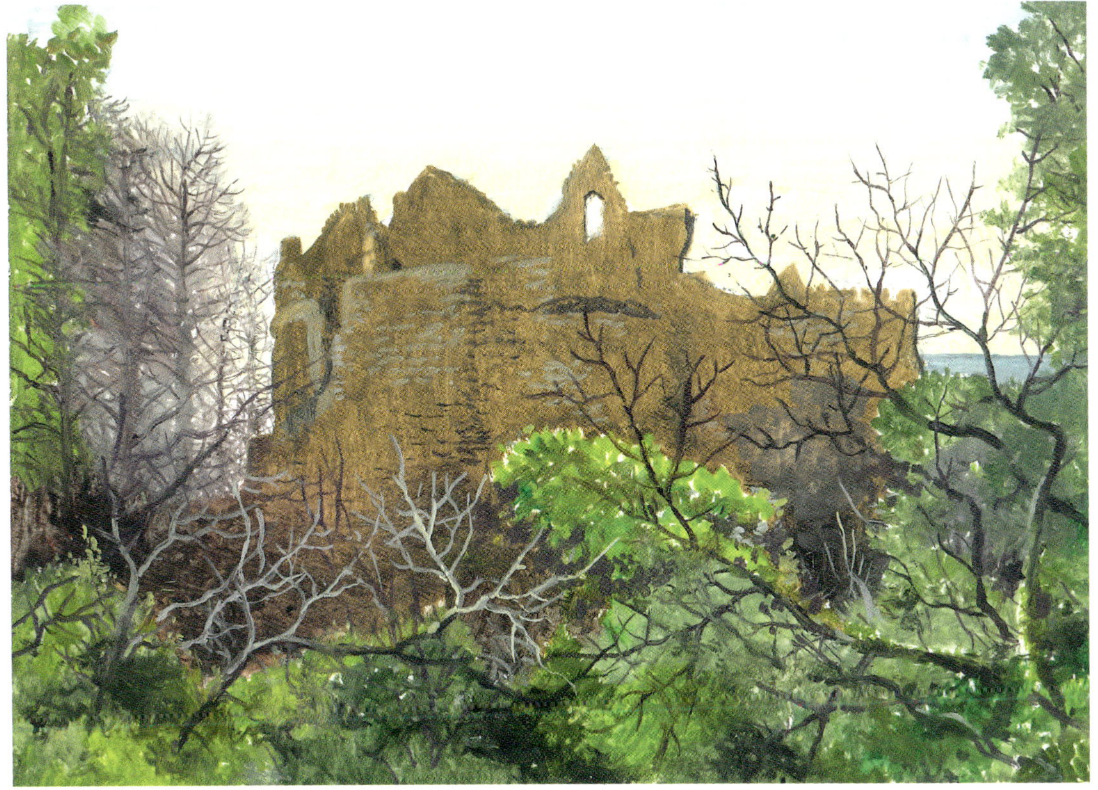

Oystermouth Castle walls

Ruined walls, like these at Oystermouth Castle in the Mumbles, Swansea, attract artists as well as historians.

Rain, rain and more rain

Next day, we drive through sheets of rain on the look-out for cafés and toilets. In Kidwelly we find a rain-drenched castle and a garage which cannot provide the hot drink we crave, but the attendant lets us use the staff loo. She tells us that Carmarthen will supply us with all we need. We drive on.

Not too far from Carmarthen's central car park is a Wetherspoons, full to the brim with people like us, warming up with hot drinks and food. Yet not quite like us. No-one looks quite as old. "We never returned to work after Covid," we're told by a couple in their early sixties. "Besides, where is the work these days?" They're looking forward to better weather when they'll be cycling again.

For us, whatever the weather, everything and anything is welcome material for a few words or a picture. The outline of a castle on a distant hill is inspiringly gothic. Clusters of primroses nestle in the margins of woodland and ranks of yellow daffodils brighten our route.

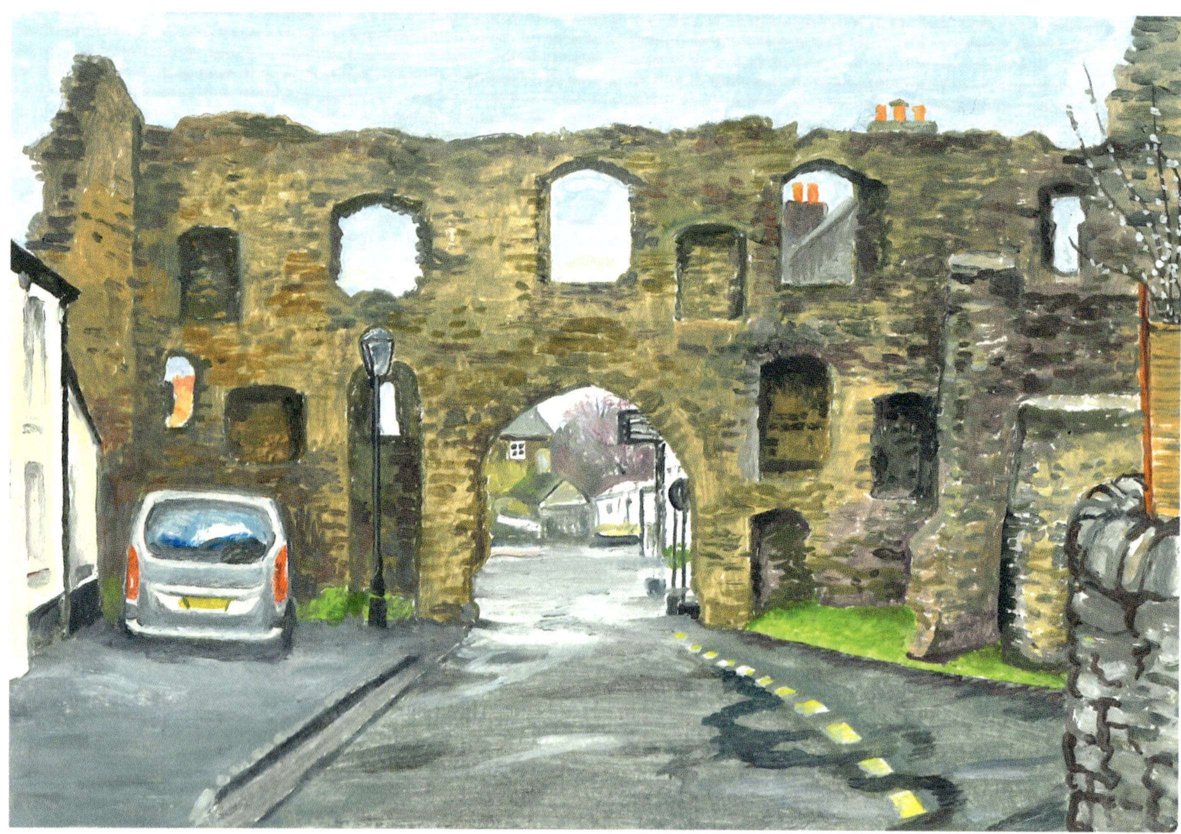

Kidwelly town walls

Kidwelly Castle was built by the Normans as a defence against the Welsh. The headless ghost of a rebel leader's widow is said to haunt the local countryside. But was it her head, or the head of her husband, which was cut off?

Llandeilo

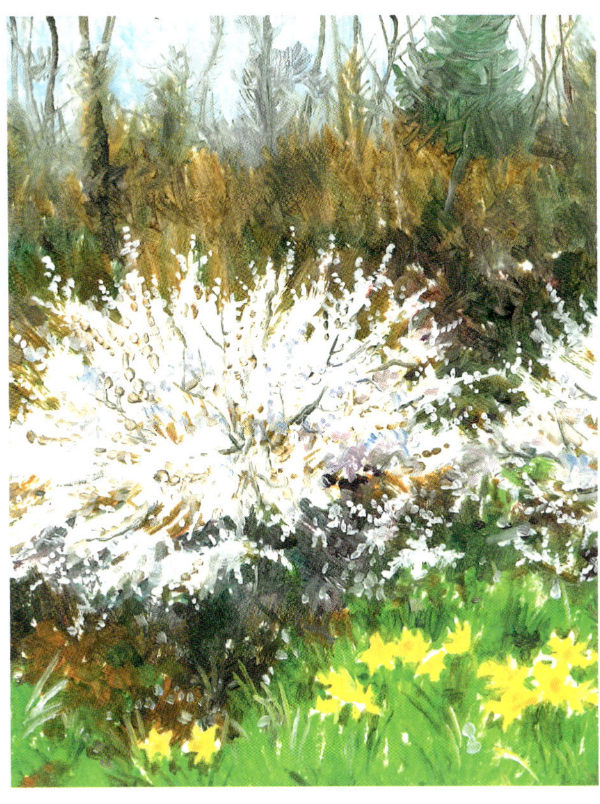

Daffodils and blackthorn blossom

Daffodils are the national flower of Wales. The sun-yellow flowers appear after long winter months, symbolising hope and joy after difficulties and sorrow.

The inn where we stayed had a modern wing attached to an old-fashioned pub. The wing gave us a comfortable room and the pub provided entertaining conversation. On the wall of the passage between the two were three identical prints: the head of an antlered deer, illustrating the inn's name. In the public bar, a great many mugs hung from the ceiling, all much the same size and shape. I imagined the proprietor filling in the order form of the wholesaler who deals with décor for pubs. "Six prints of the stag's head, 42 floral mugs and 60 bottles in pink, green and brown glass, 20 of each colour." I didn't count the bottles which were displayed on a high shelf around the bar, nor the mugs hanging from the ceiling. I was far too busy listening to the voices nearby. Entering the bar had been like stepping into a private pool. We could all but feel the ripples of attention as the eyes of the three other customers swivelled to focus on us. Slowly, the conversation we had disturbed resumed. I waited for a good moment to try my opener. By the time of this trip, I'd perfected the first cast of the bait, a judicious mixture of tactful diffidence and easy confidence. My vocabulary included vital words like *artist, writer, book on Wales, can you, is there.* In the bar that evening, it proved again to be an open sesame of an approach. Two of the three men were called Pete. The third was Daffyd. They each hoped to get a mention in the book and filled us in generously on their Welsh world. Vehicles are their livelihoods, mending them or driving them, tractors, diggers, lorries, vans. One of the two Peters had spent time in New Zealand but unlike the millions of young Welshmen who have always gone abroad to find fame and fortune, this one had come home. Unable or unwilling to work on his parents' farm, he had become a long-distance lorry driver. He now drives diggers. All three men seemed quite content. I learnt later that Llandeilo was singled out by the *Sunday Times* as the best place to live in Wales.

But many Welsh have always chosen, or been driven by necessity, to find their livelihood abroad. In 2016 a Welsh government survey estimated that there are more than 16 million people of Welsh descent living in other countries around the world.

Towards Pontneddfechan

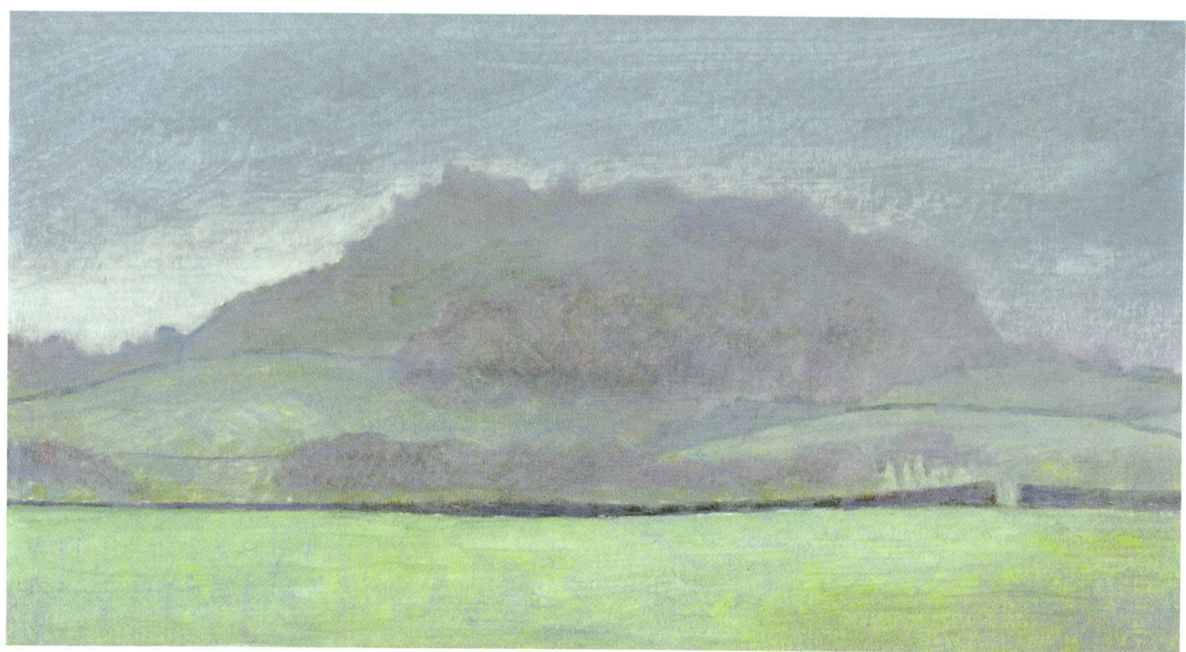

Carreg Cennen Castle in mist

Mist shrouds Carreg Castle, adding to its romance.

And still more rain. Carreg Cennen castle on top of its hill was a ghostly silhouette against lowering cloud. We dismissed the idea of getting closer. The view of the castle in cloud was atmospheric enough. We turned in the lane and drove south through a village called Trapp. I thought of the young people who are content to stay in their home territory. A honey trap? I could easily have opted to stay in Devon all my life. Having been away at boarding school, I was hungry for home at eighteen. But two years later, the more adventurous part of me drove me to London and my future husband. Peter and I, in past years, might have decided to settle in Greece or New Zealand with our son but Devon and our daughter and grandchildren pulled us back. Now we are seeing our great-grandchildren grow up. Such pleasures are precious.

From Ammanford to our next stop in Ystradgynlais, a distance of some 20 miles, there was a continuous stretch of houses snaking in terraces up and down dale. Again, we asked ourselves the perennial question: what do the householders in these built-up areas do for a living? Are they employed or unemployed? Nobody seemed to be around. If there were shops or cafés or pubs of any sort, we didn't spot them. But there were chapels, lots of them.

To our relief we found a cafe in Ystradgynlais. Like the Wetherspoons in Carmarthen it was crowded. We asked a lone man with empty chairs at his table if we might join him. He had come here from Brecon hoping his toothache would be cured by a dentist; something he cannot access in his hometown. He had to set aside a whole day for this expedition. What, if anything, he asked with a painful smile, has got better this century?

We planned to visit some of the waterfalls that tumble and gush from the high moorlands of the Black Mountain and the Brecon Beacons but the rain was creating its own waterfall from the sky. I stayed sitting in the car while Peter braved the weather to walk towards the Henrhyd Falls. But he turned back, not wanting to risk a fall himself. The next target on our list of possibles was the Four Falls trail at Clun Gwyn, not far from Pontneddfechan where we were due to spend the night. Again, Peter (to my great relief) decided against the steep, slippery path down to see the first waterfall. He may think like a thirty-year-old, but he is actually eighty-seven. Instead, we drove further on into the high moorland reminiscent of the Dartmoor of my childhood. Bog and sedge and empty landscape is coded to appeal to me. There may have been a few farms hunkered down in valleys, but they were invisible in the low rain clouds sweeping past. We recalled that, not far from the pull-in for the waterfalls, we'd seen one spot of human life: a solitary cafe bedecked with flags and a couple of covered petrol pumps. Treasure! We did a five, no, six-point turn in the narrow lane, avoiding the deep ditches on either side, and headed back.

Although Robert the owner didn't serve hot drinks, he responded warmly and soon we were hearing his life story. He used to sell petrol and diesel but no longer. Now he dealt only in sweets, ice cream and tourist information. He'd inherited the café from his mother. He was the youngest of seven children and soon after his birth his mother had left his father. He was the last straw, he said with a sparkle in his eyes and a broad smile that revealed the generous gap between his two front teeth. His mother had begun the enterprise slowly, by selling sweets in the hall to the neighbourhood's children. Now it was only summer visitors who came to the shop. Robert showed us a newspaper cutting about the chaos of summer traffic. Two yellow lines on each side of the lane now stopped people parking all along the route to the waterfalls. We took note: we would avoid high summer in Wales.

Robert had spent his life here and seen many changes. He told us what might have been the high point of his life so far: his long-drawn-out battle with His Majesty's Department of Revenue and Customs. They'd wanted him to complete his VAT return online. Robert was not going to fill in a tax form on a computer. He'd never had a computer, didn't have one now, and would never have one. It

Sheep and bog

Boggy ground near the descent to the Four Falls Trail from the Clun-gwyn car park Wet ground is not good for sheep's feet, encouraging rot in hooves. On the other hand, the grass in boggy areas makes good grazing.

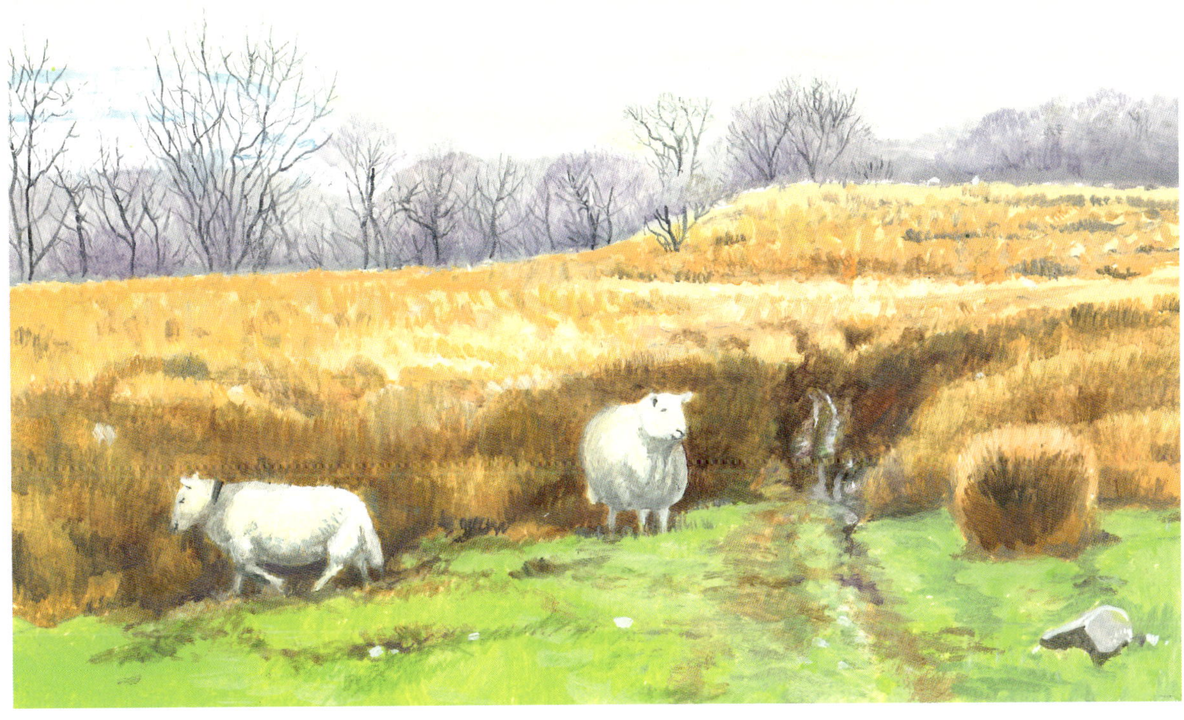

was impossible to attend an institute to learn how to use one. Each time HMRC came up with another suggestion as to how he could comply with The Rules, he had a neat answer ready. Eventually he and 79 others like him around the country were taken to court. The defence lawyer asked Robert and two others to represent the group. The case, and the story, went on and on. I sat down on a chapel pew opposite the counter. In the end, Robert and his compatriots won. Broad, sparkling, gap-toothed smile. Triumph! "I'm a Libra," Robert explained. "I'm for fairness." We are plotting to return, to see Robert and the waterfalls when it's not raining, nor high summer.

Pontneddfechan

We spent the night in the smallest room in the smallest hostelry ever encountered. Our evening meal was in the pub across the road where we'd parked. Later, back in our room, Peter remembered that he'd forgotten to switch the car lights off and went across to see to this. But he worried all night that the battery might have been drained and the car wouldn't start. Our bed was the smallest we'd ever slept in, and we woke far too early. The pub where we'd find breakfast wouldn't open until 10. Were we cheerful? Yes, very. That was because the car started without a hitch. Off we went at half past seven in the morning in a celebratory frame of mind.

Here are my notes, scribbled later at home.

Endless rain and more rain. Drove south-eastwards as best we could by the network of roads streaming southwards through the mining valleys and across the new route being constructed east-west over flyovers and under underpasses. Taking a diversion, we passed rows of terraced houses lining our route and diving off it down steep valleys, filled not with mines but light industry of indeterminate character. By good fortune we found, in a rather more focused place called Blackwood, a rare café. It was very white, clean, and stylish. A bacon twist was warmed up for each of us. A cup of tea for me, a hot chocolate for P plus a slice of choc fudge cake. The Blackwood style for men is to be over six foot tall, almost the same in width, and dressed in shiny black shorts with go-faster stripes, worn over bulging thighs. The women are equally large and most of them push prams. Our daughter Sophie's friend Anne from South Wales says that the unemployment rate in this area is the highest in Britain. We decided to head for home and return in better weather. Relief!

Later in May

As Wales lies close to us in Devon, it's easy to return if we've missed something we'd regret. In late May we returned to make good some omissions. The first was Llanthony Priory. Snow had turned us away on our first trip. Now, in May, its long, narrow valley was adrift in bridal arches of hawthorn blossom and a cuckoo called from the sheltering hills. We also caught up with a visit to a waterfall within an easy walk of a car park, the Sychryd Cascade. It was described in a leaflet we'd picked up in Robert's café near Pontneddfechen. I only managed the car park element. It was May Day, a sunny bank holiday and our first introduction to crowds. I opted to take the wheel and join the manoeuvres in the small, narrow glen of a car park while Peter, a better walker, went off to find the waterfall. He has now painted the result. I managed to squeeze our Nissan into a corner. While

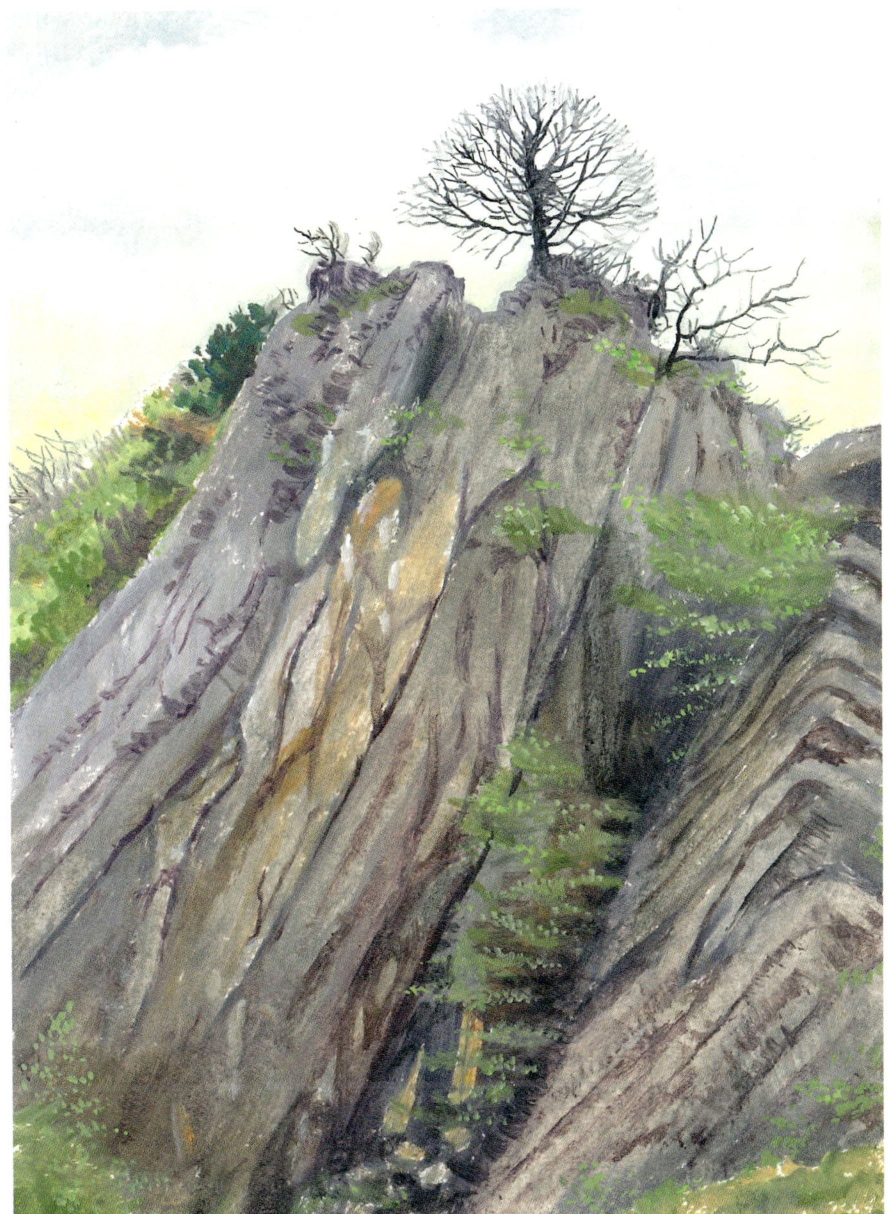

Dinas Rock

The path to the lower waterfalls of the Sychryd Cascades starts below the rockface known as Dinas Rock.

I waited, I planned another book; one which would feature only car parks with a comprehensive description of each and marks out of ten for scenery, clear signs and facilities. The Sychryd car park would come top for scenery while the car park at Cardigan visited later would be bottom on all counts.

The last omission filled at the end of May was a closer look at the mining valleys. A Welsh friend had been in our minds since starting this book. We'd planned to get Gareth and his wife Alison around to supper after our first trip. Then we heard that Gareth had drowned while on holiday in the Caribbean. This was a shocking and sad loss which emphasised our mantra: *Do what you can when you can.*

Gareth's sister Jane lives just north of Cardiff and we've now visited her twice, a welcome new friend. Their father was an important figure in the Welsh mining industry. Jane told us that she drives round a particular roundabout in Merthyr Tydfil in order to greet the statue of her father that stands there. Philip Weekes had all the qualities that make a good negotiator. He came into his own in the miners' strike of 1988, being liked and respected by both sides.

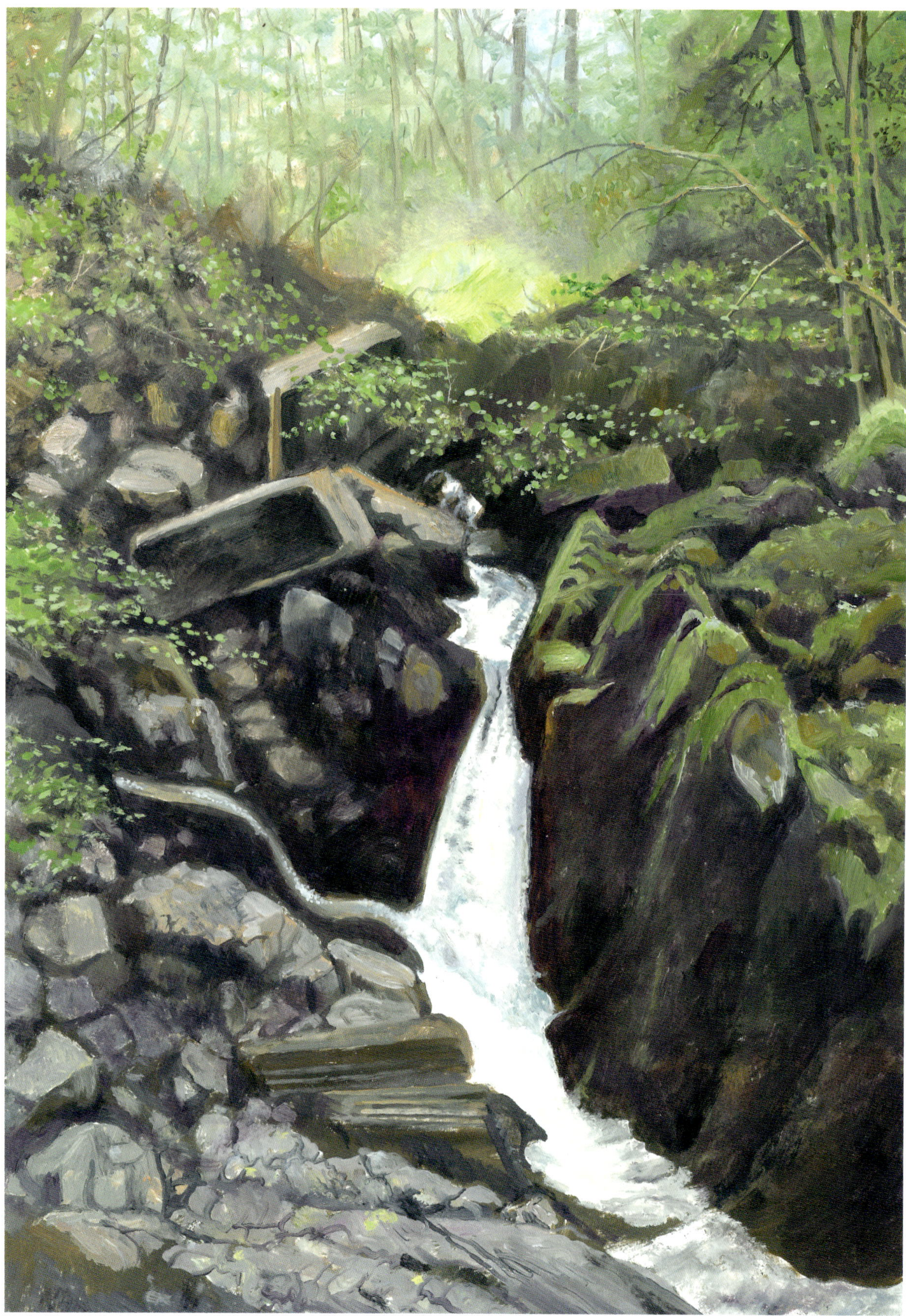

Waterfall

The waterfalls known as the Sychryd Cascades lie in a long and deep gorge accessed by paths of varying difficulty. The lower section of the gorge has an access path suitable for people who can't walk far from a car park. I opted to sit in the car, admiring the rockface known as Dinas Rock which Peter has since painted.

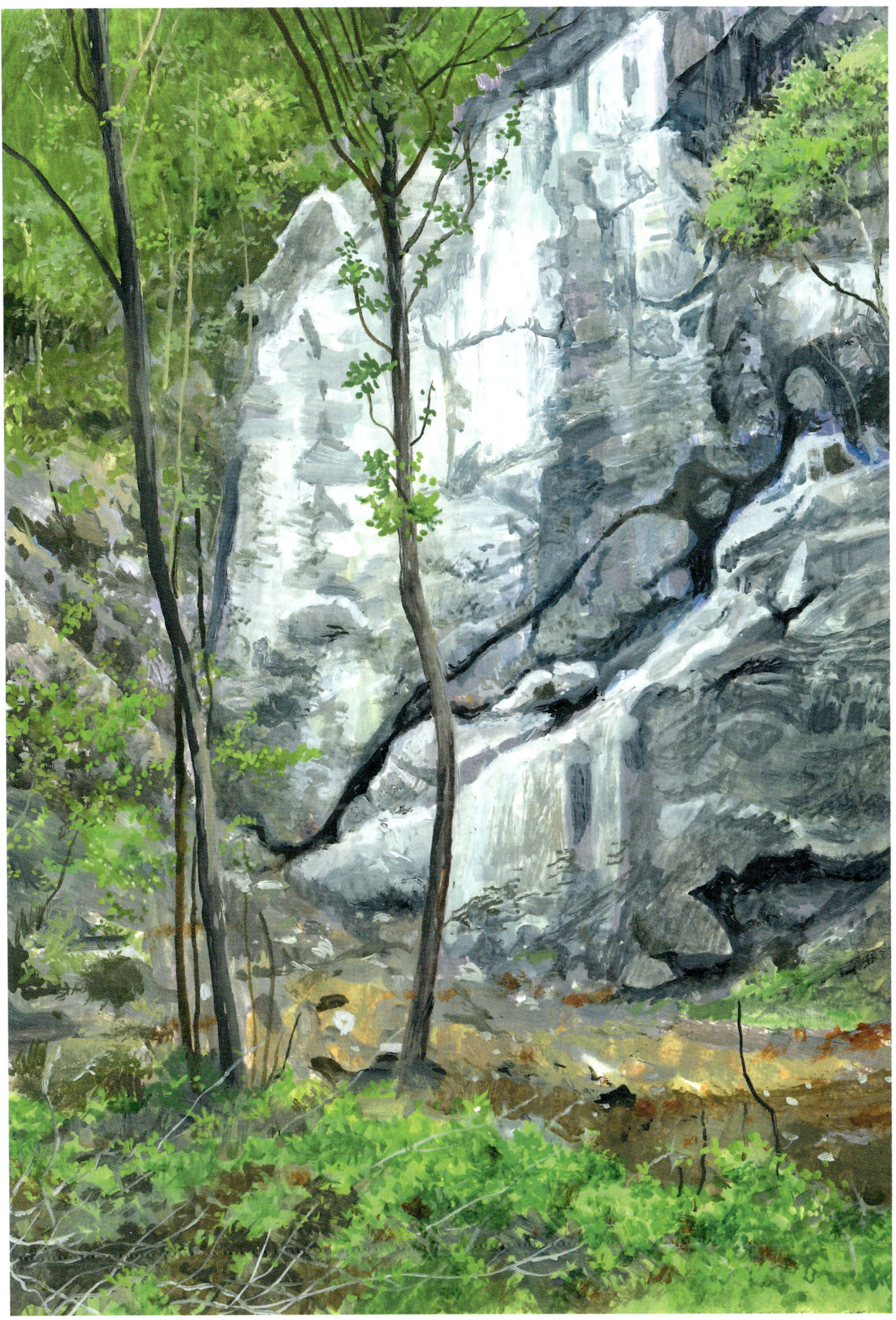

Cliff face seen from the path to the Sychryd Cascades.

Aberfan

Before our first trip to Wales in February, we had thought we might visit Blaenavon, a pit made into a visitor centre. We'd get an idea of what a miner's life was like. By May my interests had changed focus. I no longer wanted to know about life underground. My curiosity had shifted to life today, post-mining, above ground. The transition was epitomised by our visit to Aberfan. I can now banish images of those (mostly children, which makes it worse) who suffocated beneath the sliding slag heap. Instead, when I think of Aberfan, I can see the neat arrangement of flowering plants and shrubs in the Memorial Garden. I can hear the sound of children playing in the playground beside it; and – best of all – I can bring to mind the terraced house opposite the memorial garden's entrance, with its neatly painted white stucco and hanging baskets of brightly colourful flowers. Everything combines to honour the gift of life in lives present and past.

We have never felt the need for SatNav, being devoted to maps of every other kind. We both have a strong sense of direction and instinctively know where the north lies. It is only in Wales that we have spent time wandering around, wondering where on earth we are. Signs announcing the start of villages and towns are either entirely absent, or invisible. We only saw the sign to Aberfan as we left. The signpost was hidden by the burgeoning leaves of a hedgerow tree. It took us three helpers to find Lechwen Hall, our overnight stopping place. The first helper, in a garage forecourt, sent us out of Pontypridd in entirely the wrong direction. The second got us to a place with a name I recognised. Here, we

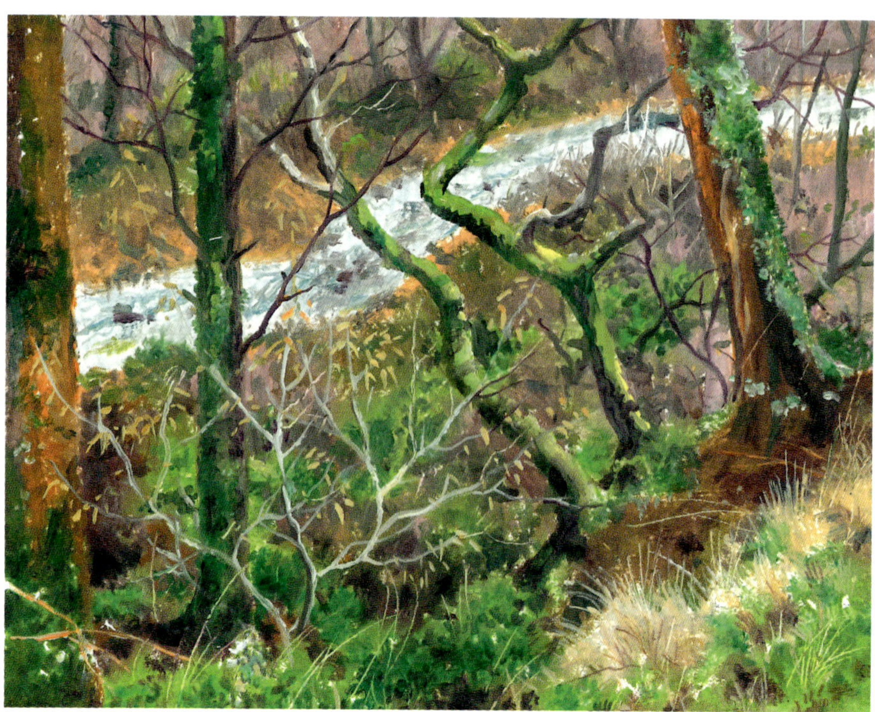

Woodland stream
In Wales you are never far from water.

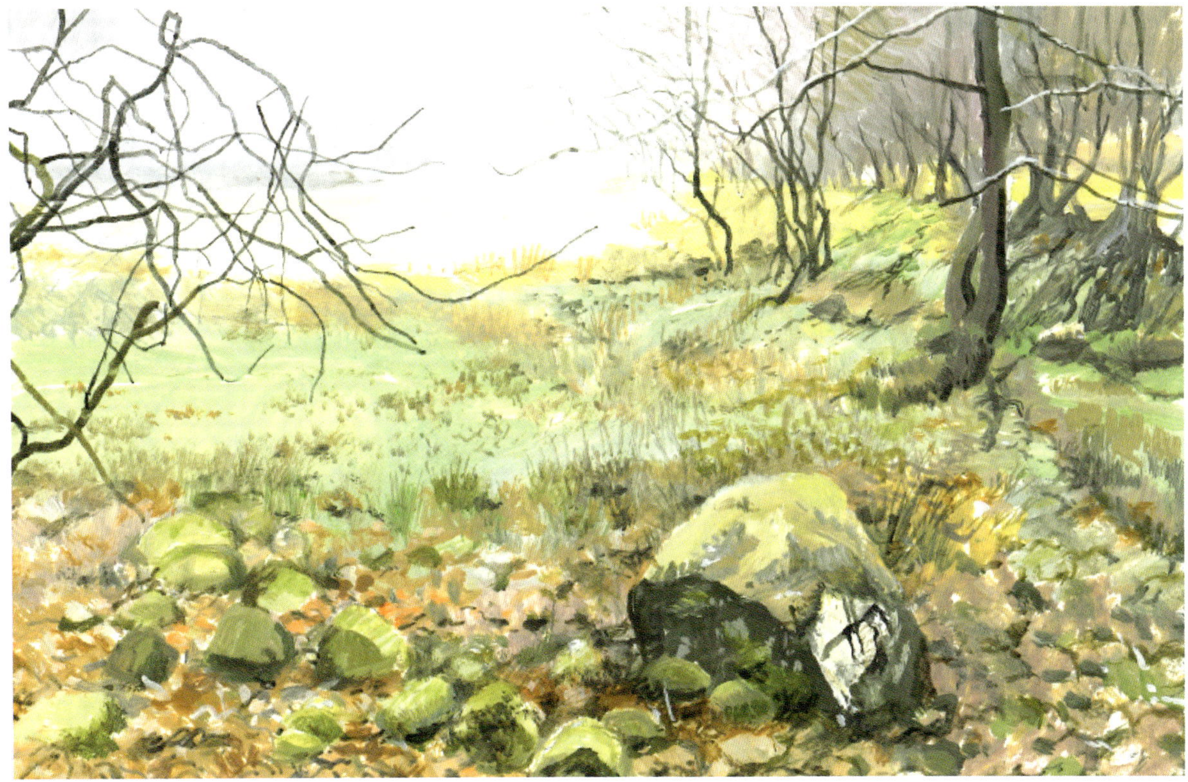

Boggy ground above waterfalls
Rainwater builds up in rocky terrain below boggy ground and descends in spectacular waterfalls.

stopped a lone jogger in his tracks – by this time we were a little fretful. He gave us detailed directions. It took us some time to wind our way up and across moorland, into farmland, then past giant pylons and an enormous electricity substation, finally doubling back on ourselves to a sign – yes, a sign! – leading us to the entrance to the hotel. I worried about the effect of so much electricity fizzing about overhead. No wonder a stay here was such good value, so close to such an eyesore. Yet, scrunching over the drive's sweep of gravel and past the fountain at the entrance, pylons and substations were out of sight and out of mind. We were in the gracious surroundings of an eighteenth-century property, built on a plateau above the distant valleys by one of the early mill-owners with his profits. It was a surprise to find a full car park in such an out-of-the-way spot. At dinner, there was a full dining room: a party of four Japanese, a family party of Americans, an elderly couple and four single people with laptops. It became clear that we'd arrived by a tortuous back lane. The normal way from the main road was much more direct and well-signed. In any case, said my informant, who'd travel without a SatNav?

At breakfast I talked with one of the single businesspeople, a middle-aged Londoner. It turned out that he was Italian, originally from the Amalfi coast, who'd come to England twenty years ago for work. His field was charity and the charity he worked for helped people with HIV. I re-arranged my assumptions as I explained our own presence here and my responses to Aberfan.

"Aberfan? Is it near here?" He'd always wanted to see it and grabbed his phone for directions. "It's only 3 miles away!" he announced delightedly and hurried to leave.

Meeting Salvatore – what a wonderful name – led me to think of the many advantages and disadvantages of having, or not having, SatNav. He, depending on his machine to find his way, had no idea he was near a place he'd always wanted to see. We, without the machine, had spent hours finding a place that was easily reached from the main road.

Our son Ben, as I write, is a red dot on a chart of the South Pacific. I have been viewing his progress over the last week from the Bay of Islands in New Zealand to Vanuatu, a chain of islands two thousand miles to the north. He was invited to crew on a Dutchman's 55-foot yacht, taking turns at the wheel. Ben has a qualification as a Day Skipper, gained in his twenties in the Dartmouth estuary. That was thirty years ago. When I see wiggles in the line being drawn on the chart by the small red dot, I imagine Ben has lost concentration at the wheel. This is the curse of an over-active imagination, as well as proof of the miracles of modern technology. How amazing that we can watch a yacht sailing on the other side of the world! At the moment, the red dot is at 19.9 degrees latitude and 169 degrees longitude, which is the exact location of Tannu, the nearest island in the chain. The yacht's speed is zero. They've arrived at the first island in the Vanuatu chain and anchored for a rest and a good sleep. They set off seven days ago north across the open ocean. Jerome, the owner and skipper of the yacht, estimated they'd take a week.

Panorama, Hirwuan Common

The view from Hirwuan Common, looking north from the western end of the Head of the Valleys road.

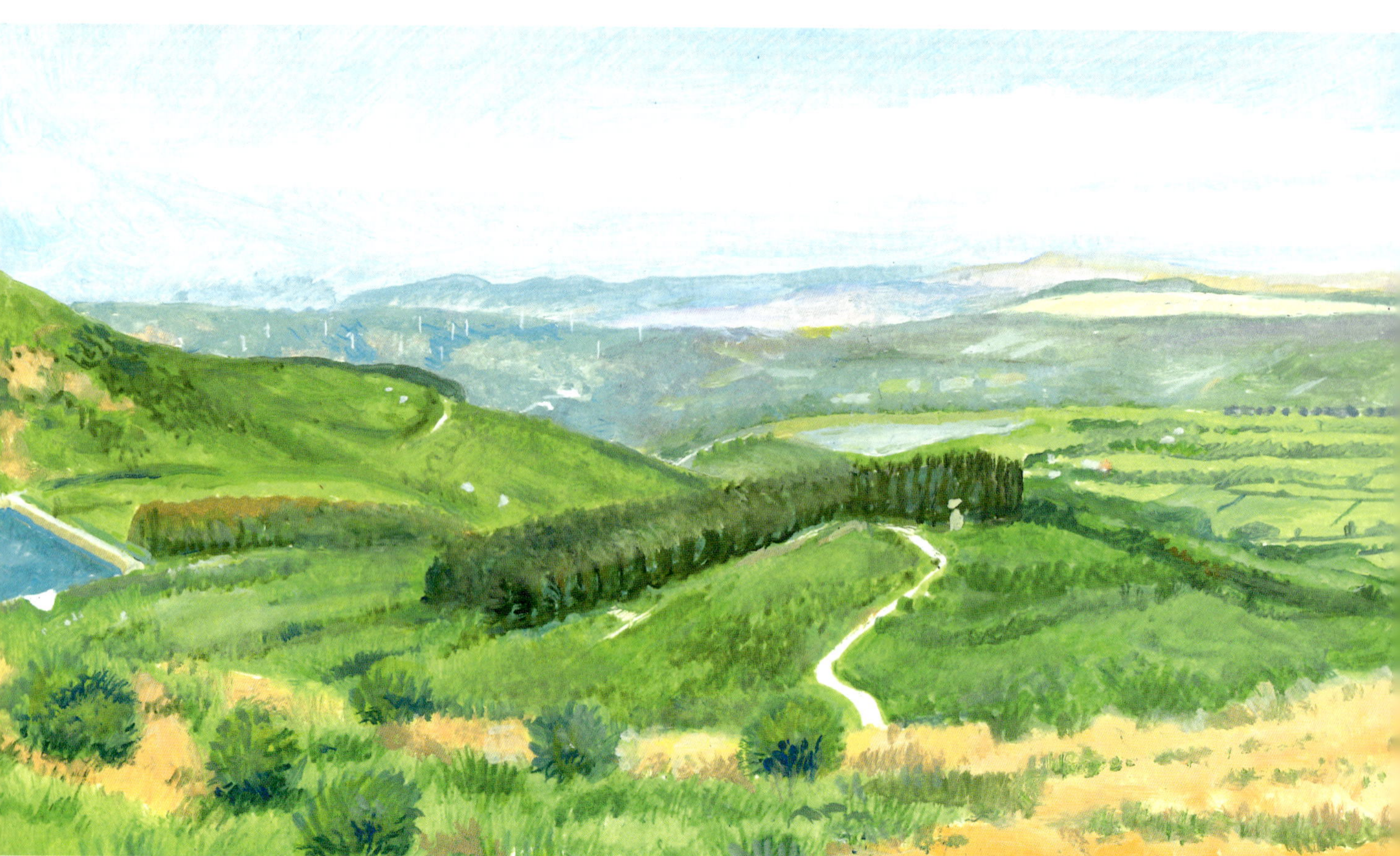

The satellite image on the screen shows the sea floor in different shades of blue. It makes clear the way the shifting, wrinkled surface of the globe is riddled with holes and rifts. We see this, too, in Wales. The area between the Brecon Beacons, the Black Mountains and the mining valleys is known as Waterfall Country. Over aeons of time, water has worn away sections of the softer rocks, leaving the harder formations. What we see today is water cascading over drops of varying height, in staircases made of hard rock known as millstone grit. South of Waterfall Country lie the mining valleys, where coal seams run through carboniferous rock. The once-industrial valleys stream south from a band of high ground, like ribbons tacked to a panel.

The Head of the Valleys road

A combination of over and under passes will make the journey across the top of the mining valleys an easy drive. But not yet. Avoiding the part still under construction, we wanted to repeat the spectacular stretch of road that curls around the head of the Rhonda valley. We stopped again at a lay-by to take in the stunning view, which Peter will paint. Down the far side, the haze of blue patches on steep hillsides puzzled us until, closer, we saw the land was covered in large areas of blue netting, laid to stop rocks cascading down onto the road. In places, it is the road itself that is falling away. Glancing down a precipice from a car window can be alarming.

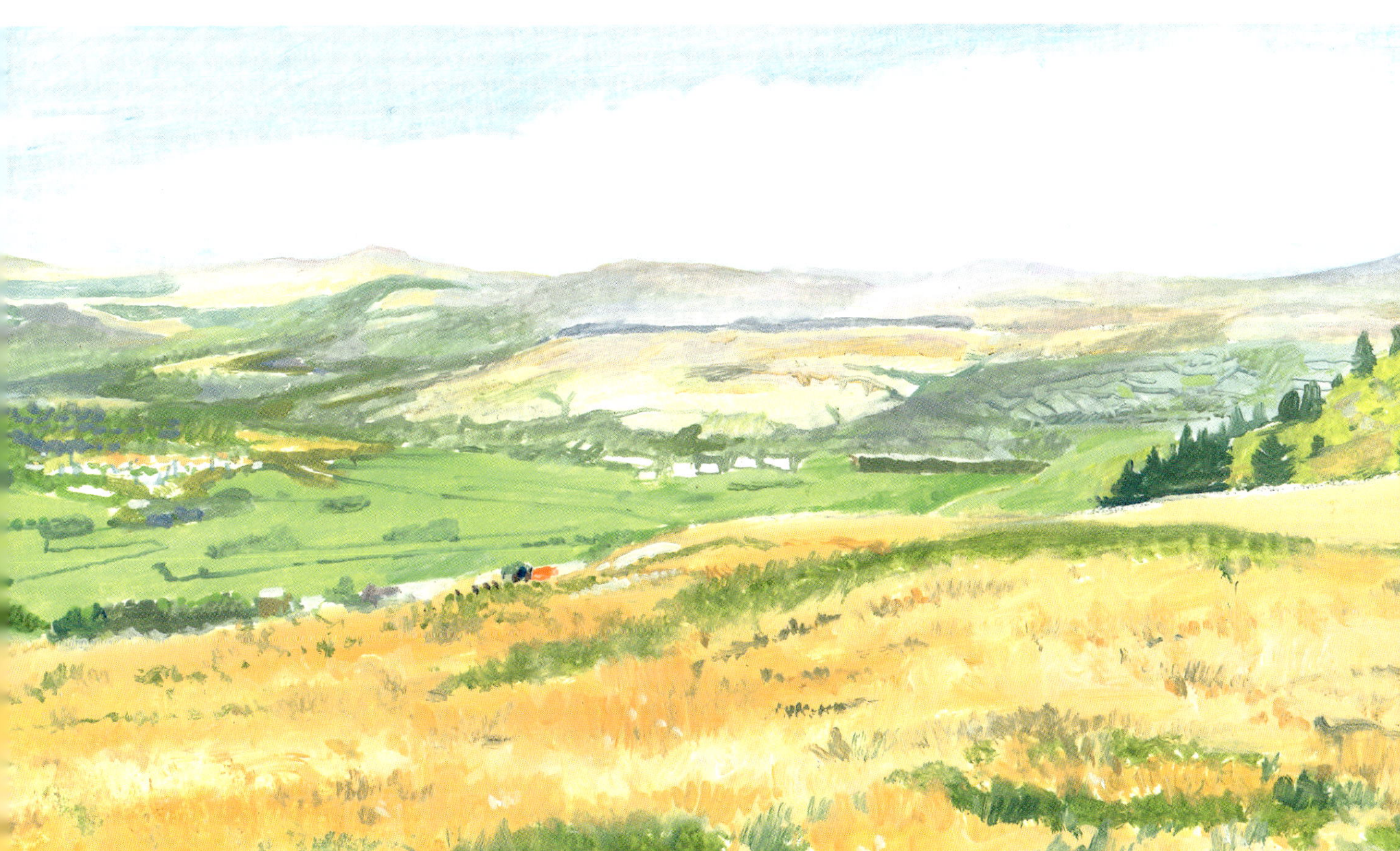

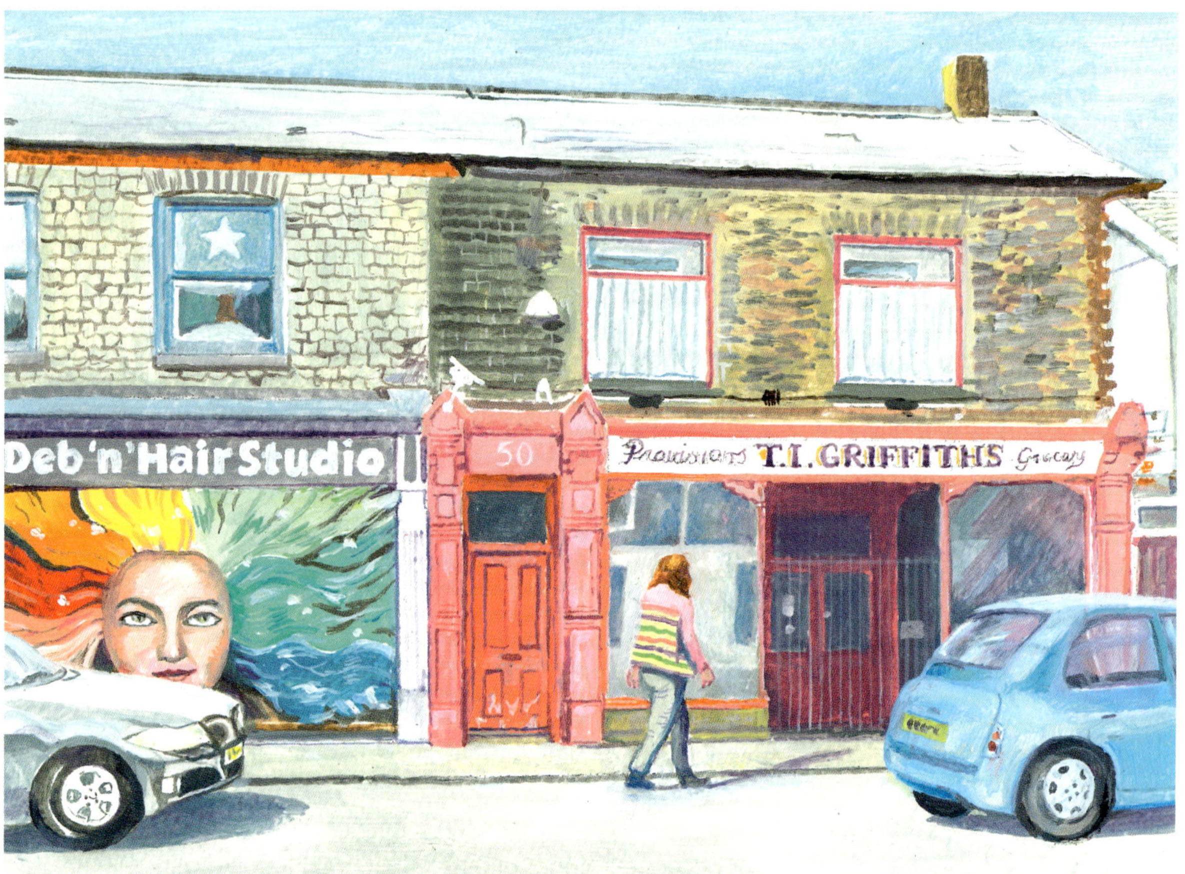

Deb-n-Hair Studio
The play on the name of a hairdresser's salon sums up the unquenchable spirit of the people in the valleys.

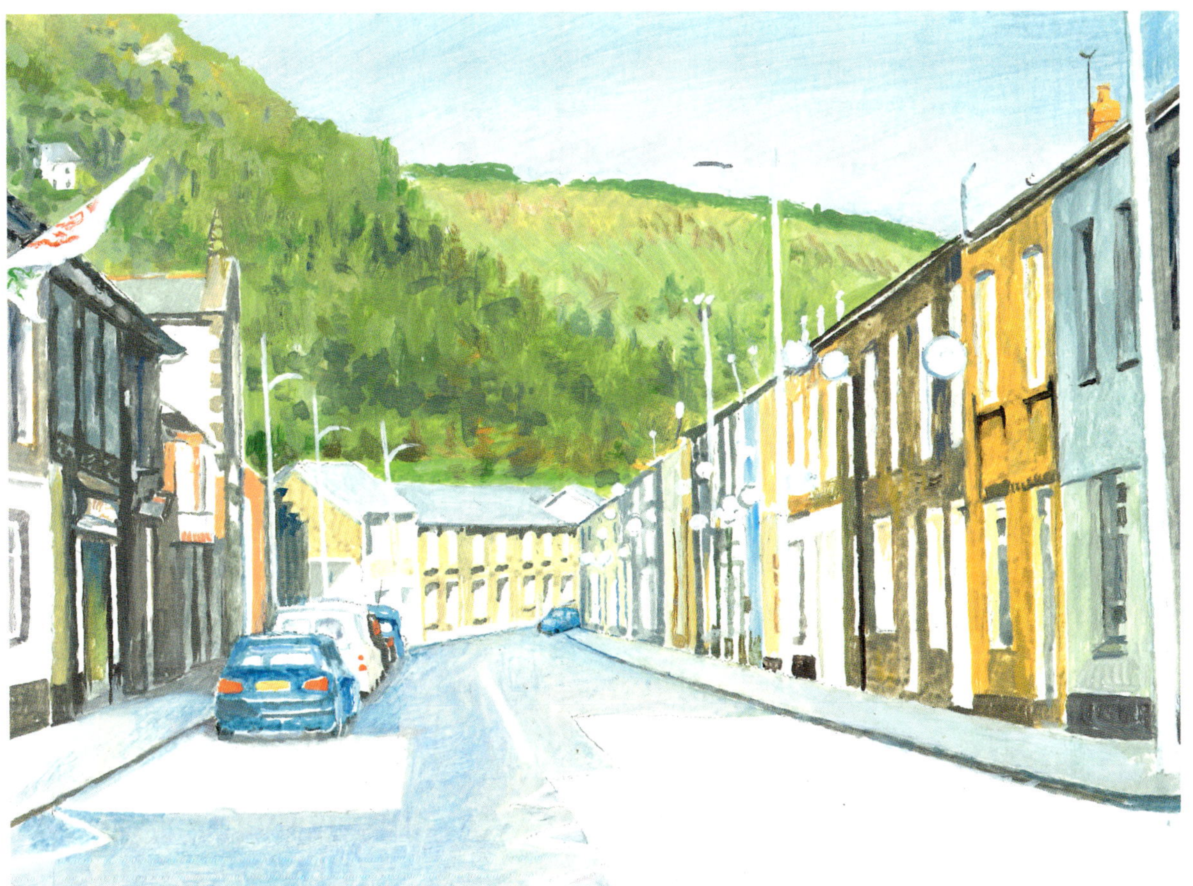

Blaenrhondda

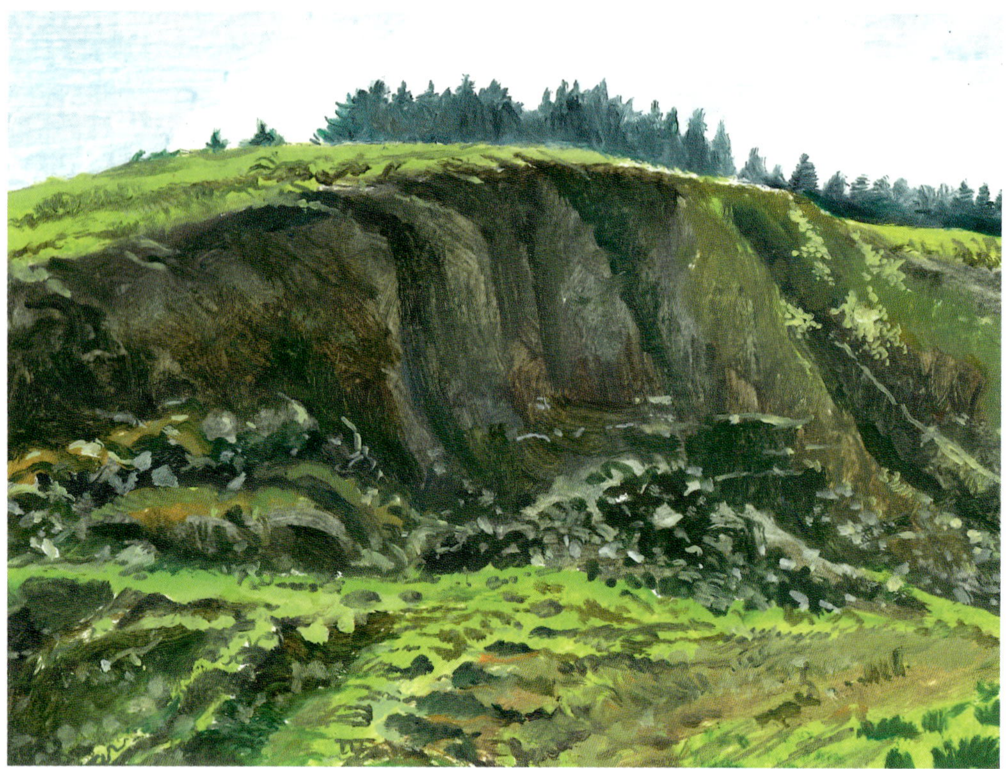

Landslips and quarried hillside
Hillsides show the instability of the terrain in the mining valleys.

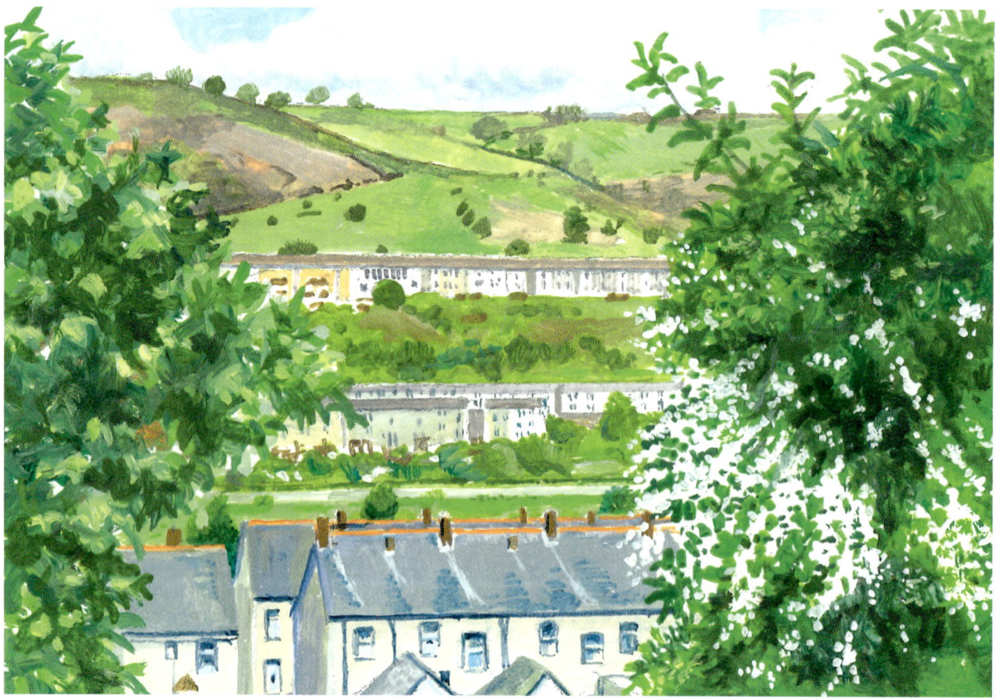

Mining valleys' terraces
Terraced houses lie in bands on the steep hillsides of the old mining villages, like the tiers of seating in ancient amphitheatres.

In Treherbert, we doubled-back on ourselves to penetrate further up a valley, keen to see the hinterland behind the rows of terraced houses. The answer turned out to be more terraced houses and evidence of a once-busy past, a rusty bridge leading nowhere at the end of a defunct lane. Mr Griffiths the butcher had long since shuttered up his shop and moved on, perhaps beyond the grave. But waiting at a bus stop at eleven o'clock in the morning stood Adele, in a sleeveless black dress, a-glitter with diamante necklaces, earrings and bracelets stacked up her plump, brown arms. Her hair was neatly plaited, coiled and held in place by a wisp of black scarf. She was on her way to Caerphilly where she works. "In a charity shop," she added. She shook with laughter, showing a generous gap between her two front teeth. I thought of Robert with his gap-toothed smile selling us a leaflet about waterfalls in his late mother's garage-shop near Pontneddfechan. The fascination of waterfalls lies in the way water continues to fall, great, white plumes of it, plunging on down, never stopping. In the same way, life goes on, generation after generation.

Caerphilly

If there is to be a ceremony on completion of this book, when we will award prizes for the best car park in Wales, the main one in Caerphilly will be a contender. It is central, ground-level, and spacious, with shops and restaurants to hand. Moreover, it has a good view of the castle. A short totter along a small shopping mall took us to a licensed cafe opposite the castle walls. Ten out of ten. The insides of castles are now beyond us; but never mind. We've seen a lot in the past.

From Caerphilly we drove to find Gareth's sister Jane, north of Cardiff. Jane was getting herself ready to go away for a few days' camping in Oxwich Bay on the Gower. We sat in the sun in her garden, the river flowing the other side of her garden fence. Every so often, her mobile phone rang, a clamorous summons from the hip pocket of her shorts. It was either Thomas or Owen, the two sons from her first marriage to a Japanese. When she returned to England after twenty years in Japan, she got a job in a Japanese car components firm in the Taff valley. She met and married an Englishman called Pete who died after eight months. Now her elder brother Gareth has died. Jane is bright; she laughs easily; her eyes sparkle. Of course, she knows sadness and loss. She also knows how life goes on.

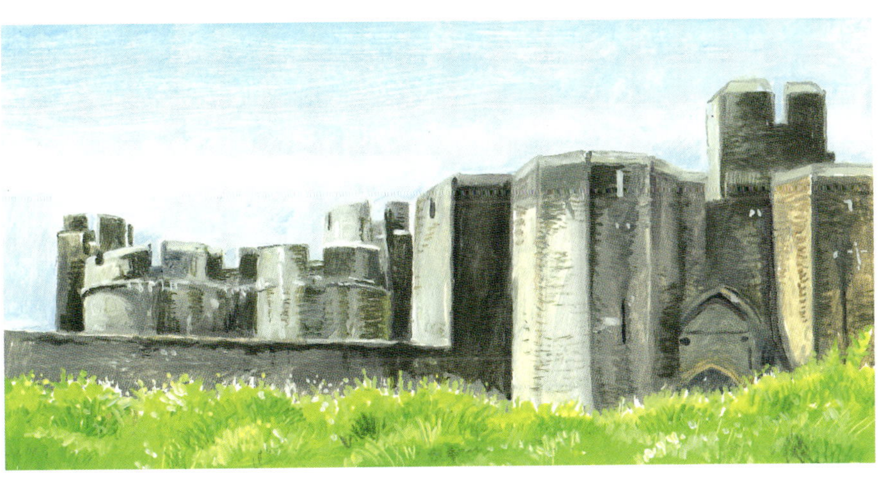

Caerphilly Castle

Caerphilly Castle, built in the thirteenth century, is the largest in Wales. Taking English castles into account as well, only Windsor Castle is larger.

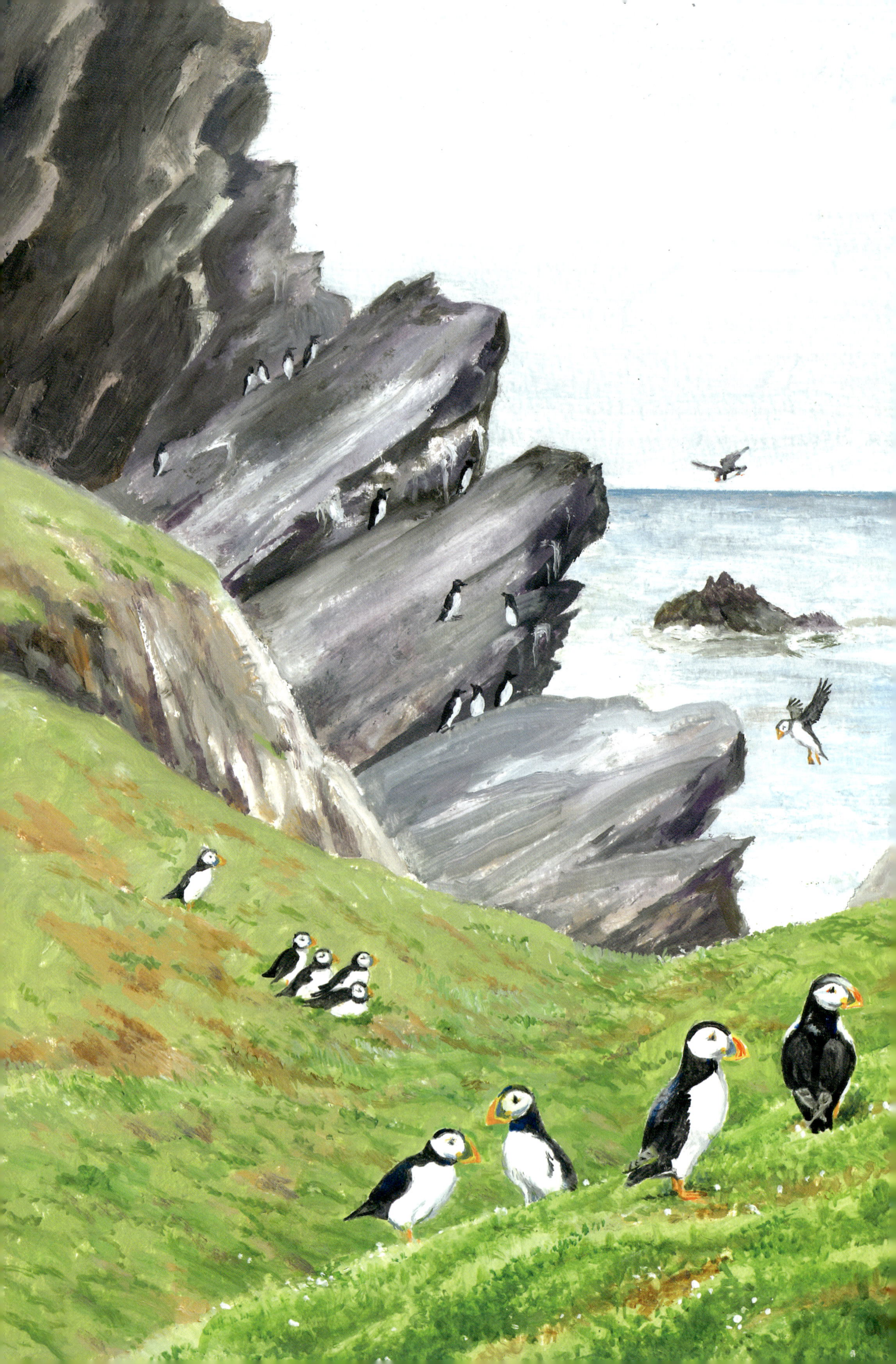

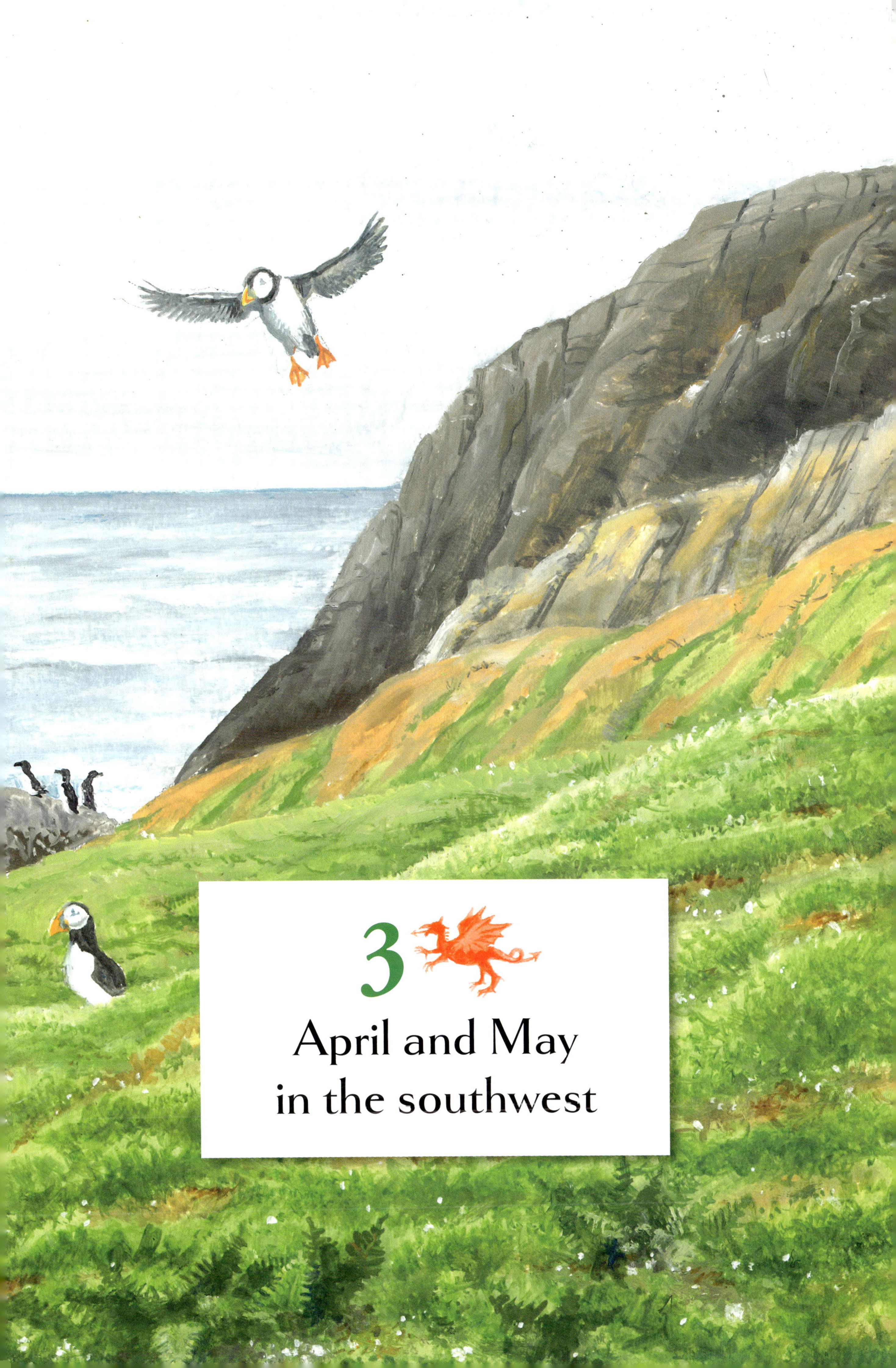

3

April and May in the southwest

April and May in the southwest

To Pembrokeshire

The Prince of Wales bridge is becoming more familiar as our trips to Wales continue. Now, towards the end of April, we are on our way to the southwest corner of the country. You only have to say "the southwest" to me and I immediately recapture my glorious childhood feeling of returning home. Like Lassie the collie in the 1940s' film of that name, I have an inner magnet that draws me in the direction of my home. However, there's another side to this. With these short trips away, I've recaptured another childhood feeling: one composed of panic and anxiety at the notion of leaving home, for however short

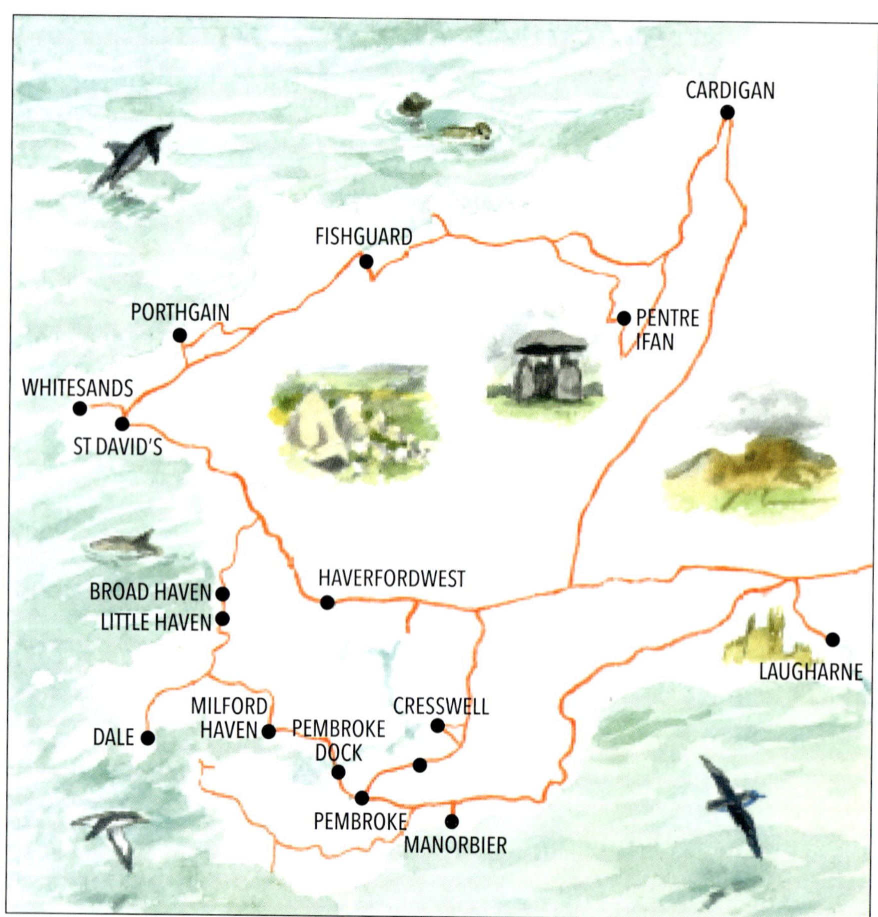

a period. On reflection, I've tracked this uncomfortable emotion to my ten-year-old self, going away to boarding school for the first time. I had my elder sister for company on the trip but on arrival in Bath she went in an entirely different direction, and I was on my own in foreign territory. Like everyone with similar experiences, I learnt to adapt to circumstances. But the scar that's touched by the act of going away remains sensitive. In my trunk there was just room, after packing the regulation knickers, cricket sweaters and uniform in general, to include Cola. I learnt much later that he was not a unique individual, but one of a kind. He was a stuffed imitation of a Koala Bear, an Australian animal, one of millions. I likened my dumbfounded astonishment at this realisation to my much earlier experience of learning that *Mummy* was not unique and special to me and my sister Jane, but one of a kind in a species called Mummy that other children had in their possession.

However short a time we're away, the anxiety of leaving behind essentials is triggered each time. How on earth do people who go through really severe crises manage? I think of everyone in the uncountable numbers of people of all ages torn from their homes by war and deprivation. At the moment, Sudan is the scene of crisis.

Laugharne

We'd visited Laugharne first in 1961, a year after we were married. No wonder it had changed by this, our second visit. The road led us down through a surprisingly large village to a car park at the foot of the castle on the estuary. We squeezed in between a bright yellow roadster and a large people-carrier. In Peter's memory the place had more marsh and less road. I had no memory of the castle, but I'd kept a clear image of Dylan Thomas's house on the estuary. More vivid than this was my recollection of the swinging rhythms of his poetry and the sound of

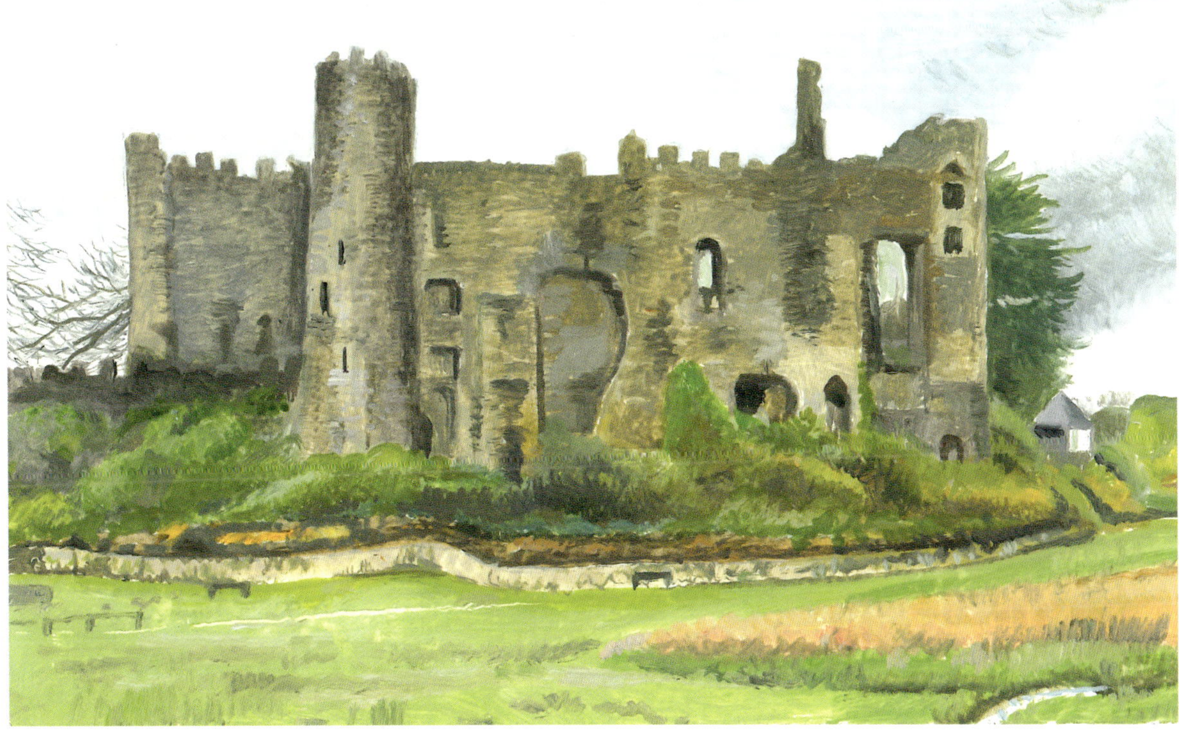

Laugharne Castle

Look carefully and you'll see the shed where Dylan Thomas, the twentieth-century Welsh bard, wrote his singsong lines.

Emlyn Williams' wonderfully Welsh voice. I'd heard him reciting extracts from *Under Milk Wood* at the Bath Festival in the early '50s.

While Peter set off over the marsh I stayed in the car, wanting to sit and stare, listen and think. I noticed a man hovering around the nearby cars holding a notebook. I wound down the window and showed him our parking ticket. He smiled. No, he wasn't a parking attendant. He was the owner of the yellow roadster, parked beyond the one we were beside. It became clear that he was hoping to have a chat with its owner. As soon its owner turned up, the conversation began. It circled around the question of gaskets before moving on to car accessories. Did the Owner of Yellow Car number 2 have a cigarette lighter? No, but he did have a 12-volt feed and so could fit one. Indeed, he'd often thought of doing so. The two yellow roadster owners had lots to say to each other. The exchange went on for some time. Dylan Thomas might have captured the rhythm in it.

The closer we get to Pembroke's southwest corner, the more the sky dominates the landscape. The hedgerow trees are permanently bowed before the prevailing wind. They look like much used witch's brooms. We descend to a wide bay

Boats, Laugharne estuary
"The mussel pooled and heron priested shore ..."
Lines from Dylan Thomas' poetry spring unbidden to mind when you look out over the estuary at Laugharne, or wander the village streets.

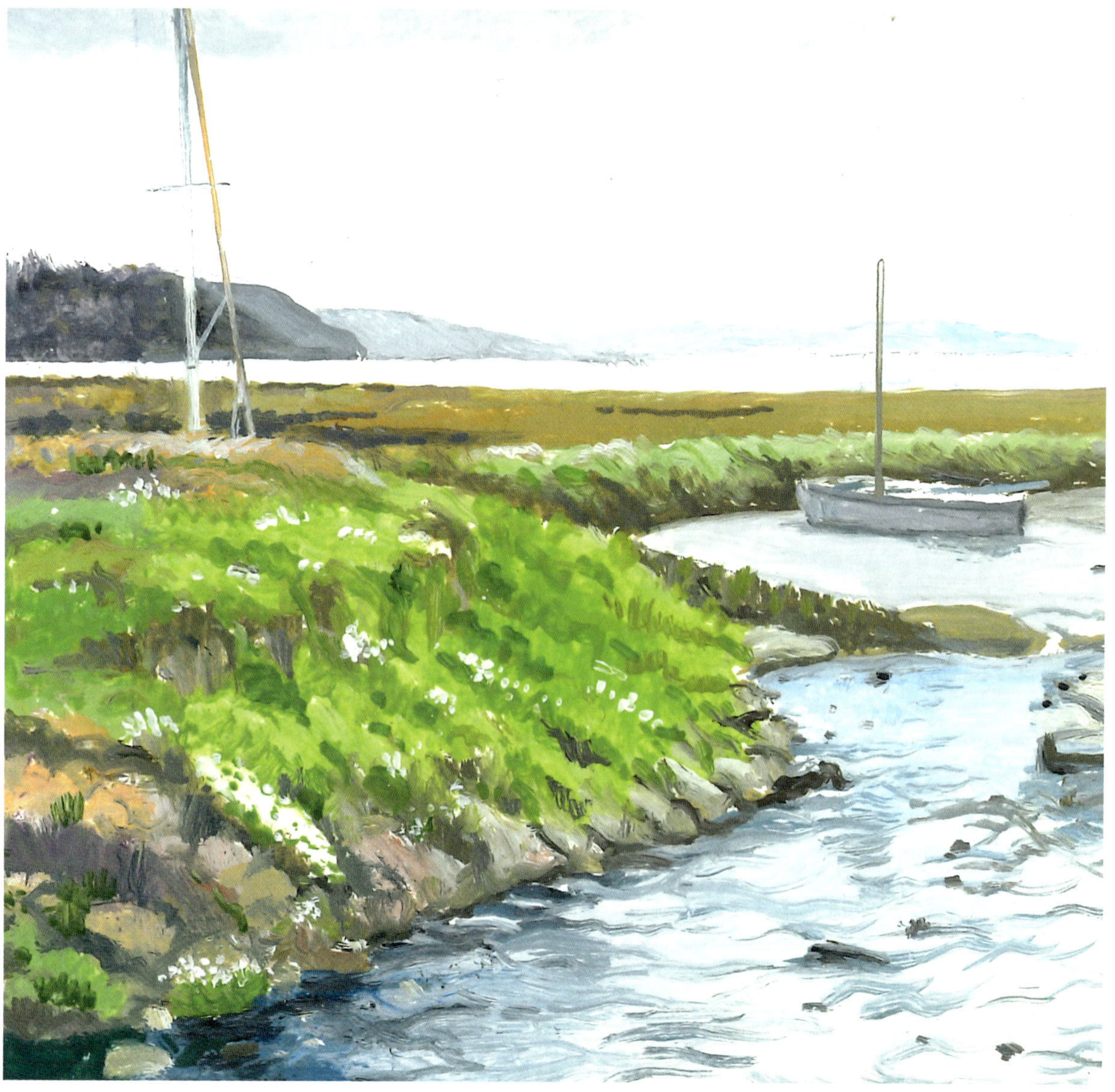

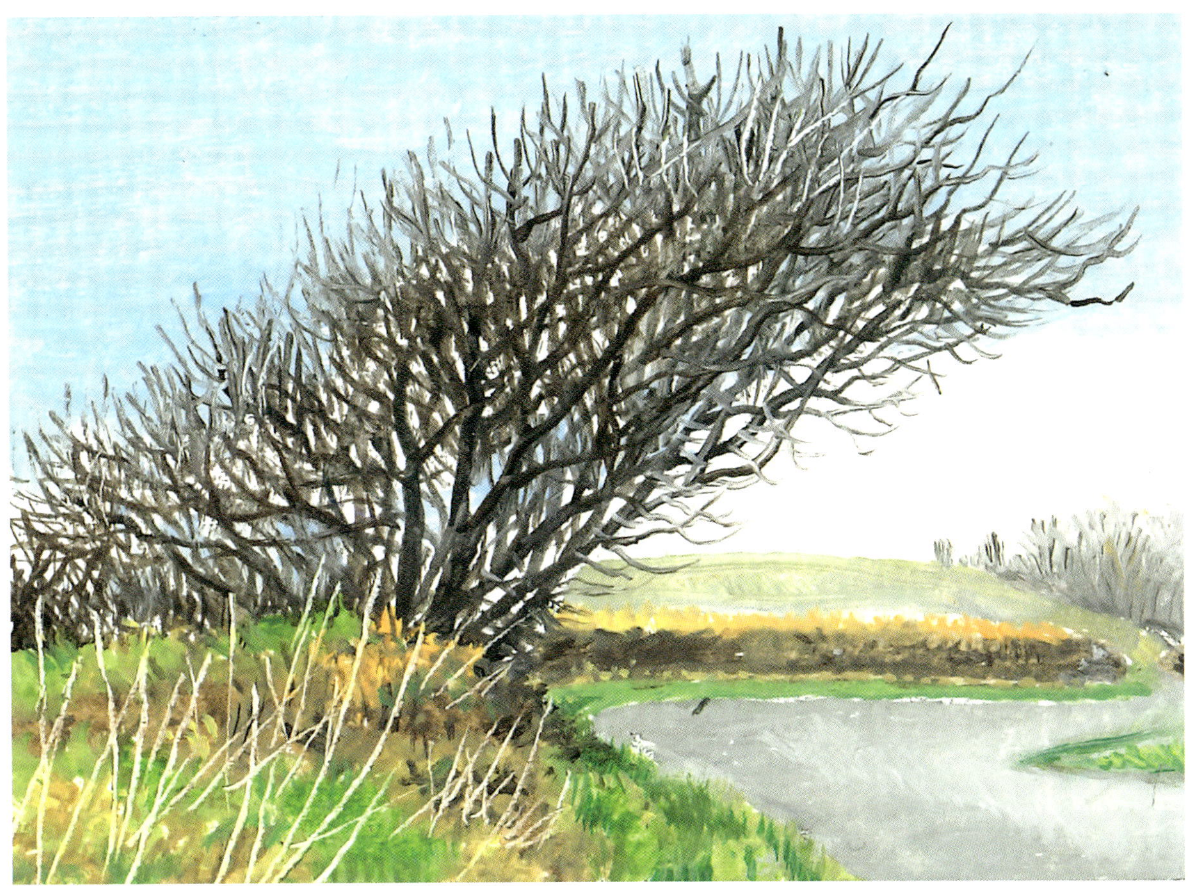

Prevailing wind
The southwesterly prevailing wind sculpts the shape of hedgerow trees.

where the wind drives waves to the shore. Newgale seems an appropriate name for this expanse of sandy beach backed by a steep bank of shingle. It must be a good place for surfers. On the inland side a number of white caravans and camper vans have started to gather for this holiday weekend.

St David's

We find our hotel, right at the start of the little town. Or might you call it a big village? In fact, it's designated a city. What is the story behind this mismatch of word and place? I take a tentative plunge into history. St David's was designated a city by virtue of the cathedral built at its centre in the twelfth century. That begs the next question: why was the cathedral built in such a small place? Answer: because the monk known later as St David founded a monastery on the spot in the fifth century. Seven hundred years passed between the establishment of the monastery and the building of the cathedral. That's as long a period as lies between us today and our forefathers of Tudor times. The Victorians decided it wasn't right to call St David's a city and removed the word. The late Queen restored its status in 1994. It has 210 listed buildings, a number surely worthy of a city.

Our hotel is called the Grove and lies in the middle of a rookery. Instead of puzzling over St David's history, I listen to the rooks quarrelling over their domain. Sleep shuts them up from dark to faint dawn. In late April, this is not a long period. The rest of the time they dispute ownership of nests. Every so often one of them gives a particularly angry squawk. It's the sort of sharp shriek we utter when someone large steps on our toes. More pigeons add their voices but,

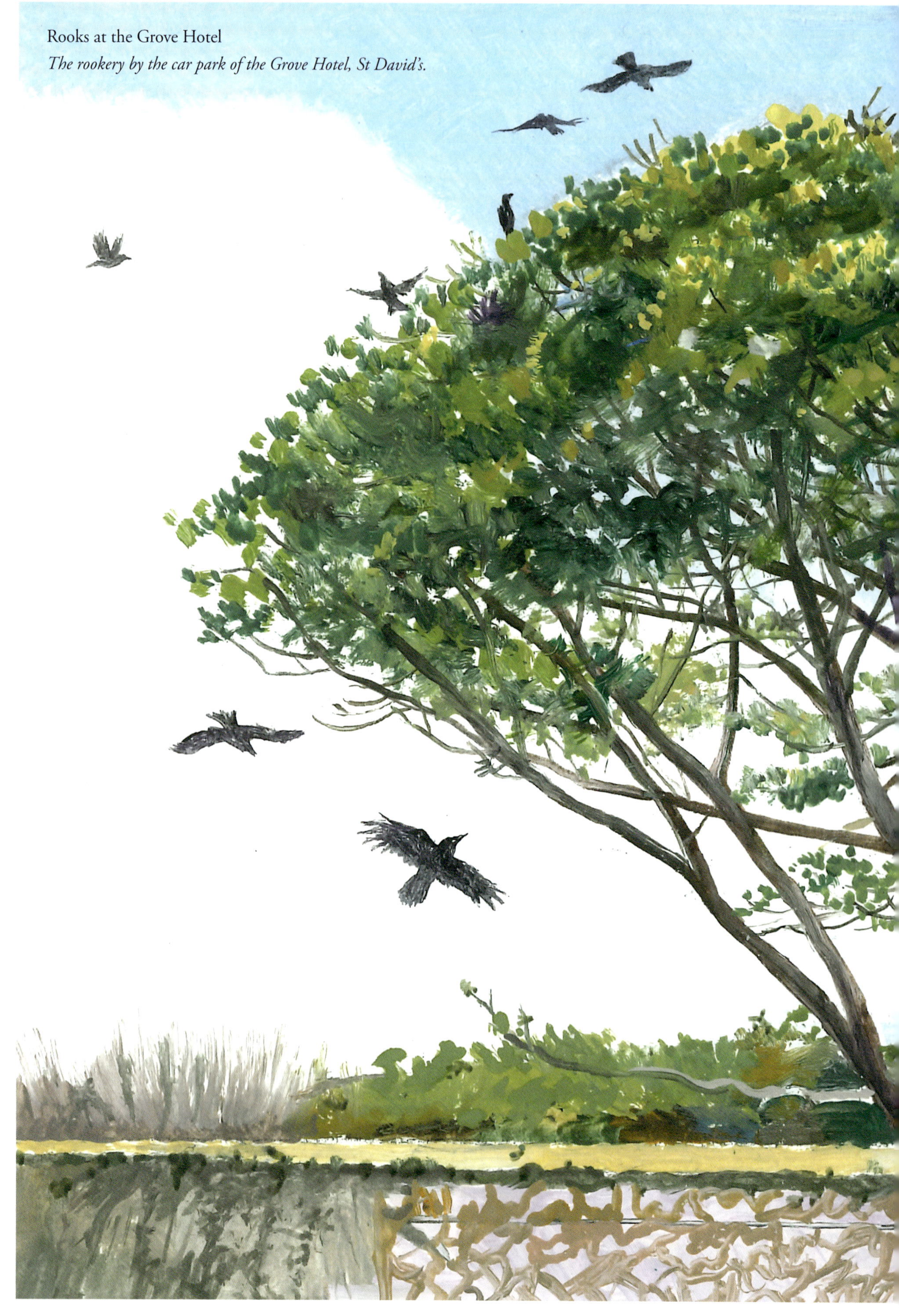

Rooks at the Grove Hotel

The rookery by the car park of the Grove Hotel, St David's.

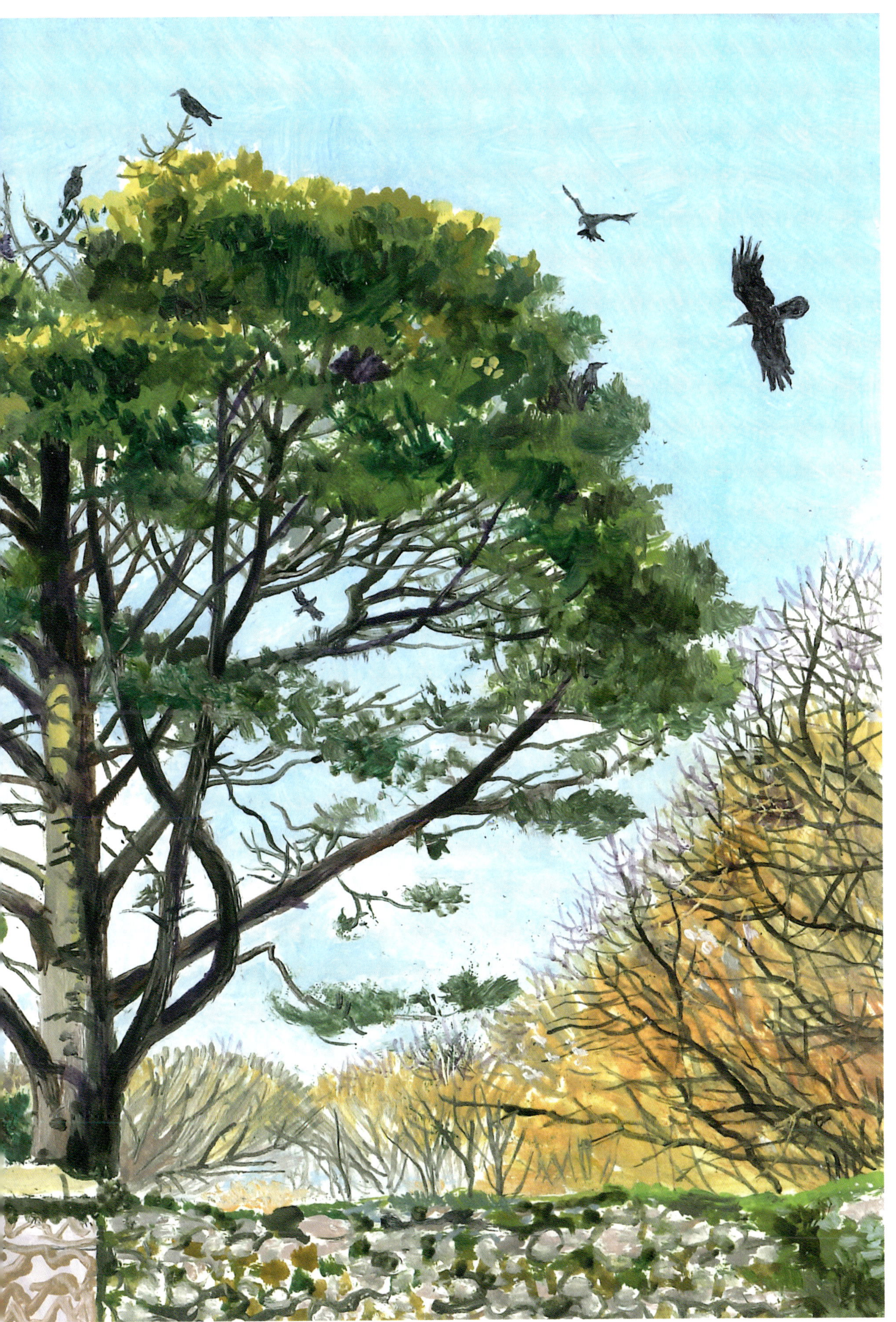

unlike the Tintern pigeons, they are not so chatty. Their conversation is confined to *"How you too? How you too? I want to answer, in similar cooing fashion, Good but would you and the rooks cool down."*

Pembrokeshire's sandy beaches

West of St David's, there is one of the best of Pembrokeshire's many, large, sandy beaches: Whitesands. In the late afternoon on the day of our arrival we went and sat on a bench as the sun sank towards the line between sea and sky. The sea glistened. The sun was warm. Like others sitting at the back of the beach, I lifted my face to the sun and closed my eyes. I recalled the acres of sunflowers on the way to Greece, in what was then Yugoslavia; the head of each flower turned in unison as the sun rode across the heavens.

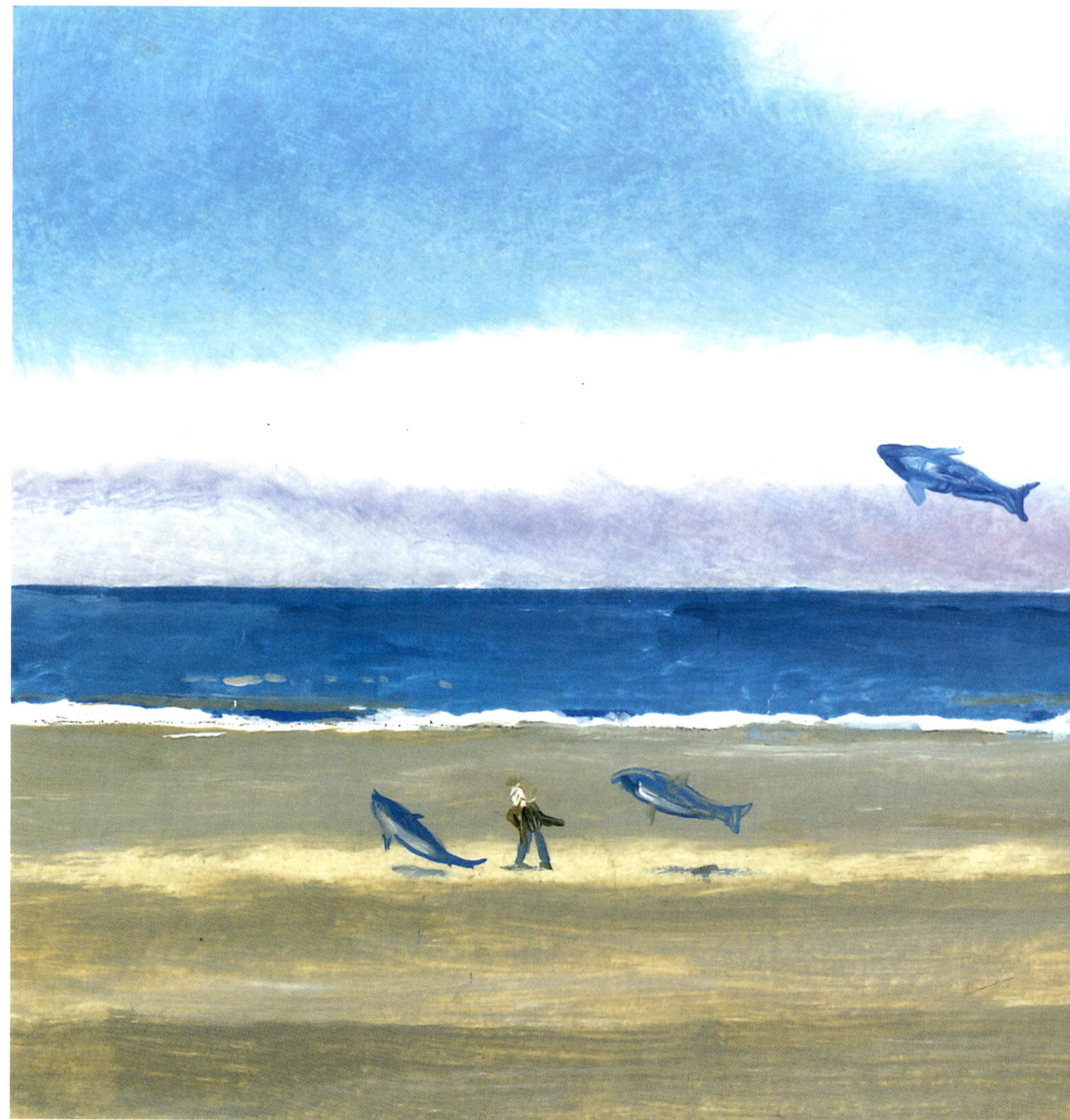

Next day we drove in the opposite direction and passed two more beaches of fine, golden sand: Broadhaven and Littlehaven. At the first beach, we watched kites being flown in the brisk breeze. For a few minutes, kite-flying looks like fun. I'm reminded of a wartime story told by my mother. My father, a serving Army officer, came home on leave. He took us out on the moor beyond our garden gate to fly a kite. A neighbour reported him to the local police for signaling to the enemy. The family responded to this with a great deal of amazement and laughter and the honing of the episode into a story for the archives. Apart from its value as anecdote material, I never saw the point of flying kites.

Kite-flying at Broadhaven
The expansive sands at Broadhaven are just what you need for flying kites.

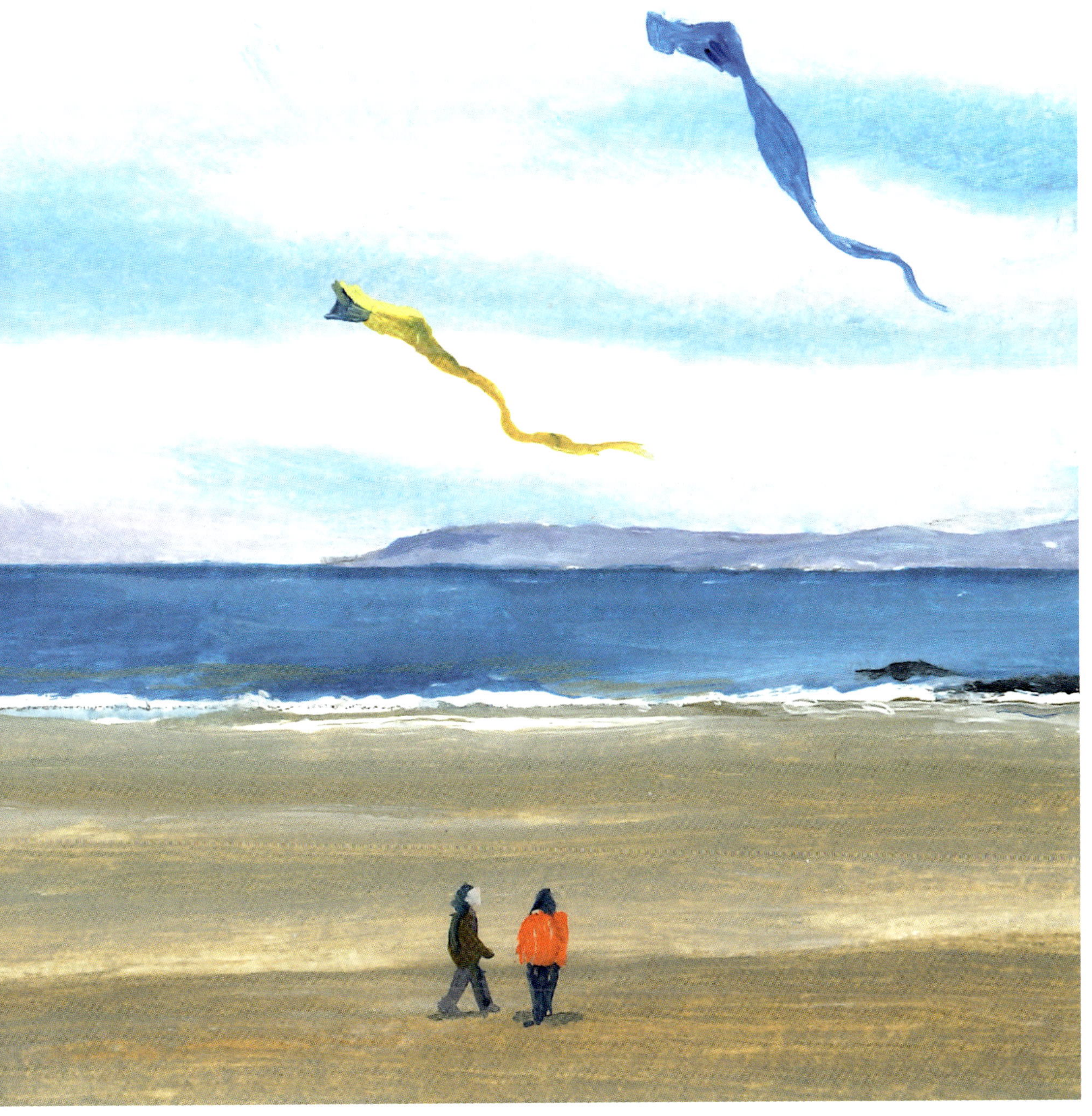

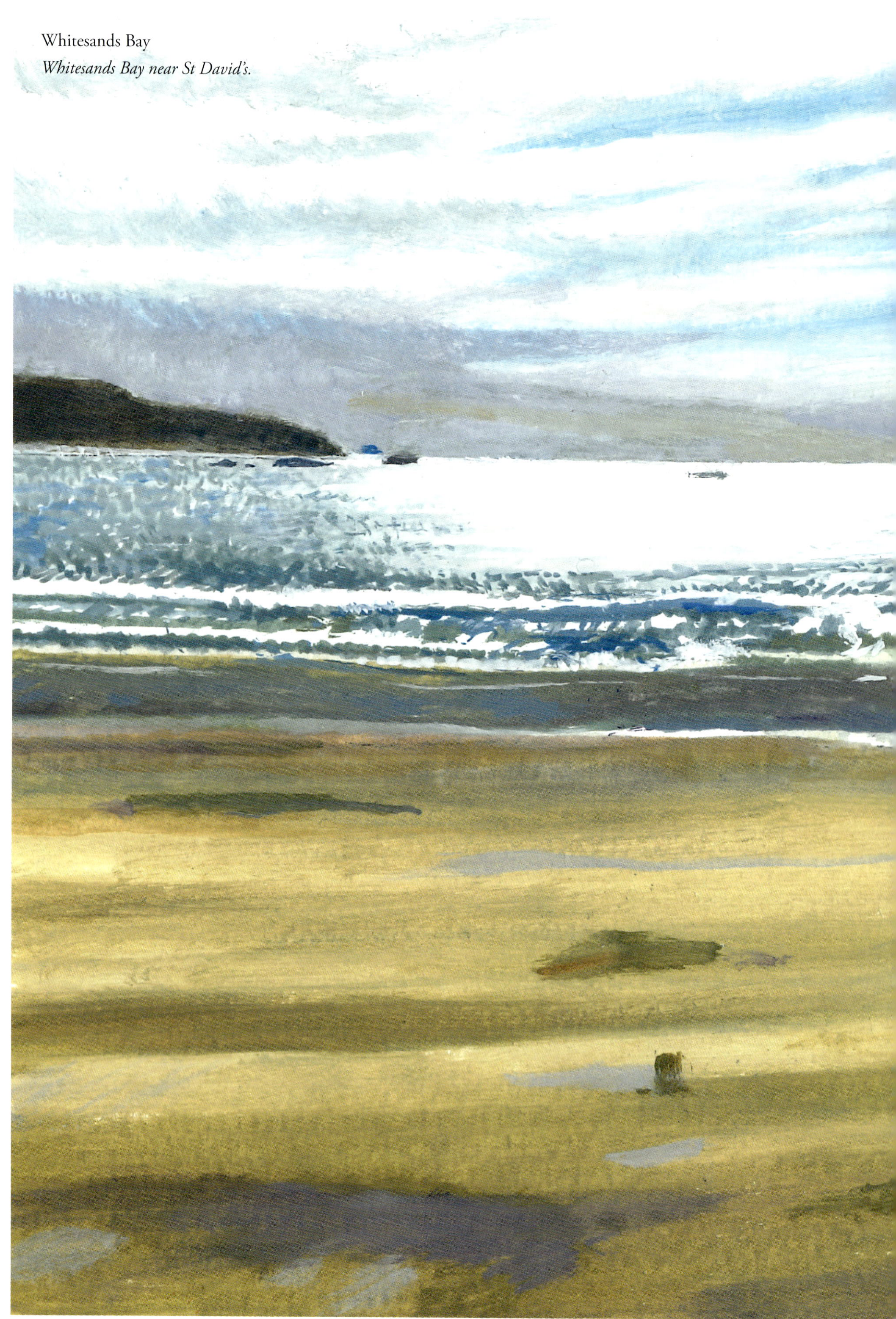

Whitesands Bay
Whitesands Bay near St David's.

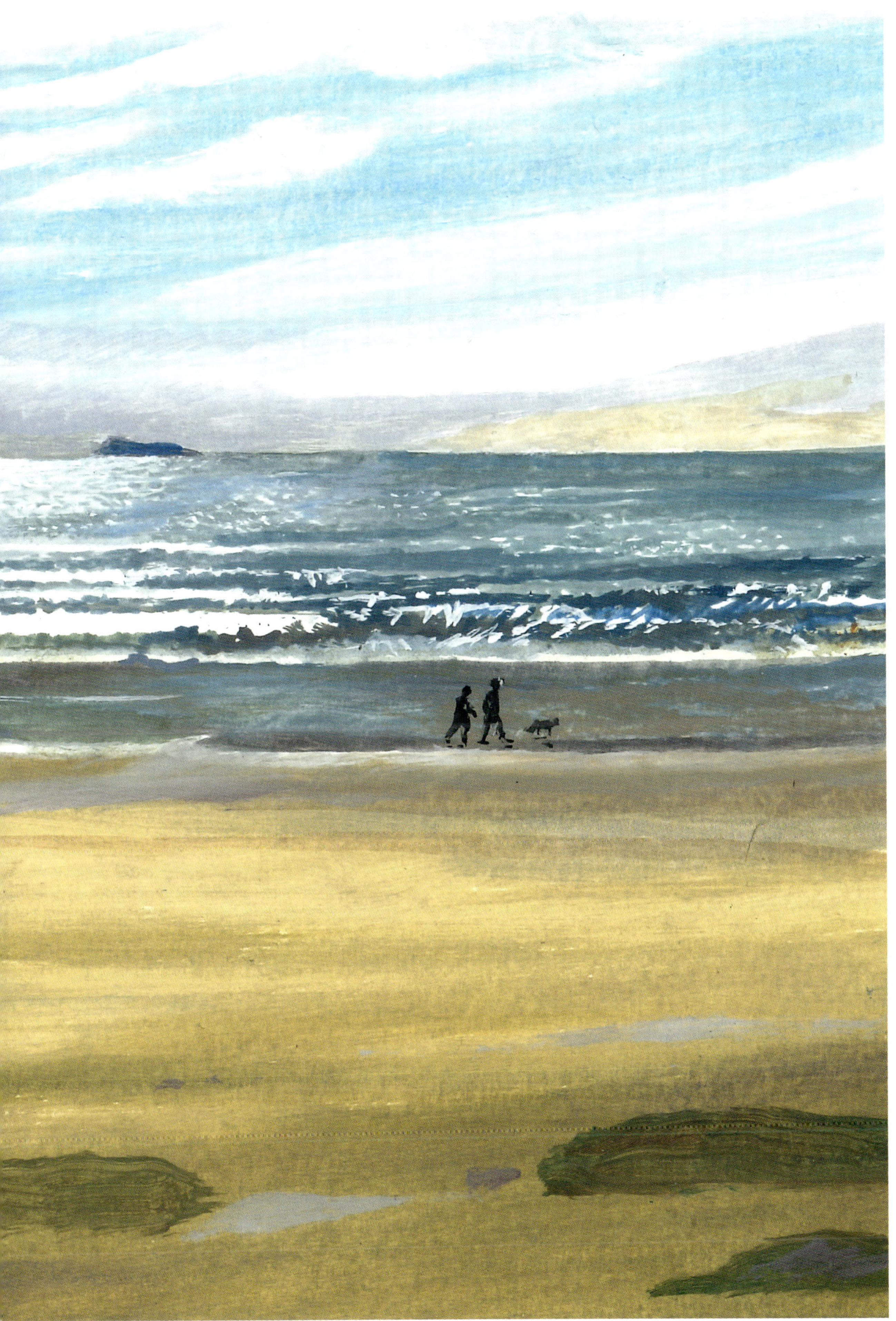

Dale, Skokholm and Skomer

Since our last trip to Wales, the daffodils have shrivelled and died, giving way in the grassy verges to bluebells, campion, wild garlic, umbellifers, dandelions and stitchwort. Stands of trees hold a misty pink haze in their bare branches, the faint tinge produced by leaves as yet unfurled. Our first target of the day was Dale, on the southern headland of St Bride's Bay. With a little imagination you can see the bay as a dragon's open mouth with Dale and St Anne's Head on its lower jaw and St David's on its upper. We passed Marloes, a place that brought back memories of trips to the offshore islands of Skomer and Skokholm. Peter had first explored Skomer with his good, childhood friend, Bill Stevenson. Bill's family were friends with R.M. Lockley, a naturalist who was living at the time in a farmhouse on a cliff in Pembrokeshire. Lockley was writing *The Seals and the Curragh,* his study of the seals on the beach below the farmhouse. Peter still has this and a number of Lockley's other books. Reading the introduction to *Shearwaters* (inscribed *To Peter from Grannie Barrett on his eleventh birthday 1946)* I take a moment to sit back and wonder at this glimpse into life's inner workings. The eleven-year-old Peter was inspired by Lockley and this influence lasted into adult life.

"Not everyone," wrote R. M. Lockley, *"has the luck to live on, to have an island to himself. It is true that before I could start this ten-year study of the shearwater, there were certain formalities to be got through. I wished to settle on this remote Welsh island in order to live simply, undisturbed and alone, but in the company of those things I most cared for; wild birds and animals, wild flowers, the sea and a wide horizon. But*

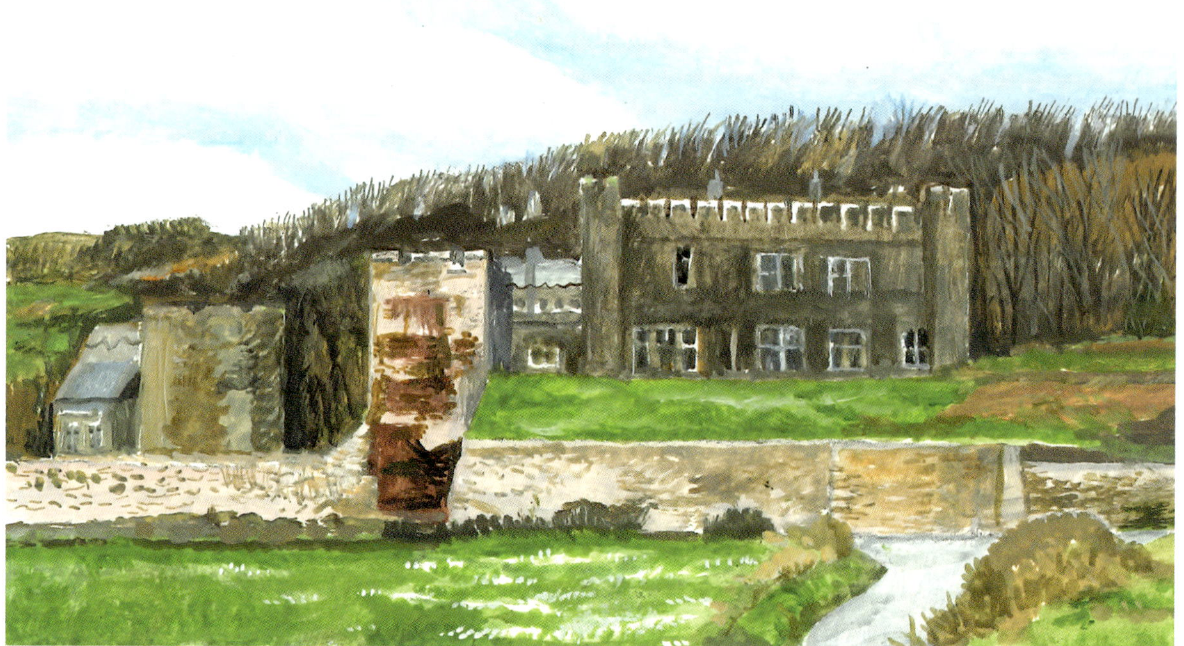

Dale's one-time castle

Dale Castle is now a conglomeration of various buildings, including a church and a kiln. It has been remodelled so substantially over the centuries, a thirteenth-century villager would not recognise it.

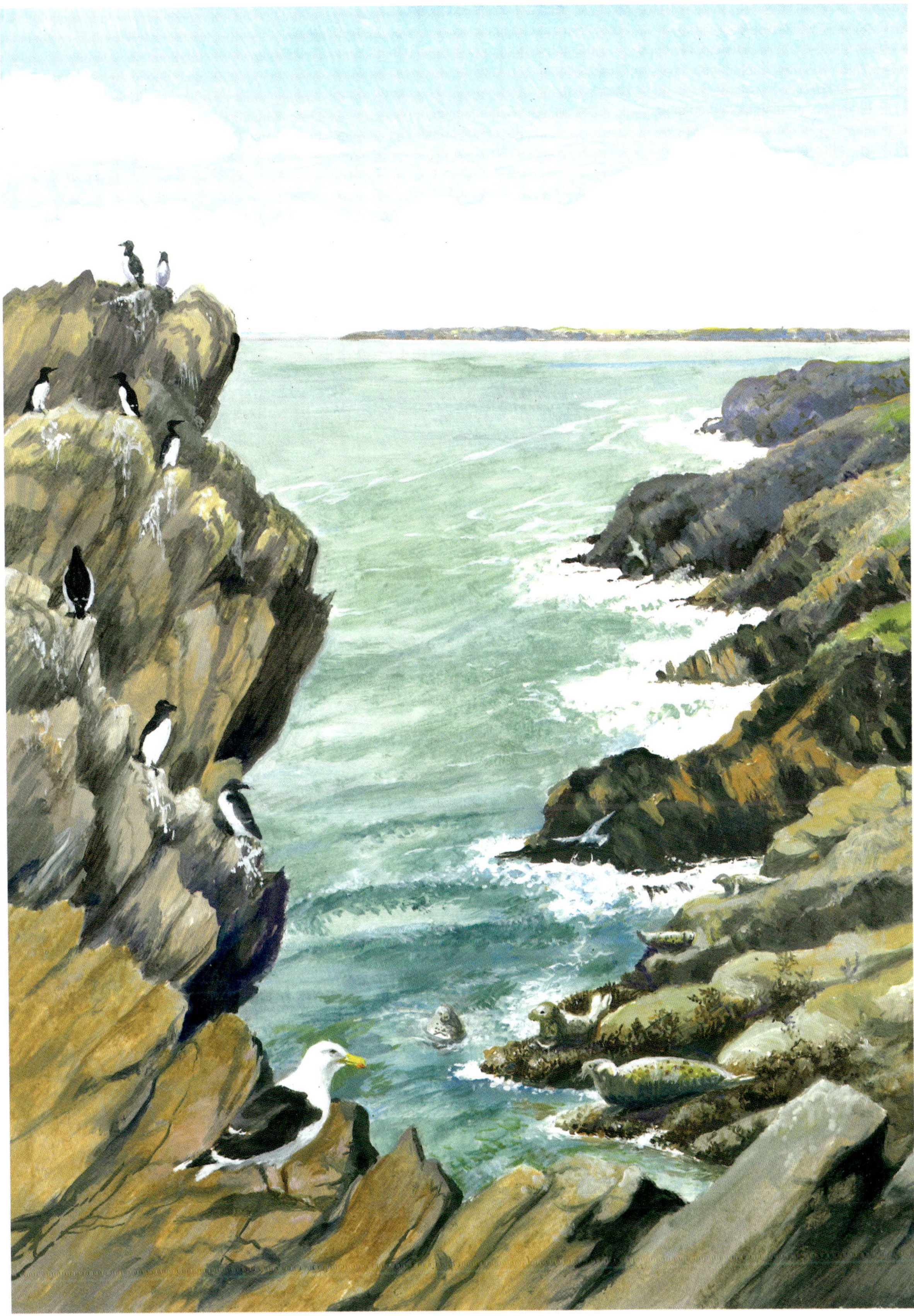

Skokholm island

The two islands of Skomer and Skokholm support the largest breeding colony of Manx shearwater in the world, as well as being important breeding sites for razorbill, kittiwake, Atlantic puffin and common guillemot.

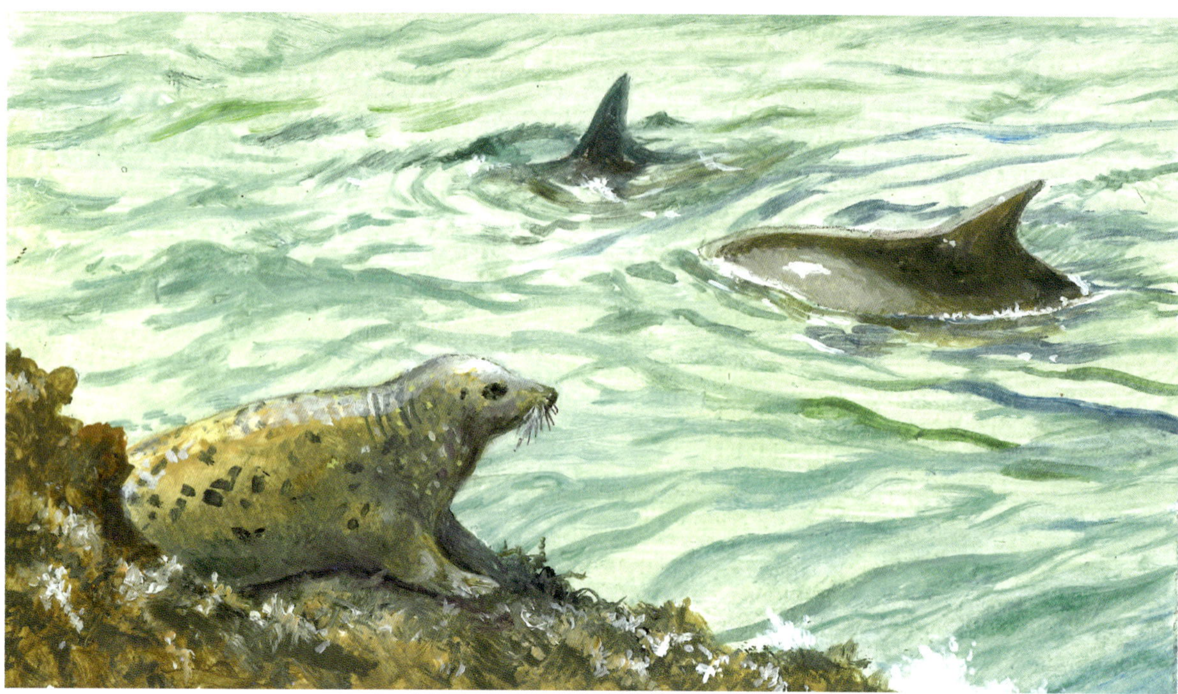

Skomer island
Grey seals and dolphins on Skomer.

Skokholm is no tropic isle where you can walk naked in perpetual sunshine, pluck your food from a breadfruit tree, and take your drink from a coconut shell. Skokholm's 242 acres lie in the path of a fierce tidal stream and in a latitude subject to heavy westerly and southerly gales. There is little shelter on the island, which is no more than a grassy, treeless plateau, rock-bound, and raised about 100 feet above the sea."

In 1961, the first year of our marriage, we went for a weekend to Wales. Peter wanted to show me the corner of Pembrokeshire where he had first met Lockley. We were walking down a lane when we stopped to pass the time of day with a man coming towards us. Extraordinarily, the walker turned out to be Lockley. He asked if we had somewhere to stay. No, we hadn't booked anywhere. Then why not stay at my place, he suggested. He and his wife were living in a large, gloomy house called Orielton, in the middle of a wood. They took in paying guests. Lockley was conducting, at the request of the Nature Conservancy, a study into wild rabbits which was published in 1965 as a book: *The Private Life of Rabbits*. Richard Adams found it essential reading when he was starting to write *Watership Down*.

We were by far the youngest in the hushed dining room of Orielton. As I spread butter on my toast, conscious of the loud, rasping sound the knife made, I strained to hear the *sotte voce* exchanges at other tables, curious as ever to know what's going on around me. Most of the sentences began "Did you see the …?" or "I saw a …." "We spotted a …" Only then did I realise that I was in the undiluted company of birdwatchers. If Peter wanted to convert me (he said he had no such motive), he failed. I had a lesson in using binoculars in the Orielton woods. But no matter how much I twiddled the knobs, altered the focus, and adjusted the width between the lenses, I never saw a single bird that Peter had patiently pointed out. By the time I was focusing on the right branch in the right tree, the bird had long since flown.

Perhaps Lockley's influence was still at work in 1962 when we went to live in Greece and found an island where we could paint and write. Many years later, in about 2004, we spent four days on Skokholm. Again, I found myself marooned among birdwatchers. This time, they didn't talk about the birds they'd seen so much as about the machinery with which they'd photographed and filmed them. Over the long communal table in the island's hostel, words and numbers flew back and forth, relating to exposures and film speeds, prices and makes of equipment. This was not quite as entertaining to overhear as a conversation about birds or the optional extras in vintage cars.

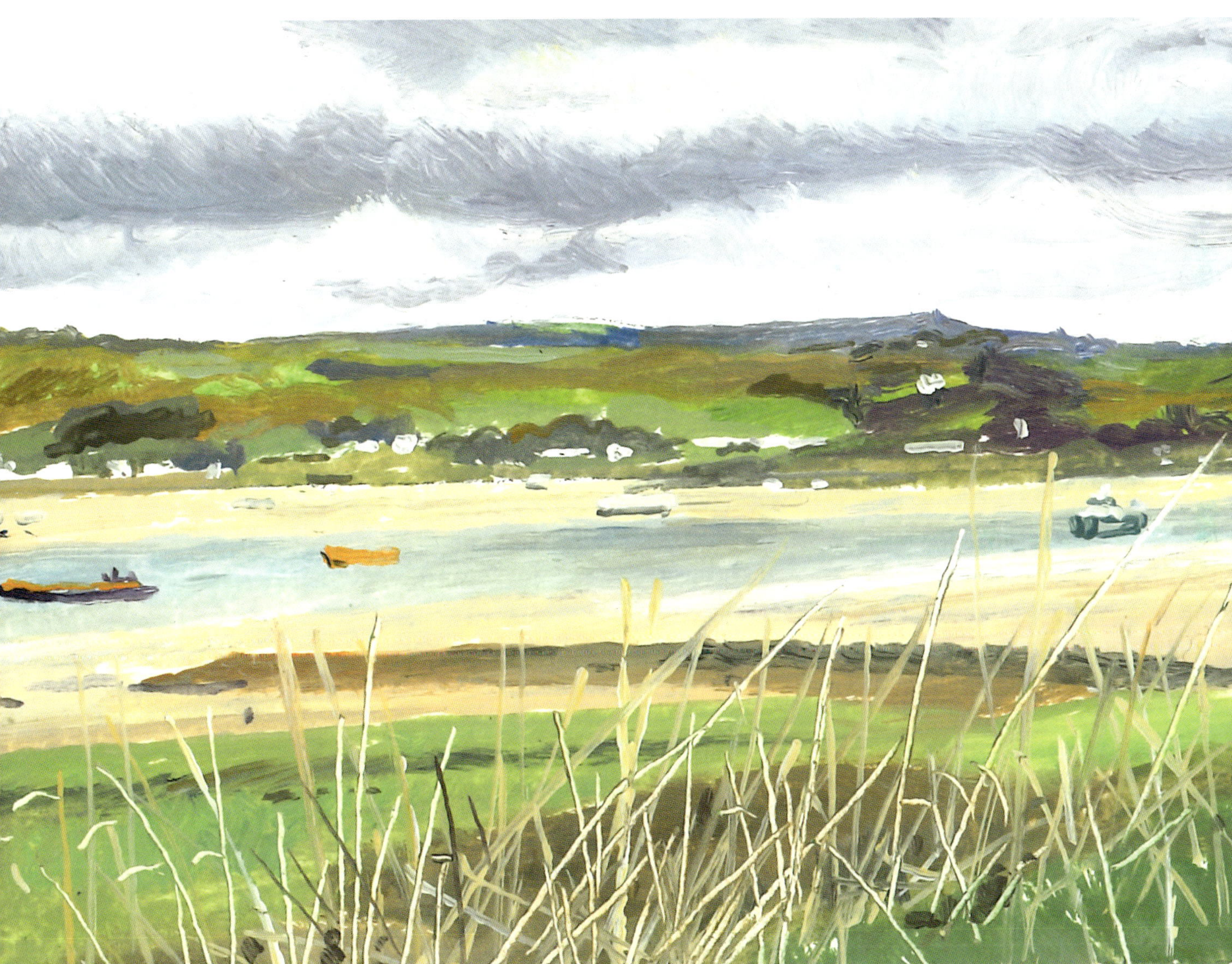

Poppit Sands

Poppit Sands in the estuary of the River Teifi is ideal for a family day out. Besides building sand castles, playing beach cricket and swimming, you can take a boat trip out into Cardigan Bay with the chance of seeing bottlenose dolphins and grey seals.

Mill Bay

Leaving Marloes and our memories of Skokholm, we came to Dale and Mill Bay, the landing place of Henry Tudor in 1485. By a rather shaky line of descent from Edward the Third, he'd come to claim the throne. He and his followers marched towards London to challenge the king, Richard the Third. They met in battle at Bosworth near Leicester. Not many years ago, in 2012 to be precise, Richard's body was found beneath a car park. What a wonderful juxtaposition between History and Modern-mundane! The cars were parked over the ruins of Greyfriars, a friary where it was thought Richard's body had been taken after he was killed by Henry Tudor's forces at Bosworth. The discovery is an instance of history surviving its transformation into legend and being proved correct.

A You Tube video recorded at the time of the discovery shows a man being interviewed. He's amused and bemused in equal quantities. He's been tracked down, or maybe he volunteered, as an inheritor of Richard's genes. What are the statistics behind that eventuality? How many inheritors of Richard's genes can there be alive in the world today? Is there a statistical expert out there who could answer that? I ask because my sister and I are, allegedly, the great to the thirteenth granddaughters of the man whose forces killed Richard the Third. A line of exclamation marks should follow such a ridiculous fact. There must be thousands of us, both male and female. I owe the claim to a Victorian forebear who was a keen genealogist and tracked down the line of descent, choosing a route that included as many females as males to get back to Henry VII. Against the rules, said a friend of mine when I ventured to claim Henry Tudor as my great 13 times grandfather. Not so unfair as male primogeniture, I could have answered. I've inherited genes from my grandmother in the same way I've inherited them from my grandfather. Why leave out my inheritance from her because we're female? The interest for me lies in my fascination with inherited characteristics, both through genetic and environmental influences. How many of us alive today in the world could claim my great to the thirteenth grandfather as their ancestor too? If all were traceable, might we become as quarrelsome as the rooks? Mine, no, *mine!*

We can be as proud and ashamed of Henry VII as of any man of normally mixed strengths and weaknesses. He united the country after years of civil war: the Wars of the Roses. He, a Lancastrian of the red rose faction, married Elizabeth of York, of the white rose side. This is the flowery message engraved on their tomb in Westminster Abbey:

The fifteenth hundredth year of the Lord had passed, and the ninth after that was running its course, when dawned the black day, the twenty first dawn of April was shining, when this so great monarch ended his last day. No earlier ages gave thee so great a king, O England; hardly will ages to come give thee his like.

What a wonderfully fulsome way to say it was the 21st of April 1509 when Henry died. Now, in May 2023, over 500 years later, our ex-Prince of Wales has been crowned King Charles III in the same abbey. Tradition and ritual can't be conjured up overnight. We can all be proud of some of our history, ashamed of

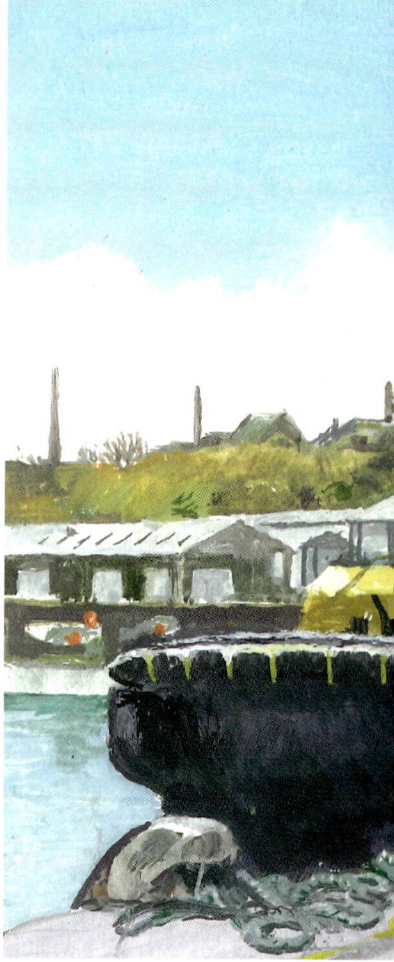

other parts of it, or choose to disagree entirely. Protestors shouted, "Not Our King!" at the back of the crowd gathered for the coronation.

The thought of Henry VII landing in Mill Bay accentuated the still, quiet atmosphere of the inlet. Nothing stirred. No-one was about. I drank it in but now, back home, I cannot describe the place. A single visit is never enough to record all the details of a scene in the mind's eye or notebook. Luckily, I have the benefit of Peter's eyes too when he has the chance to look carefully. He had no such chance when we came upon a continuous stream of tractors of every size, shape, and vintage, puffing dark fumes skywards from exhaust pipes. A big rally in a field somewhere off the main road between Milford Haven and Pembroke Dock was providing a precious day out for farmers, a carnival spectacle for us and another layer of carbon monoxide to the atmosphere.

Milford Haven

I'd expected Milford Haven to be a sprawling, industrial mess with tankers queuing in the estuary to unload their oil. But no. With a row of sparkling storage silos on the skyline and a couple of wide-hipped tugs in the harbour, it seemed a pleasant and interesting place to live with the added bonus of sailing in the estuary. The same goes for Pembroke.

Tugs, Milford Haven

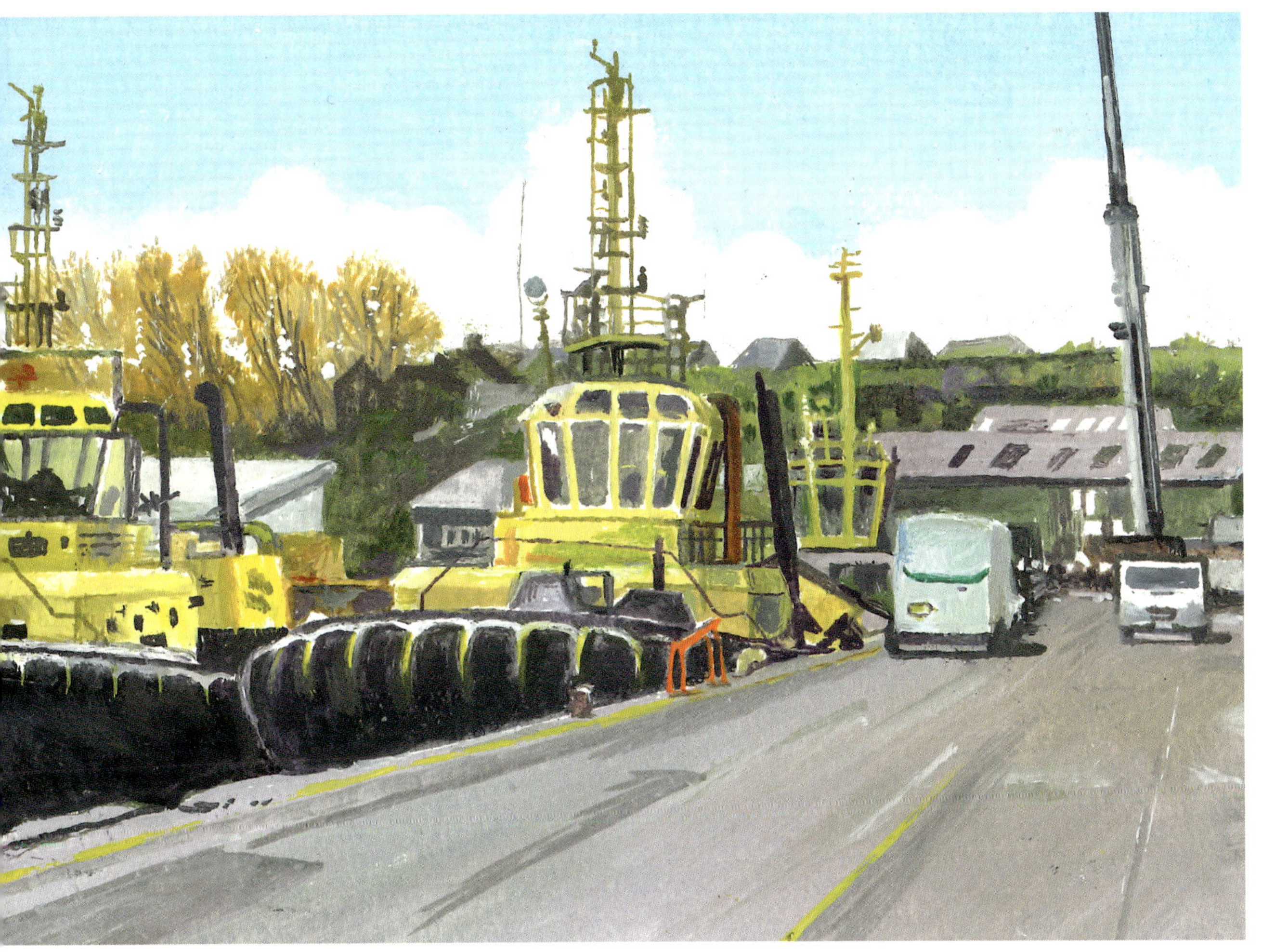

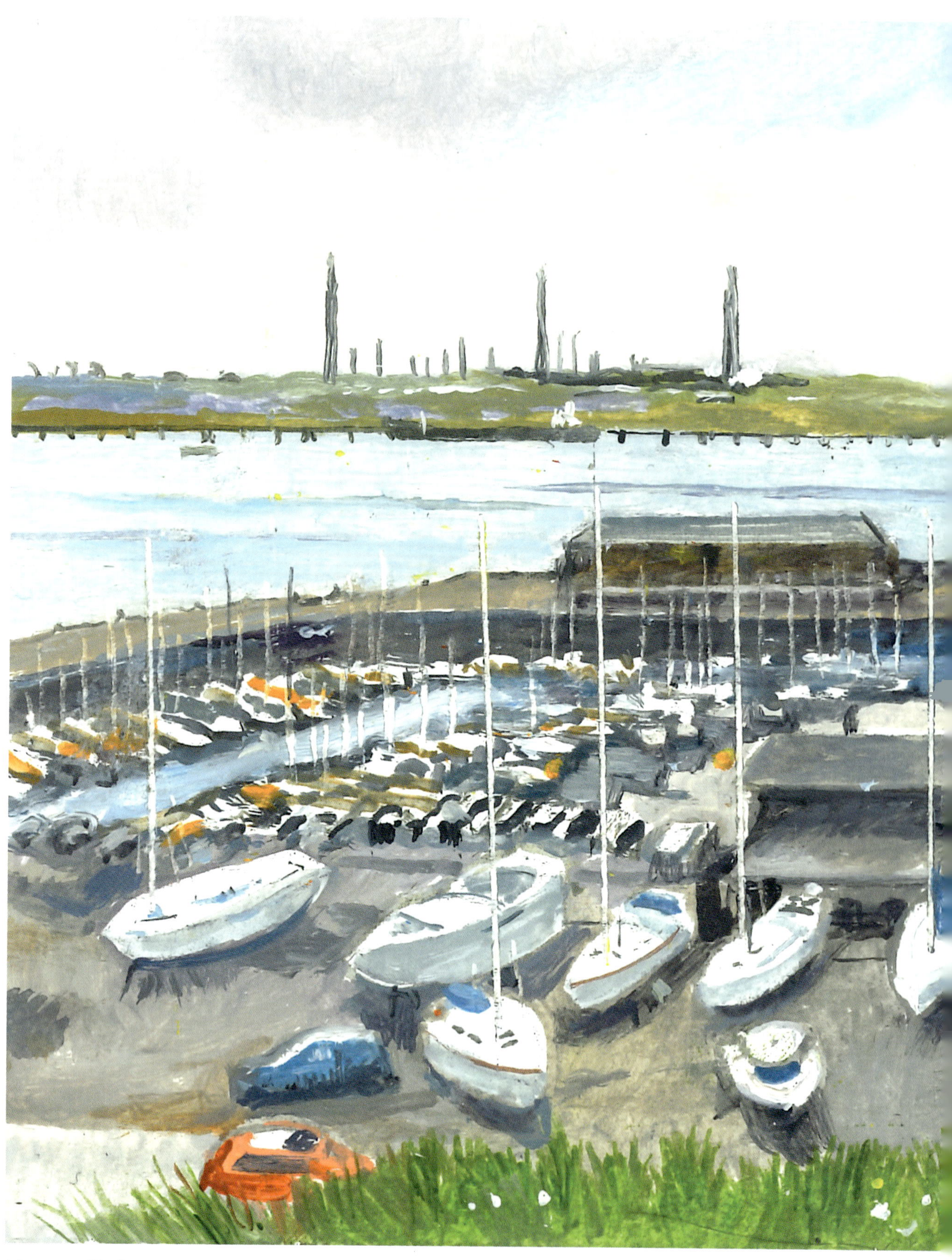

Marina, Milford Haven

The National Yachting Association gave the marina at Milford Haven its Four Gold Stars Award for its location and facilities.

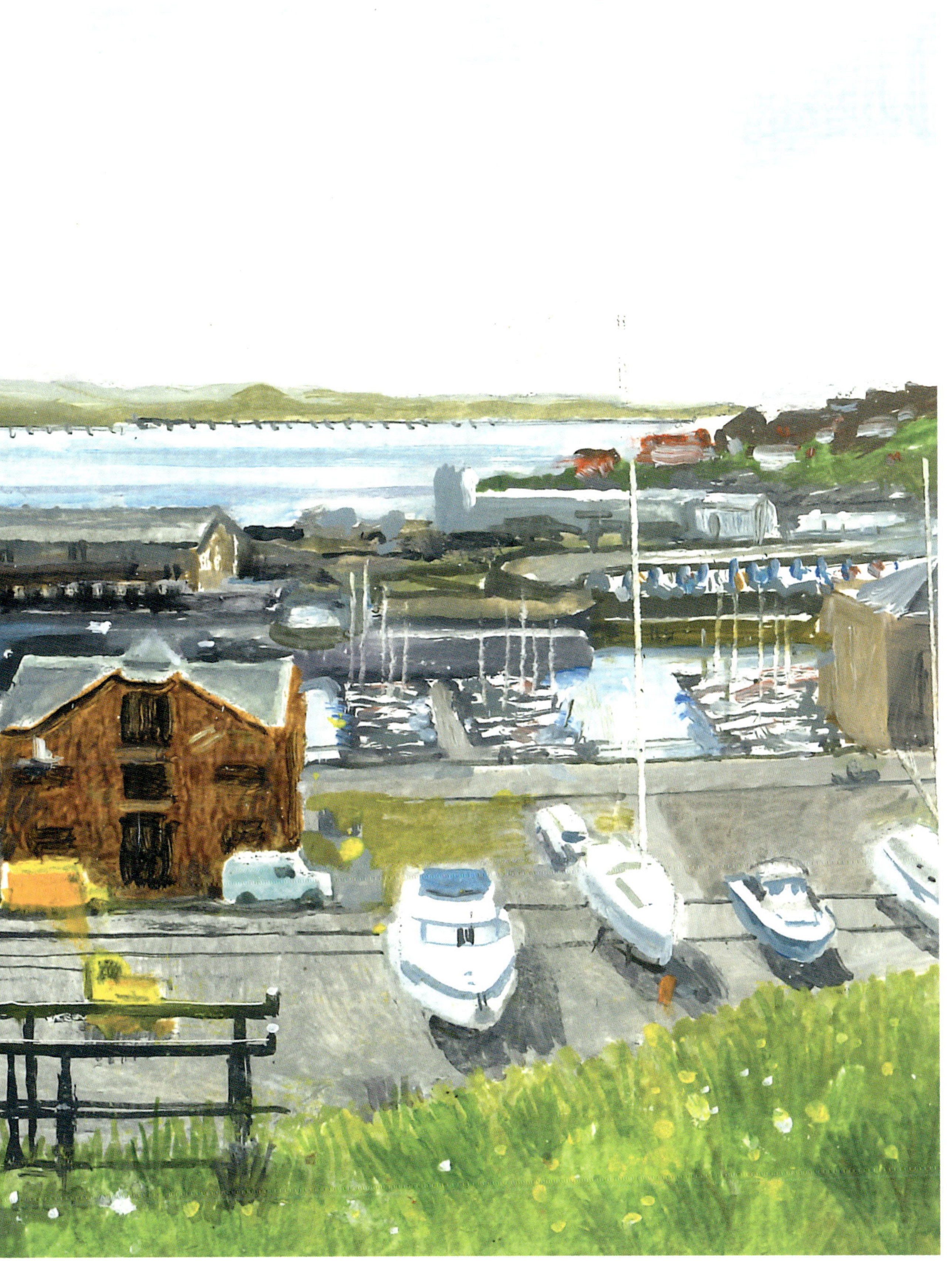

Pembroke Dock and Pembroke Castle

After crossing the bridge over the estuary, we parked to eat our sandwiches at Hobbs Point, Pembroke Dock, where two cannons pointed up and downstream at enemies that would never appear again – in cannon-fodder fashion, at least. We watched a tanker edge carefully out into midstream from the quay. Any future battle will be conducted, not over oil but microchips made in Taiwan.

From the dock we went on to find again the cafe with the view of Pembroke Castle which we'd liked on a previous visit. It was busy but we got a table overlooking the river where a couple were rowing their hired boat around in circles, struggling not to be swept up or downstream. The tidal river does complicated things under the bridge. As complex as the currents was the claim of Henry Tudor, born in the castle in 1457, to the throne.

Pembroke Dock

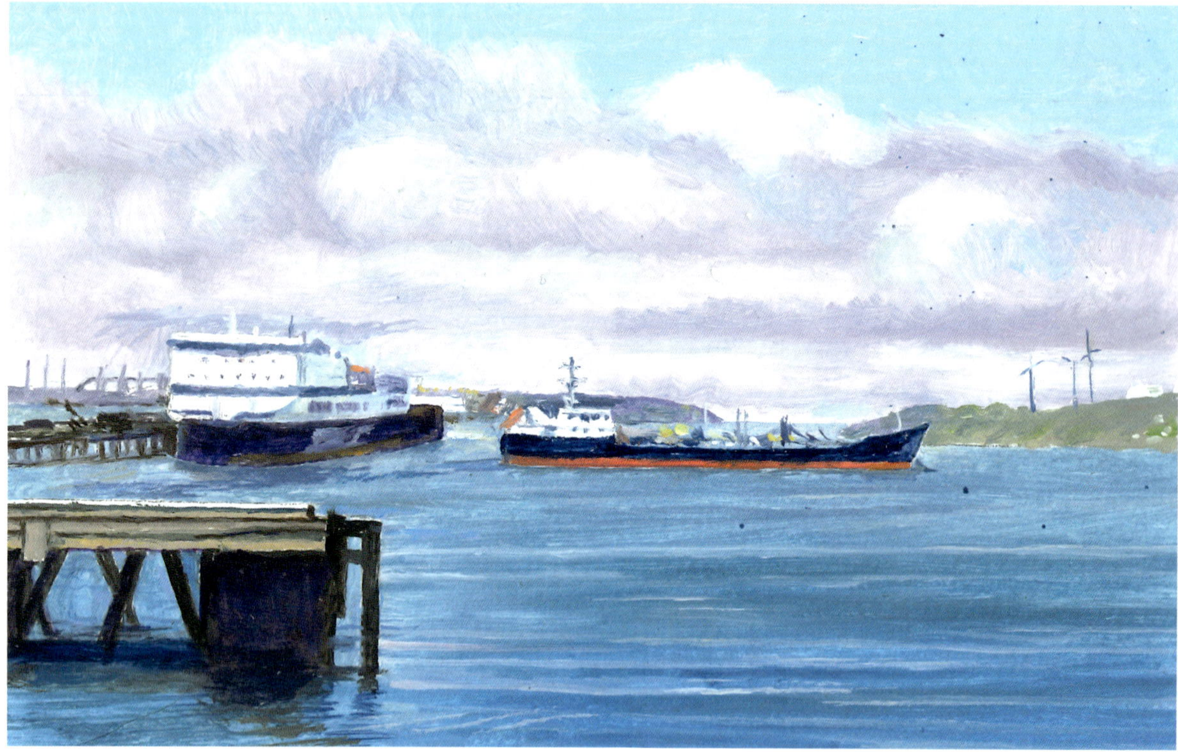

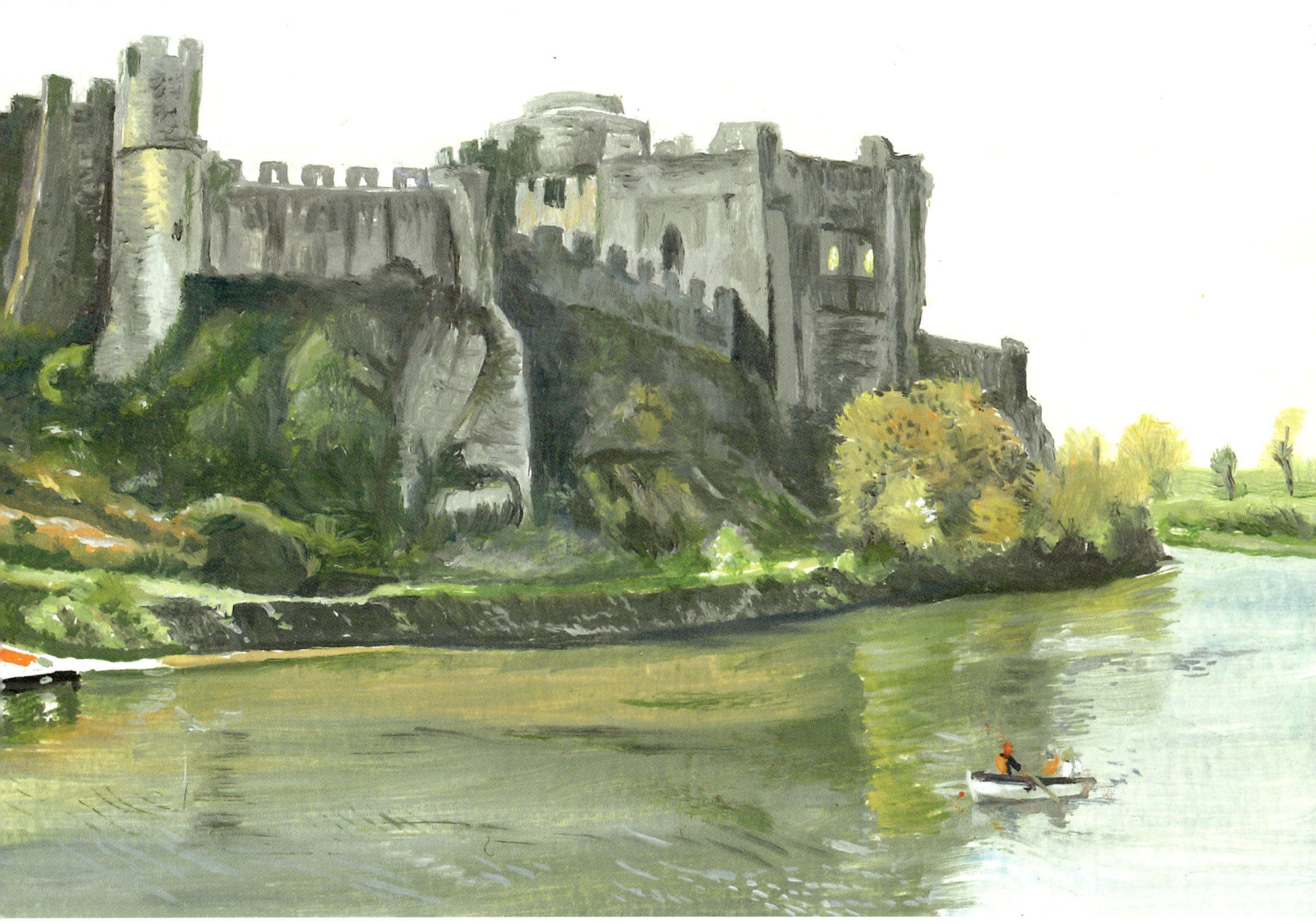

Pembroke Castle

Wogan's Cavern, a large limestone cave beneath Pembroke Castle, was fortified with a wall and a barred gateway when the earlier timber fortification was rebuilt in stone in the thirteenth century. In July last year an archaeological survey found the bones of woolly mammoth and reindeer in the cave, as well as evidence of human occupation in Palaeolithic and Mesolithic times.

Carew Castle

It's often hard to sort out legend and historical fact. So many legends serve up historical fact in a neater, more palatable form. When Rhys ap Thomas of Carew Castle heard that Henry had landed in Mill Bay and was marching to England, adding to his army of supporters on the way, his loyalty to King Richard wobbled. He'd promised Richard, so the story goes, that he wouldn't allow Henry to get anywhere near the king. "Over my belly," he's reputed to have sworn; in other words, "Over my dead body." Sensible man, he didn't want to die, nor revoke his oath of allegiance so he hid under a bridge when Henry marched over it. Mullock bridge is still there, 2 miles north of Mill Bay and protected from passing traffic by a more recent bridge built alongside. As we crossed the "new" Mullock bridge, we thought of Rhys ap Thomas and his belly. Later that day, on our way back to St David's, we admired his splendid castle which benefited greatly from Rhys's enrichment after he'd supported Henry instead of Richard.

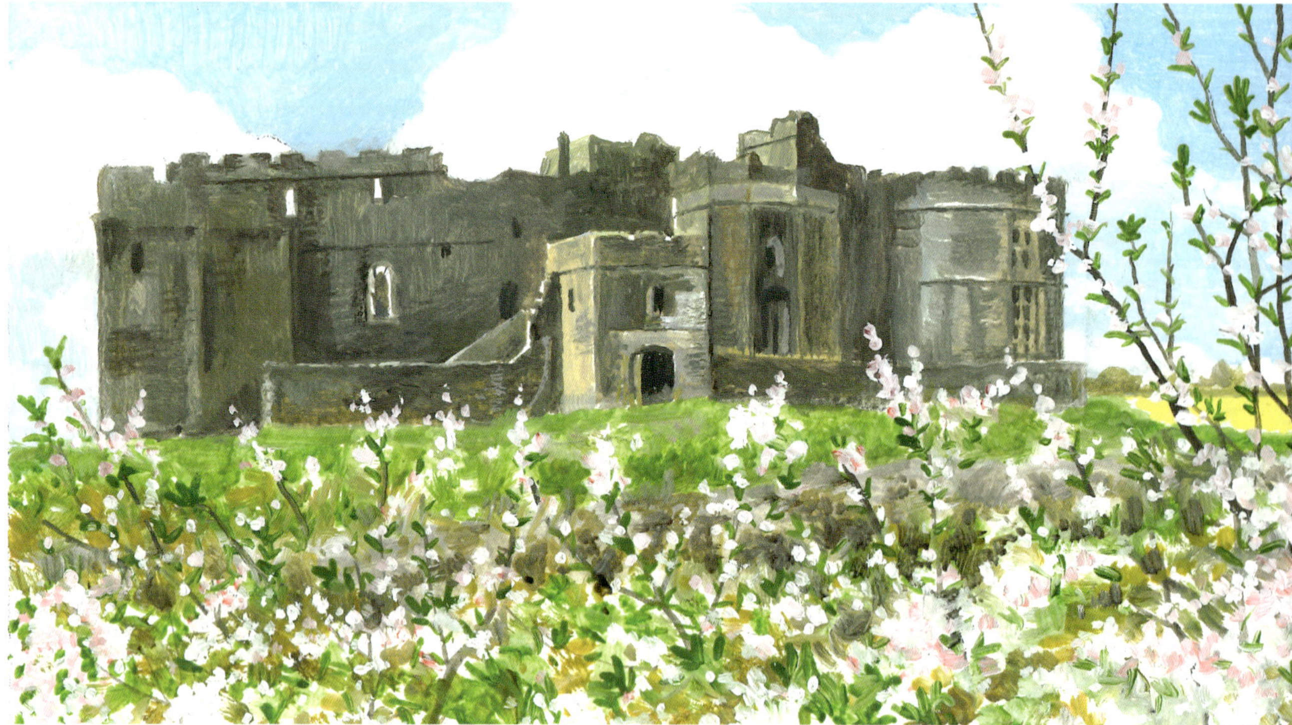

Carew Castle

Carew Castle lies on the banks of a tidal inlet in Milford Haven Waterway, a location considered strategically important for at least two thousand years. The remains of an Iron Age fort have been found here. The castle we see today mostly dates from the thirteenth century when Nicolas de Carew, who took his name from the castle, made changes and improvements. After 900 years, the family is still in possession. Both castle and family have seen many fluctuations in style and fortune.

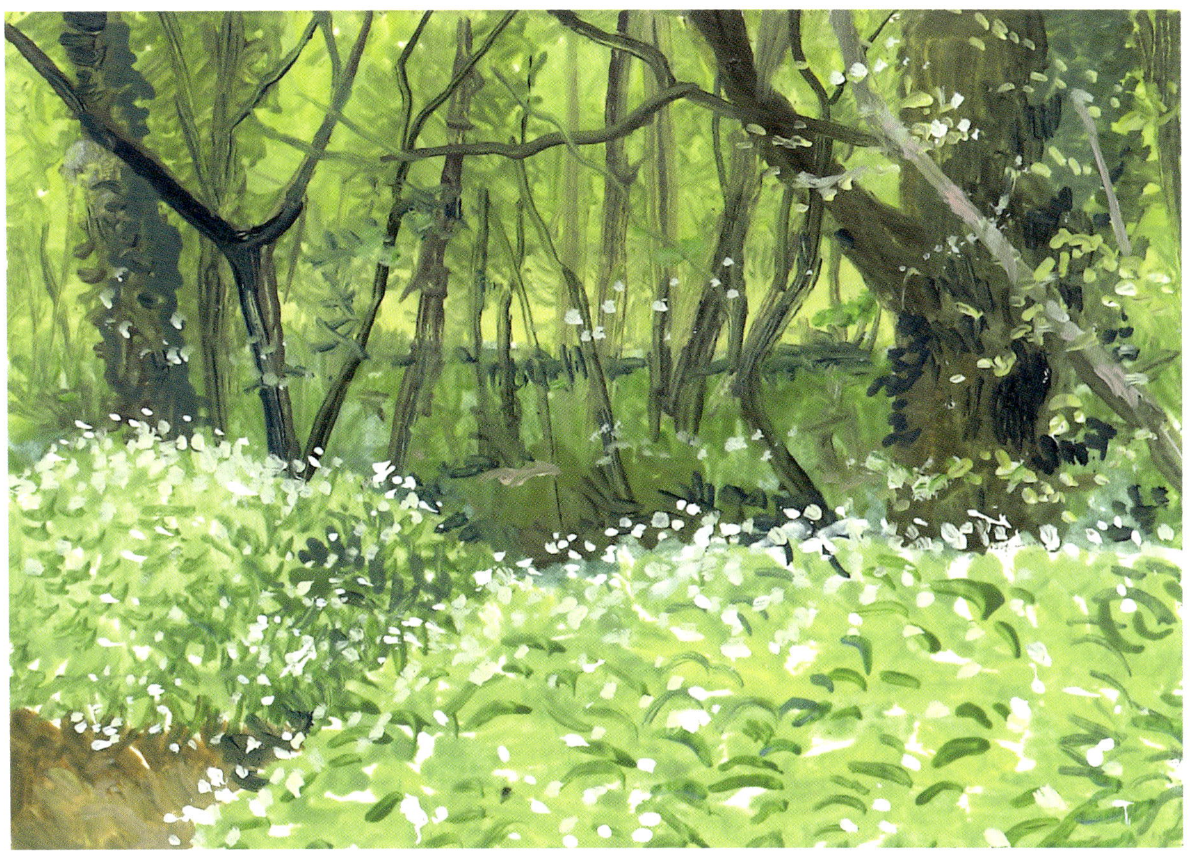

Wild garlic in a lane

The growing number of good chefs in Wales like to use the flowers as well as the leaves of wild garlic, known in the past as Ramsons.

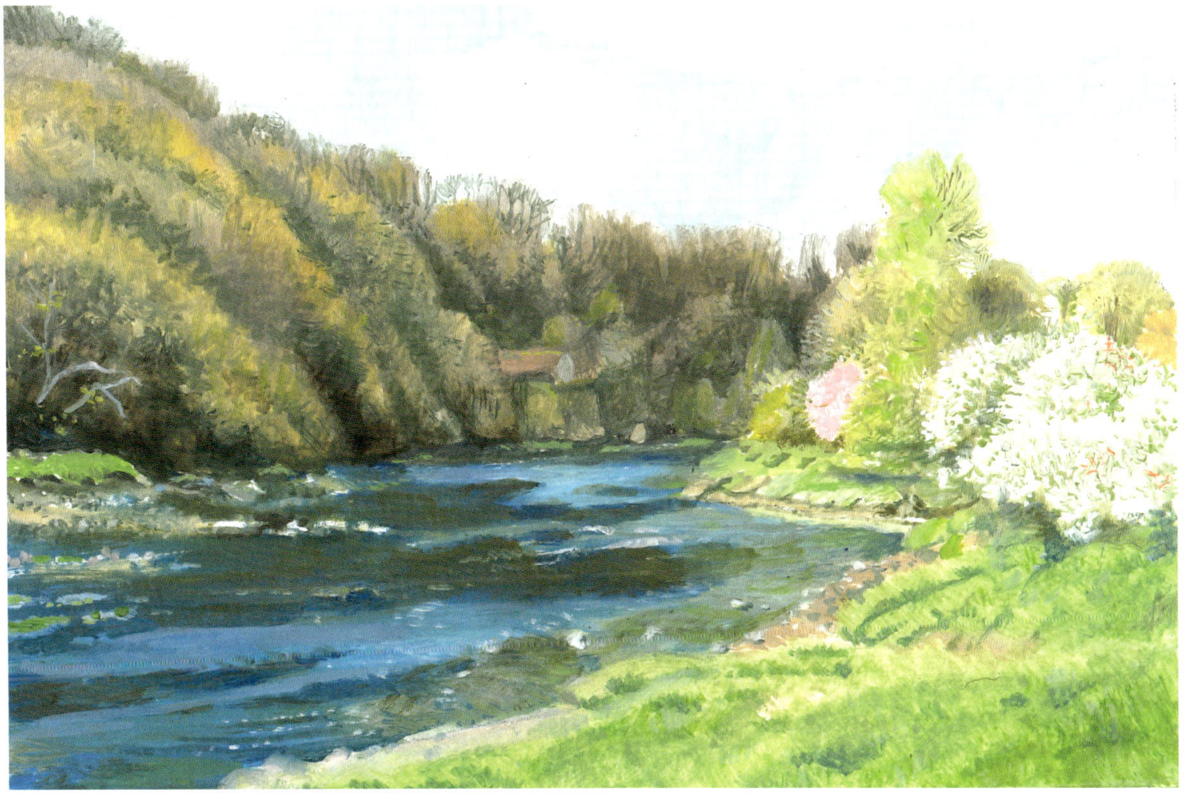

River Cresswell

Cresswell is the name for a village and its river. Derived from the early English words 'cress' and 'wella', it describes what grows in natural abundance in this area: watercress.

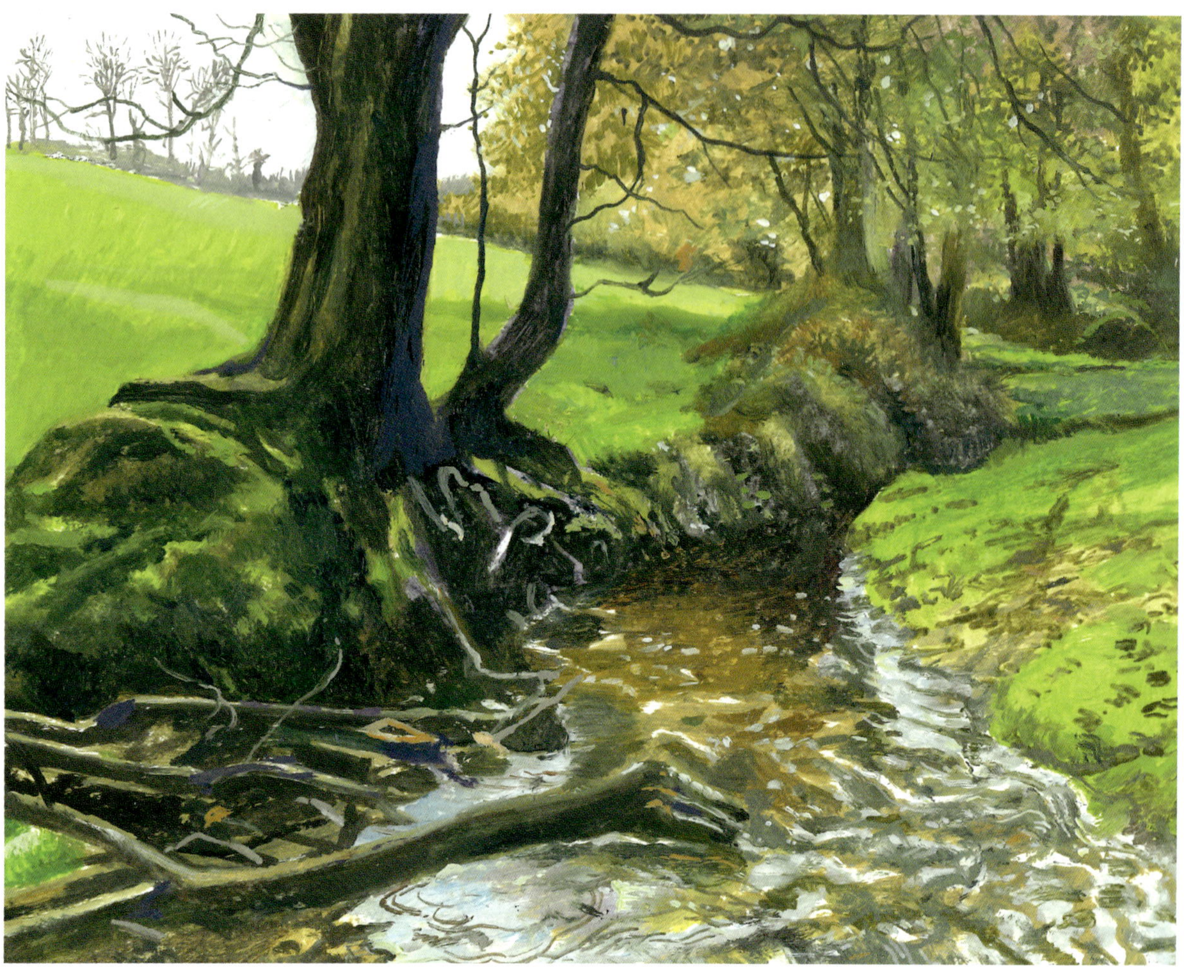

Stream on the way to Cresswell Quay

Graham Sutherland

From one of the many books Peter has illustrated, we learnt that Picton Castle had a collection of paintings by Graham Sutherland. Somewhere between St Clears and Haverford West, we turned off the A road on a Sutherland hunt. We went round and round, trying to find either a Sutherland Gallery or Picton House where the paintings might be housed. In the end we did find Picton House but were told that the collection had been moved to Uppingham. I haven't yet investigated the reason for the choice of place, but it does have resonance for me. My father was educated at the school known simply as Uppingham. The collection of Sutherlands would not include the famous portrait of Winston Churchill. Lady Churchill was so horrified by the painting, she burnt it. Sutherland received £1000 for his time. The images that exist on the internet show the portrait's brilliance.

In the Grove's dining room that evening we met a couple who reminded us of ourselves at their age, deep in the hustle and bustle of making one's way in the art and publishing world. He's a graphic designer; she's an abstract artist, with a show about to start in Milford Haven. We wish them luck.

"Do what you can, when you can" has been our motto throughout our sixty-three years of marriage. Now in Wales we travel alongside retirees. Most are younger than us, perhaps in their seventies, still able to walk the coastal paths and ride bikes for miles. Their hearts and lungs work well enough, as do their knees and hips even after replacement. They have pensions from their work; they deserve their leisure. But what's remarkable is the way many couples sit opposite each other in virtual silence, the occasional word dragged up as though from the bottom of a deep, dry well. Their good life may have come too late for animated conversation.

Cleddau river, near Picton Castle

The afternoon light makes a gothic silhouette of an oak tree on the banks of the Cleddau river.

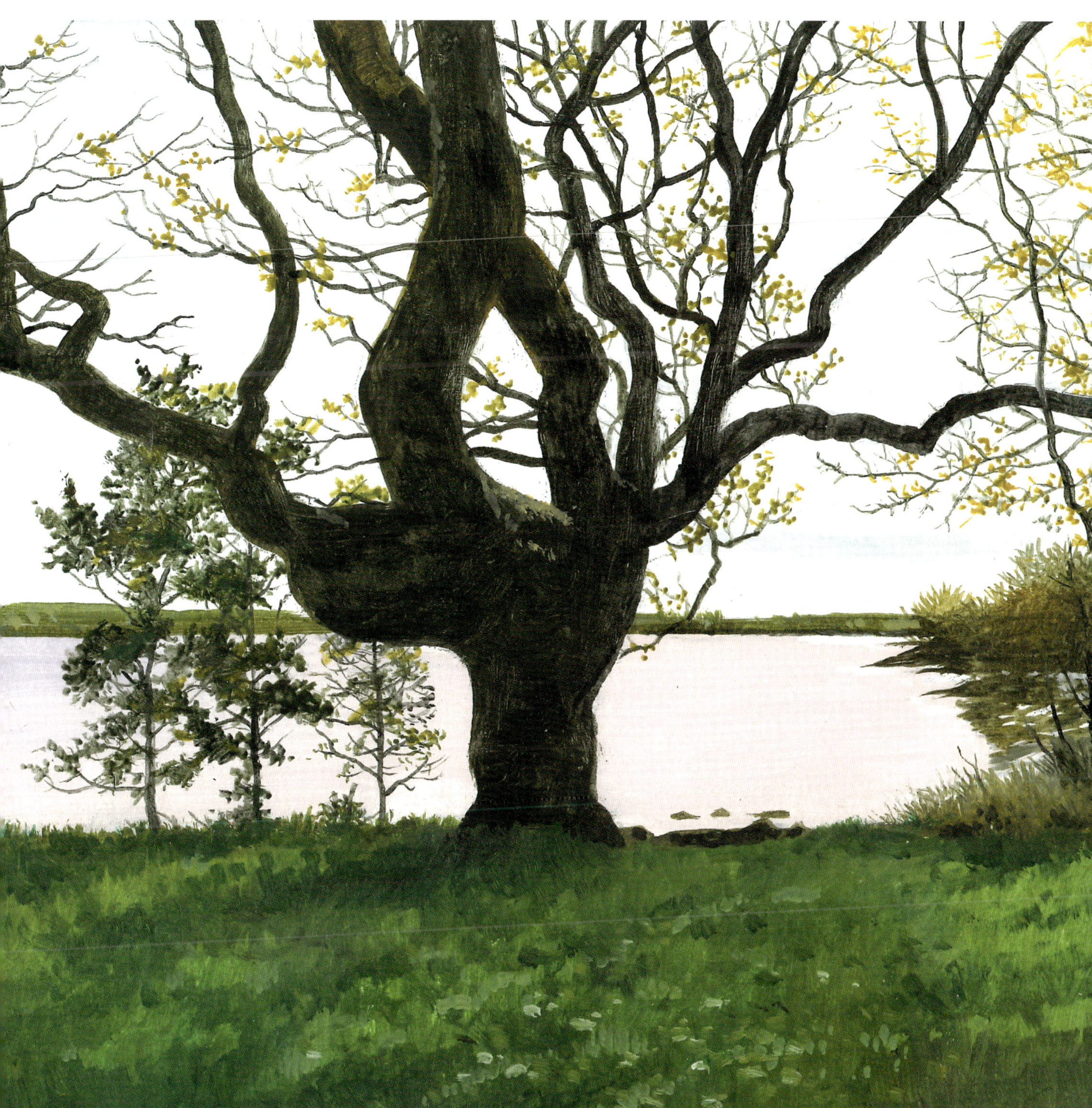

Porth Gain

On the quay at Porth Gain, two men from Swansea were squeezing themselves into their wet suits. They'd come from Swansea with their rubber dinghies and spear guns to dive offshore for bass and lobsters. Seeing their masks, I had an uncomfortable jolt of a reminder. Since February when our Welsh friend Gareth died while snorkelling in the Caribbean, I've been imagining how this happened. I banish the thoughts as best I can. At Porth Gain I concentrated on wondering about the ruins that cling to the harbour's cliffside. Scheduled as an ancient monument, these are the remains of the port's industrial past. Locally quarried slate was sawn and shipped from here. Later, the site became a brickworks. More recently, the conglomeration of buildings was used to store dolorite for roadbuilding. Now they stand empty and forbidding, frowning down on the narrow harbour where life goes on in a different way.

Porth Gain, industrial ruins
Signs of past industry in the harbour of Porth Gain.

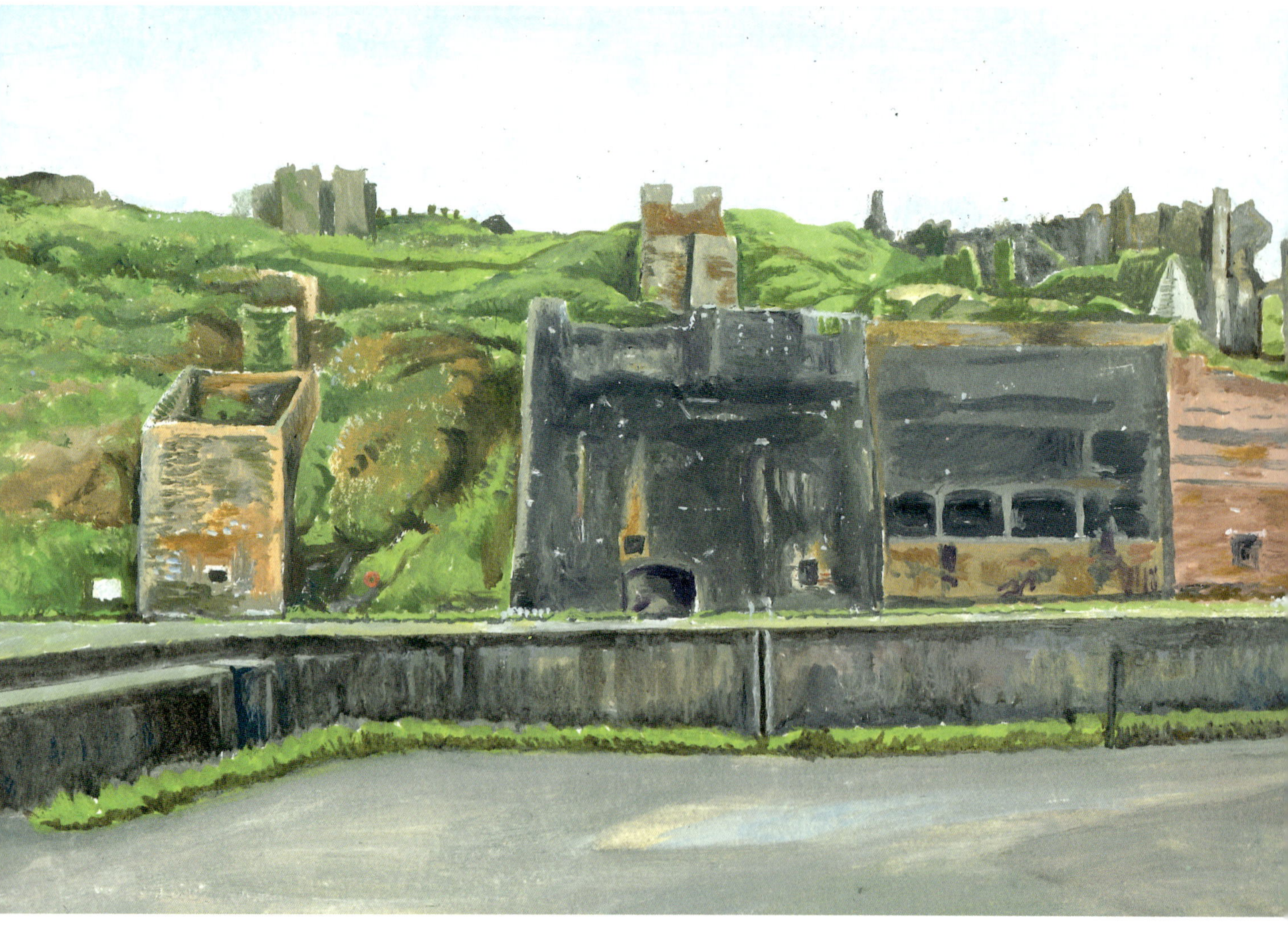

Dinas Head and Pwllgwaelod

The Pembroke Coastal Path circles Dinas Head, north of Saint David's. Walkers of this 8-mile section are rewarded with wonderful views of Cardigan Bay, and on a clear day they'll see as far as the Lleyn peninsula south of Anglesey. Closer to hand are seabirds on rocky cliffs and seals, porpoises, and dolphins out to sea. Non-walkers are rewarded, too. There is one section suitable for wheelchairs and pushchairs. This 2-mile level path links two coves, Cwm-yr-Eglwys and Pwllgwaelod. At the latter, the Old Sailor's Tearoom and Restaurant appeared closed and forgotten, but people gathered soon after its opening time. Besides serving tea and food, it's a licensed pub. Half a century and more ago, it was one of many ports of call for Dylan Thomas. Its name brings to mind the impossible mixture of letters one might be served in a Scrabble game.

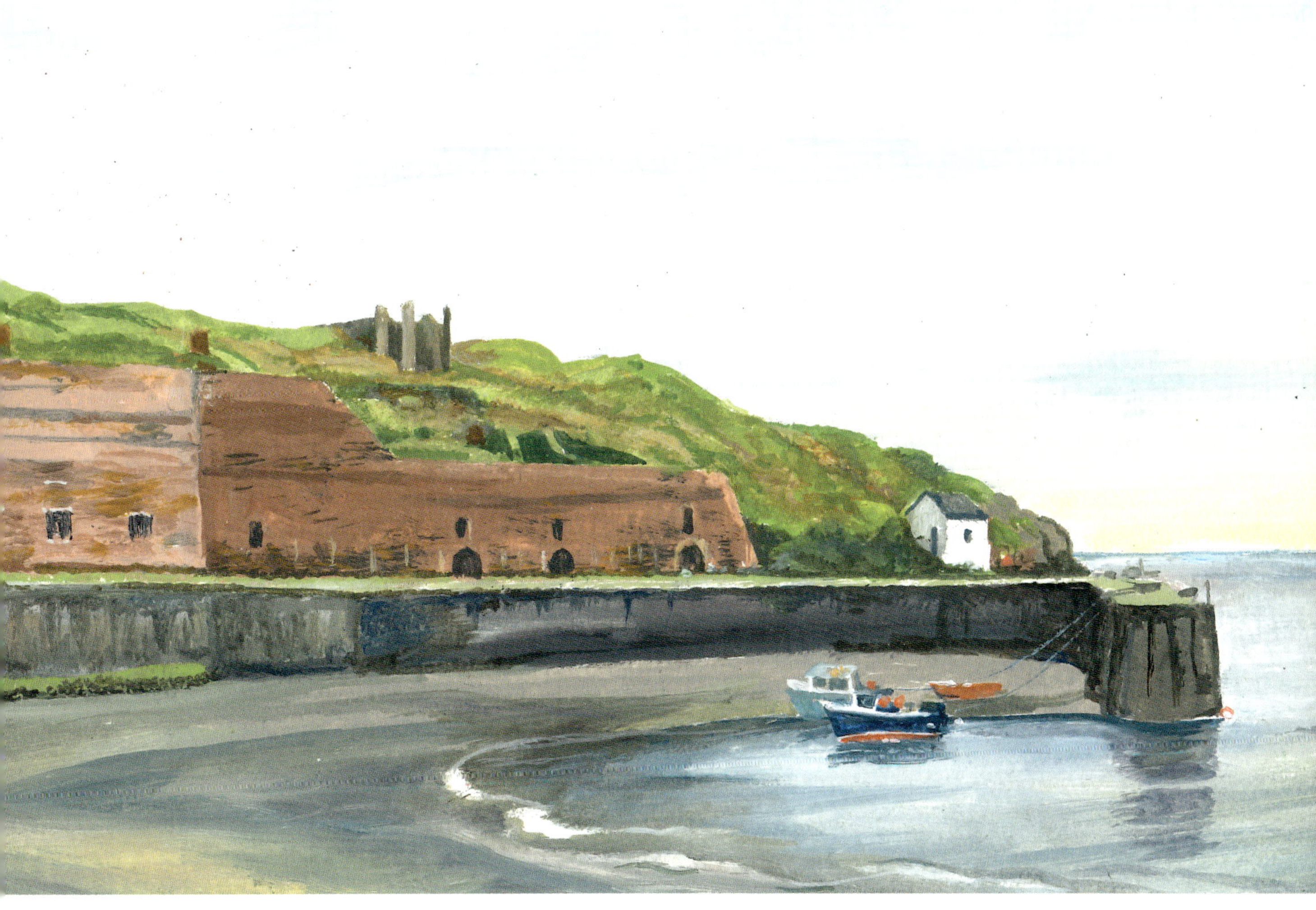

Fishguard, Cardigan and the Preseli Hills

I was astonished to find Fishguard such a small place. There was one ferry in evidence, tied up at the quay in the harbour. I'd thought the port would be twice the size it was in the 1950s when, as teenagers, my sister and I came here with our parents on our way to stay with my father's best man in County Kerry, Eire. Since then, I have become familiar with ports in Italy and Greece. They've all grown far bigger and busier. But not Fishguard. It gave me the impression of someone who has sunk back into a corner, just managing to put on a show for the sake of the company.

In the town of Cardigan my entire focus was on finding a Ladies. It took a while. I tried to distract myself with thoughts of Lord Cardigan. Not only did he wear and make famous the button-through, knitted garment easily pulled on and off, he also shared responsibility with Lord Lucan for the stupid blunders made at the Battle of Balaclava immortalised by Tennyson in the poem *The Charge of the Light Brigade*. The terrible mistakes that were made on October 5th

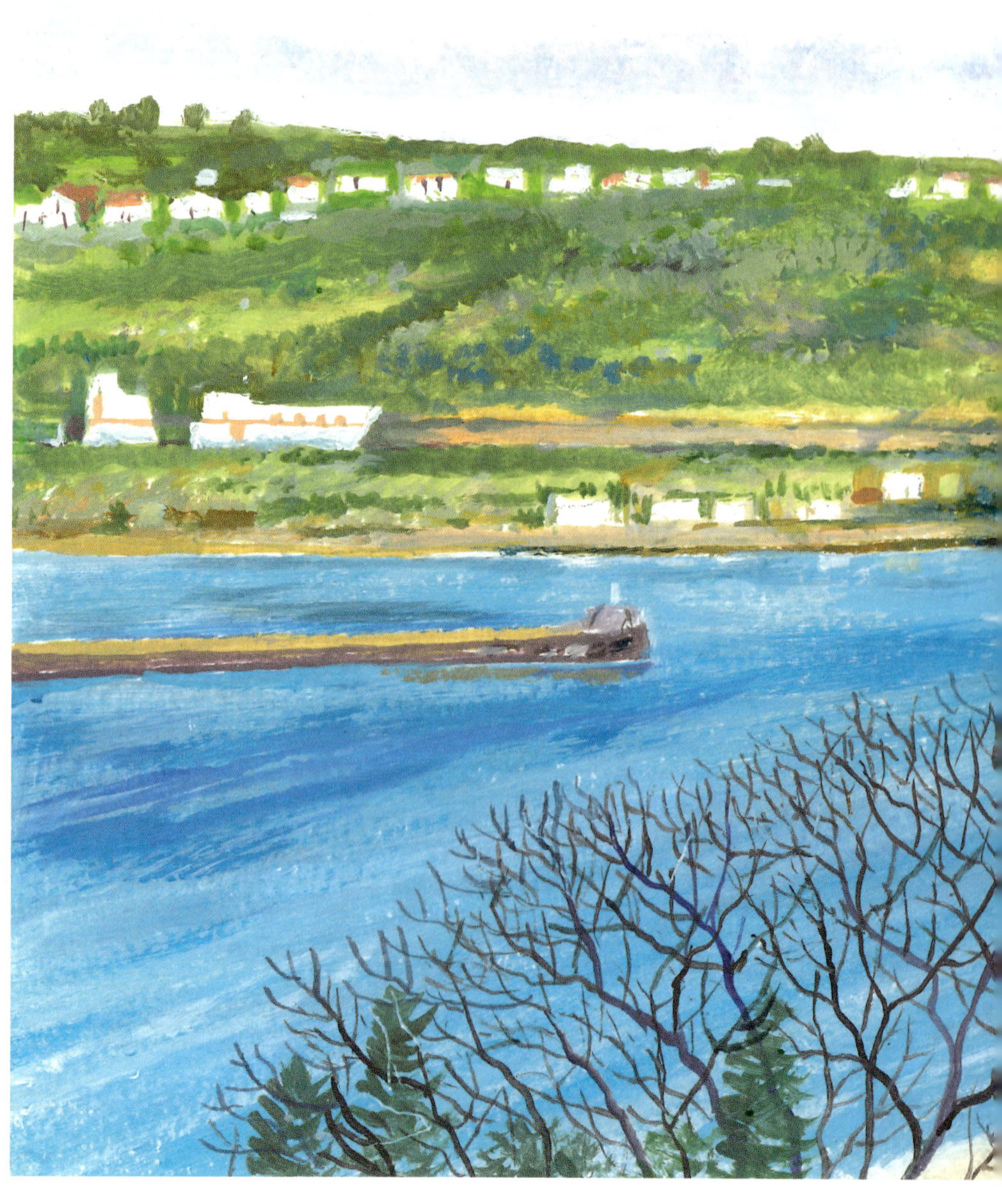

1854 might not be so well remembered, were it not for Tennyson's poem.

Cannon to right of them, cannon to left of them
Cannon in front of them, volleyed and thundered,
Into the jaws of Death rode the six hundred.

In the space of half an hour, 113 men were killed, 134 were wounded and 574 horses killed. Lord Cardigan had misunderstood orders, which had been badly expressed in the first place. He'd led the cavalry into the very mouths of the guns and trotted back to the start of the attack without suffering a scratch himself or noticing the mayhem around him on the battleground.

I prefer to think of the town of Cardigan by its Welsh name: Ceredigion. We found public toilets tucked away out of sight behind a car park. There was a long queue of ladies jumping up and down in distress. A young woman called Sophie kindly let me in ahead of her. There's a camaraderie among travellers in Wales. It's as though we are sharing an unusual experience, as we might on an ocean liner. We fall easily into conversation, exchanging travellers' tales.

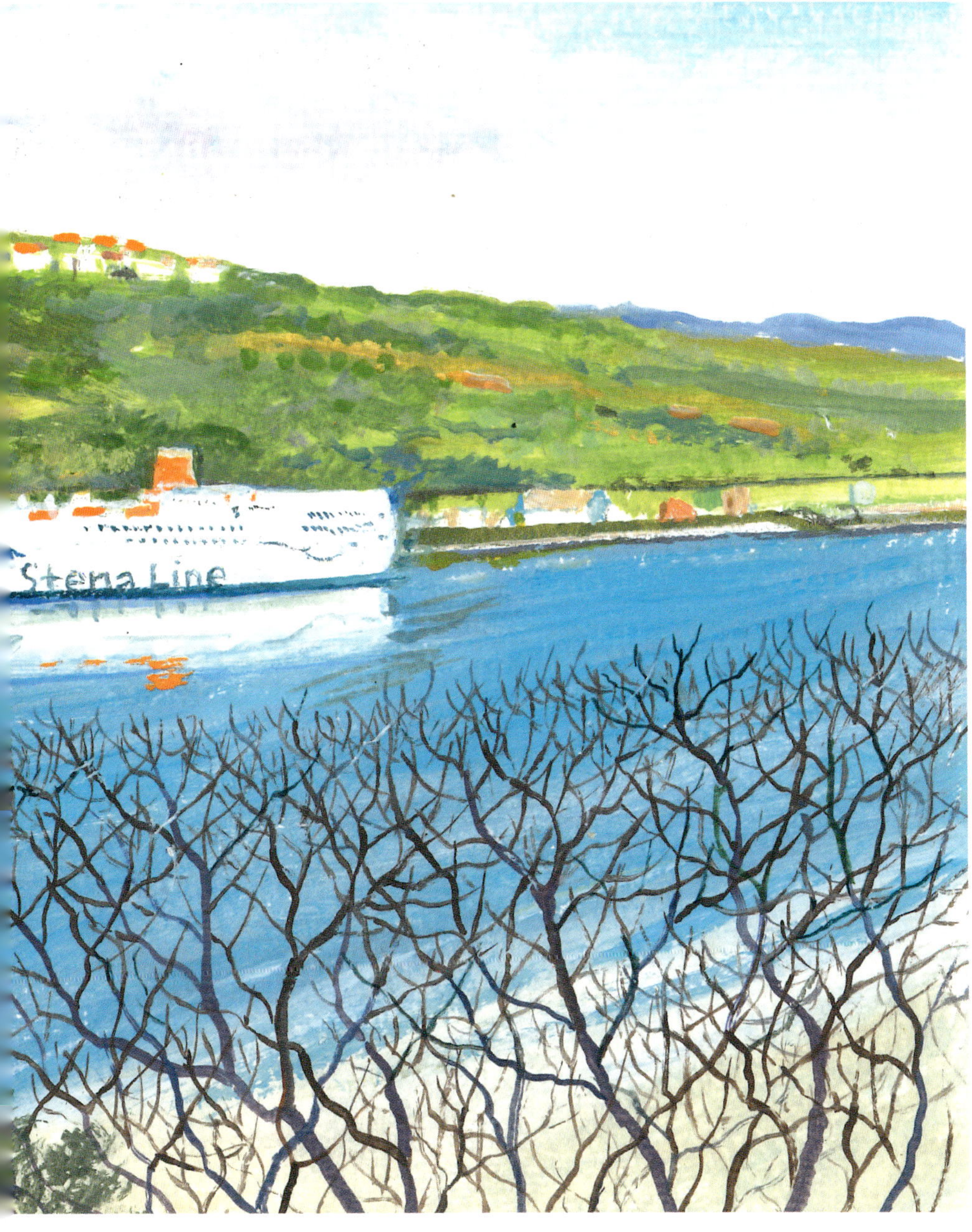

Fishguard ferry

The sight of a car ferry in Fishguard harbour brings back memories of a family holiday in Ireland.

Pentre Ifan

The sun was still shining when we turned up into the Preseli Hills to find an Iron Age burial mound. I'm certain that, if we arrange our favourite Places of Interest in Wales in order at the end of this book, Pentre Ifan will be near the top. You approach from a small parking inlet on the lane through a gate into a field. An immense quiet settles around you. The view stretches away to the distant sea over farmland. After a further field and another gate, you are among large oblong-shaped boulders half-buried in the grass. Ahead of you lies the tomb itself, an architectural balancing act perfected five thousand years ago. Beyond, white horses stand sentinel and white sheep crop the grass. The animals barely stir. The only sound is birdsong and a distant cuckoo, the first we've heard this year. Whoever it was whose bones lie beneath this stone canopy was obviously a great leader. More important than that, I guess he was a happy man, satisfied with his life's work and admired for it. I don't think he was a Lord Cardigan.

After leaving Pentre Ifan, dark clouds gathered and settled on the tops of the hills. Soon we were in the midst of pelting rain, unable to see much of the road ahead. We headed for St David's and, next day, home.

So ended our foray into Pembrokeshire but I don't want to finish this section without recalling a previous visit to the area.

Tenby and Manorbier

Tenby is as full of colour as Peter's paintbox but it's not a place for us to linger. It's a traffic trap. Reversing round corners because of delivery vans stuck in the middle of narrow streets cured us of any desire to explore. We stayed in Manorbier where there is a castle in which you can hold a wedding, a quiet and attractive beach belonging to the castle and, a little way beyond the headland, a burial chamber, similar to but smaller than Pentre Ifan's. On our first night we ate at a pub in the village. We sat next door to a large family party who slowly but steadily drew us into their congenial company. We ended up talking Greek with their grandmother, who was a Cypriot. They were celebrating the birthday of one of her granddaughters. It turned out they were all Jehovah's Witnesses. Had they set out to convert us to their religious beliefs through sheer good spirits? Whatever their motivation, we enjoyed the company of these fellow travellers to Wales and their traveller tales. I didn't know then, but I know now, that a teller of tales called Gerald was born in Manorbier Castle in the twelfth century. I raise my glass – or rather, click my computer mouse – to Giraldus Cambrensis who wrote *Chronicles of Wales.* In his opinion, "In all the broad lands of Wales, Manorbier is the most pleasant place by far."

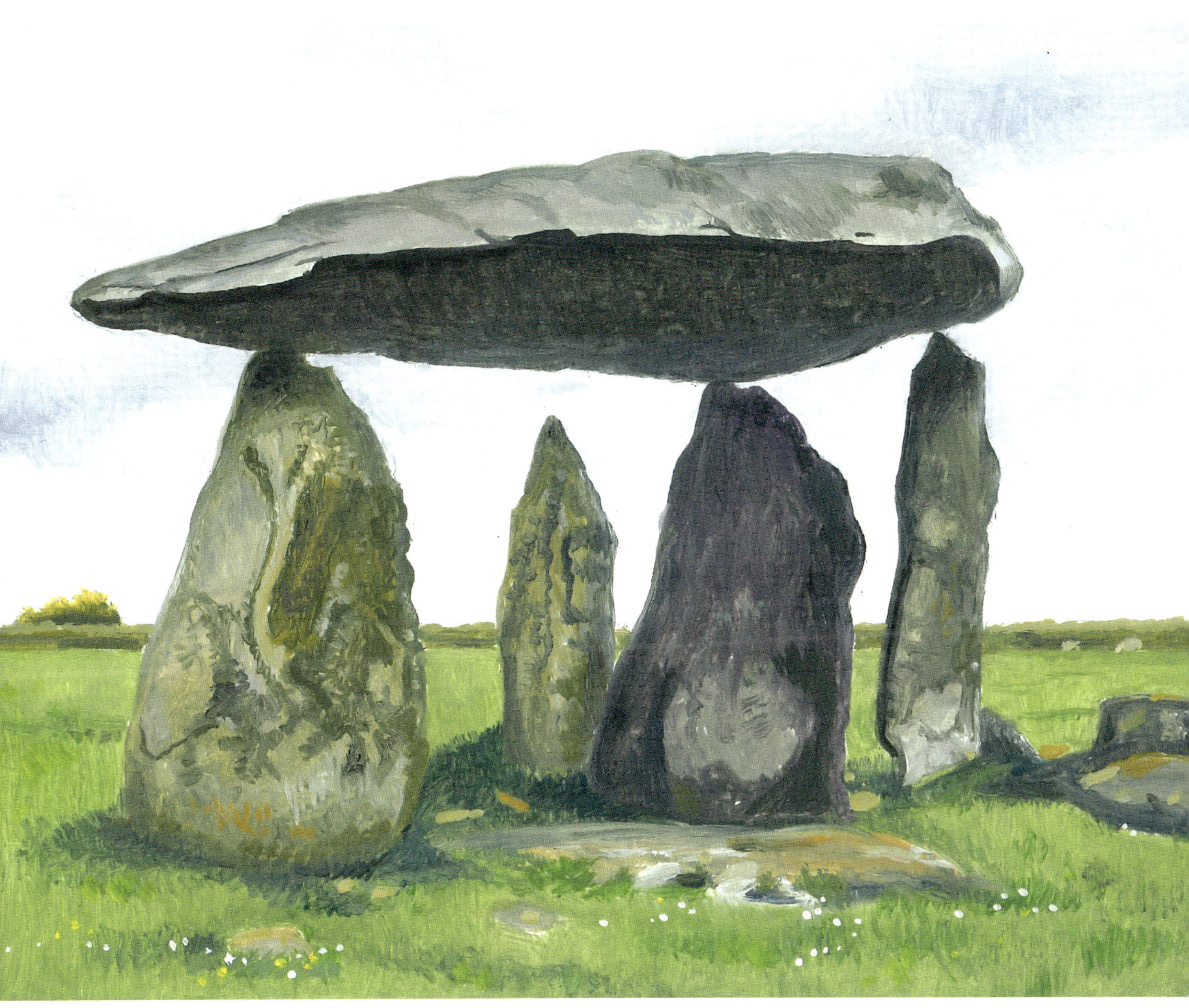

Burial chamber, Pentre Ifan

The imposing arrangement of upright stones at Pentre Ifan has disputed origins. It's either a communal burial chamber excavated from a mound of stones or a monument constructed to appear much as we see it today. Only the date of its construction is agreed: 3500 BC.

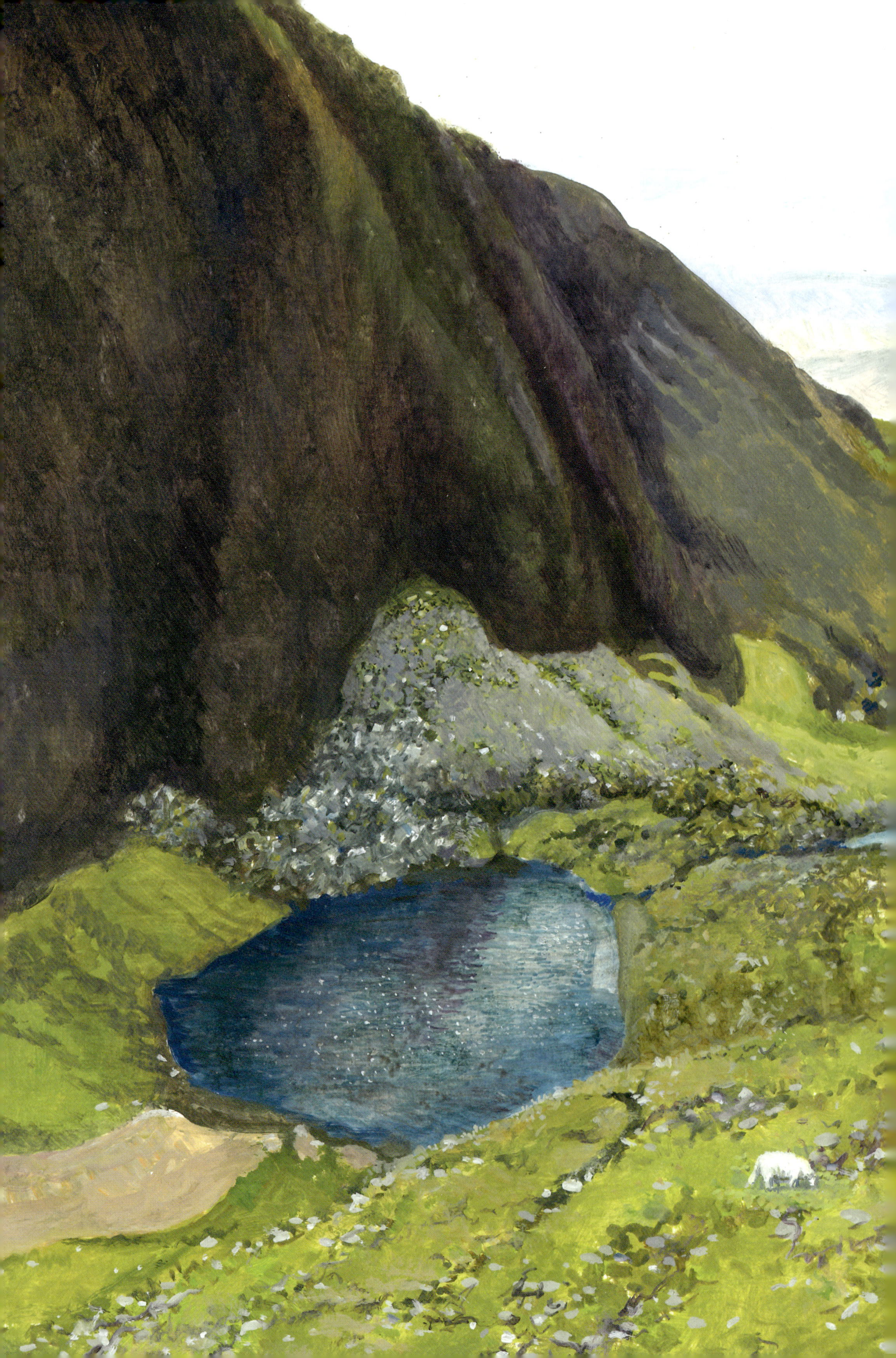

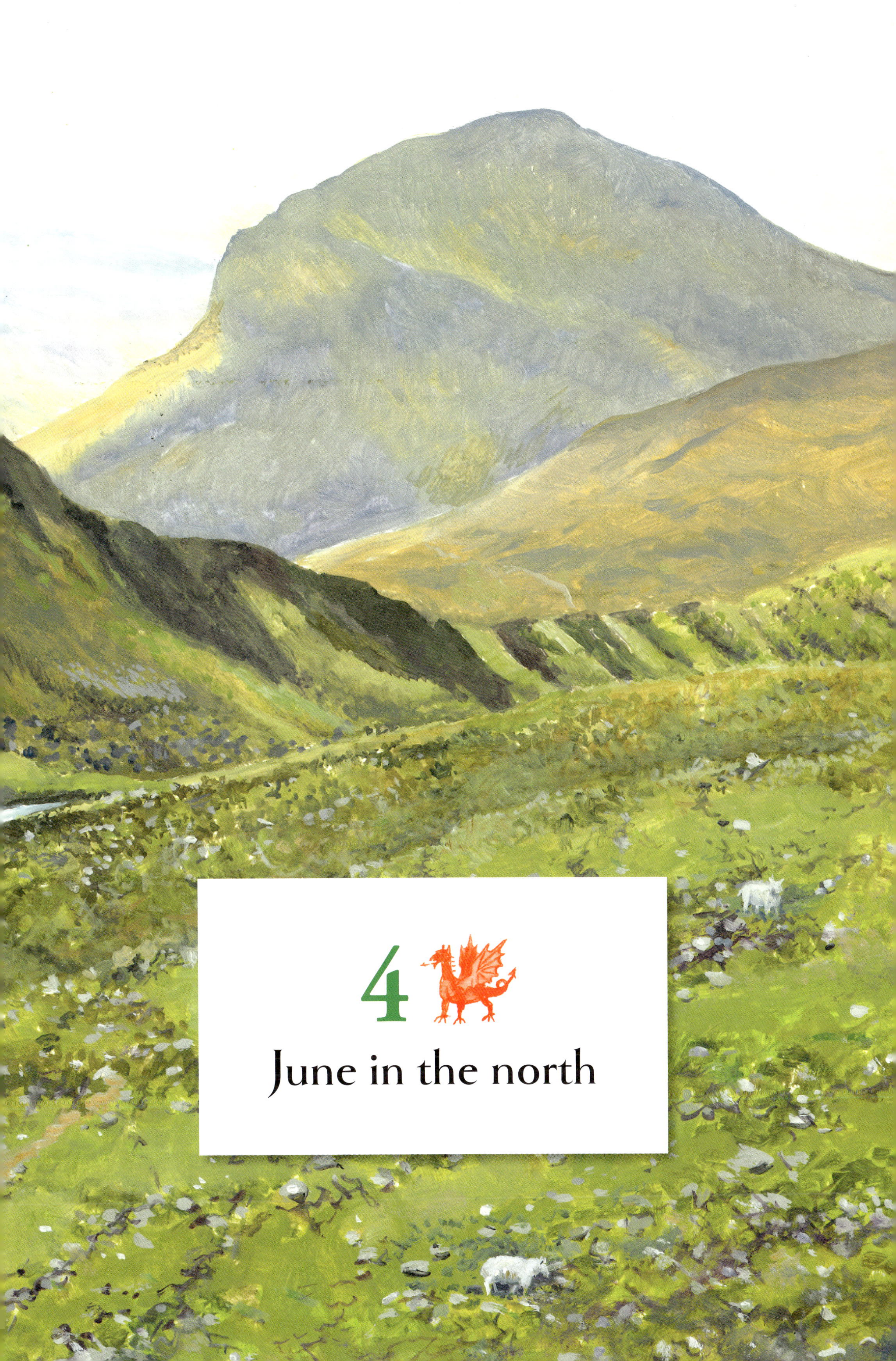

4 June in the north

June in the north

Betws-y-Coed

I'd heard of Betws-y-Coed ever since learning about Peter's Welsh childhood. He pronounced the town's name with affection. I heard it as *Betsy Coyed* and imagined it as the setting for a gothic tale as told by Enid Blyton, a beguiling mixture of everyday cosiness and weird going-on. Noddy and Big Ears would drive the train that arrived at *Betsy Coyed* station. The Famous Five would track dodgy men in loud, check jackets down the High Street. In reality, the Barrett family holidayed here from Deganwy where they spent the war years. Pa liked to fish for salmon in the Conwy River, while Peter caught salmon par, the young fish, with bait. What impressed Peter was the way the biggest "catch of the day" was displayed in the hotel's hall. Pa, sadly, was never the catcher.

We drove through Betws-y-Coed on our way from Devon to Caernarfon. It was certainly a pretty place, set on the thickly wooded banks of the rushing River

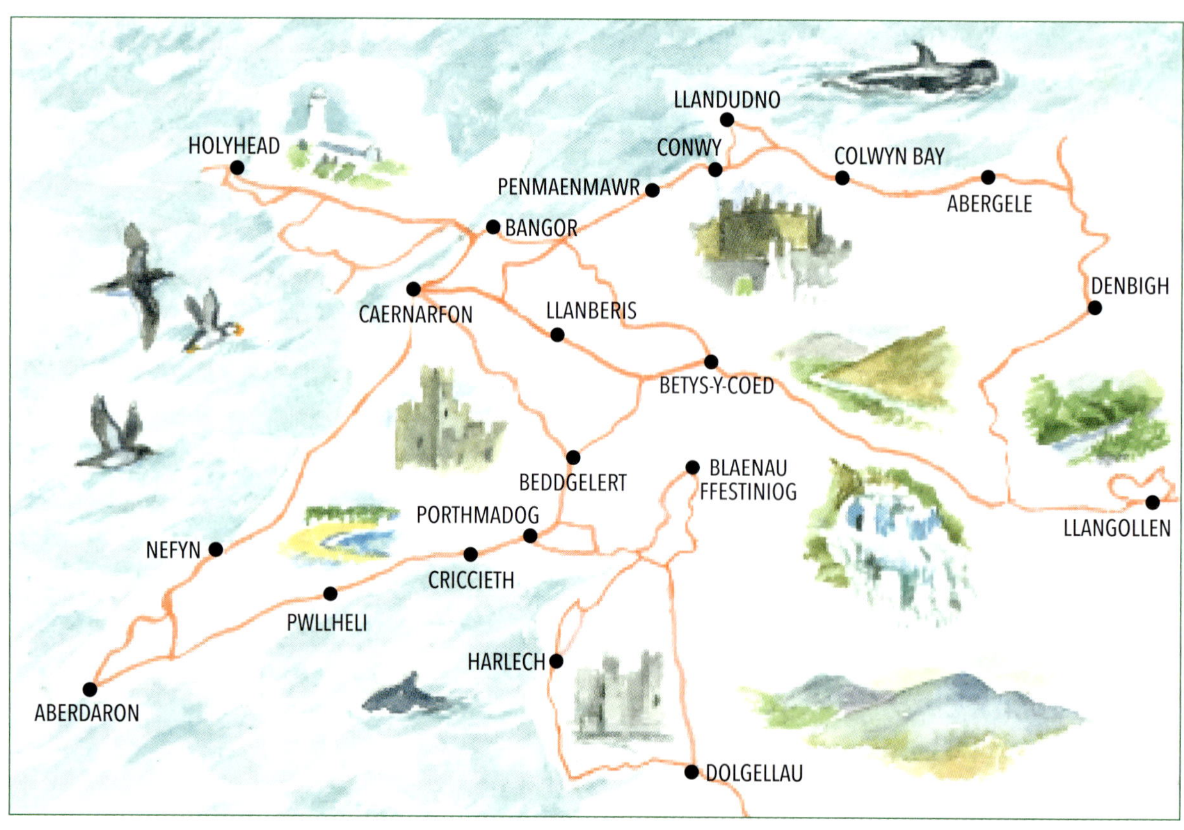

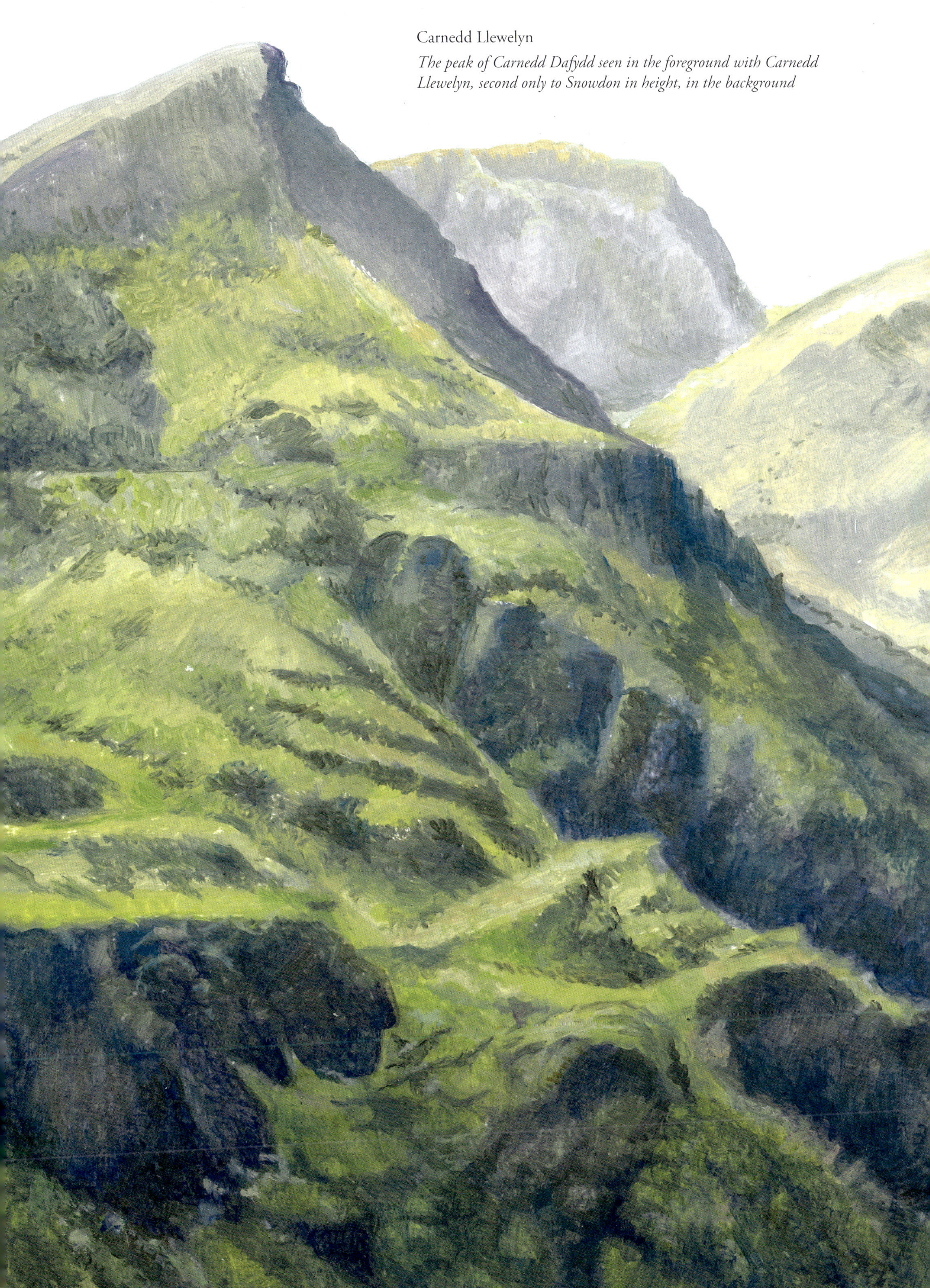

Carnedd Llewelyn

The peak of Carnedd Dafydd seen in the foreground with Carnedd Llewelyn, second only to Snowdon in height, in the background

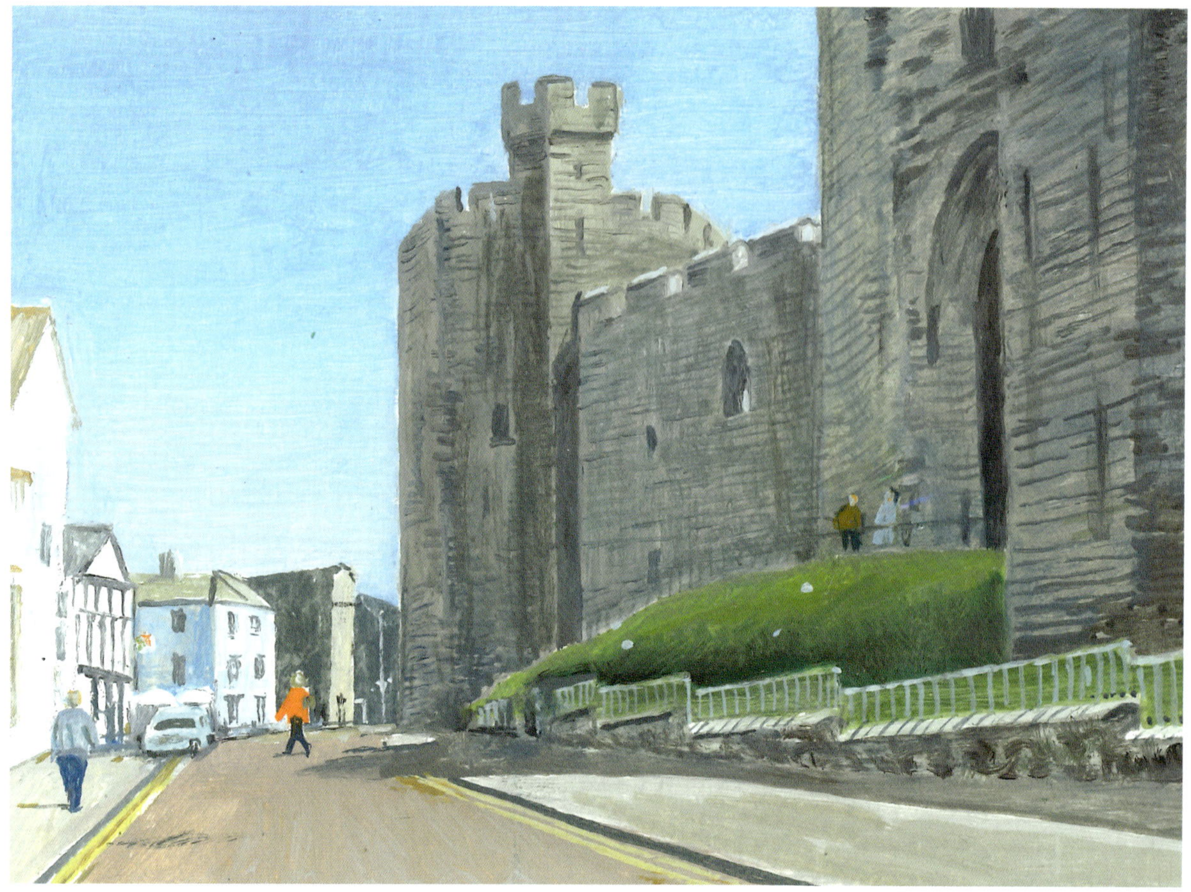

Caernarfon Castle
Originally a timber fortification on the banks of the River Seiont as it flows into the Menai Straits, Caernarfon Castle was rebuilt in stone by Edward I of England. Work started in 1283 and continued for more than thirty years. Now designated a World Heritage site, the castle forms the background to the ceremony in which the eldest son of the monrch is invested with the title, Prince of Wales. The first investiture took place in 1911. The second was in 1969 when our present king Charles was invested by the late queen. The tradition may be short-lived.

Conwy. The village was seething with people. We looked in vain for somewhere to park. Eventually we crammed ourselves into a space but our vision of sitting at a café table under a sun umbrella faded. Like the miners' terraced houses in South Wales, the buildings have their toes on the pavements with rarely any intervening space at all. The single place that looked tempting, thanks to a forecourt and cheery red sun umbrellas, was oversubscribed. Peter talked of finding a waterfall which had appealed in childhood, Swallow Falls, but our spirits failed us. We left Betws-y-Coed as though pursued by sinister men in loud check suits. It was not our Catch of the Day.

North of Betws and again reminiscent of the mining valleys, three roads lie in parallel, divided by high ground. This area in the northwest of the country is known as Snowdonia, designated a national park in 1961. It contains Snowdon itself and other peaks over 3000 feet high. When does a hill become a mountain? Climbers want a hill to be over 2000 feet before they call it a mountain; others regard 1000 feet as the dividing line. Driving north we were in among the mountains. The scenery was dramatic. In the Llanberis pass, one particular skyline engaged my full attention. *Like knuckles punching the sky*, I jotted down in my notebook.

The Celtic Royal Hotel in Caernarfon was full of animatedly chatting guests, members of the Townswomen's Guild of Maidenhead on a coach trip. Wales provides a wonderfully accessible holiday spot for anyone who lives in England and the hotels we choose are in the bracket suitable for coach groups. The groups are made up of grey and white-haired people, mostly women. "We do bring our menfolk," a Maidenhead townswoman told me, "that is, if we still have a man." She greeted her remark with jolly laughter.

Next day we had a tight schedule, worthy of a coach trip. First, we went to find out about the train that, amazingly enough, chugs to the top of Snowdon. The terminus is in the village of Llanberis, where streetlamps are adorned with hanging baskets and there are picnic tables in the station's triangular forecourt. The scene has the same Enid Blyton quality as Betws-y-Coed. We booked tickets for the 3.30 train, which gave us lots of time to revisit Peter's childhood land and seascape on the north coast.

Deganwy

Some years ago, Peter had shown me the house in Deganwy where the family lived for most of the war. Over our sixty-three year-long marriage, I've heard the anecdotes that get told and re-told. His father, John, had got away from Lancashire to qualify as an accountant and join the accounts department of the

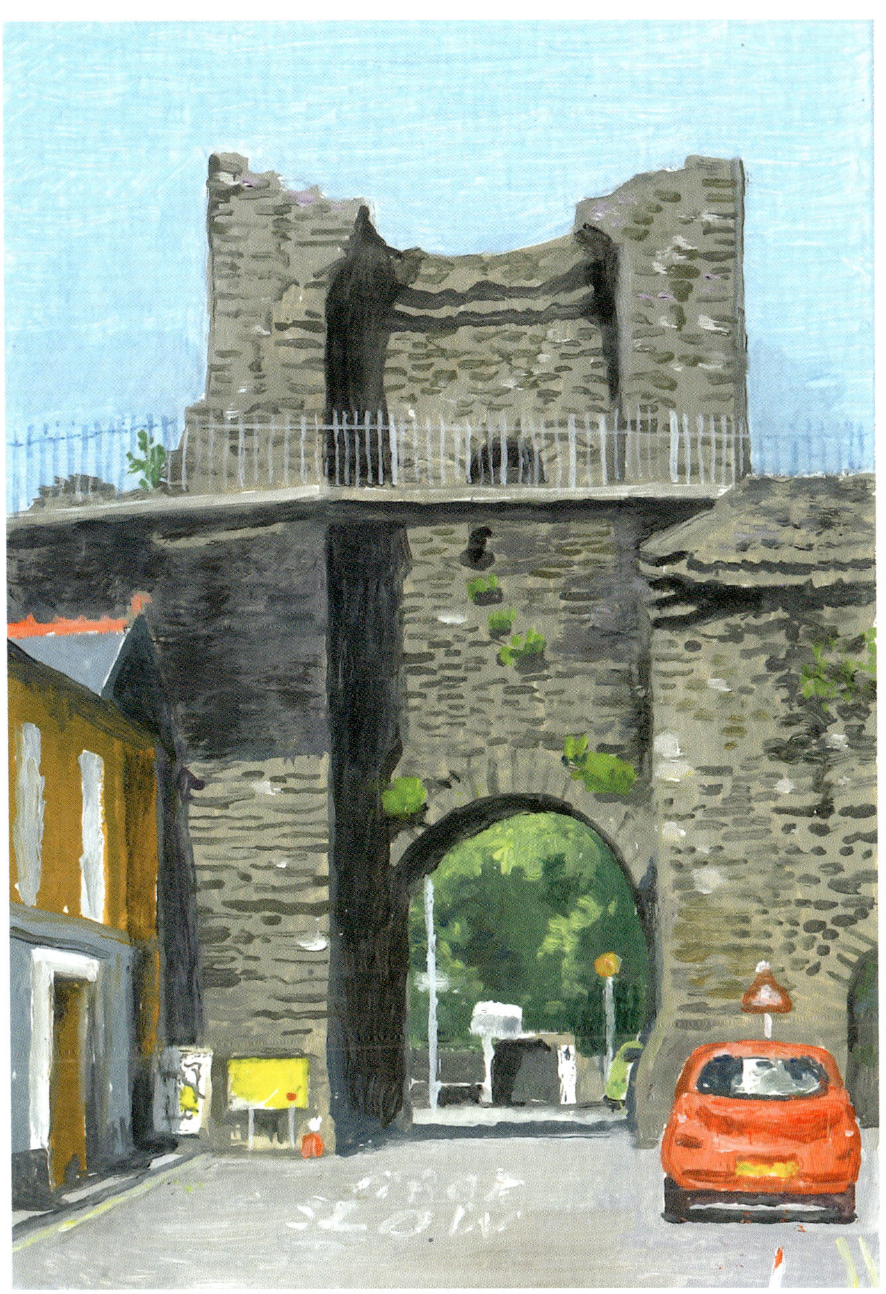

Conwy Castle

The archway into Conwy's town streets.

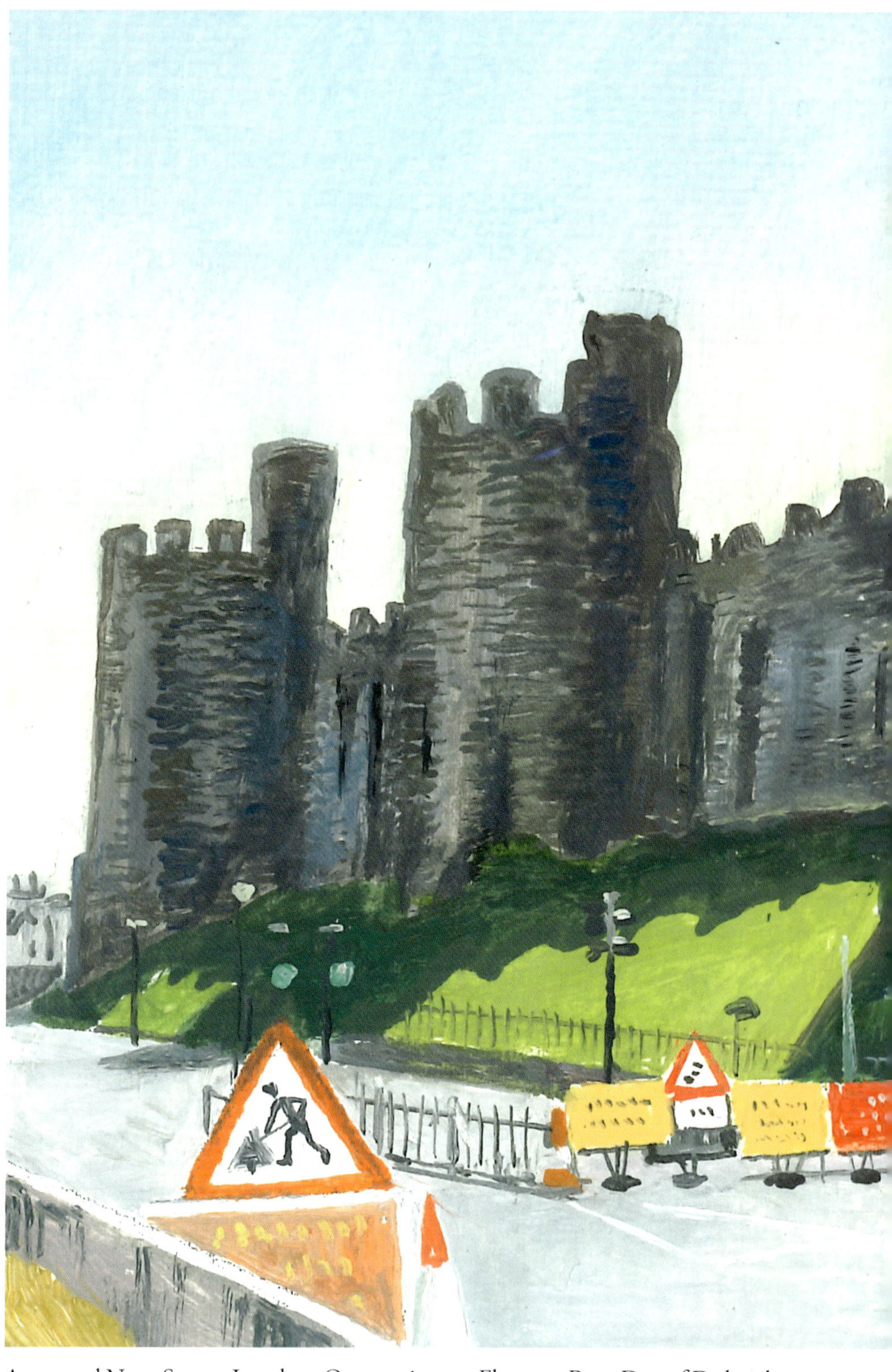

Conwy Castle

Peter liked the colour brought into the scene by the roadwork signs, the red contrasting with the grey of Conwy Castle's stone walls.

Army and Navy Stores, London. On marriage to Florence Rose Day of Dulwich, he opted for a job in the Bombay branch of the Stores. Peter was born there in 1935. When Peter was three, the family returned to England in time for his sister Jennifer to be born in London in January 1939. War was declared that September. His father was commandeered for war service in the Ministry of Food which was transferred for safety to Colwyn Bay in North Wales. Hence, the house in Deganwy.

On this, my second visit to the setting of Peter's childhood memories, I took in the details better and could relate them more accurately to the place itself. We make up our own pictures to illustrate the tales we hear, which may have

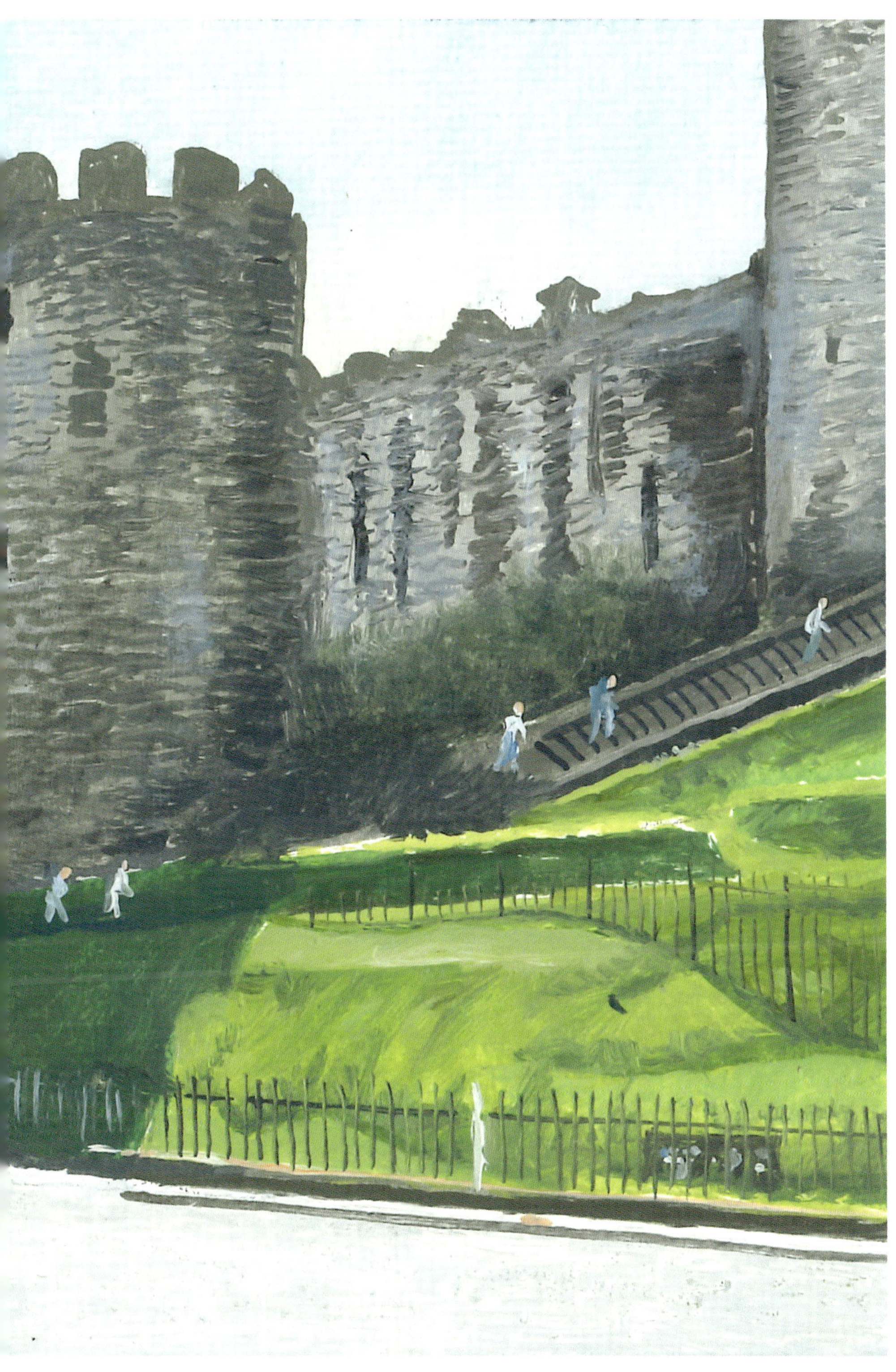

no resemblance to reality at all. In the actual setting, we shuffle pictures and places in the effort to get them to match. *This* is the gateway to the little town within the battlements of Conwy Castle. *This* is the bridge across the wide river mouth of the estuary of the Conwy River that flows through *Betsw-y-Coed*. *Those* are the hills where Peter chased and caught butterflies, something he is as ashamed of, as any descendant of an eighteenth-century slave-owner might be of a past life. The hills look to me like sandy dunes close to the back of the town. The railway line is far closer to the Barretts' wartime house than I recall from my previous visit. But I still can see Pa Barrett carrying home the family spaniel, killed by a train on the line.

From Deganwy we drove on to Penmaenmawr, the setting of one of Peter's many schools; a place so changed that Peter could not be bothered to look for his school. He had not been particularly happy there in the first place, uprooted first from India, then from London and Kent to Wales where the other children spoke Welsh. It's no surprise that he turned to the countryside, preferring the company of the natural world. His career as a wildlife artist had its origins in the war.

The fast dual carriageway along the north coast soars straight over Penmaenmawr's sea front. It runs between the steep cliffs at each end of the bay at a higher level than the beach. If you're quick, you'll spot the sign to a slip-road which will lead you down and along the back of the beach. Is this a cycle track? Yes, but cars are allowed. There are places to park at intervals and sheltered seating where you might eat an ice cream, could you but find a place to buy one. There is a couple sitting at the first bench in the first parking area. We drive to the end of bay and see no-one else. It is as though the sea front has been garrotted. Was there an alternative way to accommodate the speedy road? Were there vociferous council meetings about it? It's the old dilemma which we grew familiar with when living in Greece. Tourism tends to destroy the place that tourists have come to see. But this is not always so.

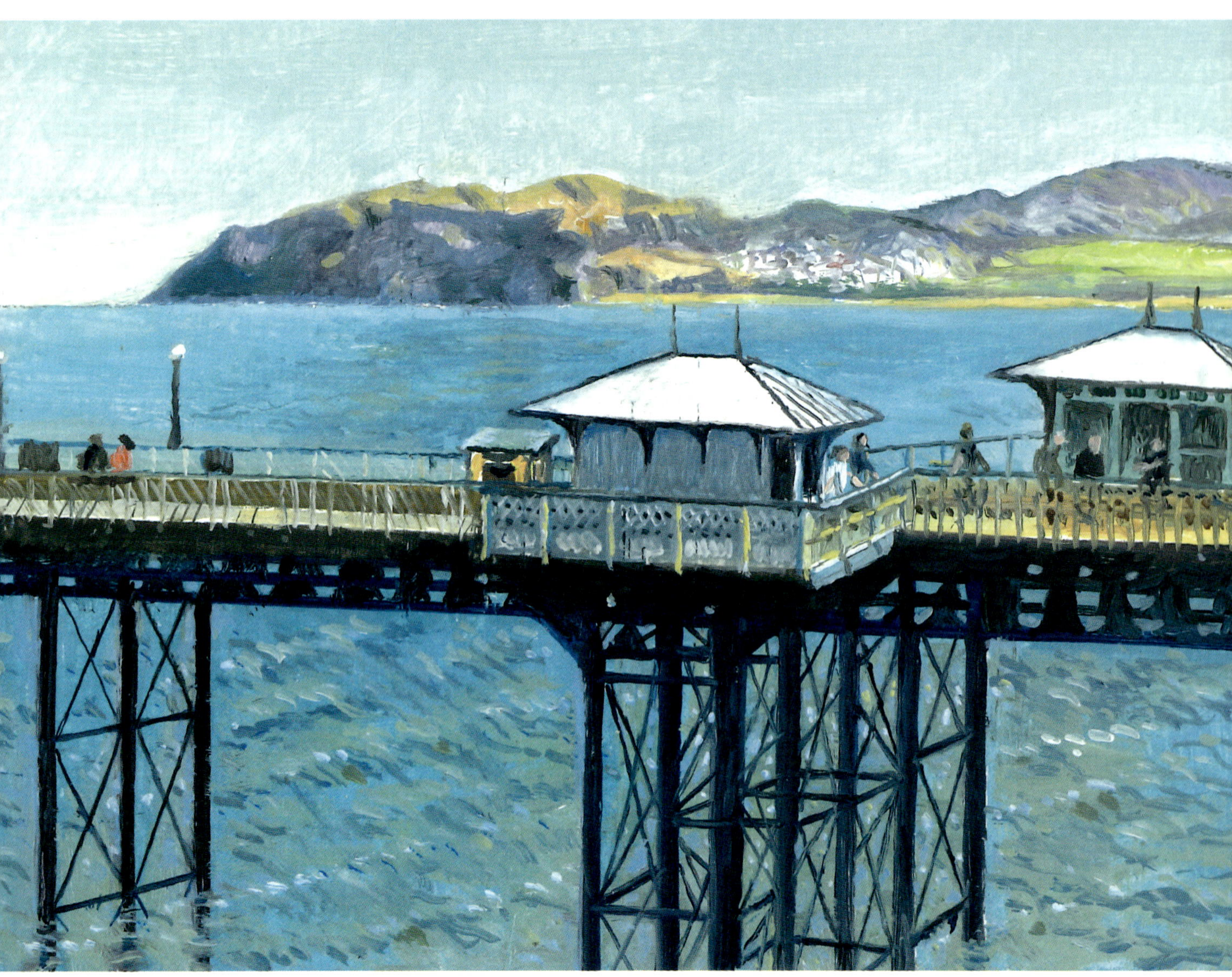

Llandudno Pier
Llandudno Pier still retains a hint of its heydays in the late nineteenth and early twentieth centuries.

Llandudno

Llandudno is a case in point. I remember seeing posters showing Llandudno framed on the walls of railway carriages when I was a child. The resort was portrayed in simple, pastel-coloured shapes. A sandy beach, tall buildings, palm trees, striped umbrellas … lo and behold, the poster's come to life, seventy-five years at least since I went to boarding school by train. Llandudno is a most distinctive seaside resort. Grand, tall, terraced buildings freshly painted in pastel colours stand in watchful attendance the length of the curving beach. If Llandudno were human, it would be as a Dowager Duchess with the hint of a rakish past, keeping an eye on present-day visitors to gauge their suitability as visitors. The Big Wheel at the far end of the beach must have gained entry when she wasn't looking.

The Duchess has a lesser sister further east. This is Colwyn Bay, where Pa Barrett went to work daily in the evacuated Ministry of Food. All Peter remembers is that Pa was not present in Deganwy on weekdays. He doesn't remember how Pa got to work. Perhaps he covered the 4 or 5 miles by pedal bike. Cars were rarely on the road in wartime.

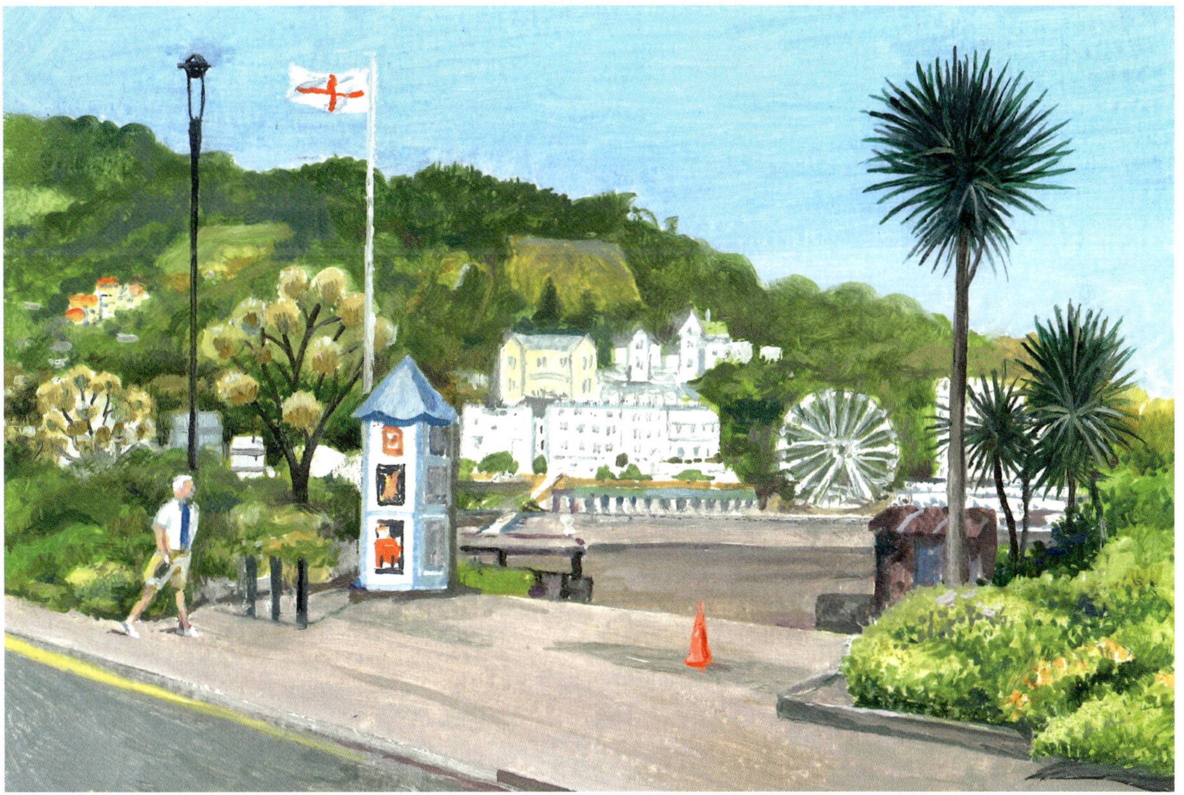

Llandudno sea front

The social atmosphere of the Llandudno sea front is not quite rakish, nor stiffly-genteel but something inbetween. You only have to blink and you'll open your eyes on a scene from the days when the railways first brought crowds to the seaside.

The train up Snowdon

We were back at the station in Llanberis by three-thirty, ready to board the train that would take us up Snowdon. I had no preconceived notions of what this would be like. In my experience, trains run, as far as possible, on the level. How could a train be hauled up Wales's highest mountain? I imagined it might be pulled or pushed by the force of steam. We might get smuts in our eyes and the smell of bad eggs up our noses, as I remembered from my childhood. Our Snowdon train was not steam-driven but diesel. We queued up and boarded the short, single coach. The driver sat at minimal controls in the front seat. He greeted us with the kind of spiel an airline pilot might deliver on a short flight; he recited facts and figures

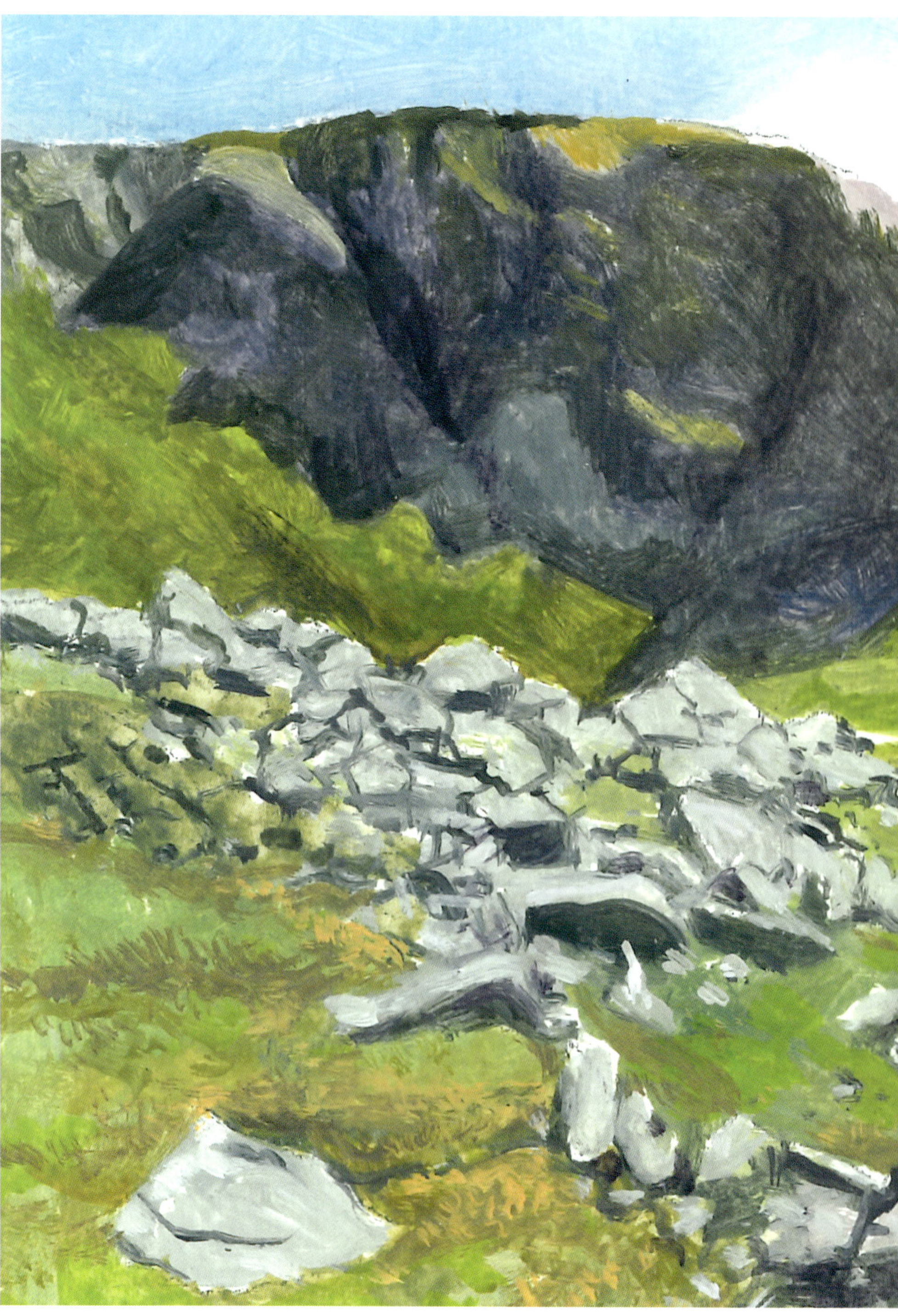

about altitude, timing and safety precautions, nicely seasoned with black humour. We certainly weren't to open doors and jump out. We were to tell him as soon as we fell from the summit. We all laughed at his jokes.

Peter and I were in compartment D, which we shared with three other couples. We could see down the length of the coach to the driver but there was no corridor. Each compartment was an island unto itself, with no means of exit, save for the firmly locked door on each side. I took in our companions as we slowly moved forward with the grind and bump of machinery. Peter, with the camera, sat by the window on my right. To my left sat a couple who could have been from Israel or an Eastern European country. Even in my outgoing, Welsh-book persona, I didn't feel up to engaging with them. Nor did anyone else.

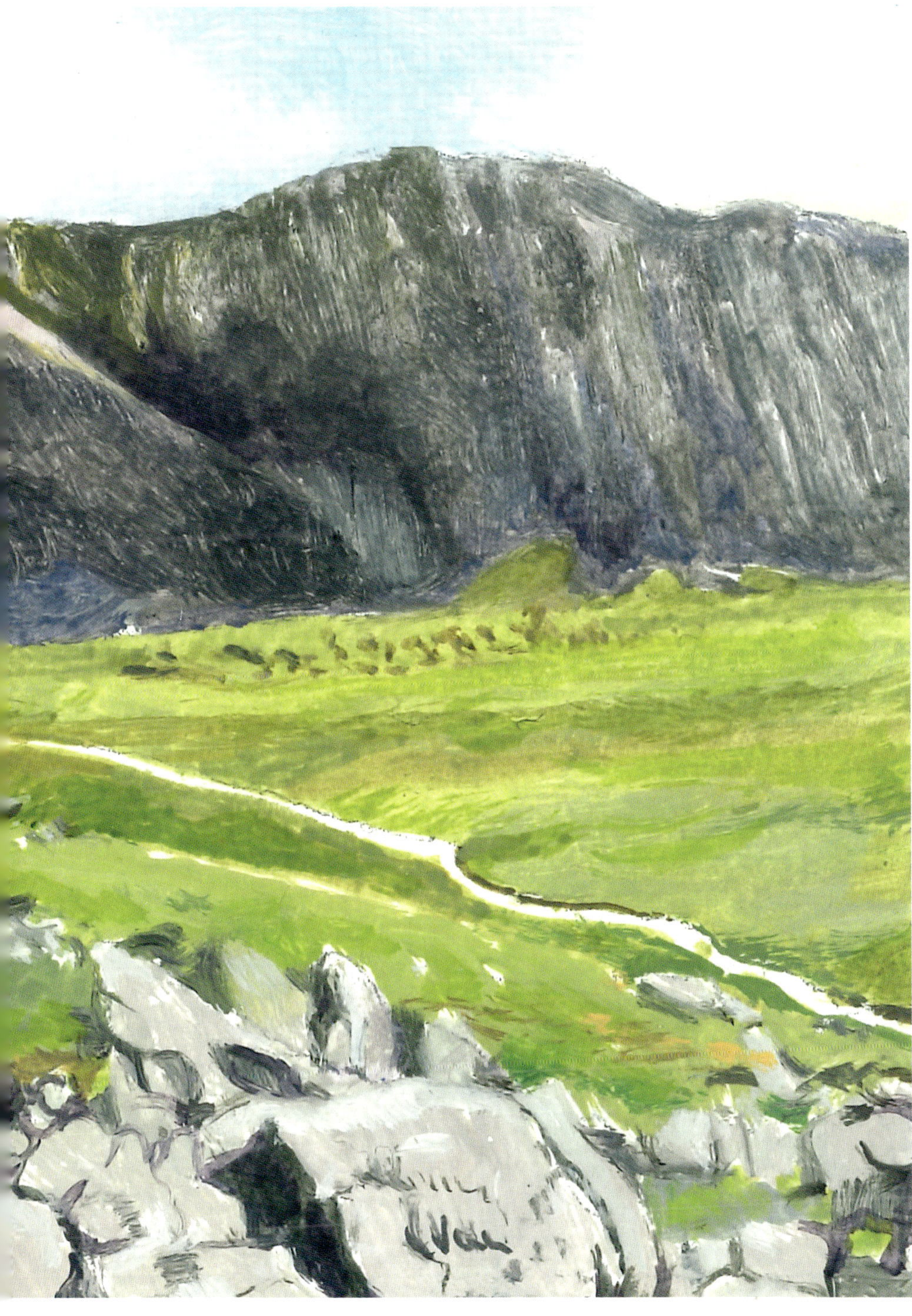

Snowdon
A section of the path up Snowdon seen from the train.

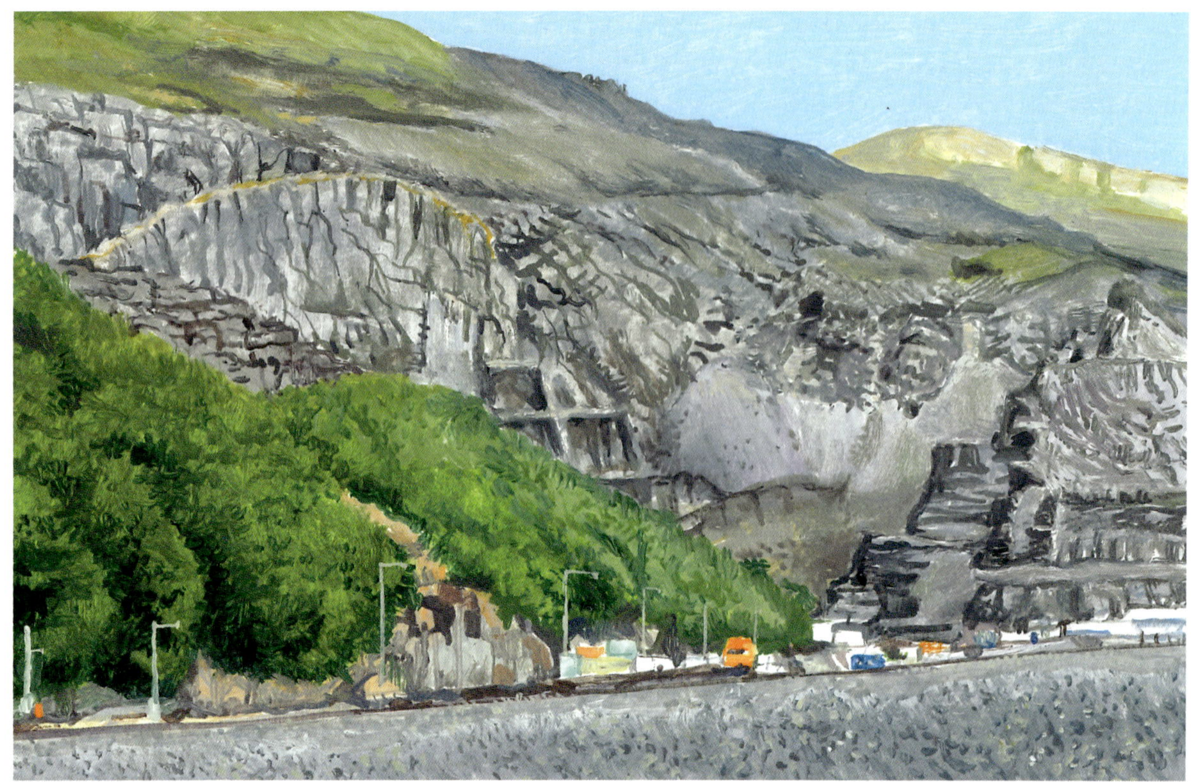

Slate quarry, Llanberis
Welsh slate was said to have roofed the world.

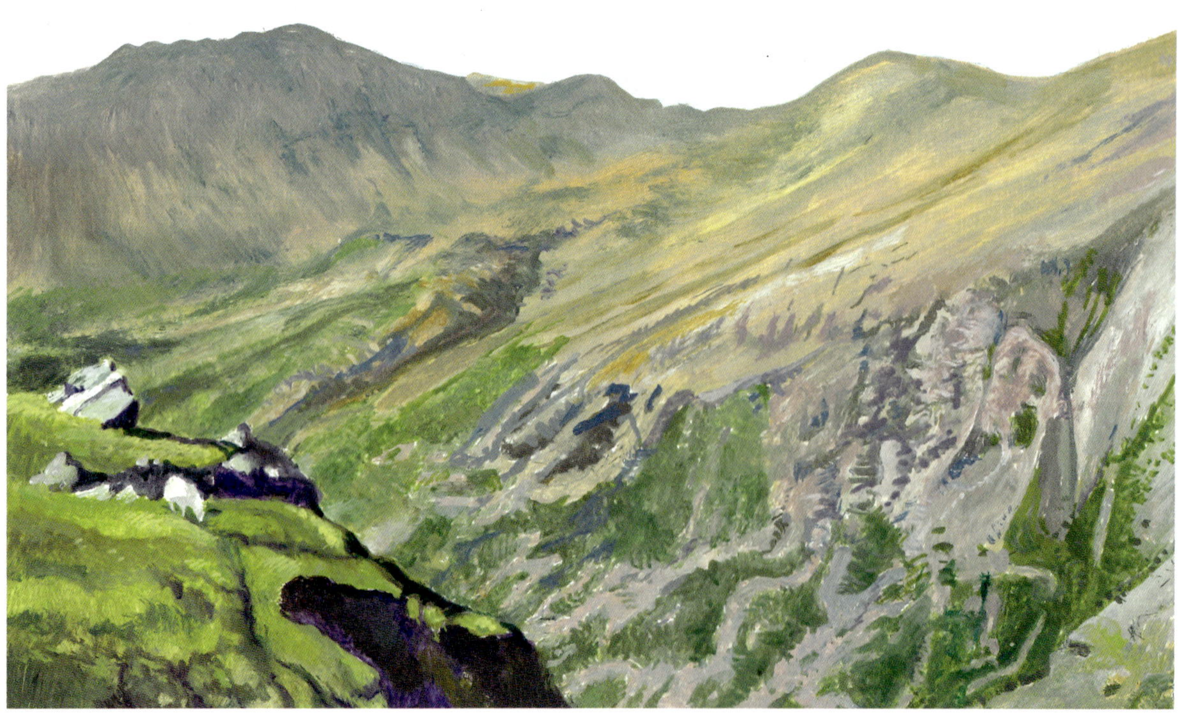

Llanberis Pass
Slowly and steadily, the train reveals new views. This painting shows the skyline of Llanberis Pass.

There was something forbidding about their expressions. Opposite them sat a father and son who looked as though they originated in the South Pacific. All the near-adult son wanted to do was lay his head against the window and sleep. His father prompted him to stay awake with endless opening gambits. He didn't respond with much more than a grunt. To the father's left and directly opposite me sat a substantially built, grey-haired Welshman eager for conversation. In his shadow sat his pale-faced wife who smiled hopefully and weakly at me as though pleading for help. Peter was busy with the views that passed by the window at 5 miles an hour. I, of course, responded happily to the man from Welshpool. However, crossing a narrow neck of land near the summit, I withdrew my attention. I was too busy imagining what it would be like if the train veered off the rails. This is something trains do, on occasion. I've seen photographs in the papers. What would it be like to plunge 3000 feet through space in this tin can of a train with these companions?

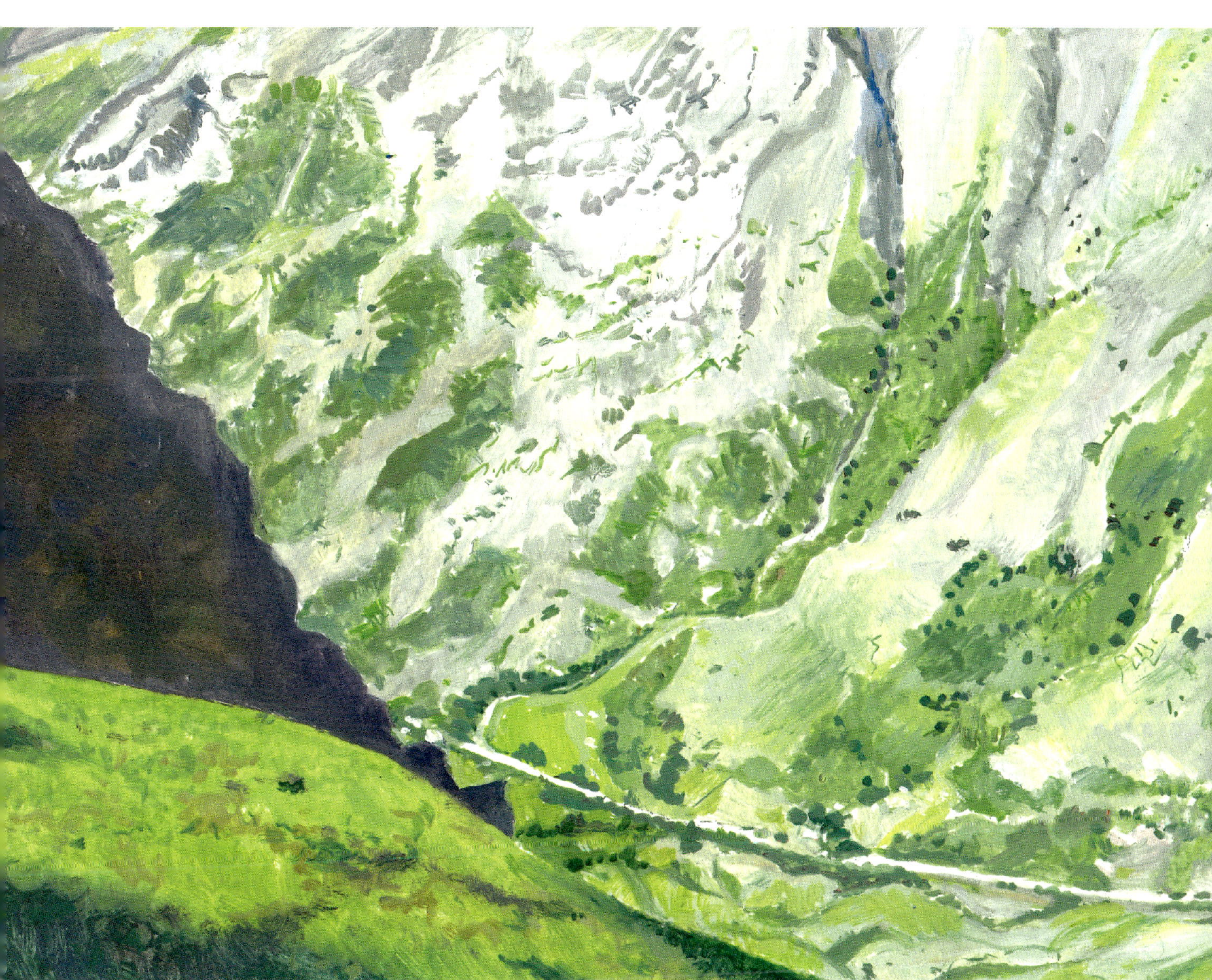

Llanberis Pass

As the train carries you higher, you catch glimpses of the road through Llanberis Pass far, far below.

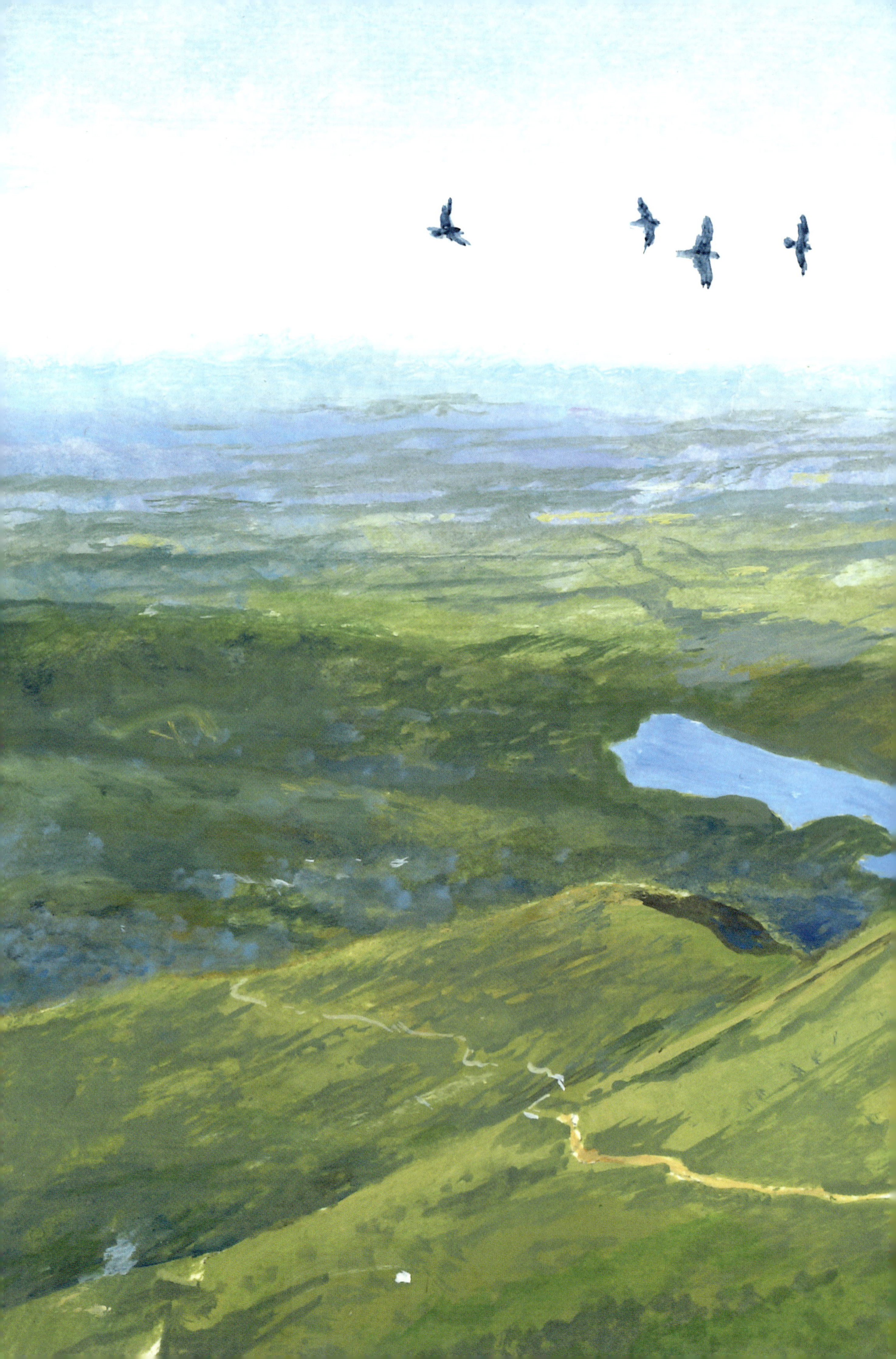

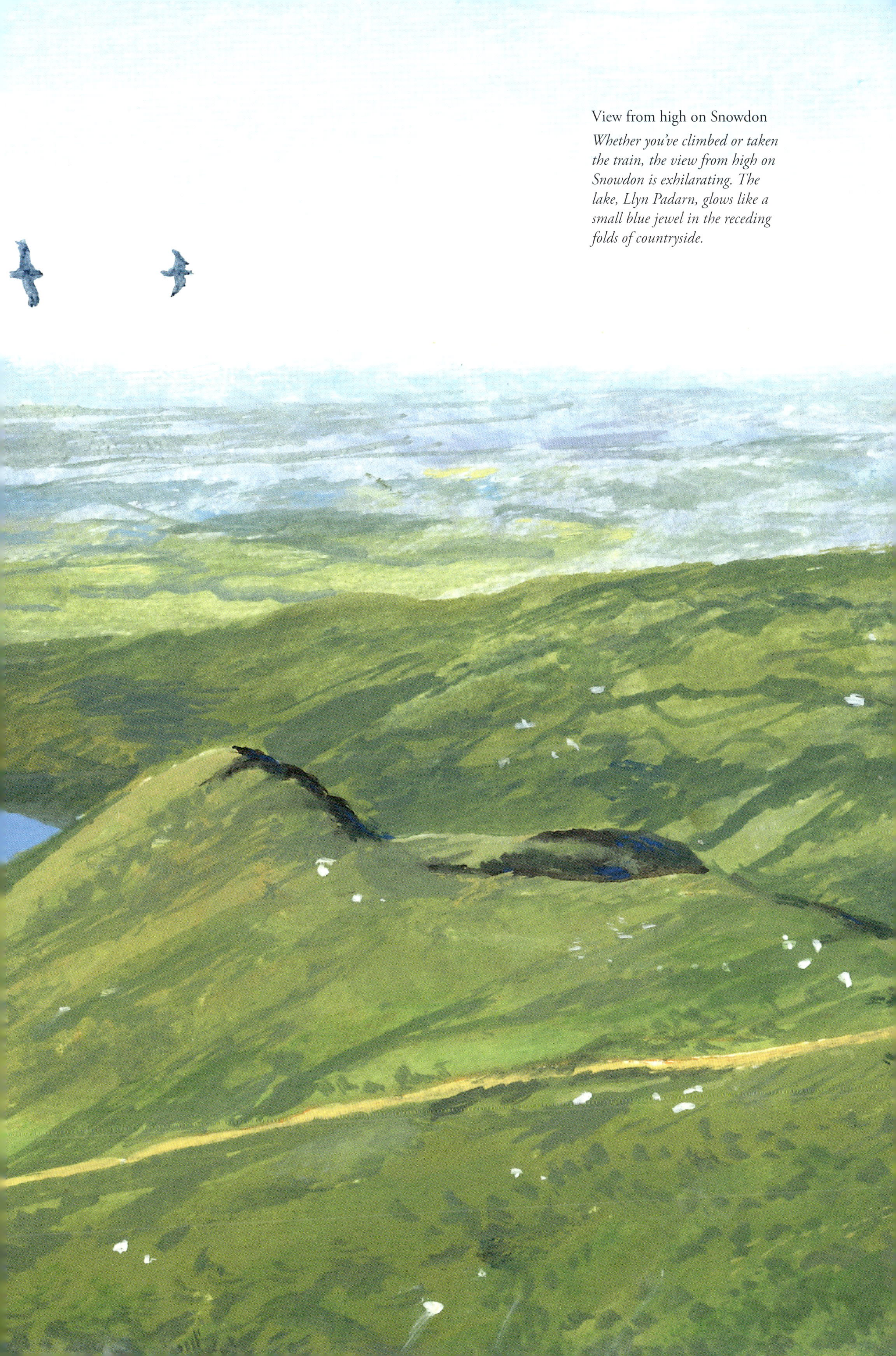

View from high on Snowdon

Whether you've climbed or taken the train, the view from high on Snowdon is exhilarating. The lake, Llyn Padarn, glows like a small blue jewel in the receding folds of countryside.

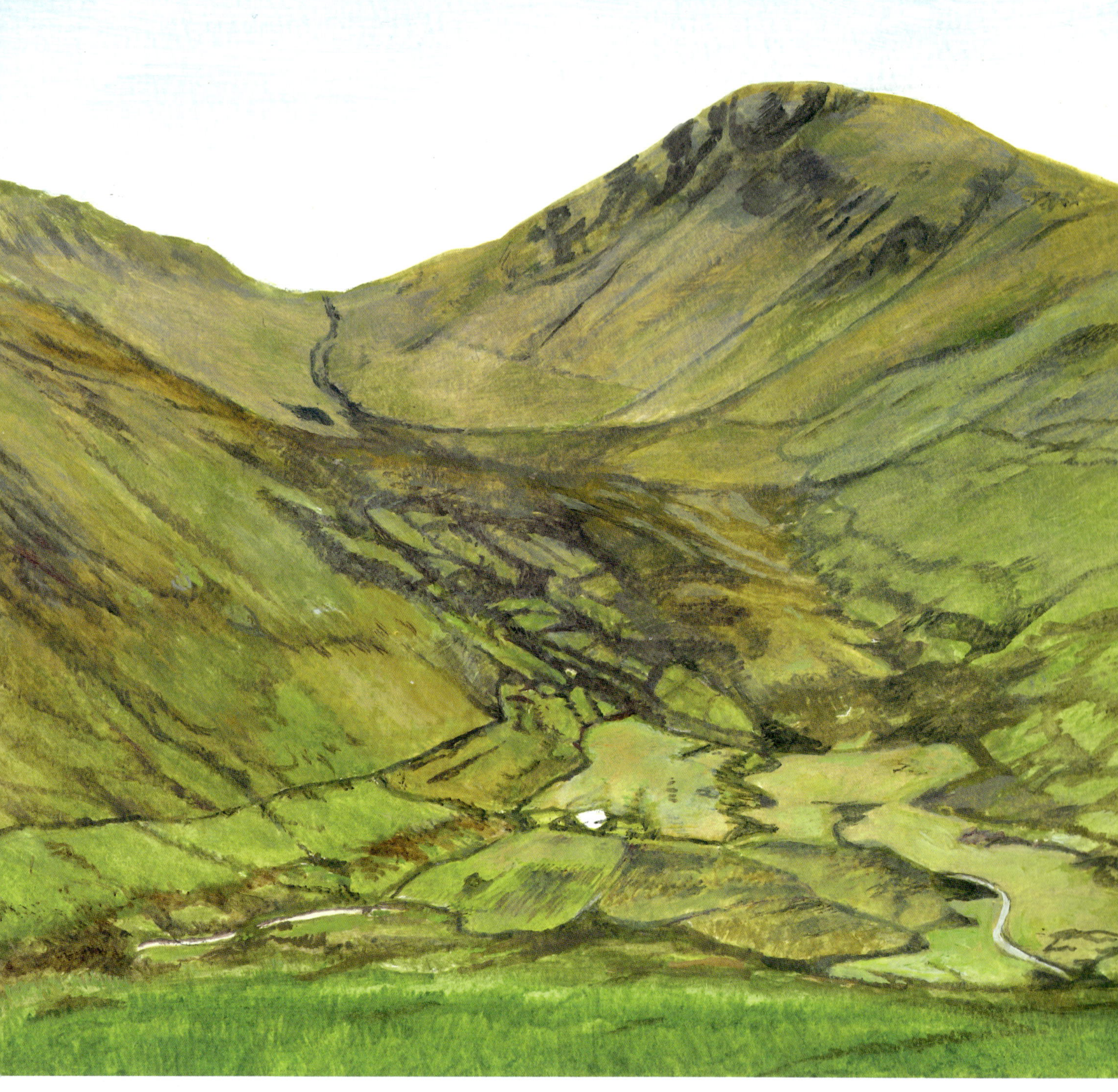

Snowdon, highland farm and fields

A deserted farm high on Snowdon. It doesn't take long for nature to reclaim farmland.

Since then, I've done some research. The Snowdon Mountain Railway uses the rack and pinion system, which was devised by a Swiss engineer in the nineteenth century. As far as I can tell, the system acts in much the same way as a zip fastener. A toothed wheel (the pinion) rolls over a toothed rail (the rack) interlocking with it and then disengaging in rotation. Picturing this might have calmed my fevered imagination. (Except zips break!)

The twin stopped at Clogwyn Station, three-quarters of the way up to the summit. The track further on was closed for repairs in 2019 and remained closed until Tuesday June 27th, a few days after our visit in 2023. Research has also thrown up the news that Snowdon, like the Brecon Beacons and other well-known national parks in Wales, is to be known by its Welsh name: Eyri.

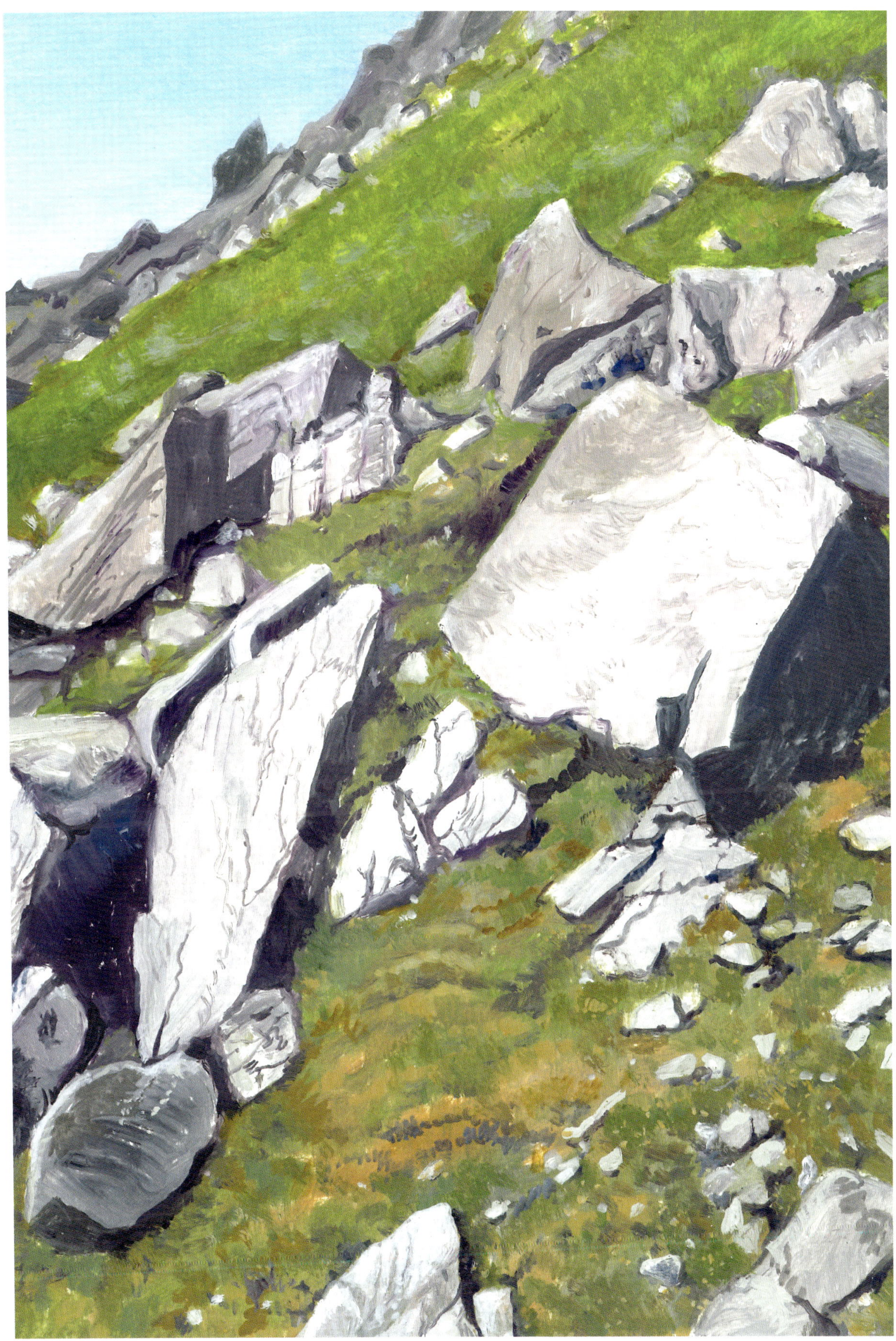

Valley of the Rocks, Snowdon

Sometimes, Wales produces sights that awaken the painter of abstracts in Peter. The Valley of the Rocks on Snowdon may have this effect.

The name of the mountain, Snowdon, in Welsh Yr Wyddfa means Rhita's tomb. The cairn at the summit is the tomb of the legendary giant Rhita who wore men's beards as a cloak. Where does the Wyddfa come in? Rhita with an h looks Welsh enough on its own, without taking the further step of an entire change of letters. Wales is a land where explanations need further explanations to explain the first explanation and, in the end, nothing feels explained.

Anglesey

More than half of the island's population are Welsh speakers. They call it Mon. Gerald of Wales, who we came across first in southwest Wales, gave its name a poetic twist: Mon Mam, the mother of Mon. But what does *mon* mean? There we go round the mulberry bush again.

Anglesey became an island when, over the millennia in the Pleistocene period, ice sheets chiselled deep valleys in the bedrock into which sea eventually flowed. The Menai Strait between Anglesey and the mainland is one such channel. Strong and conflicting currents in the narrow strait make the sea crossing dangerous. When Ireland joined the Union in 1801, the flow of people and trade greatly increased to other parts of the kingdom, with Anglesey providing

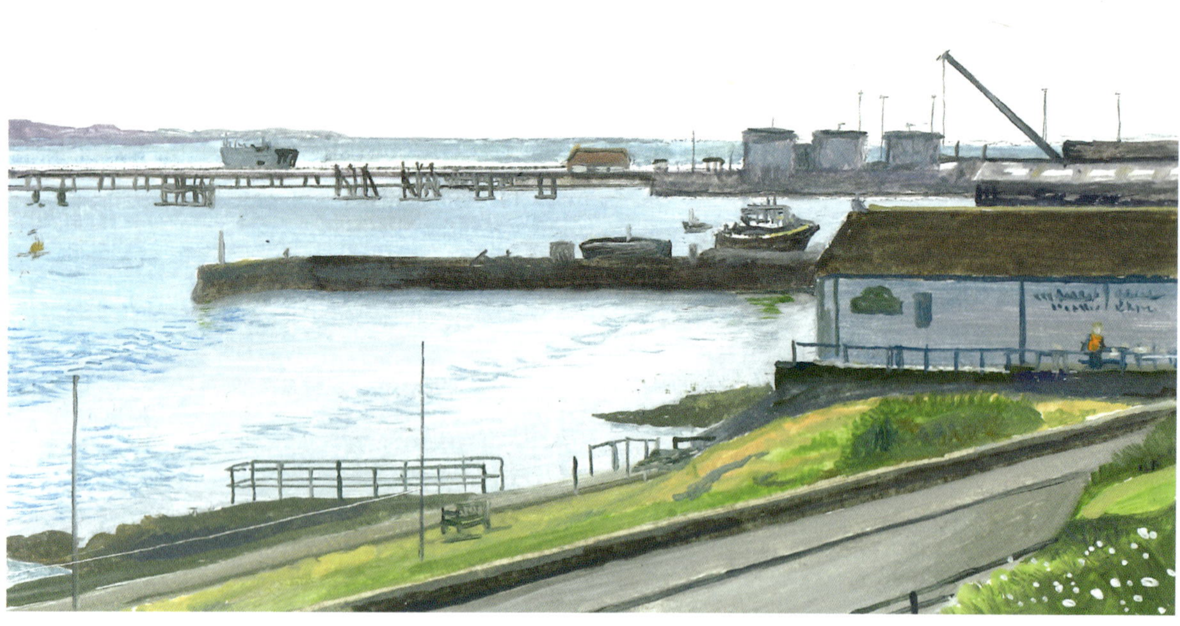

Holyhead, Anglesey

Holyhead harbour is situated in the northwestern corner of Anglesey. Although not as busy as it was in the past, it is still important as the port for Irish ferries and other passenger lines. The town of Holyhead lies on Holy Island which is separated from the larger island by a narrow strait. It's called "Holy" by virtue of the great number of ancient and sacred sites found here, dating from the Bronze Age. Standing stones, burial chambers and hillforts are evidence of human settlement over millennia. An excavated Neolithic longhouse has been dated to around 4000 BC.

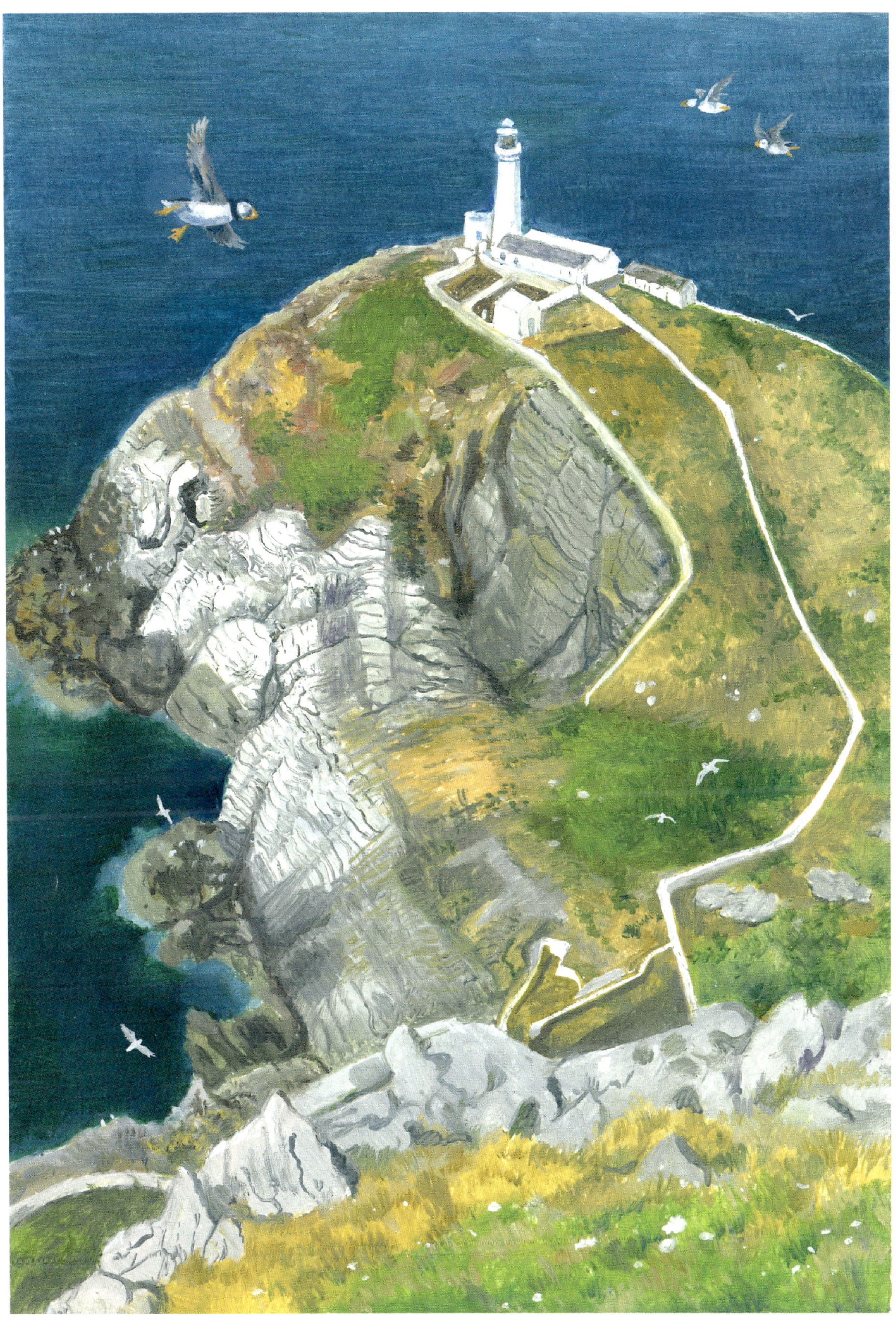

South Stack lighthouse, Anglesey
Puffins flying over South Stack lighthouse off the northwestern coast of Anglesey.

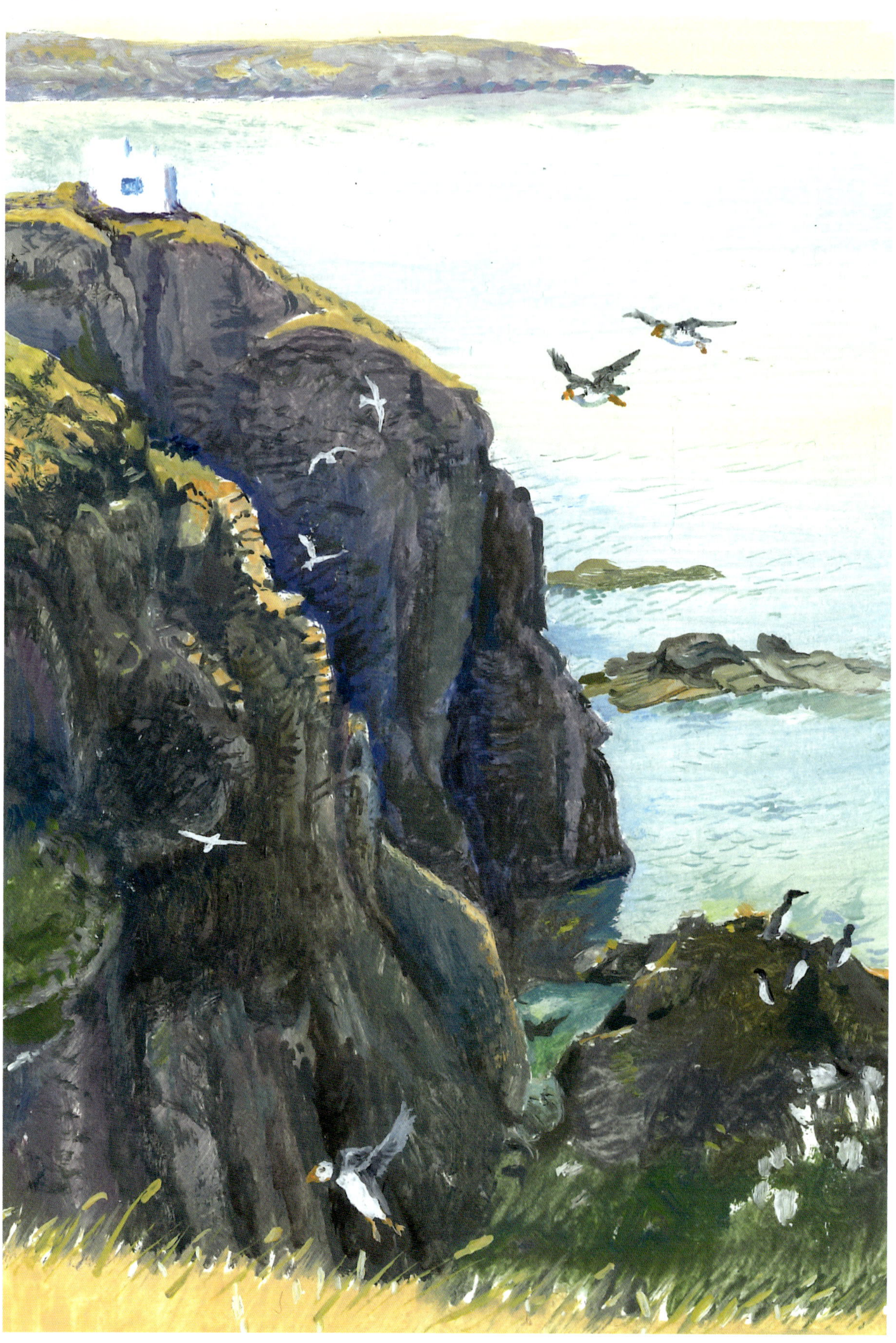

South Stack, Anglesey

A sea stack is an island formed by the sea's erosion of the rocks which once connected it to the mainland. South Stack is a place to see a great variety of sea birds.

a stepping stone. So, in the 1820s a bridge was built to make communication easier. It was designed by Thomas Telford, the Scottish engineer and architect of any number of transport projects. He also designed the suspension bridge over the River Conwy.

His Menai Strait bridge was closed for repairs. We crossed to Anglesey by a much less elegant construction further to the west. There was a marked difference in our surroundings. Unlike the terrain in Snowdonia, we drove through gently undulating farmland with no heights in view. The road was wide and empty, with stone-walled fields on either side edged with elderflower bushes and foxgloves. There was a great arch of blue sky overhead. It was yet another perfect summer's day in a run of such days.

In Holyhead we sat on a bench overlooking the stretch of bay and watched a ferry slowly approaching the harbour from the direction of Ireland to dock somewhere far to our right. A generous feeling of time and space pervades the island. We meandered on to South Stack to see the sea birds that clamour on the cliffs. While Peter found the 400 steps that drop down to sea level, I sat on a wall and listened to the mewling and screeching of the wheeling birds: guillemots and razorbills, I was told by Peter on his return. A young chap approached and asked if we'd like him to take our photograph. "You look so happy," he said. We were and are.

A series of sandy coves on the west coast of Anglesey is reminiscent of Cornwall. Peter was on the look-out for the place where he and the family had holidayed in the war years. It's hard if not impossible to match a childhood memory with the picture we see today; nor match what we see today with Wales in school holidays. Describing our Snowdon train trip to a friend, I realised what a different picture we'd see if we were here in August. She showed me photos of climbing Snowdon in high summer. The path we saw from the train, an occasional glimpse of an empty zigzag, was as full of walkers in August as a pavement in Oxford Street. It would be an entirely different mountain experience to ones we've had in New Zealand and Greece where you can walk for hours and not meet a soul. A different experience, of course, but by the look of the walkers, exhilarating in its own, communal way.

Newborough Forest

In the south-western corner of Anglesey lies Newborough Forest, a 5600-acre area of sand dunes, mudflats, salt marsh and pine plantation bounded by two rivers. Part of it is protected as a nature reserve. Peter could happily spend a month here, sketching the herring gulls, oystercatchers, lapwings, curlew, skylarks and meadow pipits, drawing toads and lizards and all manner of insects, noting and watching all the creatures flitting and buzzing, dipping and diving, scurrying and burrowing around, above and below the lichens and mosses, dune pansies, sea spurge, creeping willow and orchids of this Site of Special Scientific Interest. He'd have to disregard all the people, though. The enormous car park, mid-week in early summer, was completely full.

Lleyn Peninsula

The Lleyn Peninsula suited us better. There were no crowds until we reached the southernmost tip where there's an attractive harbour village called Aberdaron. Peter remembers his Uncle Charlie mentioning the place as a wonderful base for summer holidays. Uncle Charlie comes to mind whenever we get into a Waygood Otis lift. He was a director of the London branch of the American firm. Aberdaron attracts even more visitors than in Uncle Charlie's day. I'd talked with someone in the Snowdon railway train queue who'd had a marvellous lobster meal somewhere in the Lleyn Peninsula. I'd been on the look-out for a harbour with a fish restaurant as we drove down Lleyn's northern coast. But when we found a possible seaside village the way was blocked by a man in a high vis jacket. He explained that filming was in progress. All he could tell us, he said, was that it was for an HBO television series. The road ended in a quarry. Trefor was the village and the mountain in the background was purple with slate tips. I've looked up HBO and see it's an American pay-for TV channel called Home Box Office. Could Michael Caine be starring in it? Peter was certain that he was the man in our hotel's Waygood Otis lift who made laconic remarks about the Welsh version of "Doors Closing." Uncle Charlie would have dived into conversation with him, whether he was Michael Caine or not.

Instead of lobster or any kind of fish lunch, we ate our sandwiches parked on a steep descent down to a long crescent of sand, the beach leading to Porthdinllaen. This bay was considered once as a possible port for the ferry to Ireland, but the plan was dismissed. Somehow the "no" in this story has lived on in the place's psyche. No cars are allowed further than the point where the incline meets the sand. The long beach is a safe haven for people to enjoy, free of traffic. Not so good, though, for those who can't walk far from a car park. This is the kernel of tourism's dilemma. Rules protect as well as prevent.

Pwllheli

No such problem exists in Pwllheli on the opposite coast of the peninsula, facing Snowdonia. We found it easy to park near a café in an amusement arcade. Peter had an ice cream. I had a pot of tea. An array of one-armed bandits blinked and juddered while an argument about dustbins whirled around staff at a counter beyond an open door. Two large dogs shared a bowl of water beneath the table next to ours. The place did us nicely, but we didn't dally long, whereas I would have stayed a week at our next stop.

Criccieth

A road climbs to a castle on a hill. On one side, a terrace of houses painted in pastel colours regard the benches on the wide pavement the other side. Seated on one of the benches, we gaze over a stone wall at the view. Below the wall is a long sandy beach and the sea. This is the gulf between the Lleyn Peninsula and, a good distance away, Snowdonia. The bench we sit on is painted blue. Each of its arms and the rails on its back and seat has a picture of the scenery: the terraced houses, the waves, the seagulls, the castle, the blue sky, clouds, and flowers. The scenery itself and the pictures of the scenery make us glad to be there. I hope to be back one day.

Criccieth
A terrace of colourful houses leads uphill to Criccieth Castle.

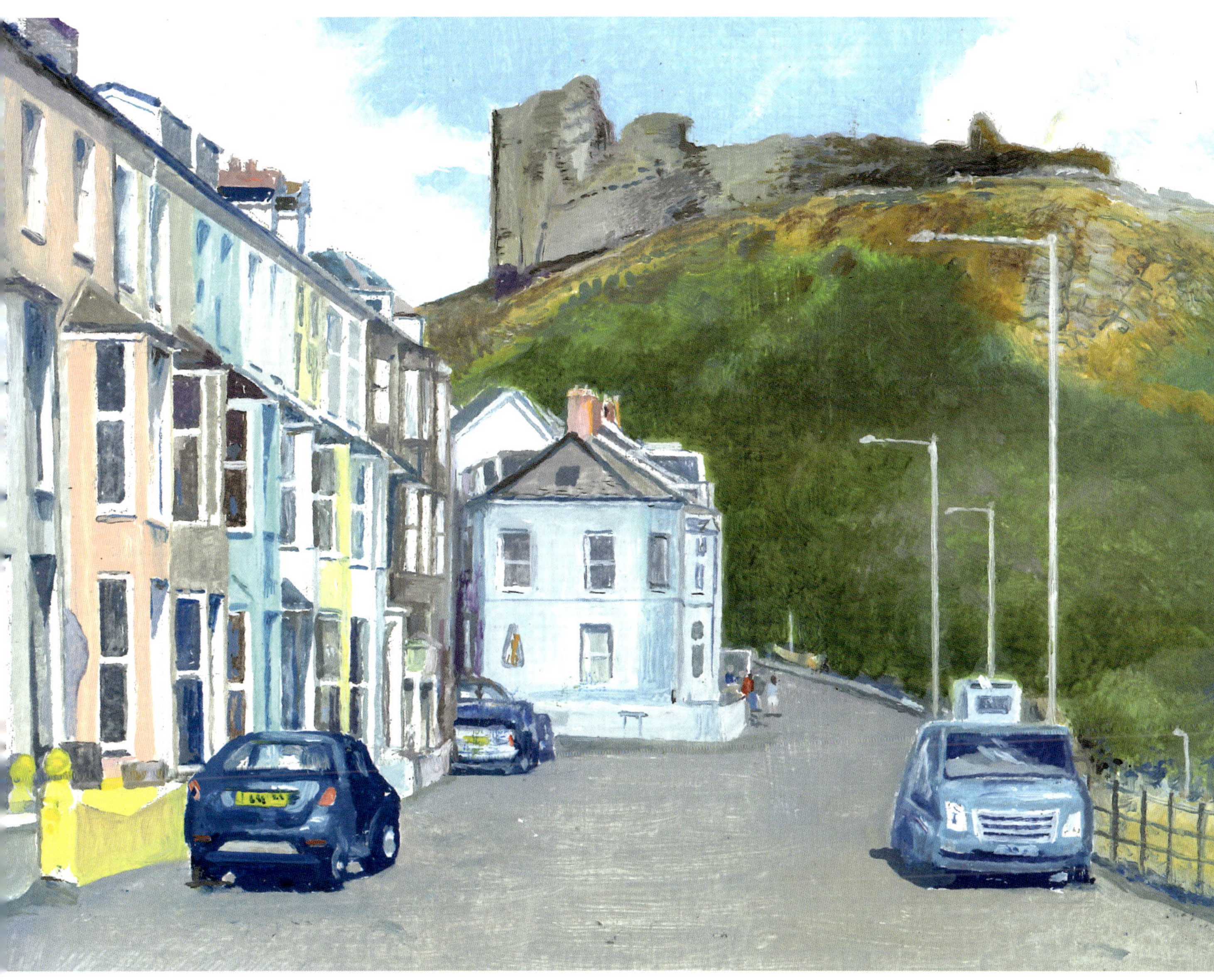

Beddgelert

There's a legend about a faithful dog known by the name of Gelert. It's one of those sorrowful tales of an animal killed, in this case by its owner, as the result of a misunderstanding. True or not, the story has lasted. In the village there's a mound known as Gelert's grave and there's a statue and shrine to the dog-hero. An accompanying story tells us that the legend was made up by the eighteenth-century landlord of the village's Grand Hotel to boost visitor numbers. Which tale is more likely to be true?

The village is attractive enough without resorting to the lure of legend. Two rivers, flowing fast down thickly wooded valleys, meet here. The dark stone of the houses is repeated in the dark stone of the bridge over the Glaslyn before it joins the Colwyn. It is soothing to sit by water of any sort, but I particularly like the sound of a rushing river. Perhaps that's an effect of my Dartmoor childhood.

Later, from the comfort of my study, I followed walkers with their video cameras on the rocky path up Dinas Emrys, a wooded hill overlooking the Glaslyn valley, the site of a medieval fort steeped in history and legend. It looks enchanting, a distillation of all that Wales offers in stories and scenery. It provides me with a hard lesson, too: how to accept gracefully the effects of old age.

Bridge, Beddgelert

The two-arched bridge in Beddgelert, a village made famous by the tale of a faithful hound mistakenly slain by its owner. Some say that this popular story was fabricated by a nineteenth-century landlord to attract visitors to the village and his hotel. The ploy worked. The legend still attracts visitors in their thousands.

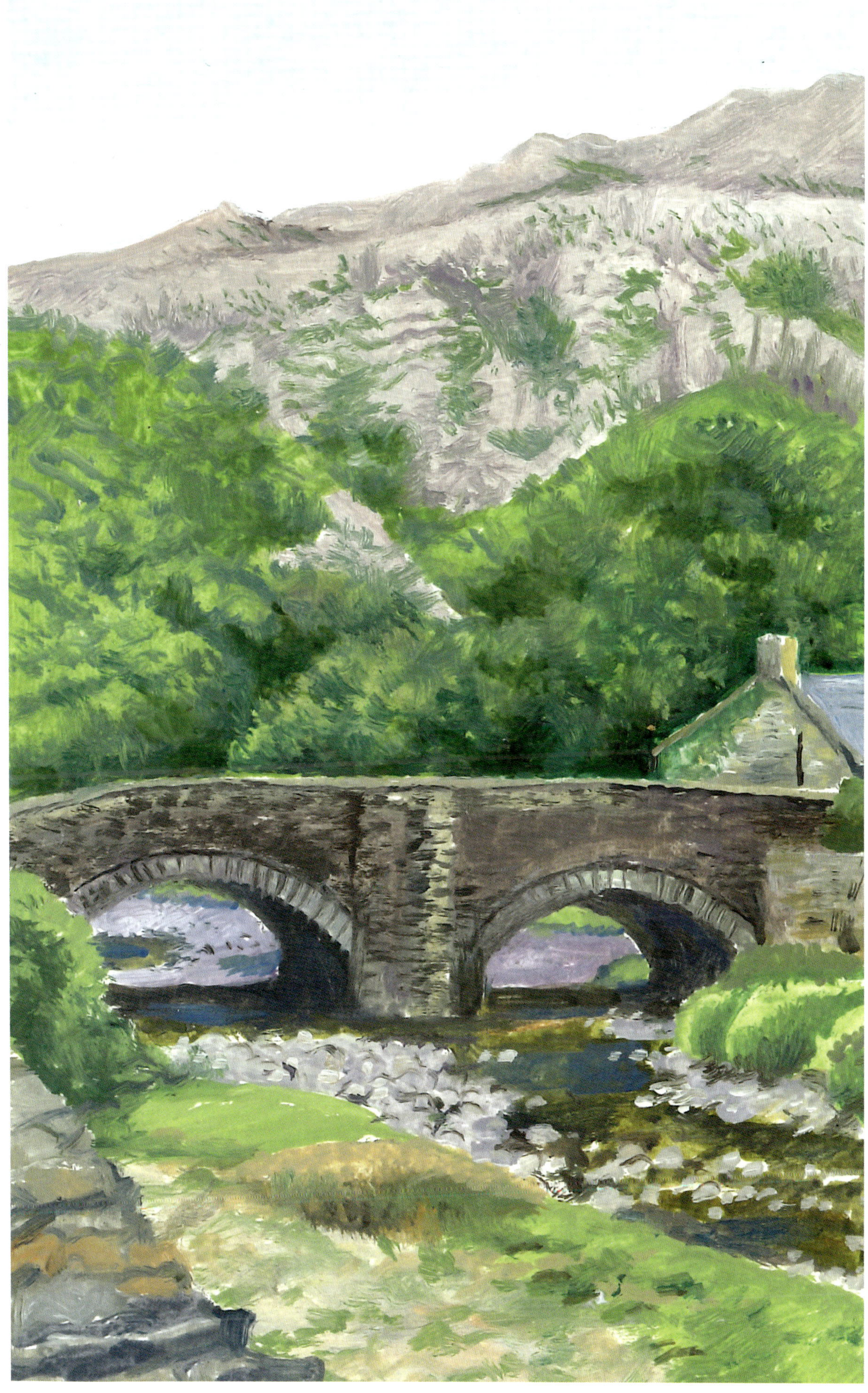

Blaenau Ffestiniog

The size of the car park at the Llechwedd slate mine shows that, in the summer holidays, this is a popular visitor attraction. Today at the beginning of July there is only a sprinkling of visitors. Some, in crash helmets, head for a few linked, yellow carriages tilted down at a steep angle towards a dark opening in the hillside, just big enough to swallow them. This, I learn later, is the steepest cable railway in Europe. It descends an abrupt 500 feet to the caverns below where slate used to be blasted from the rock face. We stay on the surface, forewarned about the 61 steps we'd have to negotiate in the tunnels below. Instead, we learn what we can in the visitor centre.

Local slate was used by the Romans as a roofing material for their garrison at Caernarfon. In the heyday of slate quarrying and mining, 17,000 men were employed in the industry. They worked in teams. There's still a small market for slate. We've considered slate for floors and roofs in various renovation projects. The closest we've drawn to owning slate is to inherit a slate-shelved larder in a Victorian house. It's an attractive and covetable material, one of the many such mineral gifts stored in the Welsh mountains. Outside the centre's café there are two linked wagons in which slate is packed tightly in rows, like stone playing cards. But this is a museum exhibit. Like coal and copper, there are other places in the world that can extract the material more economically than is the case in Wales. However, it's still possible to buy Welsh slate, in a range of fruity colours: plum purple, grape green, and coffee-grained grey.

A black-uniformed school party turns up. The boys come first, making for the trestle picnic tables outside the café. They sit on top of the tables, their feet on the benches, and keep changing places, ties and jackets flapping. Then come the girls. They are in small, cohesive groups. They sit down neatly on the benches and lean on the tables in animated conversation. They all speak Welsh. I approach a couple of girls for a lesson in pronunciation. "Cool," they say when they hear we're working on a book. "What's cool in Welsh?" I ask them. "Coo-el," they answer. Well, that's easy. Were the whole language a matter of breaking up vowels like that, we'd be fluent in no time. But let's remember for a moment the name of that famous village in Anglesey:

Llanfairpwllgwyngyllgogerychwyrndrobwllllantysiliogogogoch.

This translates as *Saint Mary's church in the hollow of the white hazel near the rapid whirlpool and the church of Saint Tysilio of the red cave*. The village achieved fame through the length of its name, which was the sole purpose of the publicist who composed it. He was the owner of a local hostelry and wanted to drum up custom. That was in 1869. Saying the name aloud is a tongue-twister, best not attempted. Locals talk of Llanfairpwll and have done with it. The publicity stunt is still working, though. Two hundred thousand visitors a year come to the village to see the place name displayed at the railway station. Last month we passed close by and missed visiting the station near Britannia Bridge to see the 58-letter place name for ourselves. However long we spend in Wales there will always be more to see and learn. The secret is to be content with what we do manage.

Blaenau Ffestiniog
Steep, quarried hills dominate the village of Blaenau Ffestiniog.

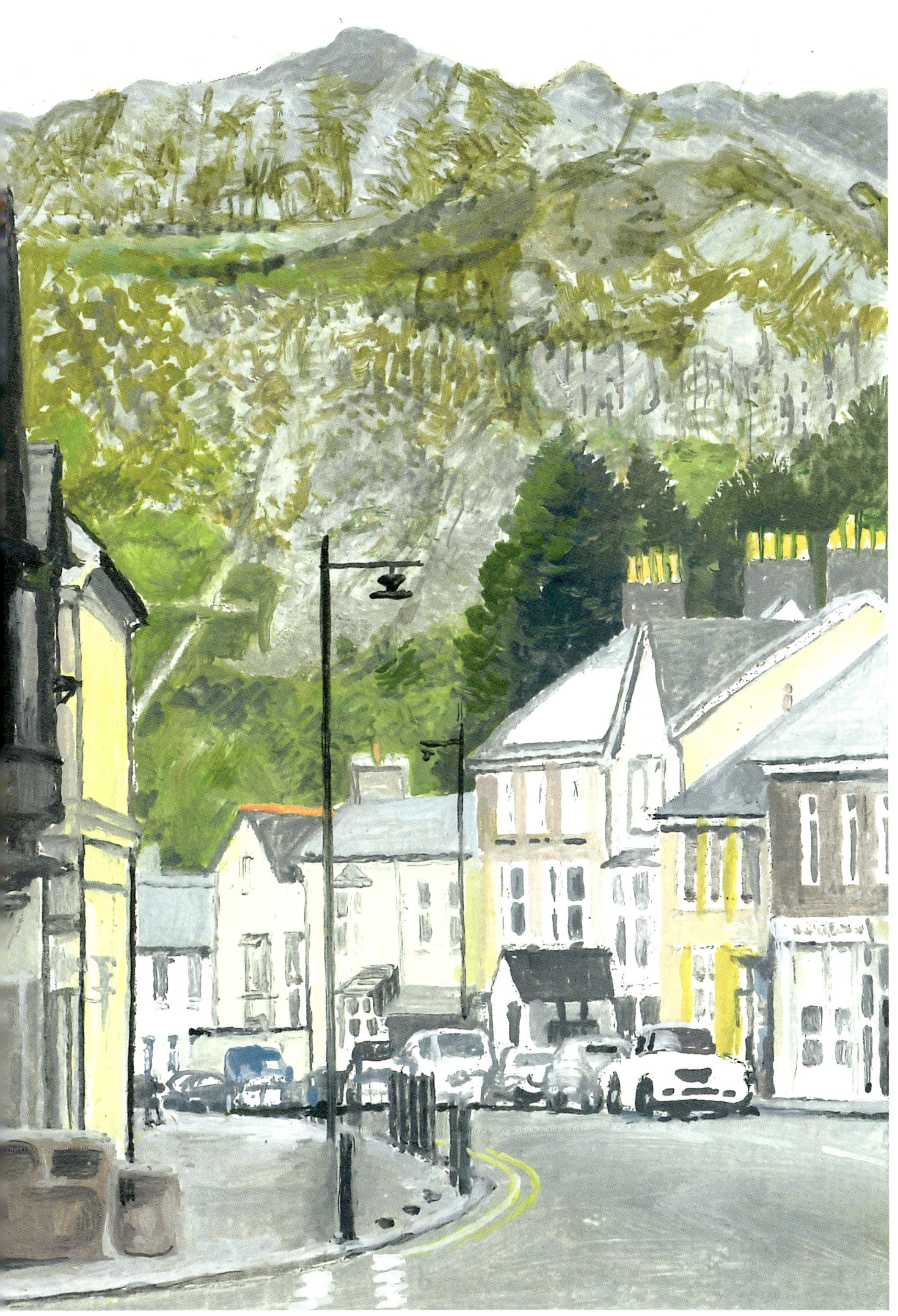

Slate mine trucks

Trucks used to carry loads of packed slate on rails around the processing yards.

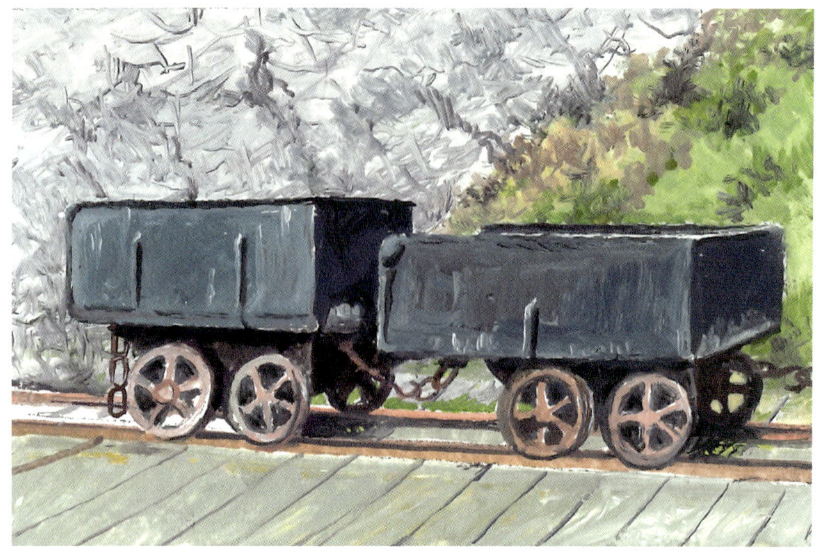

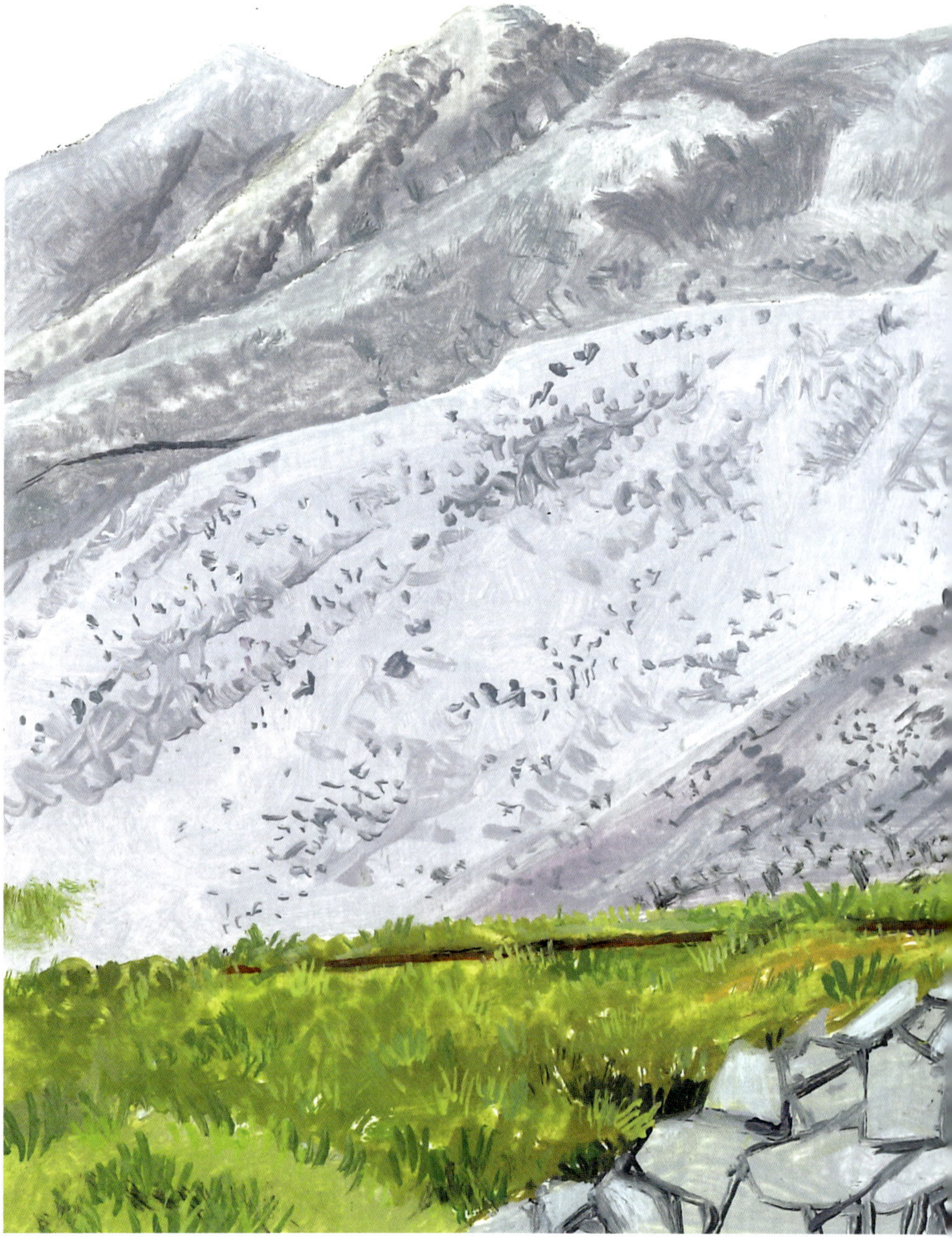

Slate tips

Any quarrying or mining operation leaves great heaps of waste on the surrounding countryside: the price of industrial gain.

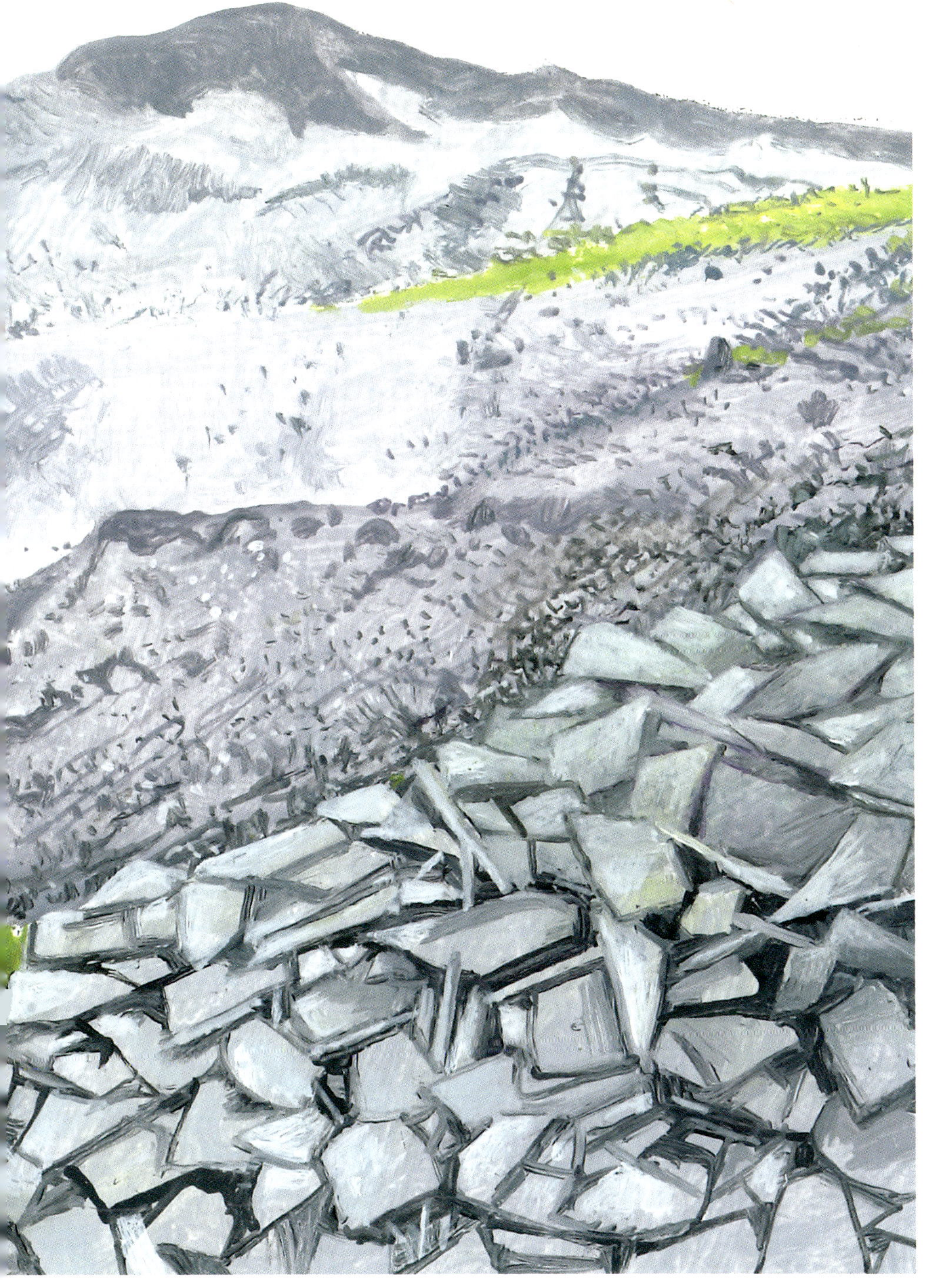

Llangollen

A visit to Llangollen reminds us of the vital importance of water. Not only is water necessary to keep us alive, it can also be harnessed as a source of power and a means of transport. Llangollen is a place that demonstrates this reality. The 'gollen' of the town's name derives from the name of a monk called Collen who came here by coracle up the Dee, the river which runs through the centre of today's town. The Ellesmere Canal passes close by. Eleven miles of the canal have been classified as a World Heritage site. Thomas Telford designed a weir, known as the Horseshoe Falls, to marshal water into the canal from the river. He also designed the aqueduct which takes the canal over the steep river valley. When we first visited Llangollen some years ago, we stayed at the Chain Bridge hotel which is built on a narrow strip of land between the river and the canal. Revisiting this year, we watched people stepping gingerly into the modern version of coracles: canoes. In the canal basin at the nearby village of Trevor, we watched people boarding barges for trips down the canal. One of the barges is run by a charity which helps disabled people enjoy a trip. It has special arrangements for people in wheelchairs. Generally, we are kinder today to people with disabilities than we were in the past. Travelling by barge is slow and soothing and there's time to appreciate the scenery, unlike being in a bouncing coracle.

Coracle, canoe, barge, river, canal, aqueduct and mill (there's a 600 year old corn mill opposite the railway station) – mental and actual images make Llangollen a picture book example of the power of water.

Horseshoe reservoir, Llangollen

Designed by Thomas Telford, the weir known as Horseshoe Falls was constructed in 1806 to supply water to the Shropshire Union Canal Local mills suffered as less water flowed in the River Dee. The resentment felt as the result of a loss caused by another's gain is summed up in the famous song, The Miller of Dee. "I care for nobody, no, not I, if nobody cares for me."

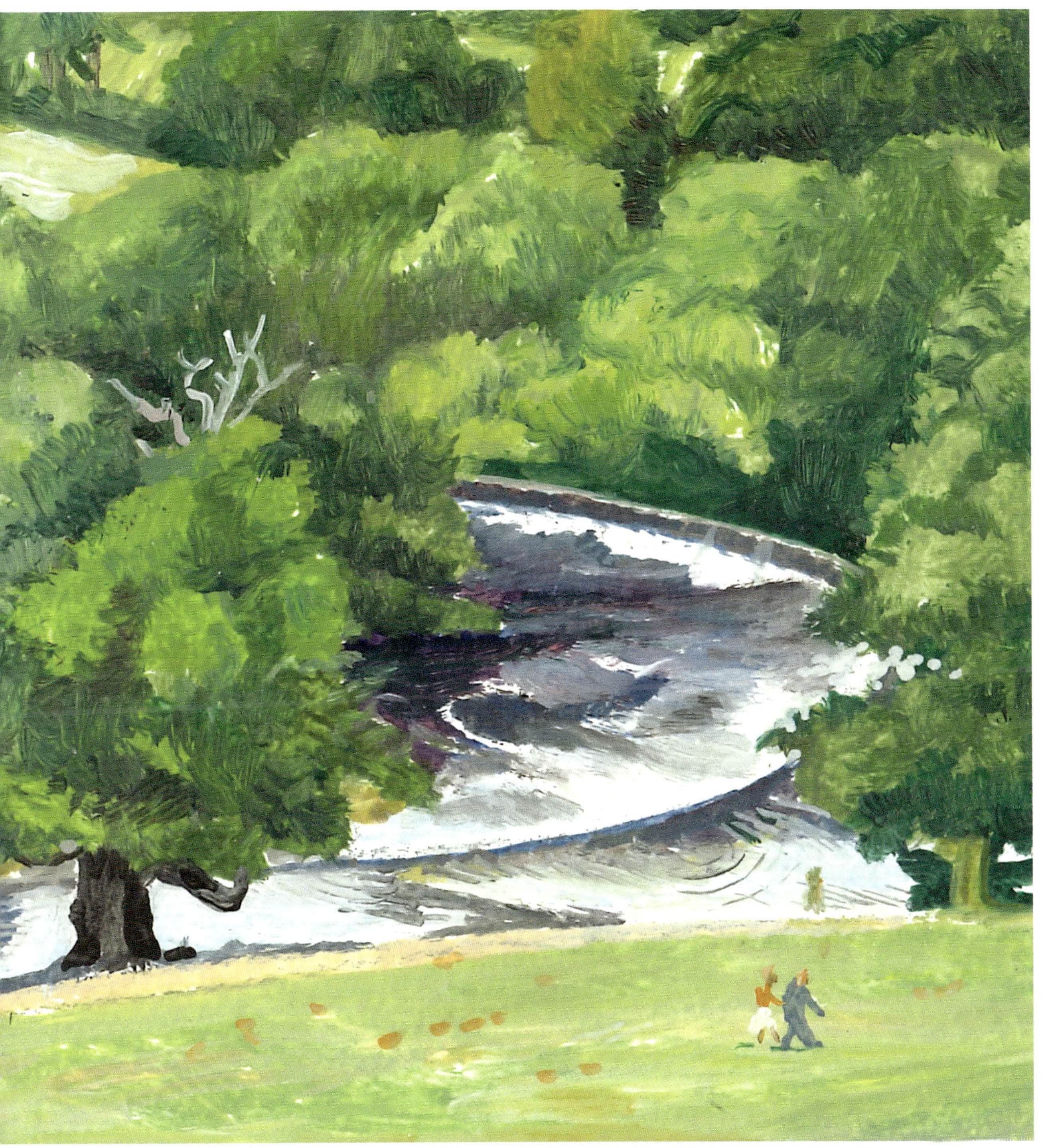

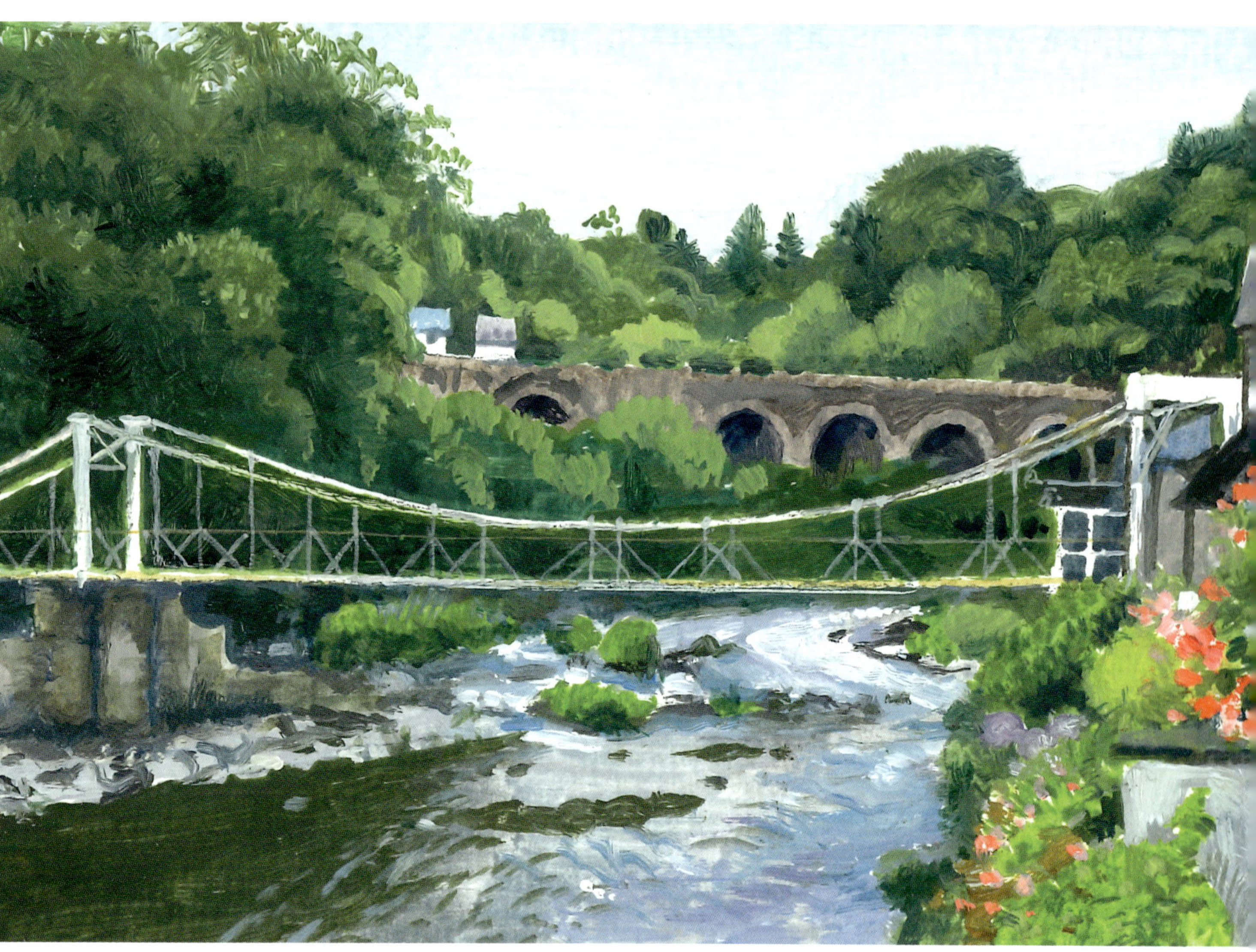

Chainbridge, Llangollen

Llangollen is a town of water and bridges in various forms.

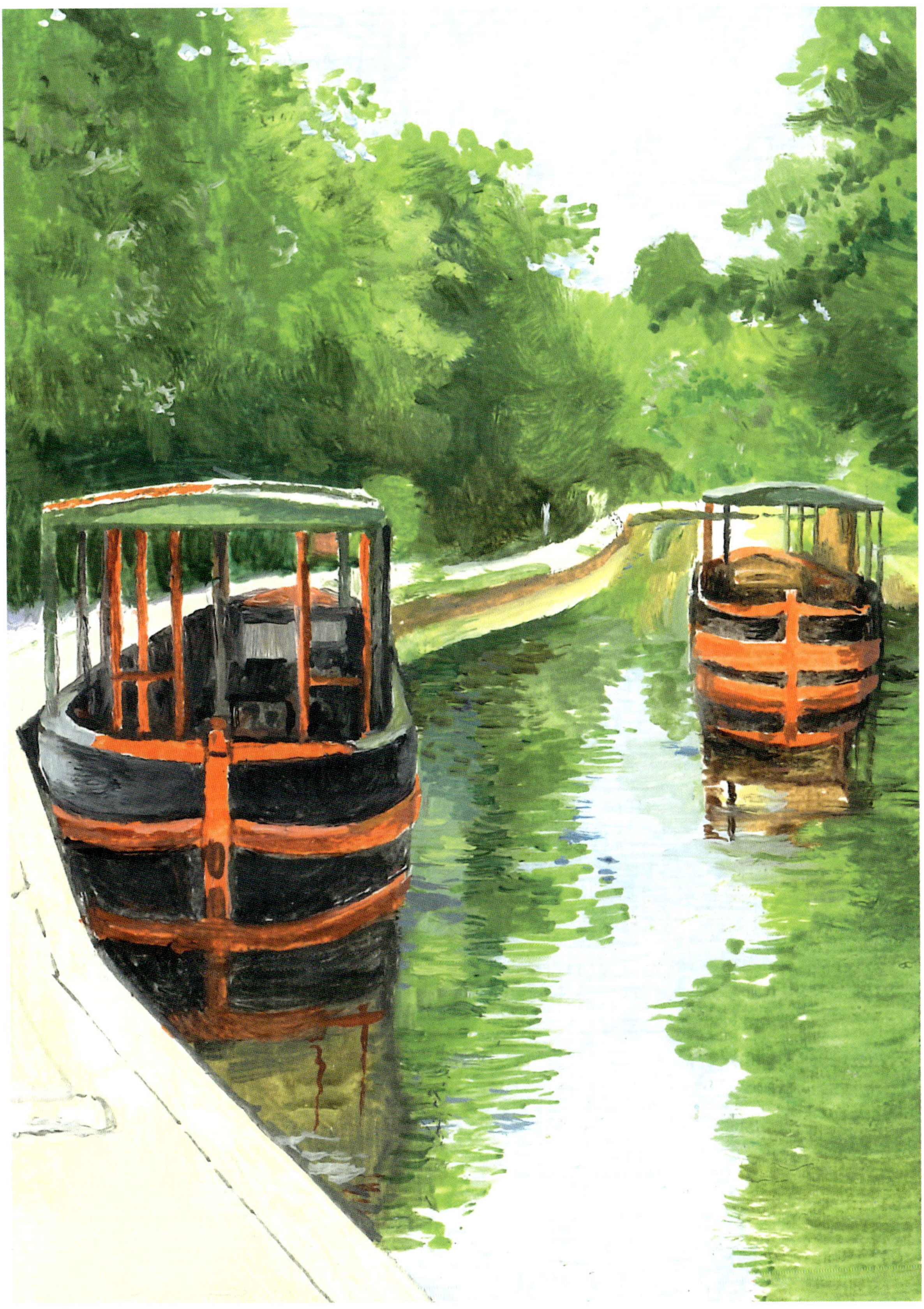

Llangollen barges

Colourful barges wait for passengers on the still waters of the Llangollen Canal. Mesmerised by the tranquillity of the scene, I recall lines from Leisure *by the Welsh poet W.H. Davies:*

"What is this life if full of care

We have no time to stand and stare."

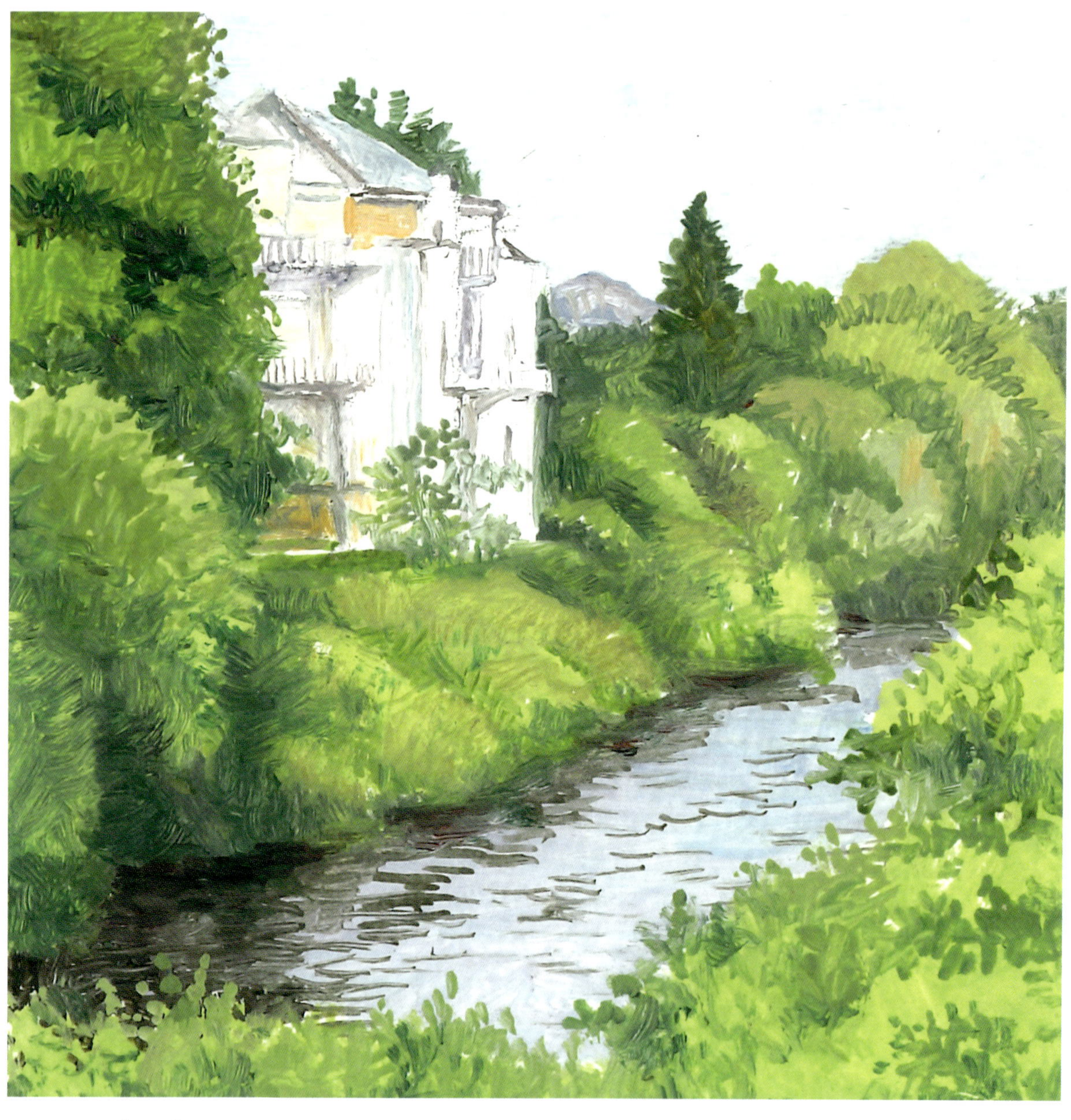

River Dee, Llangollen
View downstream of the Dee as it flows through Llangollen.

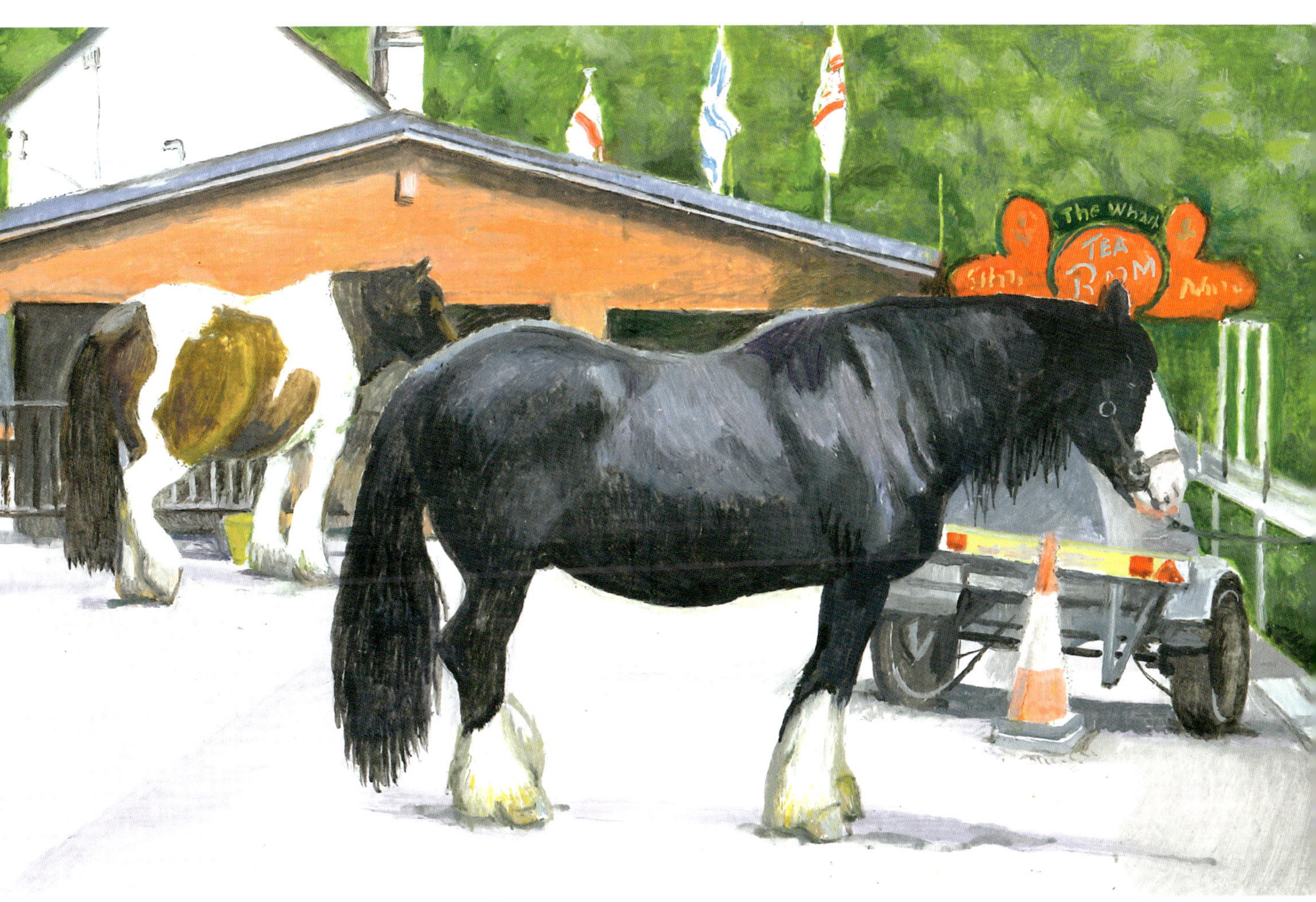

Shire horses, Llangollen Canal
What could be more unhurried than a horse-drawn barge trip.

On the way home

We took a detour from the main road and found Erwood Station Café and Craft Centre, a private enterprise set up in the 1960s after Doctor Beeching axed the line between Brecon and Llanidloes. The word "axed" sums up the anger felt by many rural communities by the government's line closures. The station dates from the early nineteenth century, when transport links were developing apace. The Mid-Wales Railway was established as a consequence of plans to connect London with Ireland, via a ferry port on the Lleyn Peninsula, Porthdinllaen, a place we'd just visited. Discussions about the port's location lasted in Parliament from 1806 until 1810 when Holyhead in Anglesey was chosen instead, thanks to Thomas Telford's influence and engineering experience.

We ate our picnic lunch at a table in the shade of trees beyond the car park and on the banks of the River Wye. The car park was beginning to fill and a couple lingered to chat. Ron and Edna were keen to tell us about a cannon still to be seen on a nearby hill. It was given to the community after the end of the First World War. Which community in which county, Brecon or Radnorshire, was the focus of a long-running dispute, with the cannon being taken from one hill to another in the immediate area of the river, a natural boundary between the two. Eventually the cannon came to rest on Garth Hill, close to Erwood Station. Edna's father had been brought up on a farm in the hills behind Erwood. He'd walked to the station to catch the train to school. Ron and Edna had met at school, but they'd spent many years in Malaya and the East Indies before coming to rest near Erwood, like the cannon on Garth Hill.

Two motorcyclists also chatted in a friendly way. I said something about my father's BSA Bantam which I rode aged seventeen, skimming over Dartmoor, free as the wind. It was the time of the Suez crisis and its aftermath when driving tests were discontinued to conserve petrol supplies. To compensate for this, the government allowed learners to drive on their own without a licence. When I see a motorbike screaming around a corner on the outermost rim of its tyres, I remember the feeling of freedom. No holds barred! My new friend reminisced in turn. He'd been in the stores department of Oakwood colliery for a year before the mine closed. With his redundancy money of £12,000 he was able to buy his terraced house, now worth £145,000. He talked of the many Londoners who have bought up miners' cottages and commute daily from Blackwood. He worked locally for Panasonic and, later, at a firm with a row of initials I didn't quite catch. At Panasonic, he said, you do what you're told. At IRW you find your own way to carry out an order. I can see how biking in Wales appeals.

At home we were greeted by a riot of roses in full bloom. It's been, we're told, the hottest, driest June on record. Llangollen, send us some of your water! We need Telford to engineer a connecting canal.

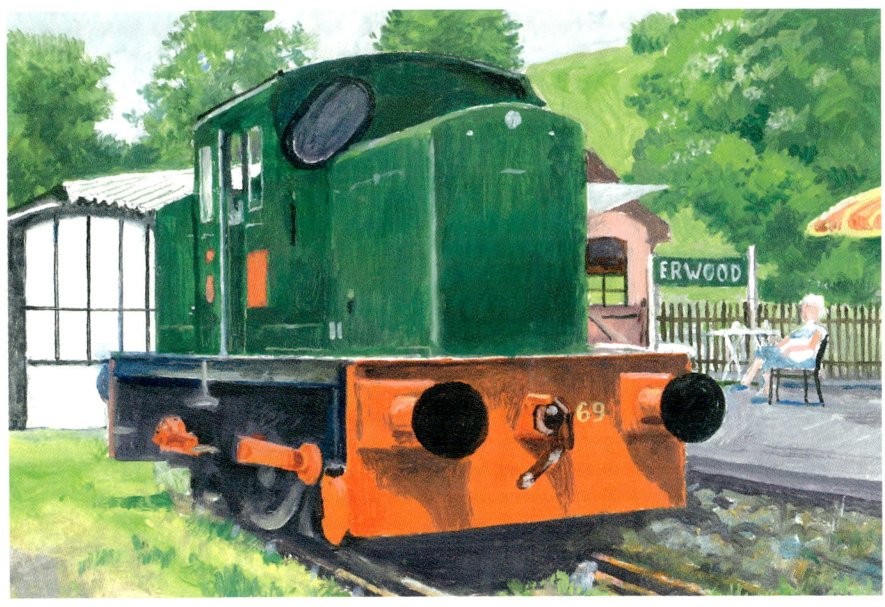

Erwood Café

Erwood Café and Craft Centre was once a station on the Mid Wales Railway between Brecon and Llanidloes. A restored industrial diesel engine, named Alan after the Craft Centre's founder, seems to be waiting while you eat a cream tea at a café table on the platform.

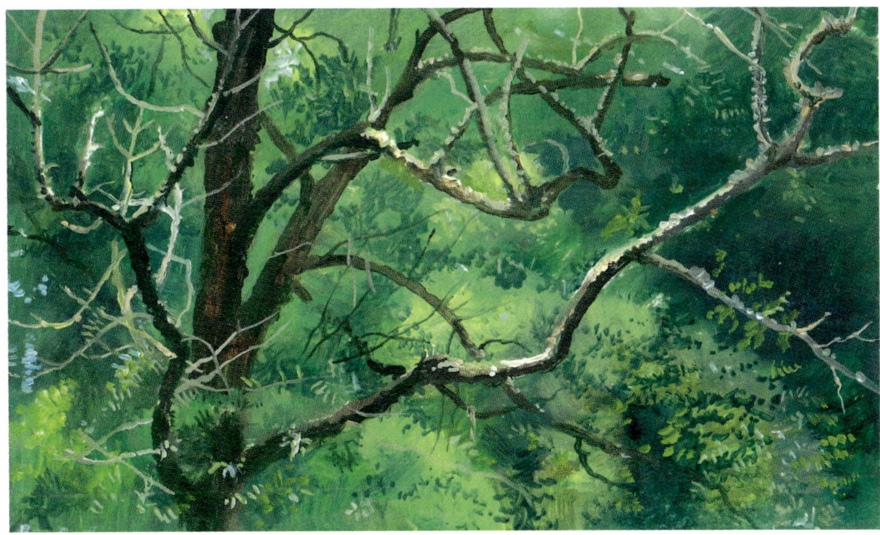

Ash tree dieback

A leafless ash tree in summer is a sad sight, increasingly prevalent due to a fungal disease that originated in Asia. The hope is that our native ash will slowly build up resistance to dieback.

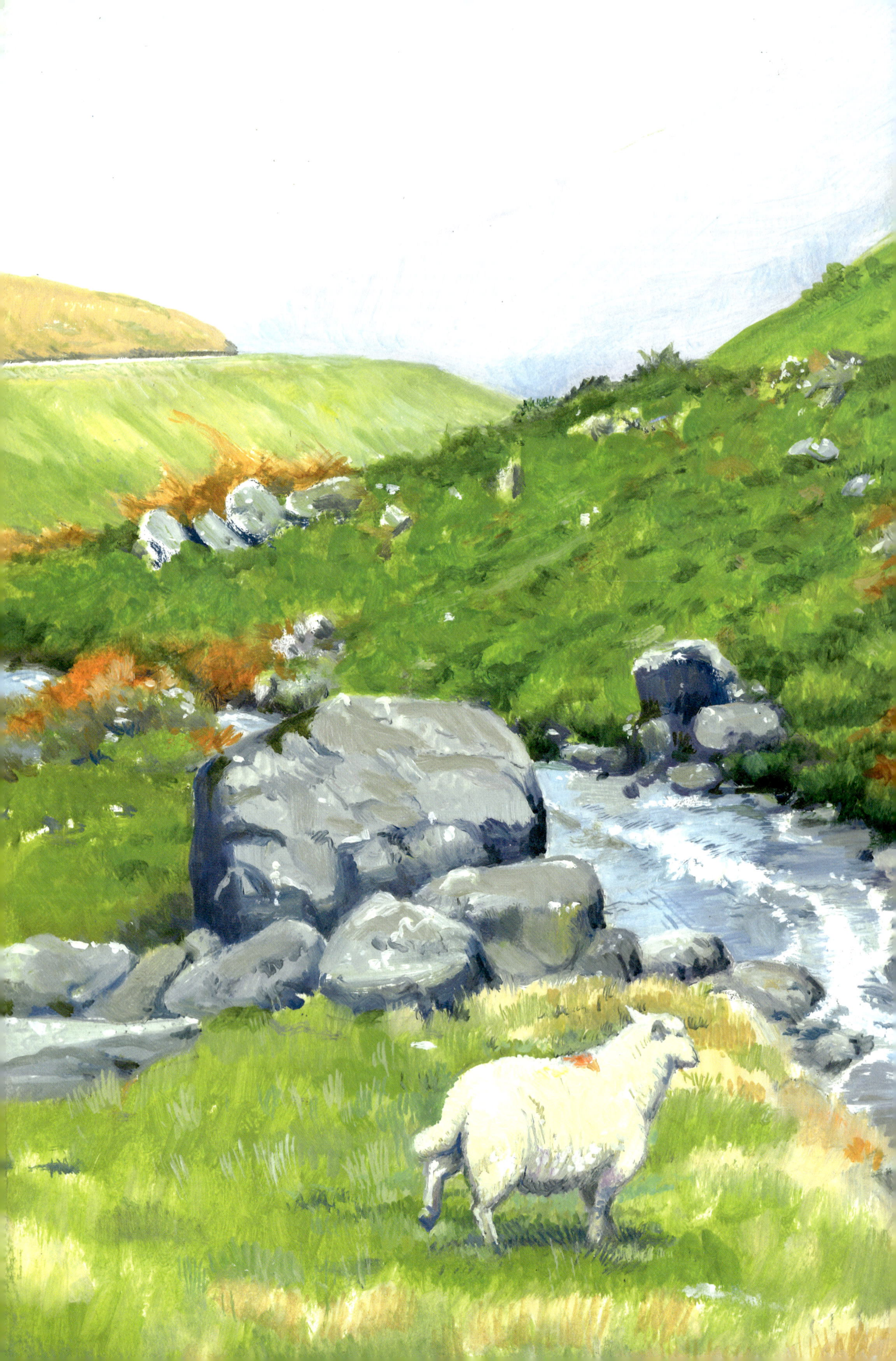

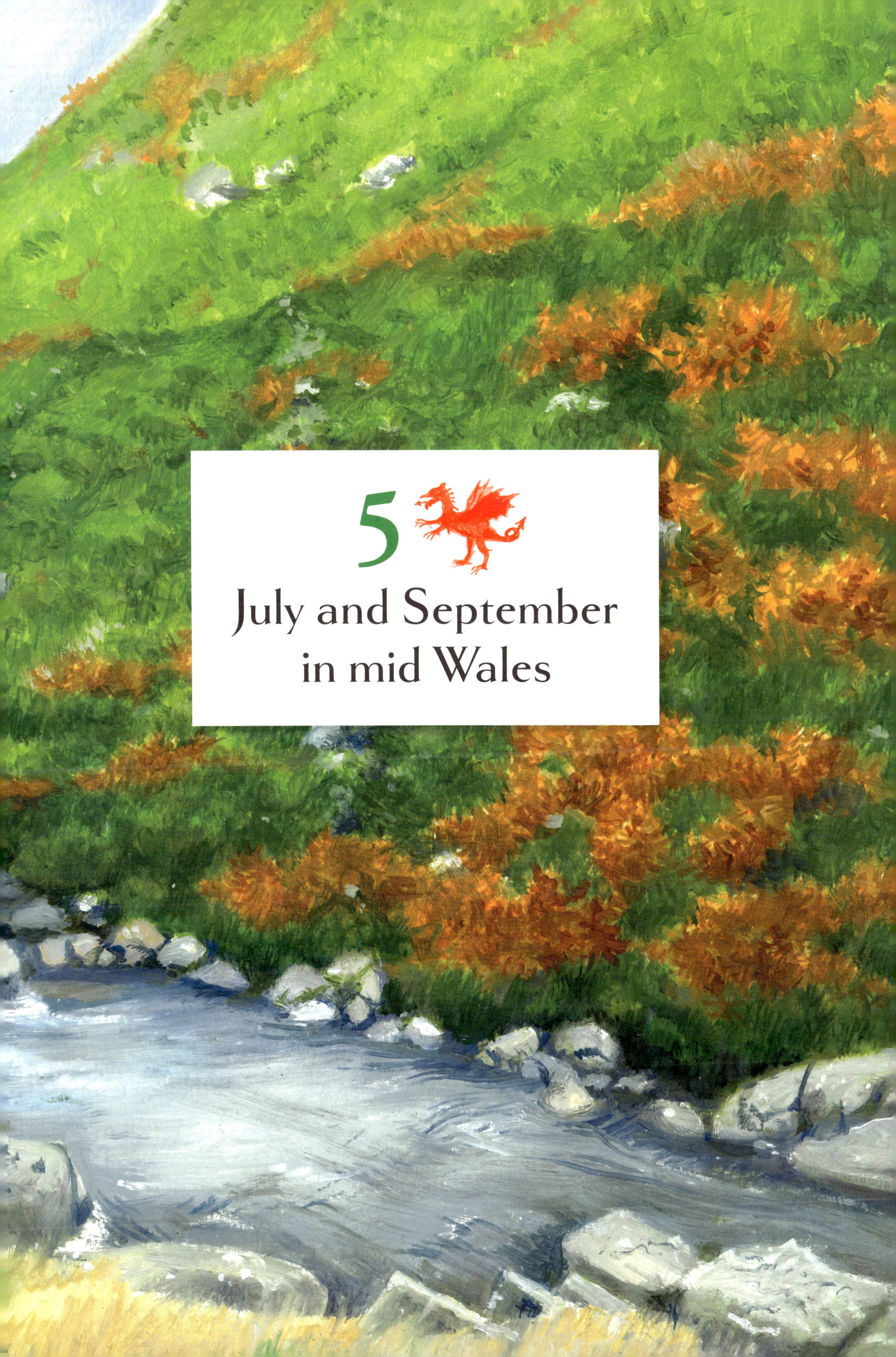

5 July and September in mid Wales

July and September in mid Wales

Llyn Clywedog

Going northwest from Llanidloes on the B4518, we caught sight of the sign to Bryntail lead mine. This pleased us. Brown tourist signs are not always spot-able in summer hedges. We were directed down a lane to a parking space at the edge of a wood. Unlike the generous parking space at the Blaenau Ffestiniog slate mine which could hold any number of coaches, the lead mine does not have room for more than four or five cars. On our arrival there was one other car.

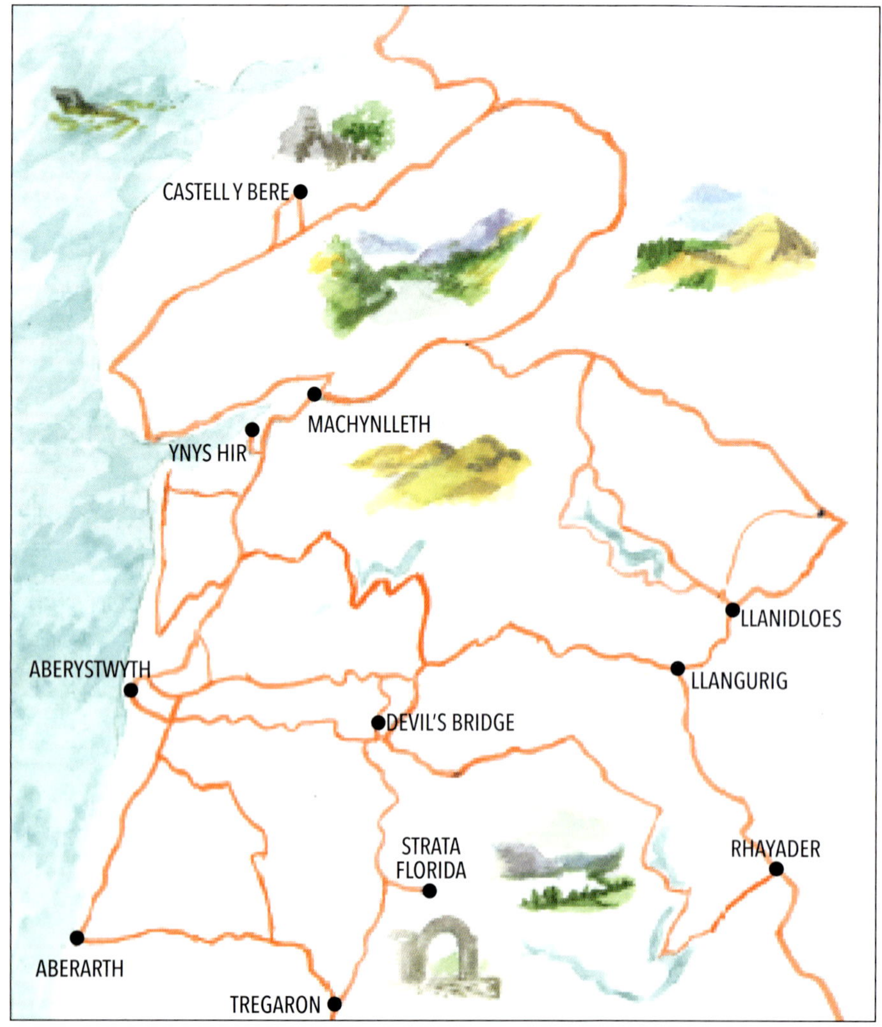

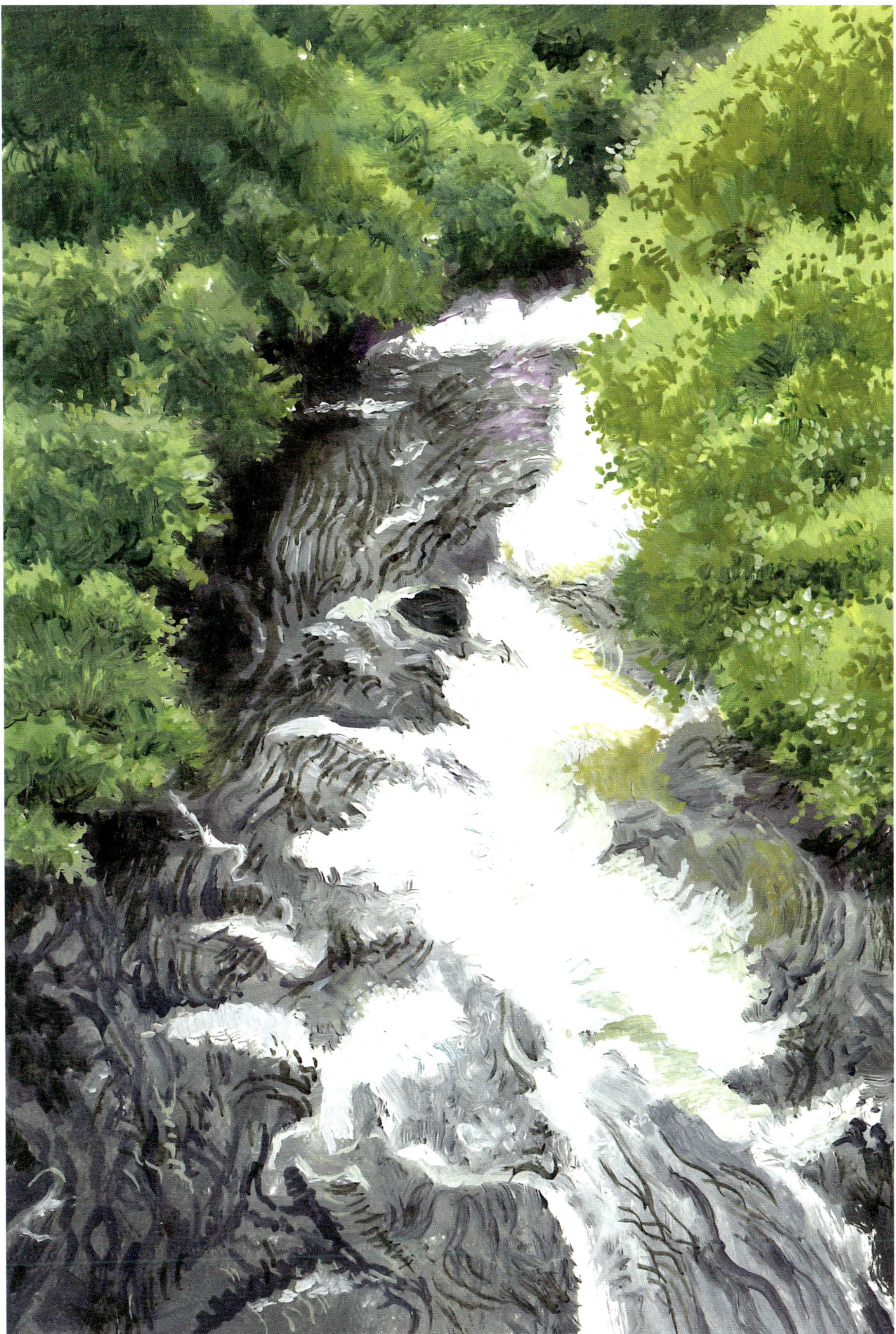

Torrent from Clywedog dam

The Clywedog Reservoir was created in 1967 to regulate the flow of the River Severn to prevent flooding downstream and ensure the supply of water to the West Midlands. It has the tallest concrete dam in Britain.

We could hear the thunder of water as we followed a path through the trees and down to a wooden bridge. The dark brown river below was hurling itself over boulders creating a churning mass of froth like the head on a glass of stout. The dam that causes its pent-up force was visible above and beyond the ruined stone buildings on the riverside meadow.

The dam was built in the mid-1960s to regulate the flow of the River Severn, which has its source in the nearby moorland of Pumlumon Fawr. The aim was to prevent winter flooding and summer shortages. It's a surprise to learn that the river whose estuary we cross to reach Wales starts its life so far away. In fact, the Severn, at 220 miles long is the longest river in Britain. The Wye, which rises in the same moorland and flows for 155 miles on its own route into the Severn estuary, is the fourth longest. The Wye and the Severn are like old friends from home, happened upon when travelling abroad.

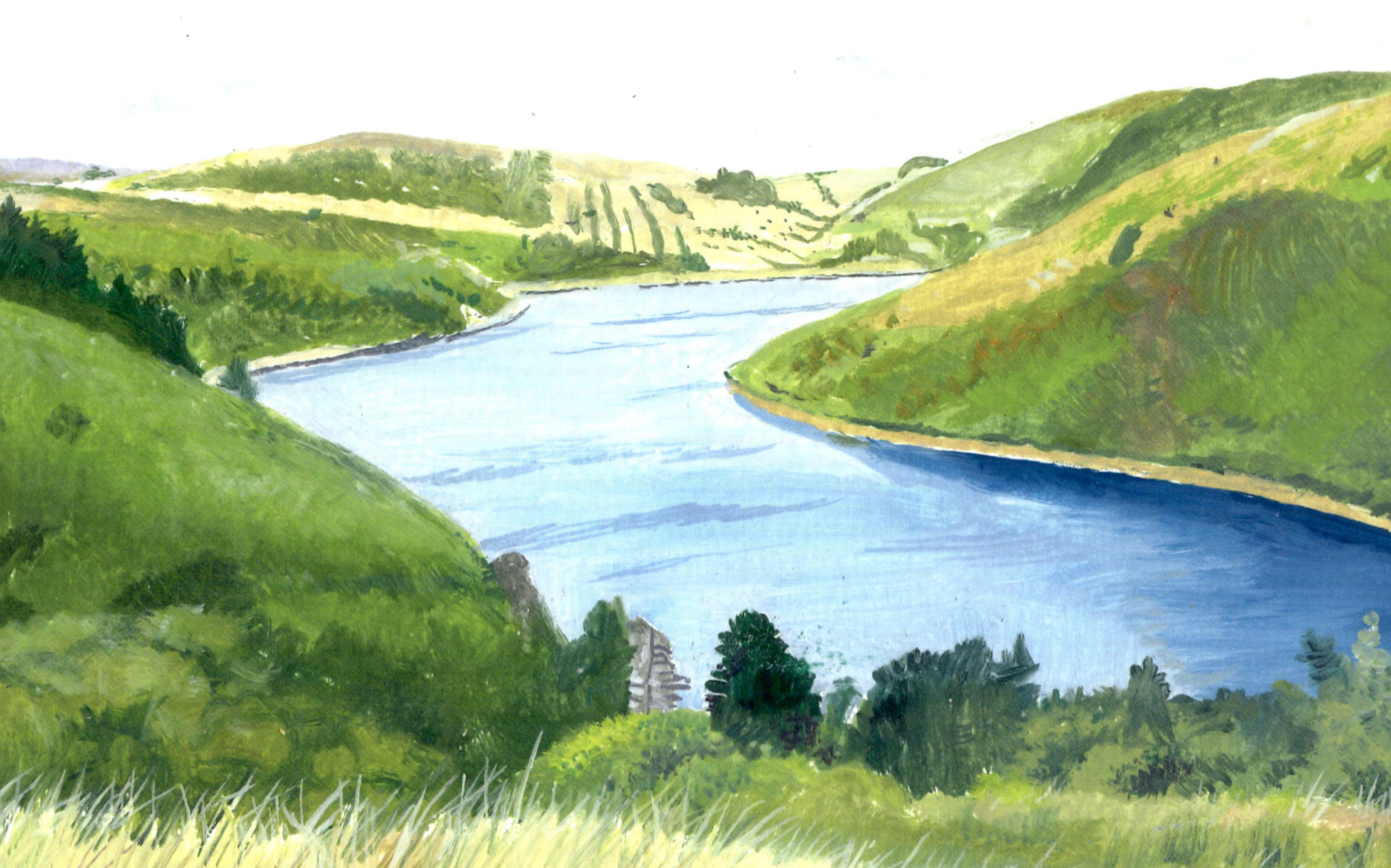

Lyn Clywedog
The lake above the dam.

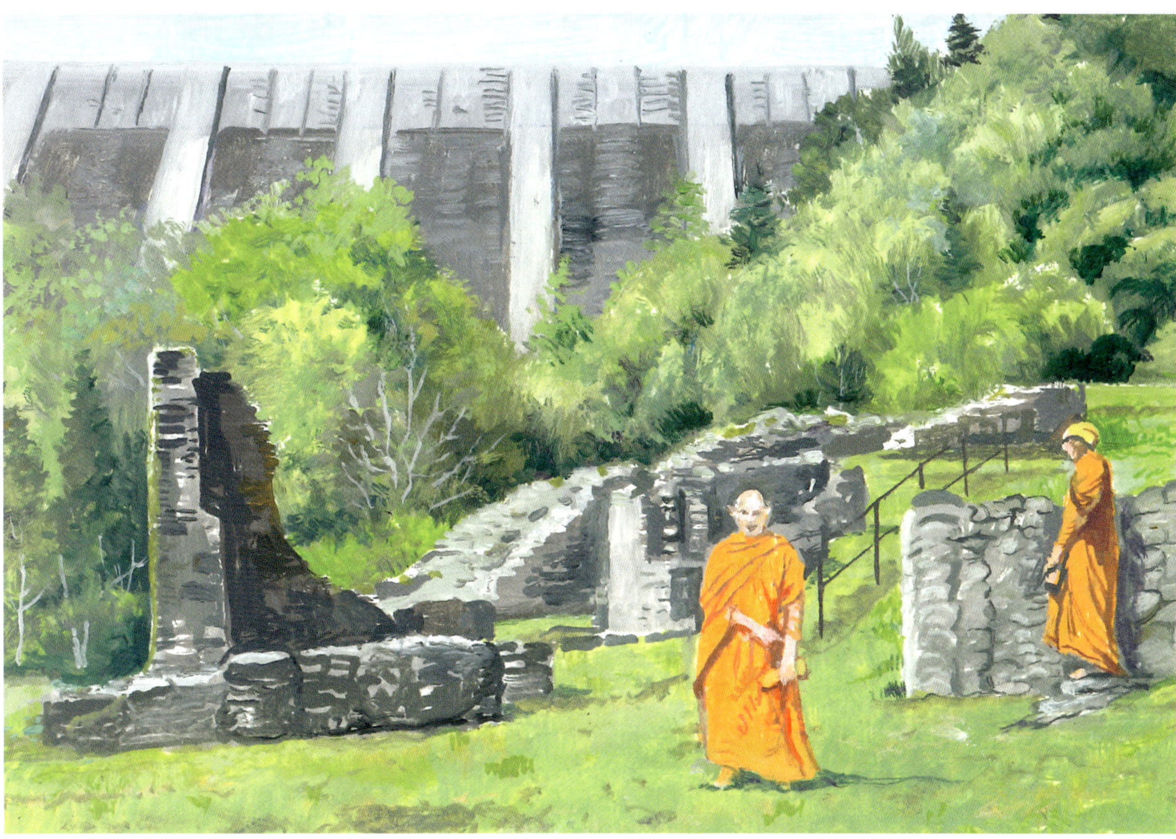

Buddhist monks

The flame-coloured robes of Buddhist monks stand out against the grey stone ruins of the Bryntail lead mine.

There was one other couple and a dog wandering around the ruined buildings. When they left, we were alone for a while with the river and birdsong for company before more visitors arrived. Two of the group of six men wore saffron-coloured robes. Here was another surprise: Buddhist monks in the ruins of a lead mine. As they moved slowly here and there among the grey stone walls, their robes shone out like candle flames. The guide for the group, an Englishman from London, told me they were here from a monastery near Gatwick, which they were visiting from Thailand. He would ask the monks to talk with me when they were on their way back to the car park. There was no hurry. I sat at a trestle table which had a plastic surface printed with a photographic montage of the faces of miners and their wives, and a short text about their lives. Some who worked in the mine were as young as nine or ten.

When eventually the monks were ready to speak with us, I learnt that one of them was fourteen when he joined the monastery. What does a Buddhist monk who has spent the majority of his life in a Thai monastery make of a Welsh lead mine? I guessed, having watched them pace up and down within one of the ruins, they were comparing the miners' quarters with their own. But in fact, the ruins had once been crushing houses, ore bins, roasting ovens, a smithy and the mine manager's office. The miners had to find lodgings in nearby farms, walking a distance to and from work. None of them lived long. They suffered from lead poisoning. Their health was said to be 'not worth a snap of your fingers.' Rather be a Thai Buddhist monk at fourteen than a Welsh lead miner at ten.

Cader Idris

When our children were twelve and ten we were invited by my sister and her husband to join them camping in the foothills of Cader Idris. We remember it as our Wet Week in Wales. It can't have rained all the time, but it was a marked contrast to our life on a Greek island in the children's early years. They are now in the second half of their fifties. At the same moment in 2023 as we were wondering which Welsh field had been our camp site, our son was co-skippering a 55-foot yacht in the South Pacific and our daughter was on holiday in Corfu. The sun was shining on us all. Our visit to Cader Idris prompted us to remember that 1978 holiday. We remember one of my five nephews running down the field waving the envelope he'd picked up from the farmhouse containing his exam results. This was either the eldest of my sister's five sons with his A Level results or the second eldest with his O Level results. Today the youngest son tells

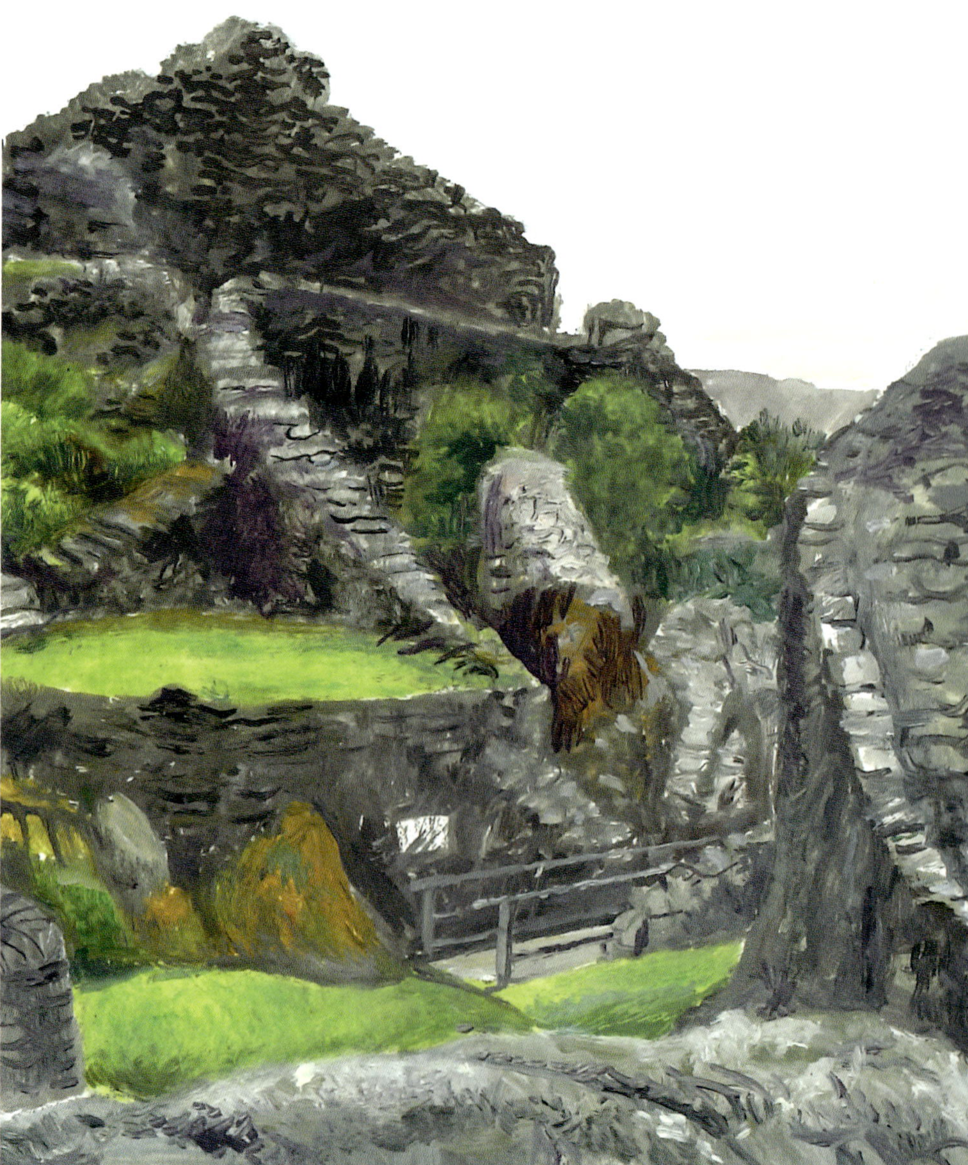

Castell y Bere

After their invasion of England in 1066 the Normans extended their power base westwards into Wales, establishing defensive strongholds is the borderlands Gradually stone castles replaced earth and timber fortifications. Castell y Bere is one of these, built by the Welsh leader known as Llywelyn the Great and used to defend against rivals as well as the Normans.

me he remembers his father towing us to a garage with the very thick rope we apparently carried in our boot for the purpose. We must have broken down a lot. Nowadays my nephews are taking it in turns to spend time at home, caring for their parents who are bedridden. The thought of my sister and her husband lying side by side in hospital-type beds and reclining chairs fills me with clammy horror. Jane's footsteps have always been planted firmly in front of me. I remind myself that I stopped following them when I was nineteen but I fear I could still follow Jane's fate today. Walking and seeing I'm finding increasingly problematic.

In July we identified the farmhouse and maybe the field but our prime target that day was Castell y Bere further up the narrow valley. I stayed in the car while Peter walked the reportedly ten minutes to the ruined castle. Meanwhile, I watched someone on a quad bike rounding up sheep on the far hillside. He sped up and down through openings in the hedges until he had the flock gathered where he wanted them. He then drove them along the valley to the farm. The

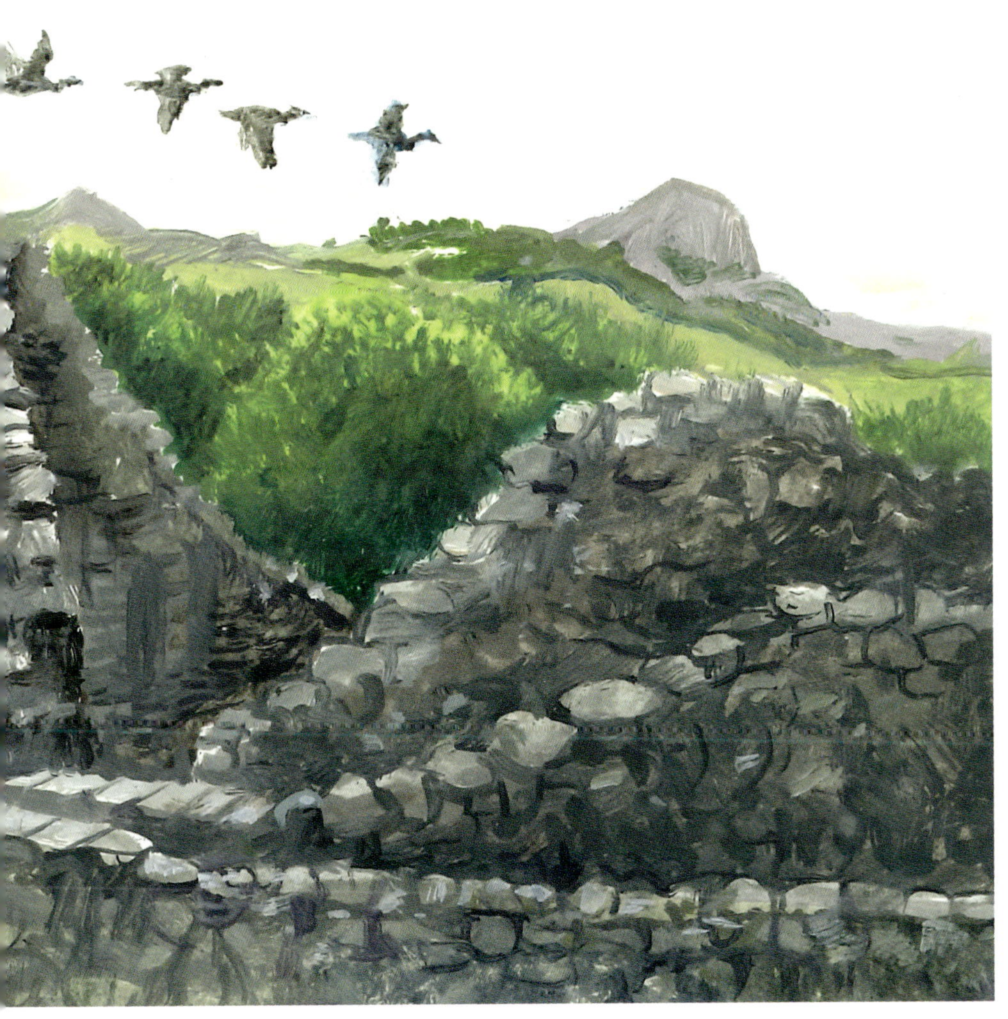

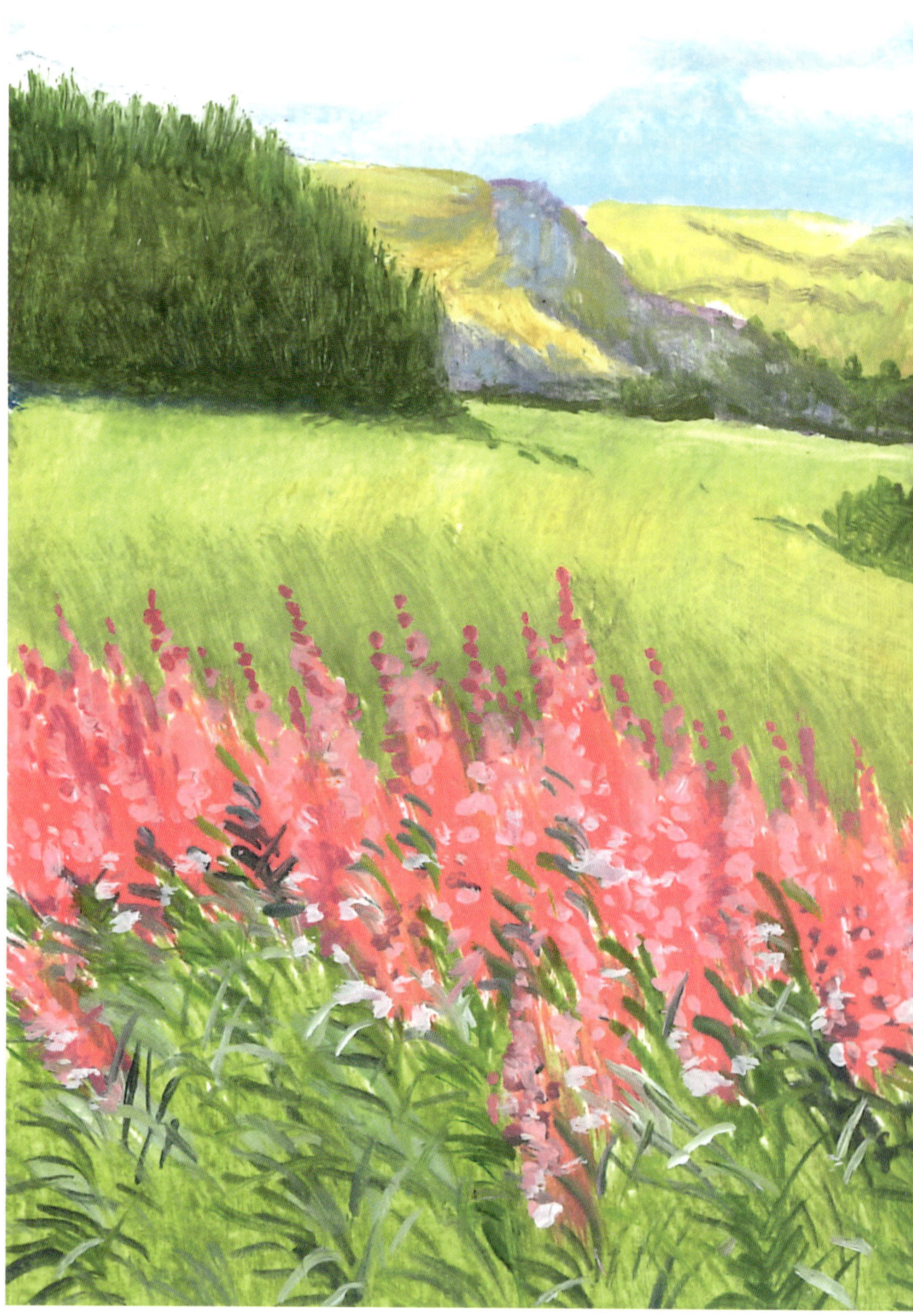

cacophony of bleats, throaty and shrill in various registers, slowly faded into the distance but there were still a few sheep left in hollows, complaining bitterly. Like me, I have to say. I'd begun fretting at what was proving a long wait. I tried to stop watching an imaginary film of Peter lying senseless on a rocky path while I flapped my arms in an attempt to stop non-existent cars in the deserted lane.

The few remaining sheep returned to grazing and quiet filled the valley once again. My imagination was brought up short when the profound peace was broken by a low-flying jet, appearing out of nowhere and screaming down the valley, like a knife slicing through silk. The sky above Snowdonia is the training ground for pilots in preparation for what? Attack or defence? Where and why might conflict occur?

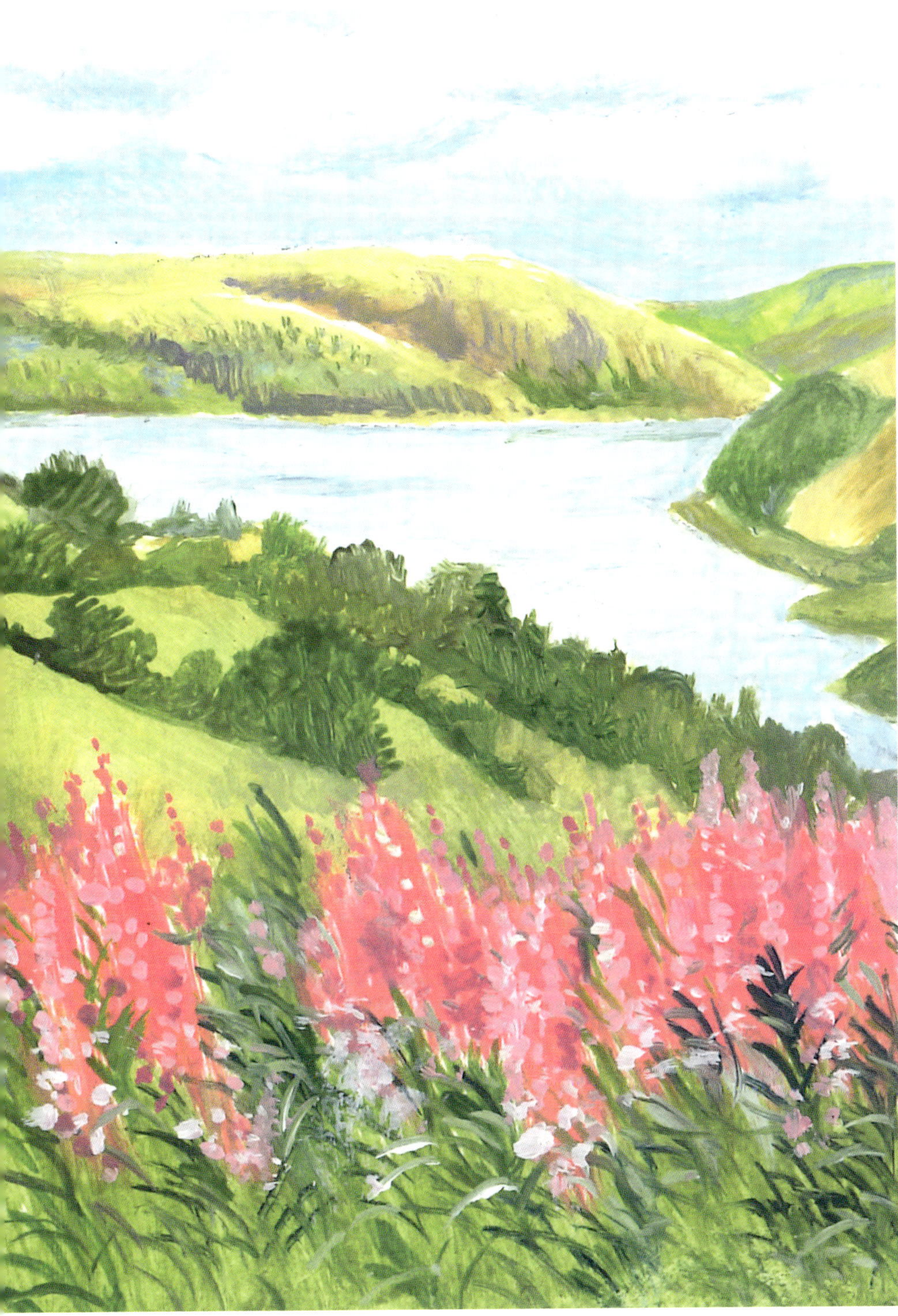

Rosebay willowherb
Known as fireweed in America, Rosebay willowherb springs up on cleared ground, particularly after forest fires. It was a familiar sight on London bomb sites in the post-war years.

Present dissolves into the past as the sound of the jet fades. Castell y Bere was built in stone in the 1220s by Llywelyn, later known as the Great. The castle's purpose was to defend against the Norman invaders on one side and, on the other, the local chieftains whose land he'd taken in battle. After his death in 1240, the Norman king of England, Henry III, regained much Welsh land but this, in turn, was taken back by the inheritors of Llywelyn the Great. Conflict continued, within the family and with the kings of England. When Llywelyn ap Gruffudd, the grandson of the Great, became Prince of Wales in 1255, he put his brother, Owain, in prison. He was a rival, not an ally. Thirty years later Llywelyn was still fighting the English. He died in battle against Edward I in

1282. The castle was finally re-taken by the Welsh in 1284. Remnants of the walls still stand, serving as backdrop to sheep and jets. A reader of Welsh history can get confused by the proliferation of similar names. The imprisoned Owain was not the grandson of the Great but the grandfather. Known as Owain the Great, he was the first to be given the title Prince of Wales. Eight hundred years later, the title is still given to the king's eldest son.

At the southern end of the valley stands Craig yr Aderyn, a high, rocky hill which bears the traces of an Iron Age fort built in two stages with an upper stockade and a lower one. The sea used to lap at its foot and cormorants nested here. They still do so, even though the sea has retreated and today the hill lies several miles inland. Besides cormorants, the promontory is a haven for choughs, owls, redstarts, wheatears, and linnets. It's known in English as Bird Rock.

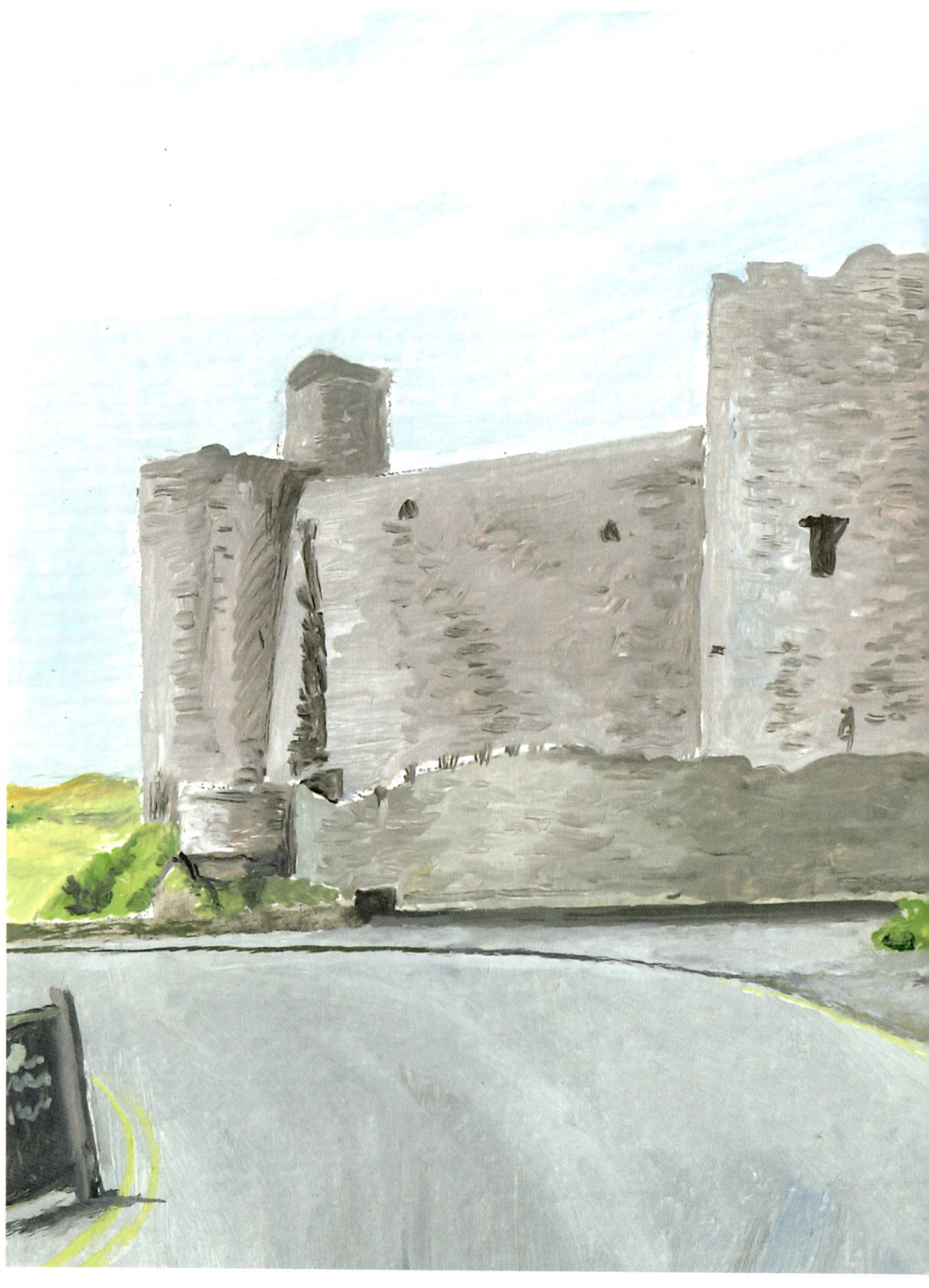

Harlech

The town of Harlech, with its castle made famous by its rousing battle song, *Men of Harlech,* stands on the slopes of a hill above what was once the seashore. It has two approach roads, one from the north and one from the south, making it the apex of a triangle. We drove up to the town from the south, then through the town looking for somewhere to park and found ourselves leaving the town before we could stop. It was tempting to accept defeat and drive on. Towns, however attractive, are not our overriding interest. However, we don't give up easily. I, as driver at the time, took a sudden decision on seeing a lay-by and dived in with the idea of turning around and going back to the town. We were in a kind of bosky dell, with a metal field gate on the far side. By the entrance

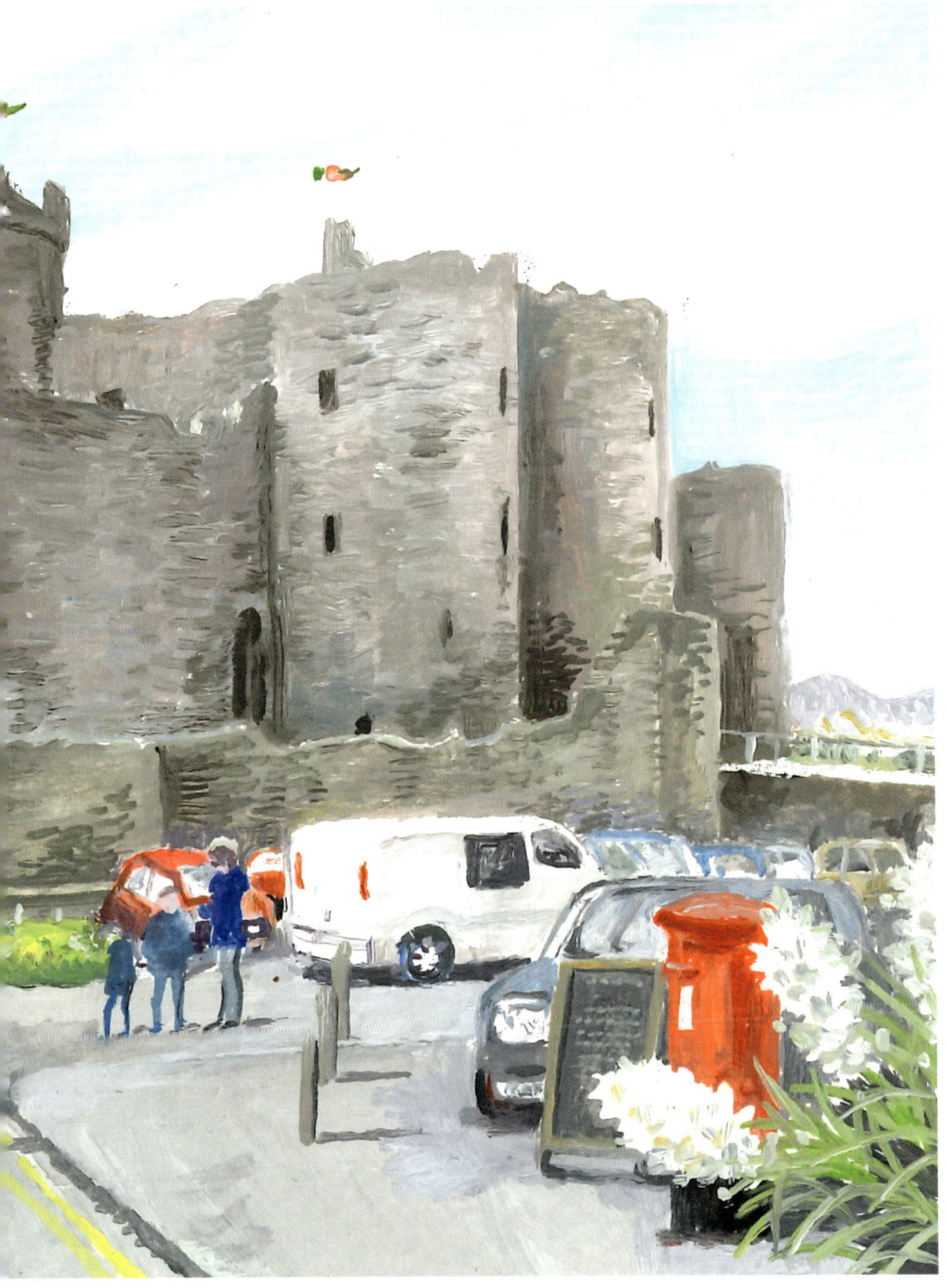

Harlech Castle

Built on a rocky knoll overlooking the Irish Sea, Harlech Castle was the scene of a number of sieges. In the fifteenth century civil wars, the Lancastrians held out against the Yorkists for seven years, the subject of the famous song "Men of Harlech." In the Civil War two hundred years later, the castle was held by Royalists against besieging Parliamentarians before succumbing to their armies in 1647.

was a sign that looked informative. A historical residence lay beyond the metal gate, open on Thursdays and Fridays. It was Thursday. We drove in.

A stoney track led across a marsh and then stopped at the entrance to a field. On the far side, where the ground rose to the brow of a hill, stood a tall, square, grey stone house. A couple of cars were parked by the field entrance, and we slotted in beside them as a woman approached from the direction of the house. "Yes, do go on up," she said. Her colleague was in attendance. When we were still only half-way across the field, her colleague, dressed in red, began waving at us. She greeted our eventual arrival with enthusiasm and immediately launched into her role as guide with information about the place, its history and the Reverend Ellis Wynne who had lived here in the late seventeenth, early eighteenth century. Two hours later we came away with a University of Wales 1984 publication, a treatise on Ellis Wynne's *Visions of the Sleeping Bard* on which his reputation as a Welsh literary figure is based. Our guide was keen that we should understand how well Wynne had written, proved not just by his handwriting (very neat) but by his poetic and witty style. As far as I can make out from the booklet, his *Visions* were loosely based on translations of the work of a Spanish writer of the seventeenth century, known as Quevedo. Besides his adaptation of Quevedo's satiric poem, Ellis Wynne reconstructed the family home which had faced south. He doubled its size by building an extension and rearranging the rooms. The house now faces east across the flat land to the wooded hills of Harlech. The hillock on which it was built was virtually an island, as in Wynne's day the field we'd tramped across was flooded at high tide. Here, as at Bird Rock, the sea had retreated. It would have been a life of solitude had Ellis not had a family. His first wife died young leaving him with one child. He married again and had ten more children. A creative man. While Peter

Eighteenth-century house

The eighteenth century home of the Reverend Ellis Wynne near Harlech.

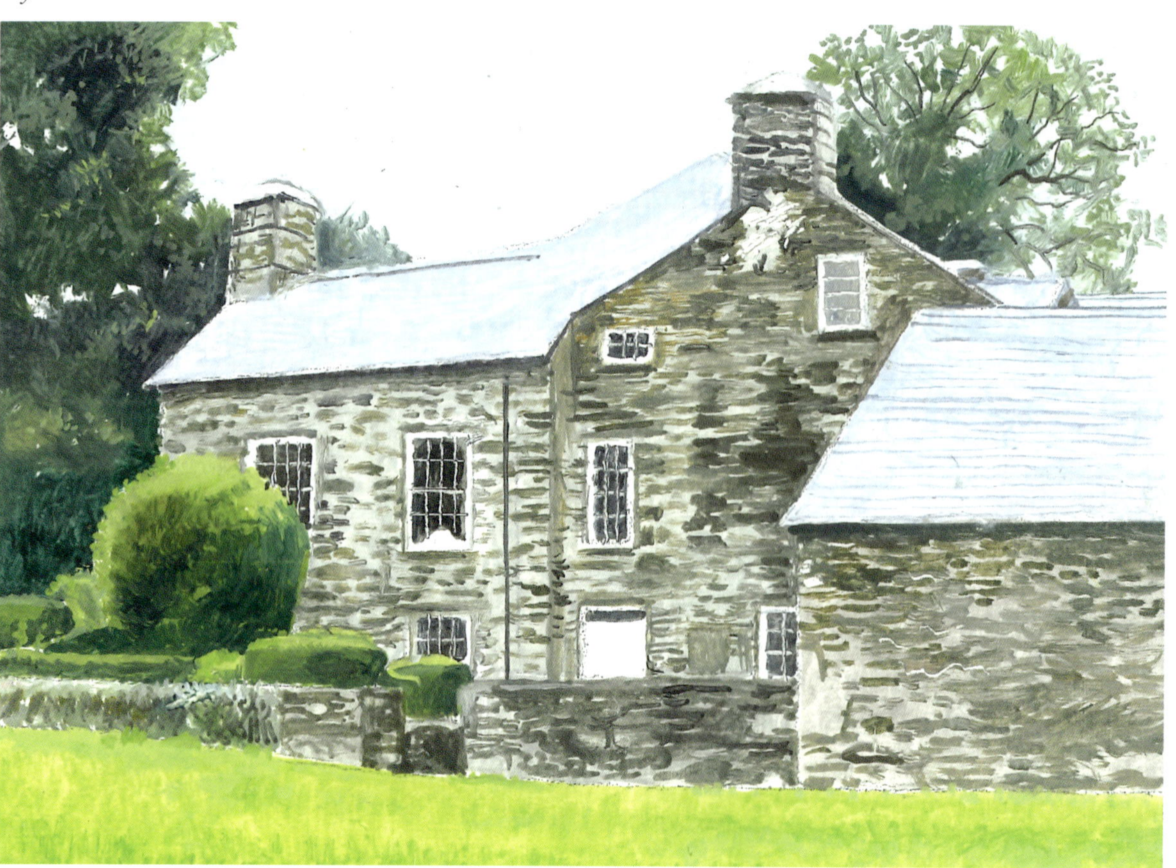

went with our guide to the top floor, I sat in the main, first floor room listening to its peaceful silence. I wondered if Ellis Wynne had sat in the same wooden armed chair by the fireplace, thinking up a verse for his sleeping bard while his eleven children ran around the rest of the house. Although there were eighteenth and nineteenth century tales of noisy visitations, I found the present-day atmosphere quietly benign.

I regret not learning the name of our excellent guide. She had been a primary school teacher and talked clearly and fluently with a pleasant Welsh lilt. But her days as guide may be numbered, even though she does it for love, not money. The house belongs to a preservation society with sharply decreasing funds. It costs a large sum per year to keep a damp house open. There aren't enough visitors We happened upon it by chance. To attract tourists, you need the kind of publicist who turned around the fortunes of that long-named town in Anglesey. Ellis Wynne, had he been alive today, might have come up with an equally creative plan.

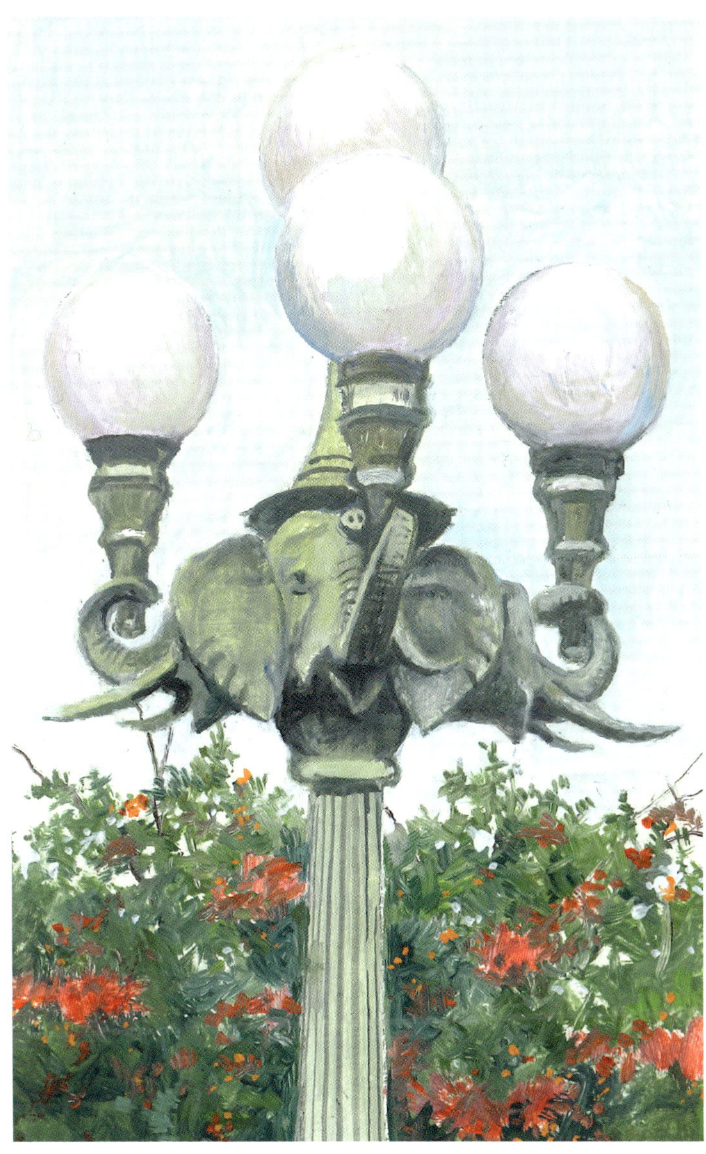

Elephant light

In the garden behind Y Talbot Hotel is the decorative lamp made to mark the burial mound of the circus elephant that died in the town of lead poisoning.

Not too little, not too much, but just right with Erasmus shaving soap. This advertising slogan, which engraved itself on my memory in childhood, could have been dreamt up to warn of the effects, not of shaving but of tourism. When we lived in a stone-built village in the Pindos mountains in Greece, we became involved in the local debate about the benefits and dangers of attracting visitors to its fragile environment. Unlike shaving soap, it's difficult to achieve just the right amount of tourism for the healthy life of an attractive place. We decided not to visit Wales in August, even though there are tracts of the country where you can avoid crowds, if that is your preference. We waited until September to return and complete our explorations for this last section of our book. I had originally booked a room in a hotel in Aberystwyth but thought better of it when I learnt about the steep staircases within the tall, colourful, lift-less, seafront hotels. Instead, we stayed at what turned out to be our favourite Welsh inn: Y Talbot in Tregaron. The evening meals are cooked by one of four chefs who all know what they are up to. The management and staff are relaxed and helpful in just the right way. Our room looked onto the hotel's garden where an elephant lies buried. The table mats in the dining room tell the story. A circus elephant died of lead poisoning in 1884 and the hotel's garden provided the space for burial. Lead poisoning? The story raises more questions than it answers. Could death have been caused by the elephant being fed hay from grass grown in the nearby central ore mining valley? We were to visit that later.

On the day of our arrival, we'd left home before ten and were passing Newport after an hour, nodding in recognition at landmarks and place names that have grown familiar. Caerleon has a particular significance as it was the first place we visited with this book in mind. We followed the M4 until we reached Junction 45 where we went north to Ystalyfera and from there we turned northwest to join the A4069 at Brynamman. Fairly soon we lost confidence in our surroundings. The map promised the Black Mountains ahead, yet the road was taking us in a wandering kind of way through an indeterminate landscape, neither entirely countryside nor habitation. We stopped by a post van. The postman – how pleasant they are as a species – reassured us. We had not missed a turning. We were exactly where we hoped to be. Soon we were up high in moorland and pulling into a lay-by where we ate our picnic alongside sheep cropping grass with keen concentration. A brisk wind chased fluffy white clouds across the blue sky. We breathed again after the morning's long drive.

The A4069 led us over the mountain to a point where the far side was revealed. A vast expanse of hedged fields interspersed with wooded valleys lay spread out before us. We stopped beside a cattle grid which marked the boundary between moorland and farmland. A large flock of sheep had been driven into a pen. They crowded to the fence on the road's grassy verge and regarded us with vague questioning in their sheep's eyes. Were they wondering

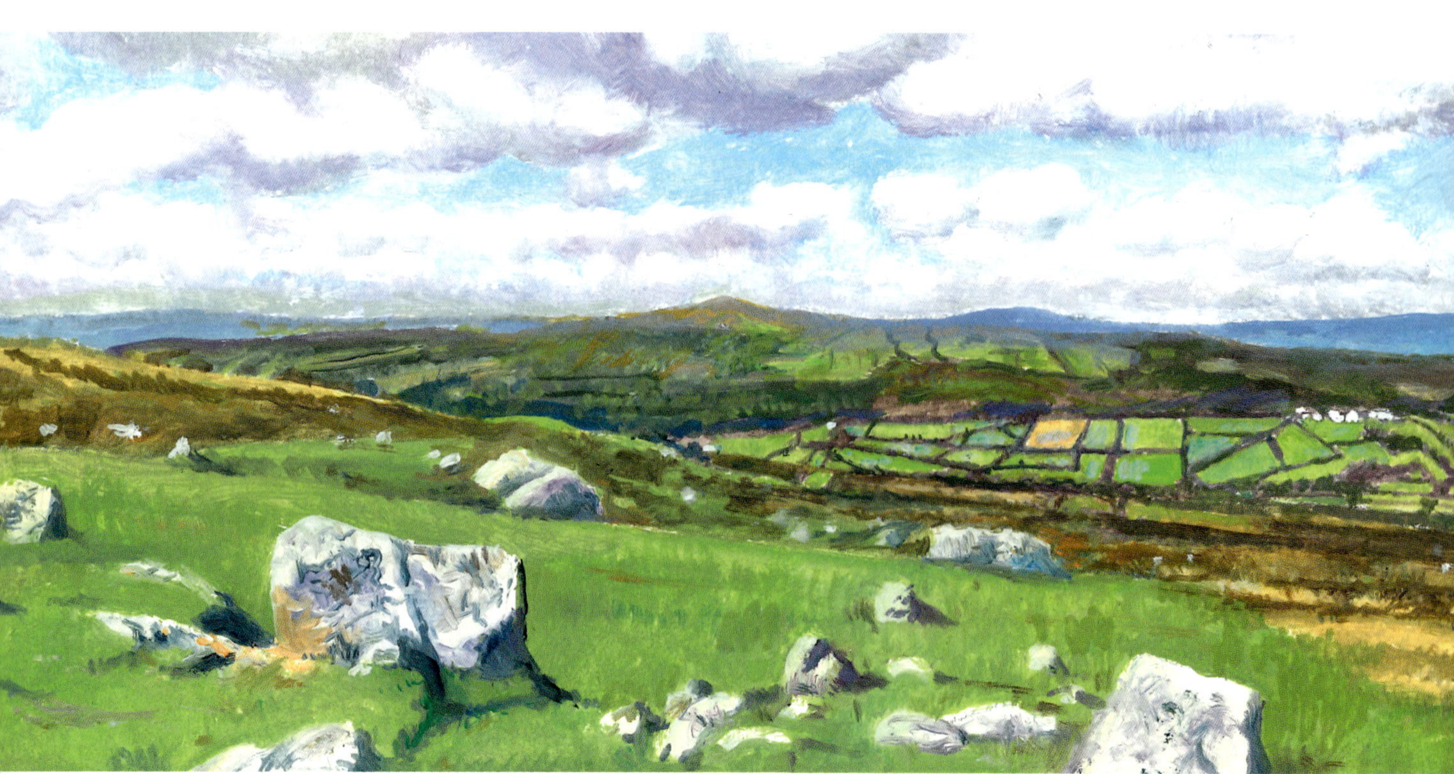

if we'd come to do the next thing that was expected of them? Who knows what goes on in a sheep's brain.

There's a wonderful café in Llandovery that we'd happened upon once in the past but had never managed to visit again, never passing at a suitable time for a stop. Again, it wasn't time for a break. We bypassed the town by continuing our line northwards on the A482 to Lampeter and then on the A485 to Tregaron.

Tregaron

We were immediately pleased with the Y Talbot hotel, its cooking, our room, the elephant story and the hotel's symbol – the head of a fox hound. A Talbot was a medieval fox hound. How and why the Talbot gained its name I haven't yet found out. But dogs and places are often linked. There's the Beddgelert hound and Swansea Jack, both famous for rescuing people from danger.

The next day was Peter's birthday and Jennie Tierney joined us in the evening to celebrate. Jennie lives in Talgarth when she's not in India. We met in 1971 when she helped us with the children on Amorgos, Greece, for a year. Now in 2023 we spent Peter's 88th birthday exploring Aberystwyth, the Devil's Bridge and the coast around Borth. For non-walkers the Woodland Tea Rooms at Devil's Bridge are a lifesaver. We didn't need to negotiate hundreds of slippery steps to appreciate the waterfall. Instead, we peered over a stone wall on the road bridge to the thundering water far, far below. Impressive enough.

View from Truman Point, looking north west.

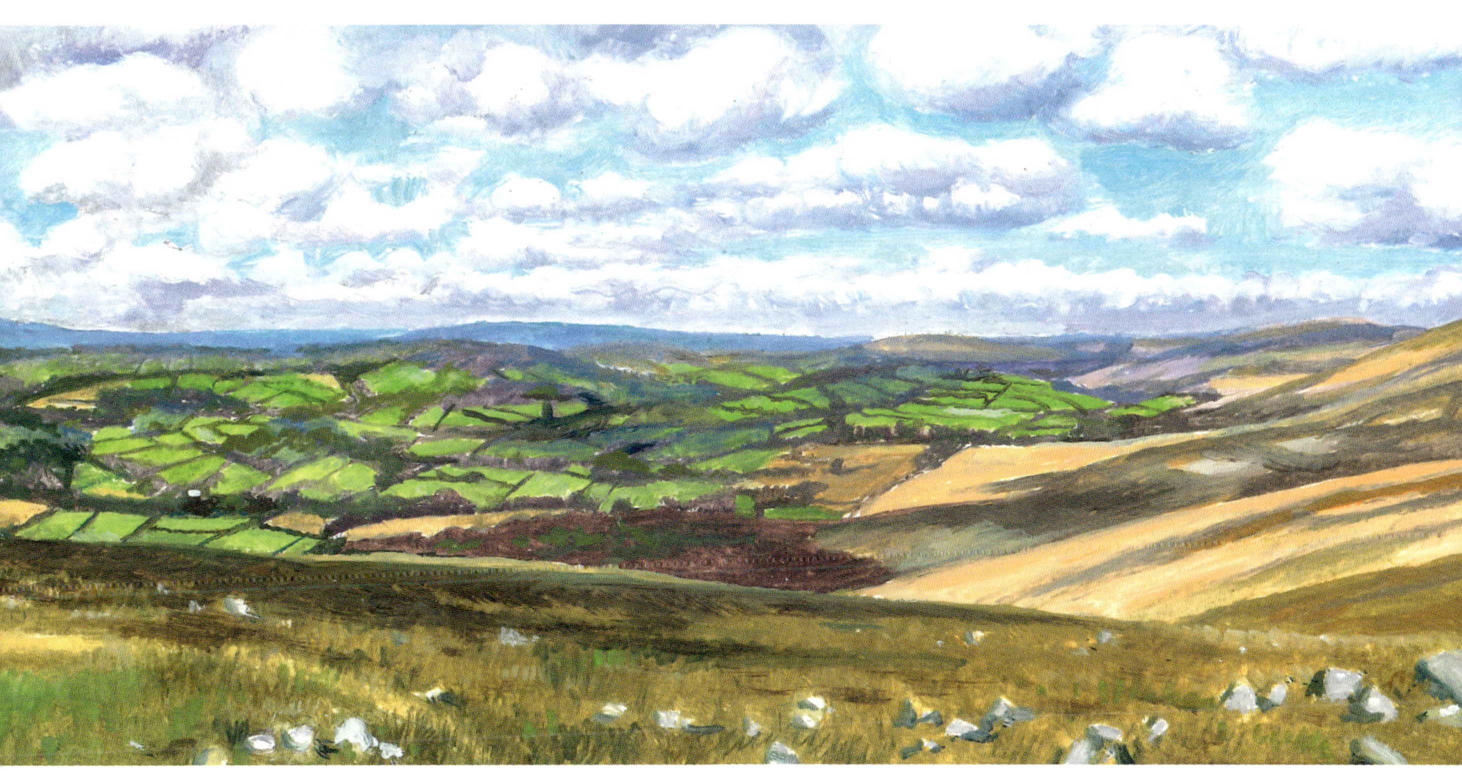

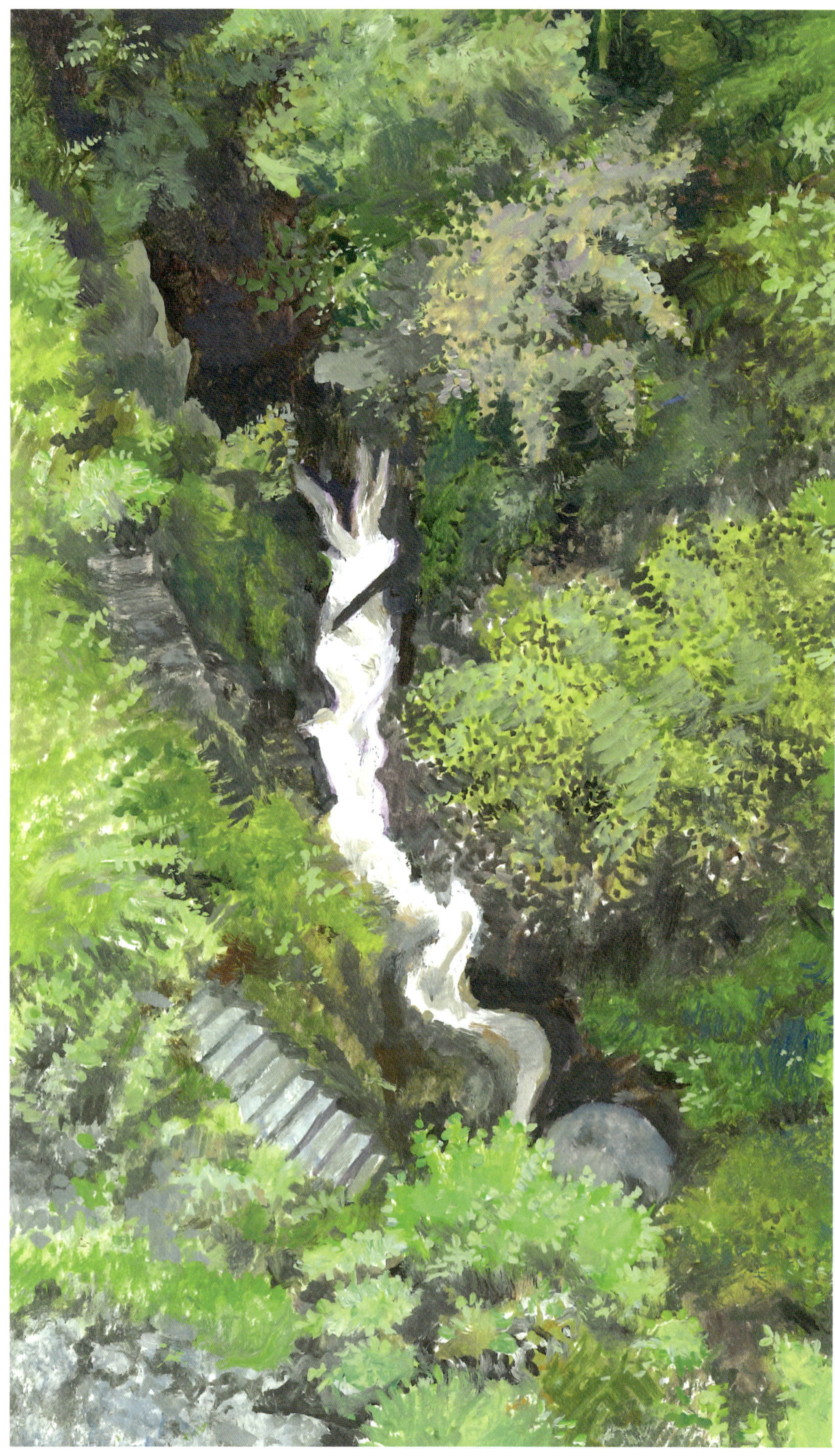

Waterfall at Devil's Bridge

The sight of the tumbling torrents of water far below the Devil's Bridge is dizzy-making.

Nant-y-Moch

We went on to the Nant-y-Moch Reservoir on the western slopes of Pumlumon Fawr. The reservoir's name in English is "Pigs' stream". Wikipedia tells me that, before the dam was built in 1964, the bodies buried in Nant-y-Moch's graveyard were moved to the chapel in nearby Ponterwyd. Even more impressively, cairns built to memorialise the dead and dating from the Iron Age were also moved, stone by stone. We slowly crossed a glorious stretch of moorland rising to a height of 2467 feet in the Cambrian mountains. We revelled in the remote and wild landscape, not meeting another car for an hour and a half. The hillsides were riven by streams hurtling down over boulders. Pockets of bright green grass contrasted with sedge-coloured slopes. Bracken stood out in reddish-brown patches. The road twisted and turned and eventually led over a dam from where we turned westwards to find our way to the coast.

Crags near Nant-y-Moch

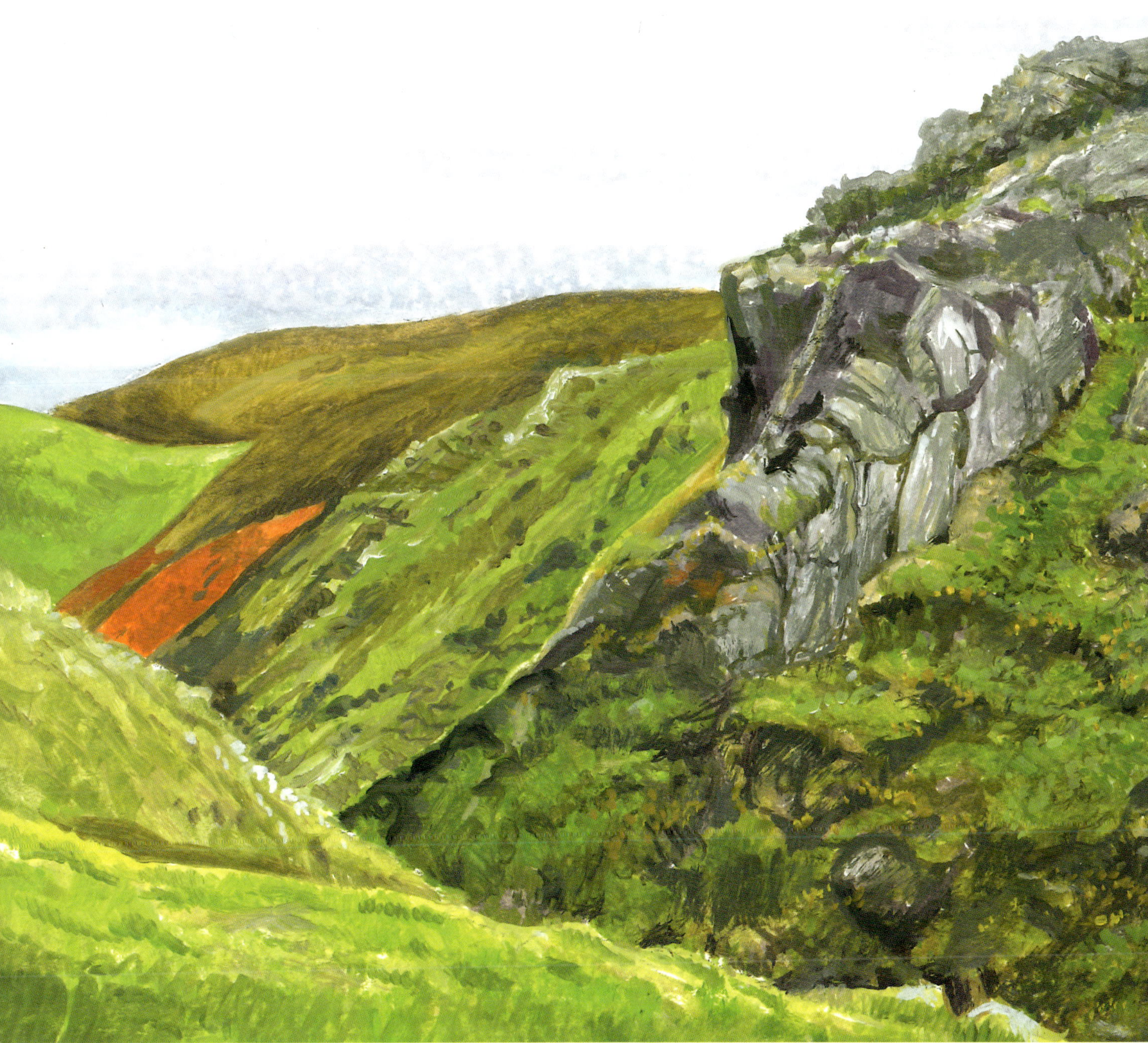

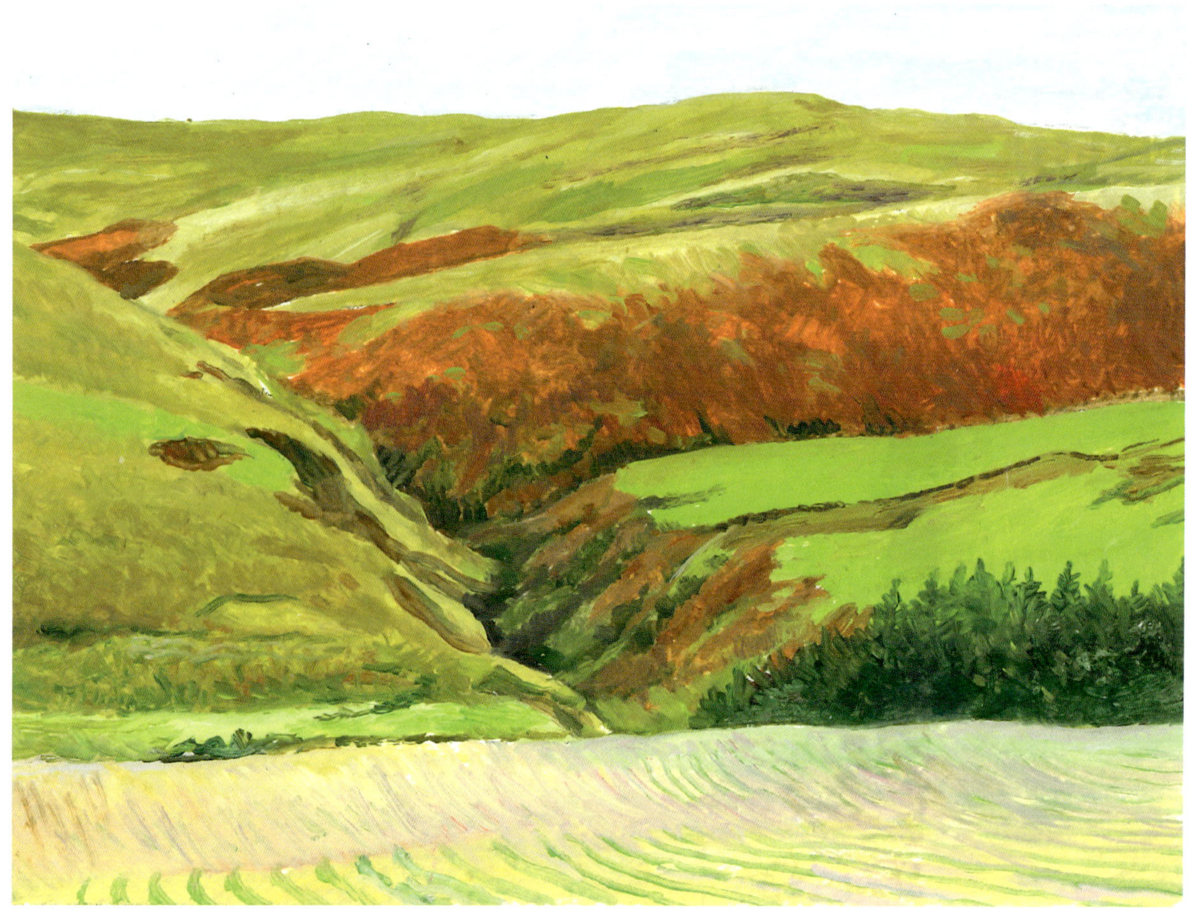

Countryside near Nant-y-Moch
Moorland near Nant-y-Moch reminds me of the Dartmoor of my childhood.

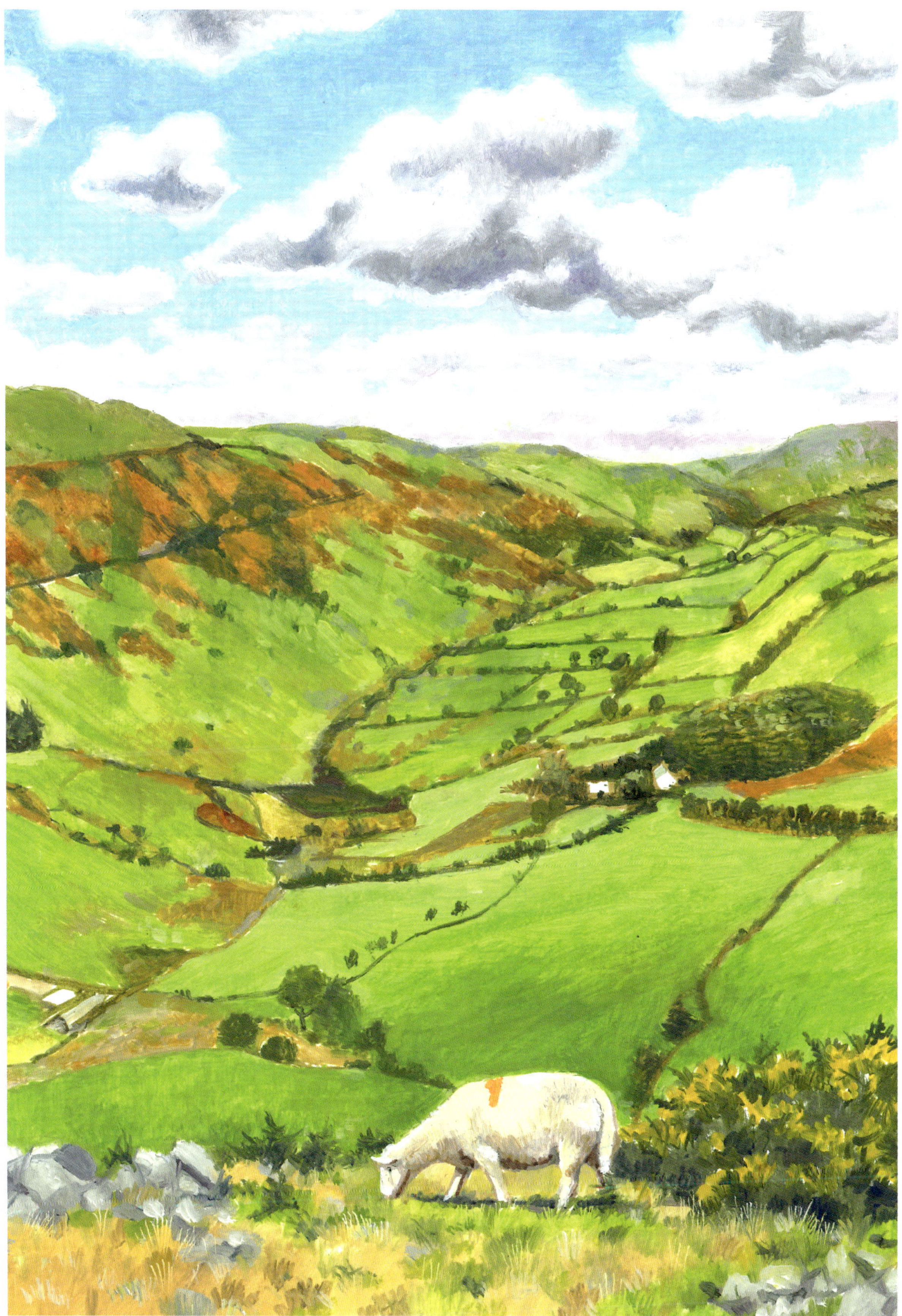

Valley near Nant-y-Moch

Bracken gives this view of the Nant-y-Moch countryside a warm, coppery tinge.

Places built for tourists often deflate into plain ugliness when the tourists are absent. The coast around Borth and northwards to the estuary leading to Machynlleth might have sprung to attractive life with the appearance of happy summer holidaymakers. In September the straggle of bungalows and caravan parks looked abandoned and dismal. We were eager to return to Y Talbot and Tregaron. In the evening, we ate another chef-cooked meal as we picked up the never-dropped threads with Jennie. We've been friends for fifty-two years. As readers will know from their own experience, long-term friendships have a quality all their own.

The following day Jennie left after breakfast. A ruined abbey with a strange name was at the top of our list of places to visit. Strata Florida lies not far from Tregaron. Wikipedia tells me that the name is the Romanisation of the Welsh Ystrad Fflur, 'Vale of Fflur'; the Welsh word ystrad being synonymous with dale or valley, while Fflur is the name of the nearby river. The word sounds like the French word for flower – fleur. Flower Valley, then. The abbey was founded in 1164 by Cistercian monks. Today the ruins make a kind of ground plan of the one-time abbey and contain within its bounds a profound peace and quiet. There was one other couple contemplating the abbey's past while a robin sang to the accompaniment of chaffinches. The birdsong served to emphasise the prevailing silence. Religious ruins hold this kind of intense quiet within their stones. Next door to the abbey lies the graveyard of a more modern church. Rows of identical, shiny black headstones intrigued me. A noticeboard held the information that, in the area's mining past, most miners couldn't afford decent burials. A more recent philanthropist funded their re-burial in graves marked by standardised stones.

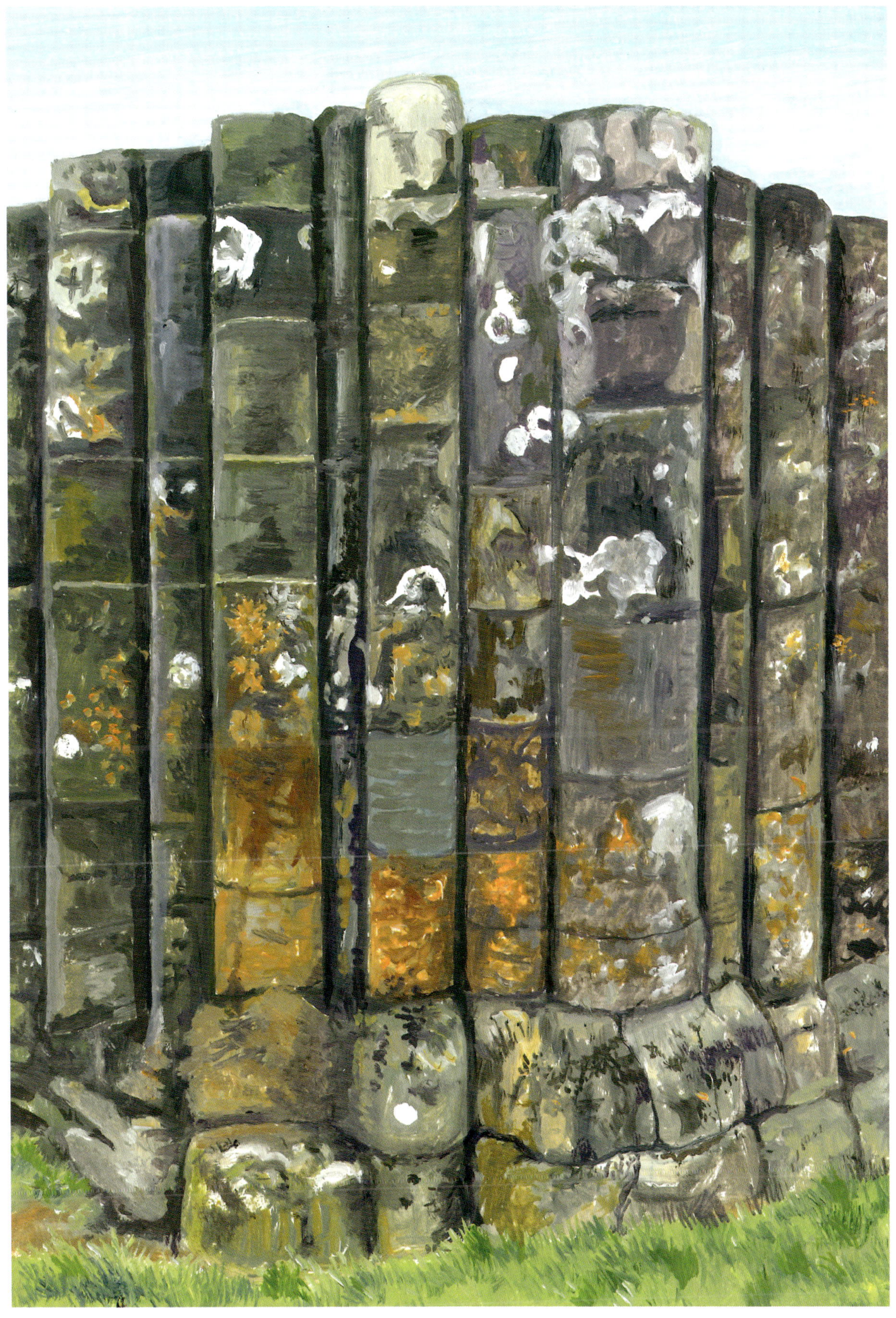

Ruined column, Strata Florida

Peter was attracted by the patterns created by lichen on this broken column at Strata Florida.

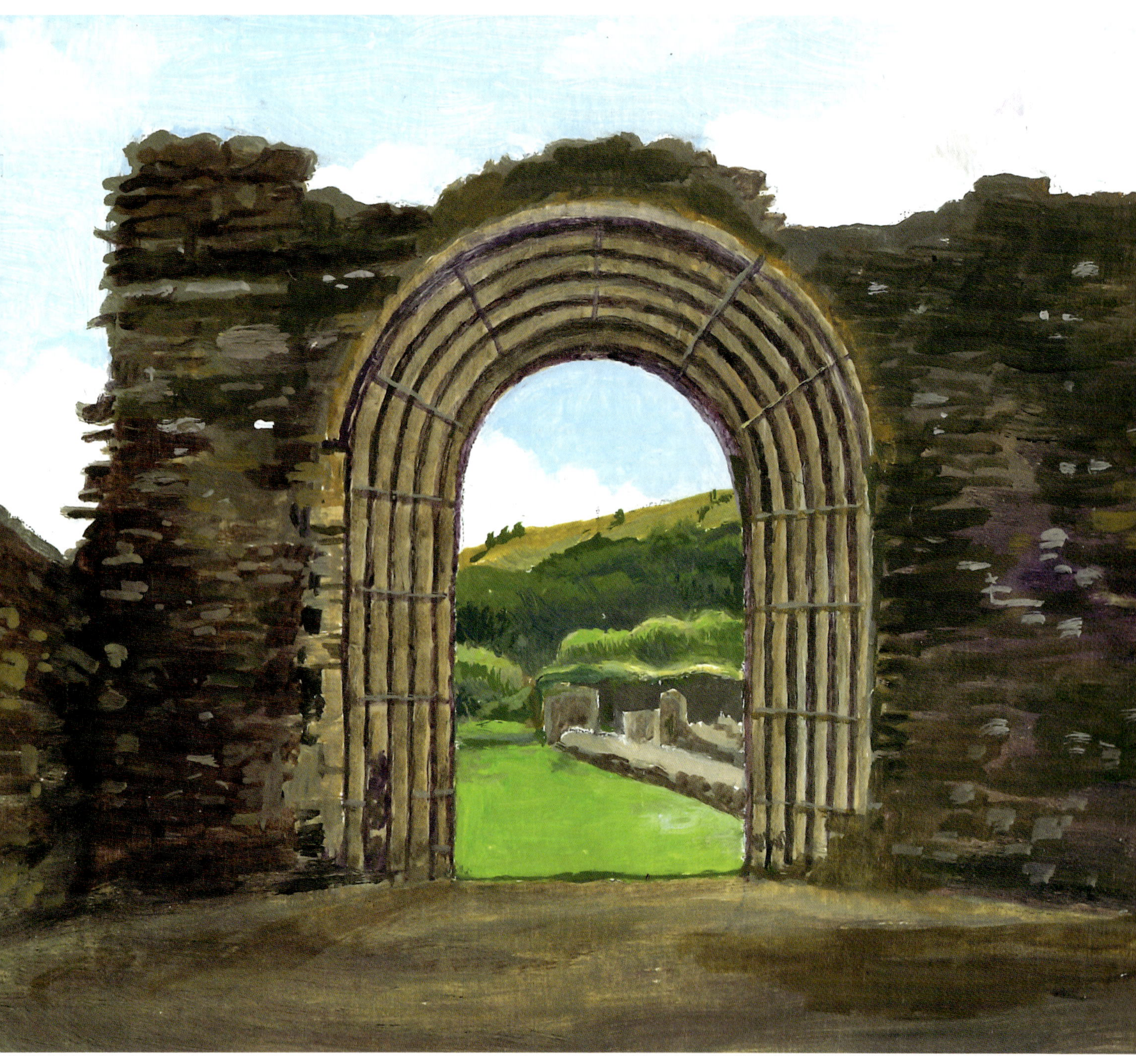

Strata Florida arch

Not only the flowery name of this ruined abbey is graceful but so is its architecture.

Ynys Hir

We returned to Devil's Bridge for another look and another hot drink in the tea rooms – very welcome – before turning eastwards towards Llangurig. We planned to retrace the route we'd taken in July when we met the Buddhist monks at the lead mine at the southern end of Llyn Clywedog reservoir. Perhaps we were paying for the good time we'd had laughing and talking with Jennie the evening before. I, as map-reader, failed to spot the turning for the reservoir and we found ourselves joining the A470 where we headed north-west towards Machynlleth.

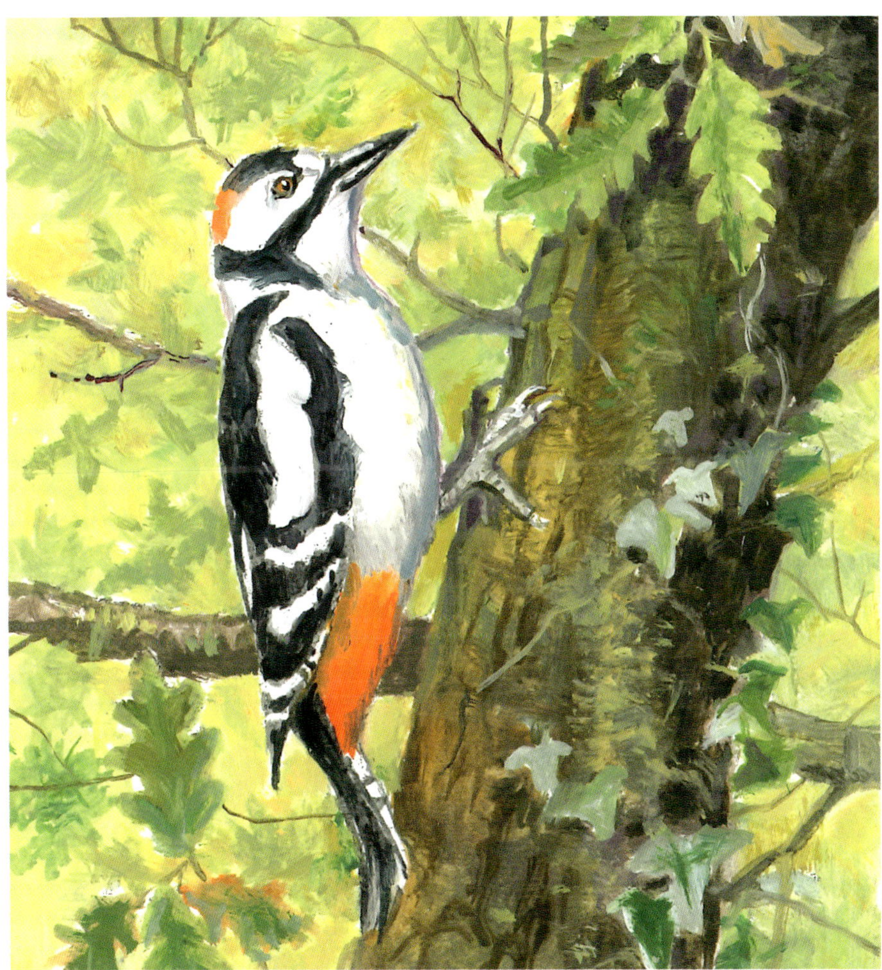

Great spotted woodpecker
Great spotted woodpecker seen at Ynys Hir RSPB reserve.

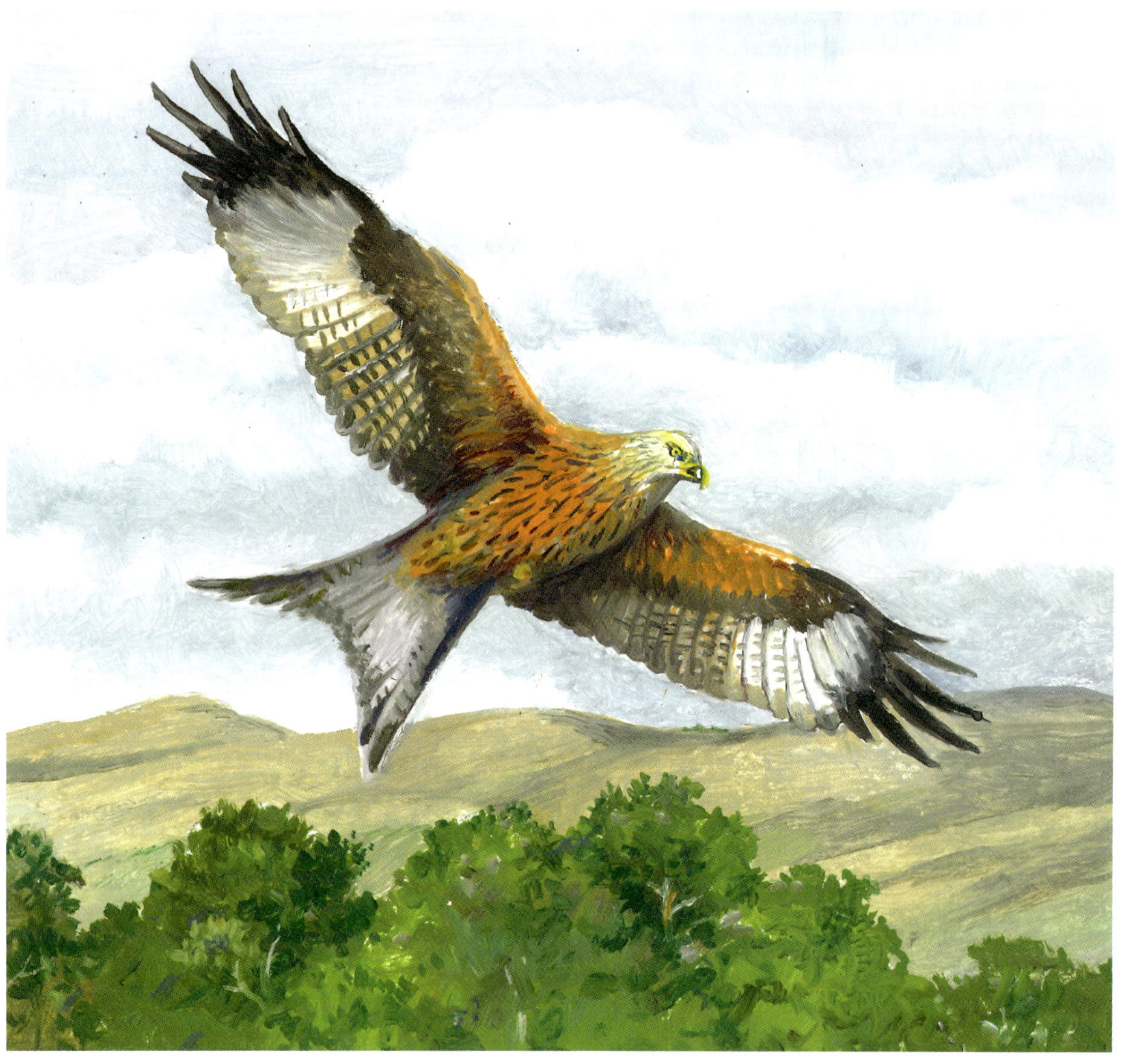

Kite

Not so long ago, a Kite was a rare sight. Brought back by breeding and feeding centres, it is now common.

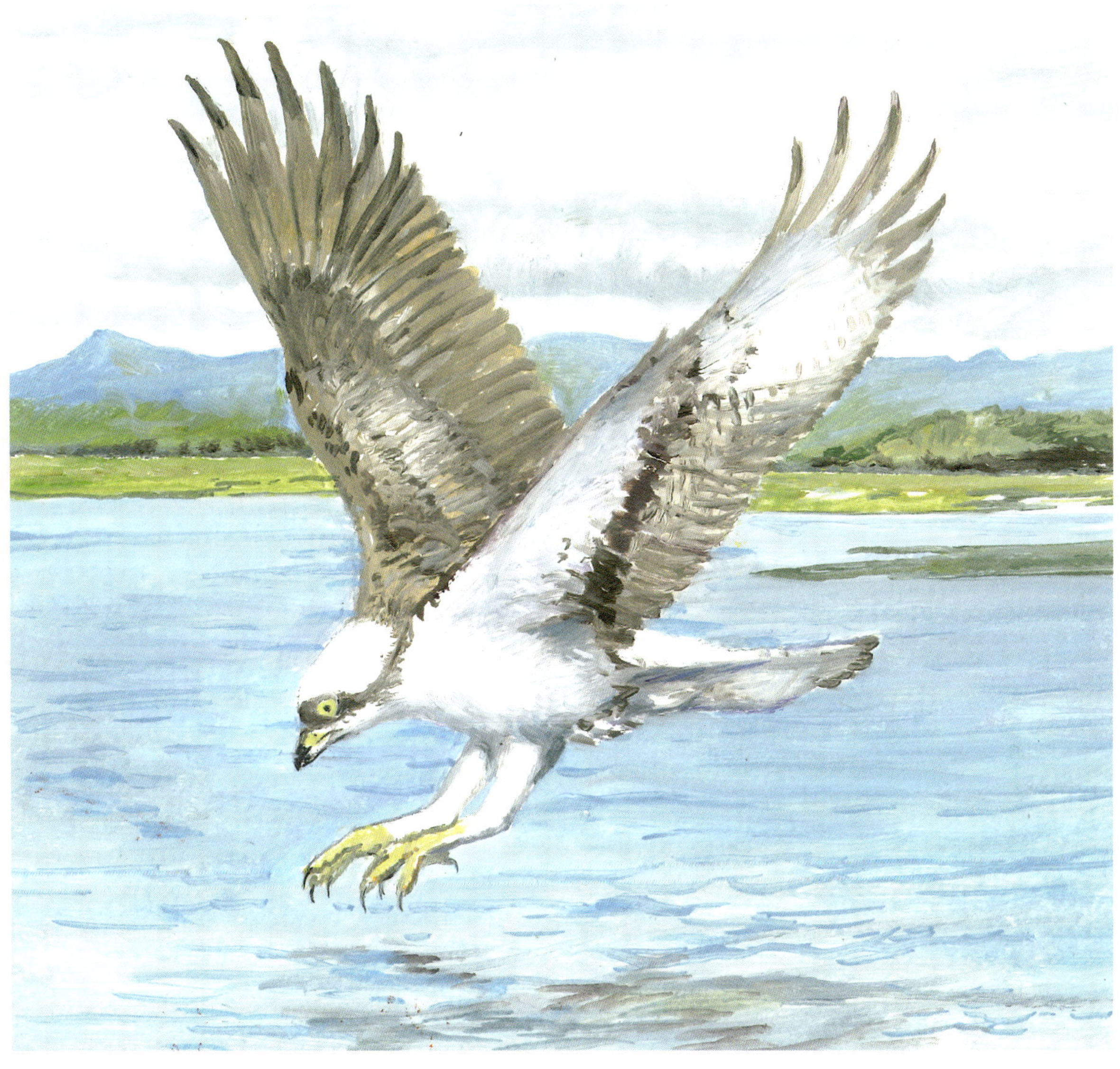

Osprey

Two cameras were set up by Natural Resources Wales to monitor an osprey nest at Llyn Clywedog. The fascinating, livestream footage can be seen on YouTube.

Missed targets might have to be the title of our book. We failed to visit a watermill at Furnace. We just caught sight of its enormous wheel on the side of a building as we drove past without any chance of stopping. But we did manage to visit the RSPB reserve at Ynys Hir. In the past Peter had illustrated a book titled *Birdwatchers' Diary*, written by Roger Lovegrove who was the head of the RSPB of Wales at the time. Beverley, the helpful guide on duty at Ynys Hir, had worked for him. Did this connection influence her view of our fitness, I wonder. She was confident in our ability to follow the blue trail through the woods. Off we set. By

Industrial ruins, in the area north of the Elan Valley

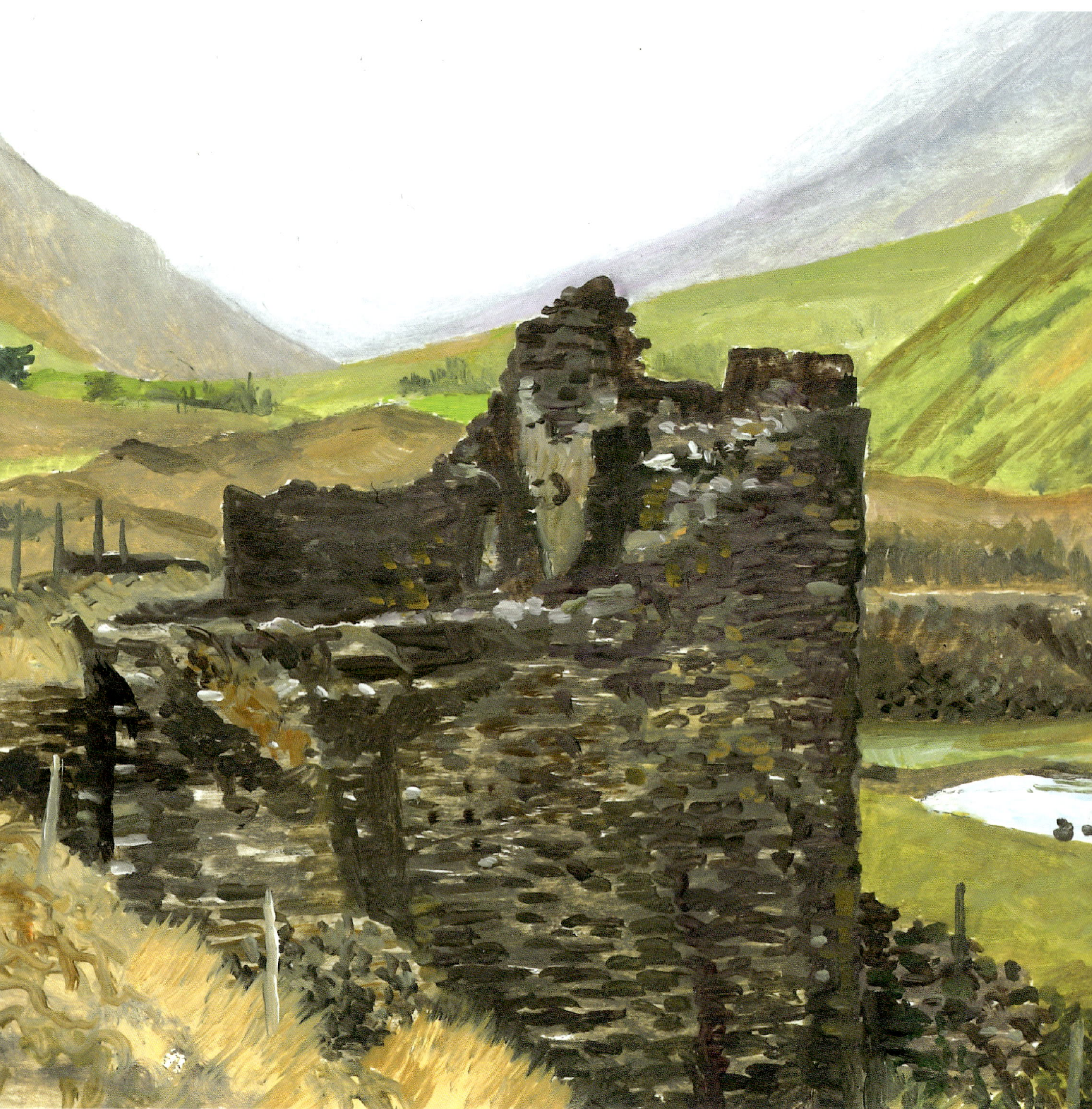

the time we reached a wide expanse of boggy marsh bordering the estuary we had lost any confidence in our ability to go an inch further. We returned to chat with the only other visitors, a couple from Swansea who were typical of the very many who explore the country in a leisurely fashion now they are early retirees. They talked enthusiastically of the red squirrels they had watched feeding in the middle of an Anglesey nature reserve, a special sight we'd missed. But we can't cover everything, we tell ourselves. We don't discover our limitations until our limitations interfere with our plans.

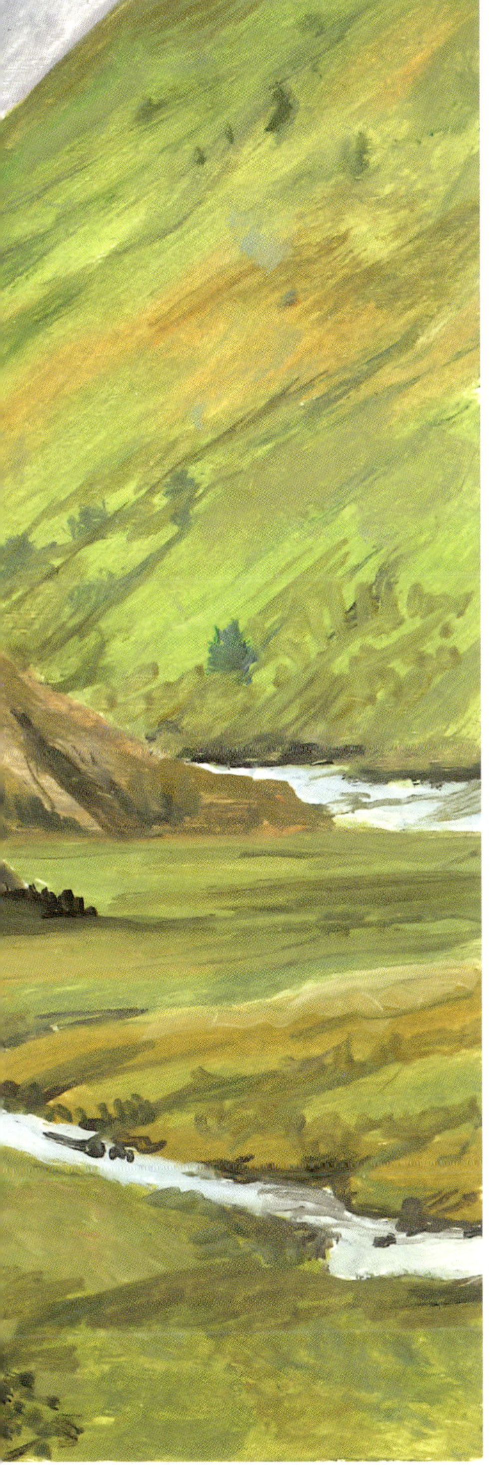

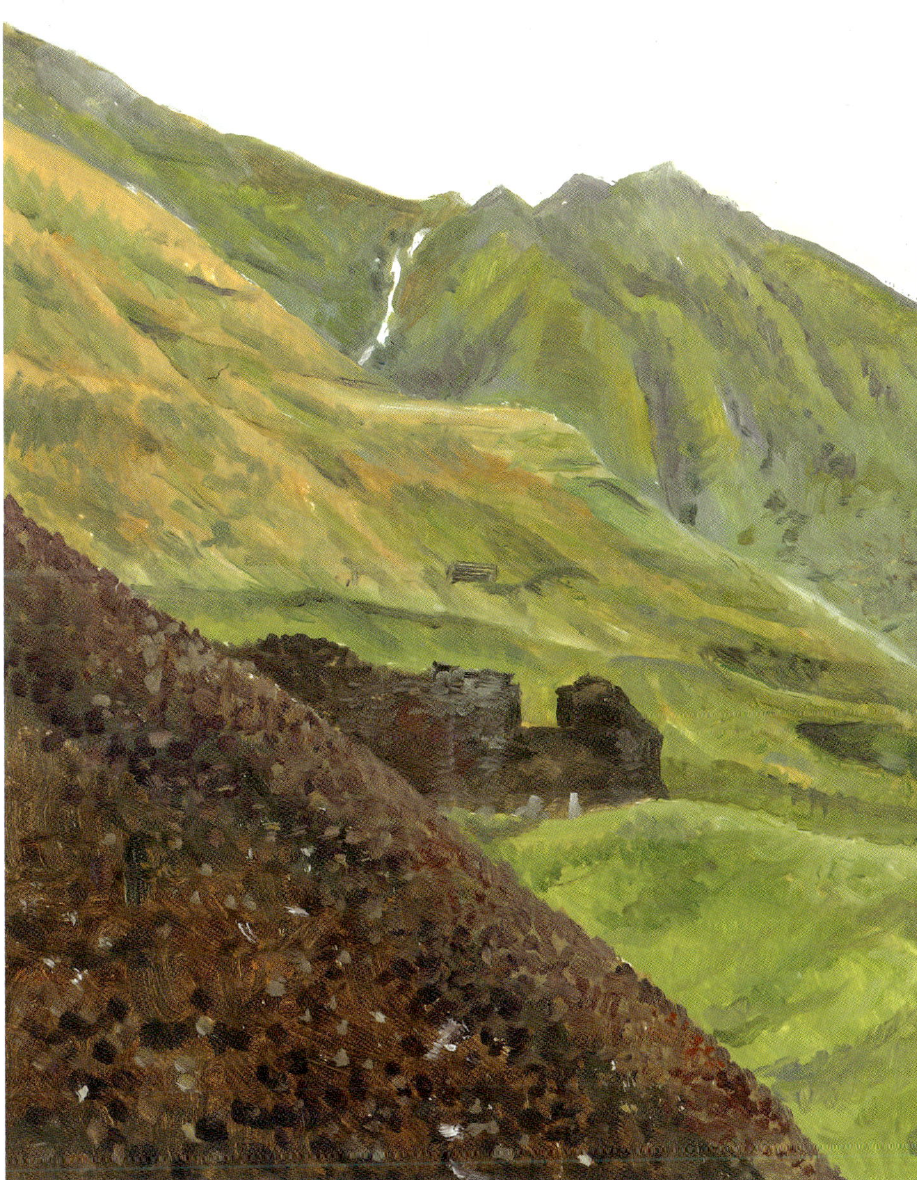

Industrial ruins
Signs of past industry litter the hillsides.

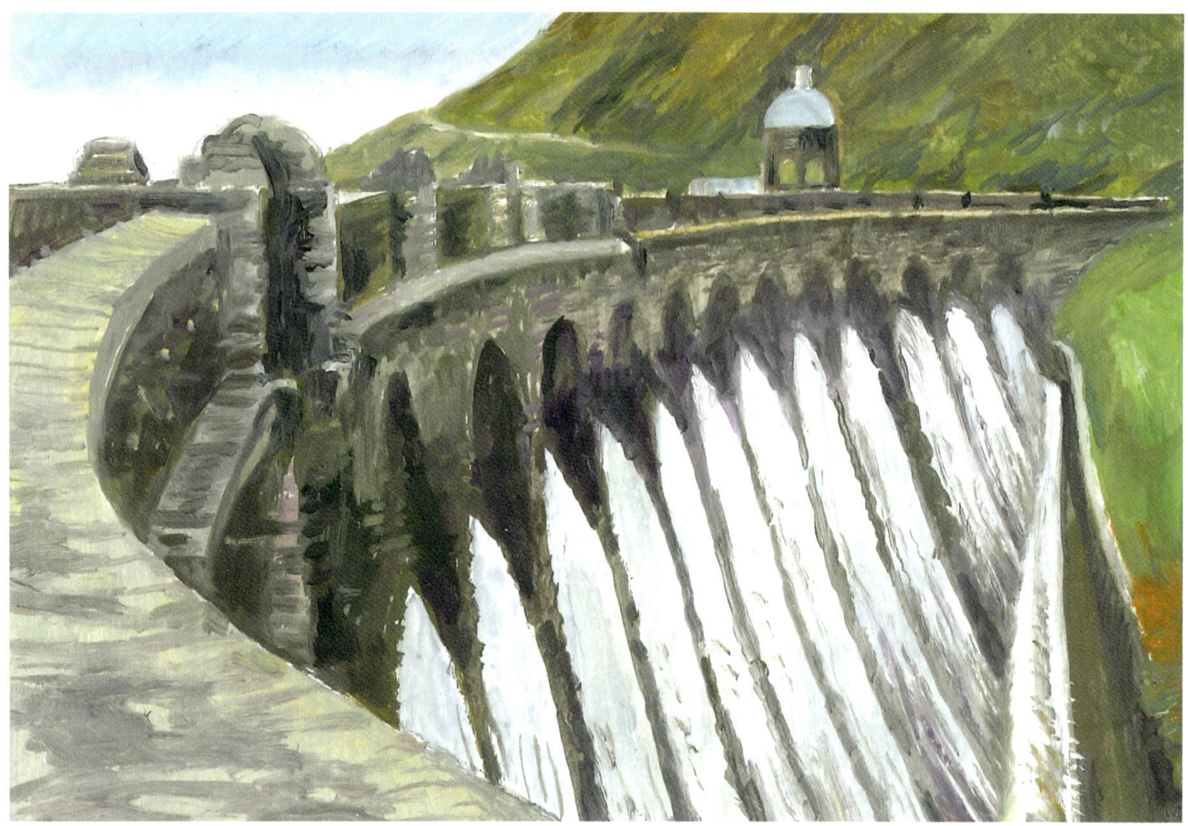

Elan Valley dam

The Elan Valley is a 70 square-mile area of lake and countryside, much of it designated an SSSI, a site of special scientific interest.

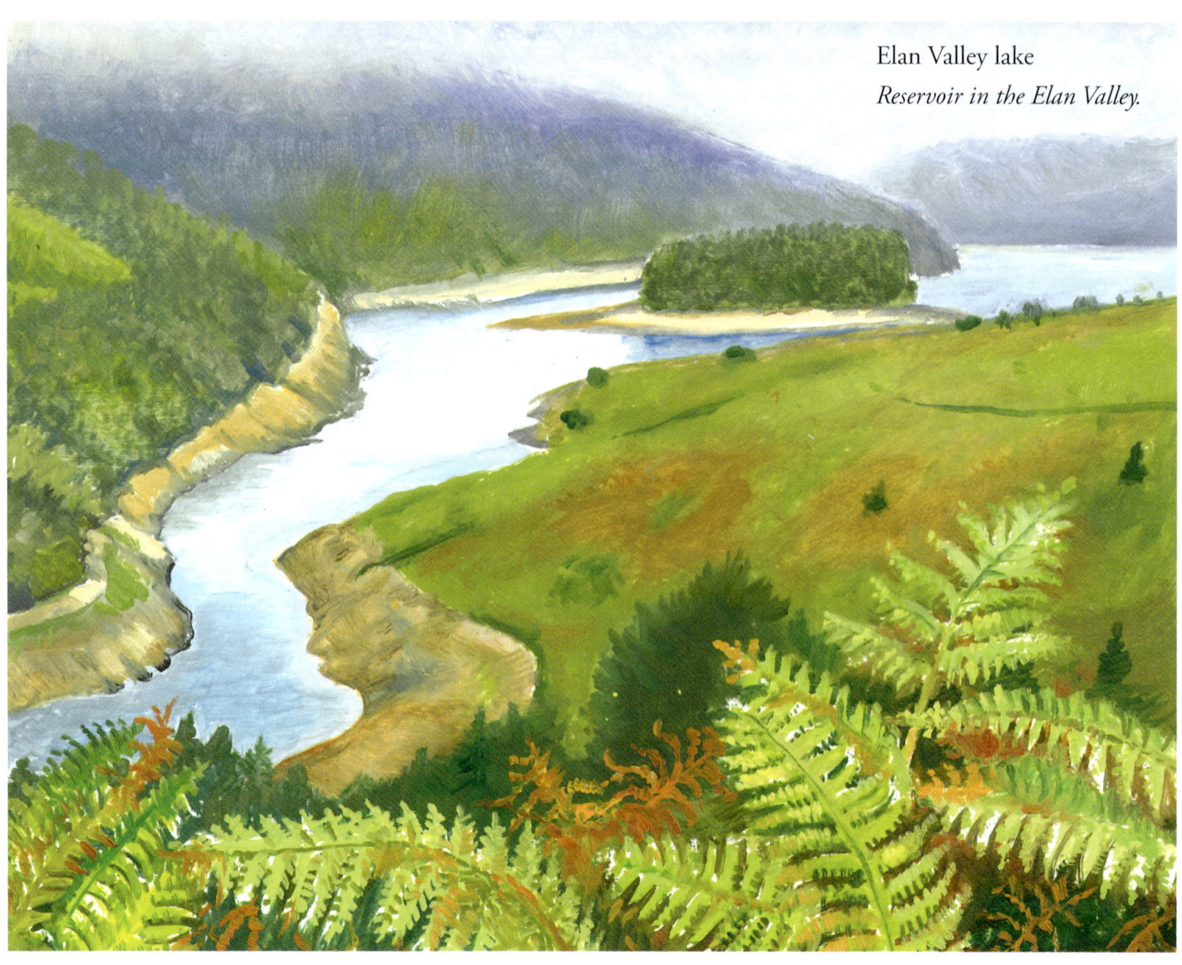

Elan Valley lake

Reservoir in the Elan Valley.

Our plans for the next day were easily carried out. First, we drove through a high, long valley bounded by debris-strewn hills. A noticeboard in a parking area opposite a lone pottery gave information. This high glen is known as the central ore mining valley. Here, minerals of various kinds were mined over centuries dating back to the Iron age. How did the minerals become part of the rock strata? Meteorites containing gases that solidified into minerals hit Earth and left deposits of lead, gold, silver, copper and who knows what other substances that humans could mine and fashion into artefacts for use and decoration. Have I got this right? Should I become a geologist before daring to present information? The potter in the pottery opposite the parking would do a far better job. I didn't stay in the pottery to listen to whatever he wanted to tell me but tried to read the noticeboard in the parking lay-by through a veil of hair blown across my eyes.

The countryside was wreathed in atmospheric low cloud. The fine weather was being blown away in the path of a low front heading in from the Atlantic. In the Elan Valley we kept stopping to take in the stunning views and weirdly wonderful light effects. Wales is the place to appreciate the ever-changing nature of a temperate climate. Do the 16 million Welsh who live in other parts of the world hanker for a mild, damp day and verdant, green grass?

Rain started to fall as we ate our picnic in the car park of Erwood's railway station café. It marked a fitting end to our seven months of Welsh travels in almost continuous sunshine. Yet there was one more missed target to try and fill in. In all our visits to Wales we had barely spotted a single kite. On the way home we stopped in Talgarth as Jennie had told us that this was the place to see them. Don't bother with kite-feeding centres, she said. You can see them at any time hovering over the butcher's shop in town. Correct! Here's Peter's painting to prove it.

Kites over Talgarth

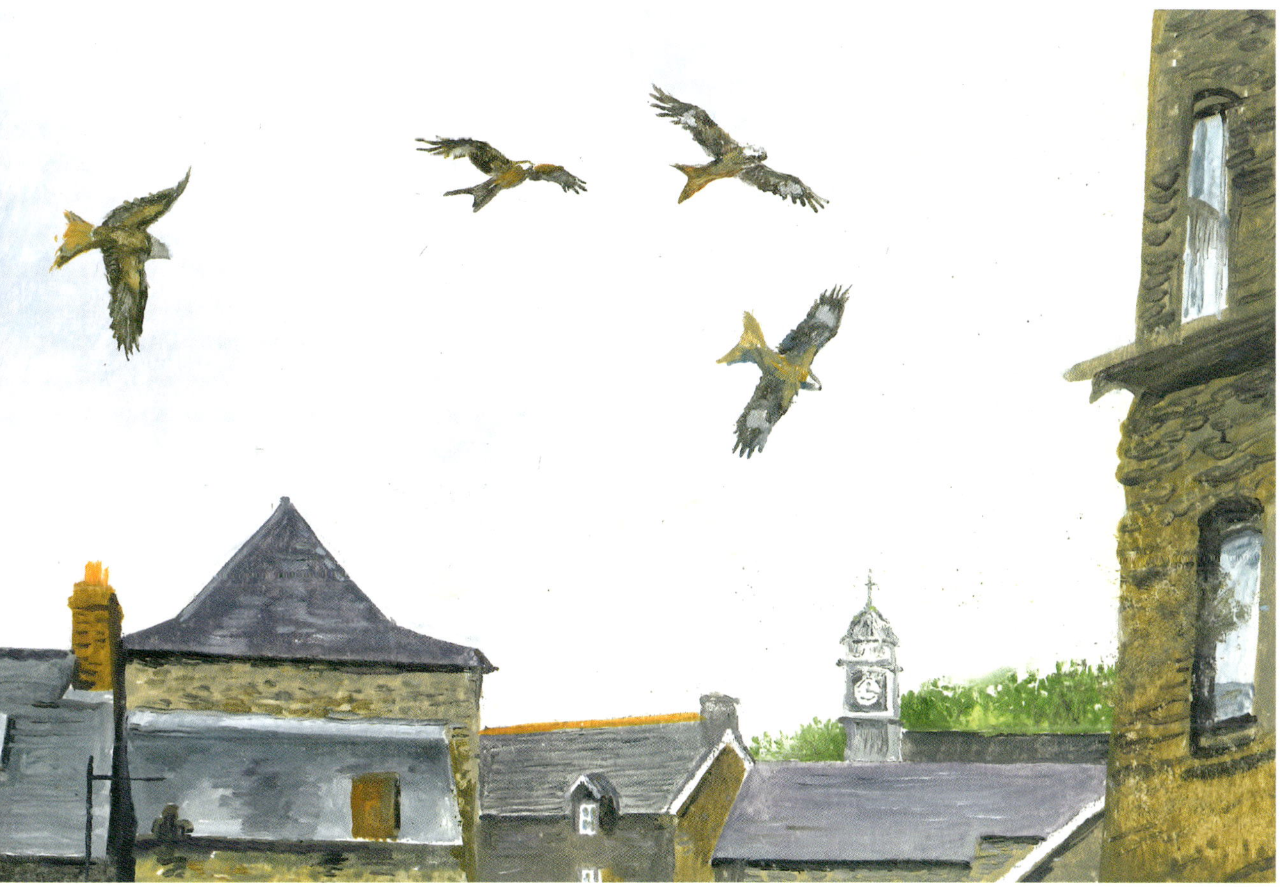

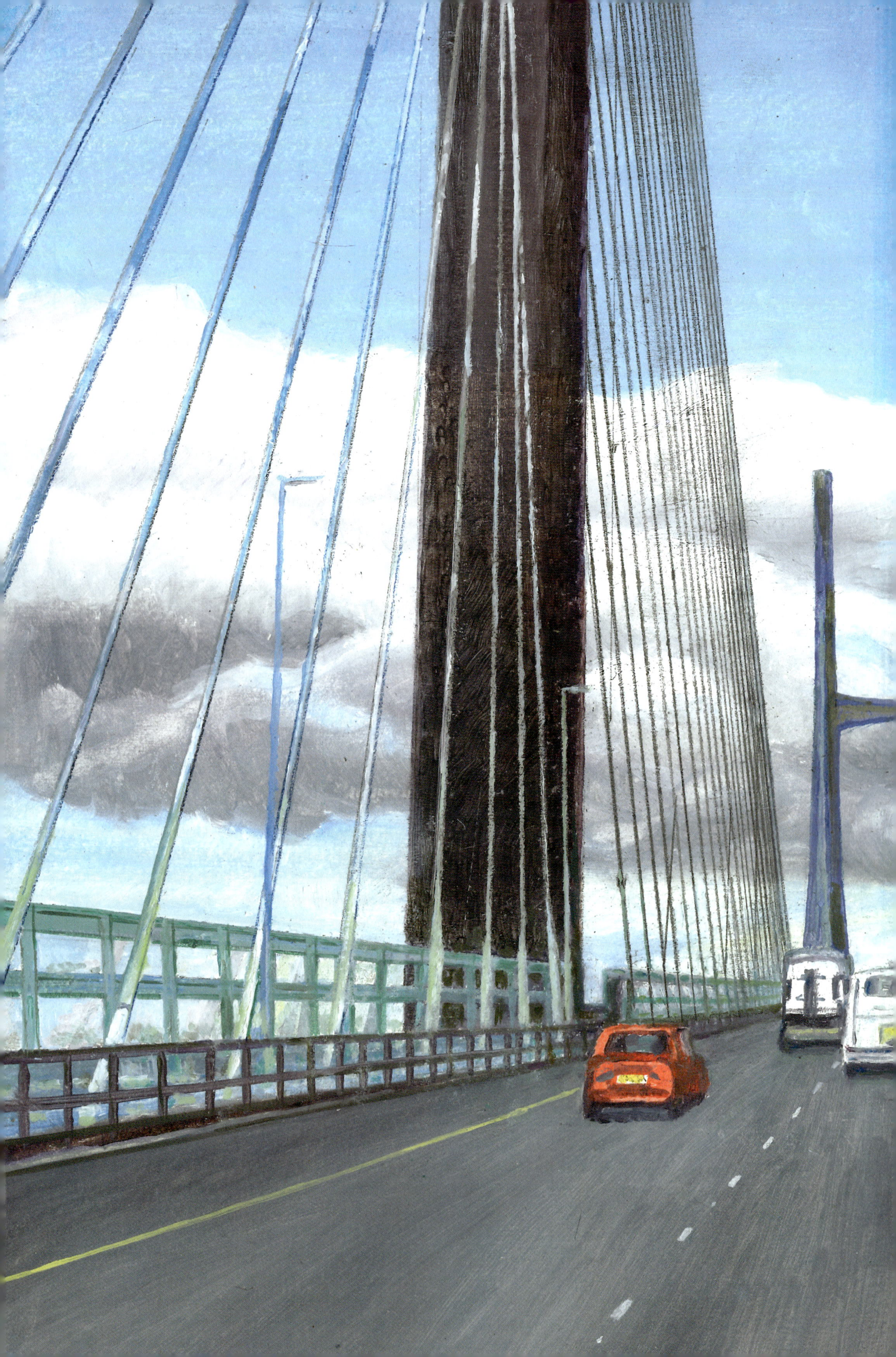

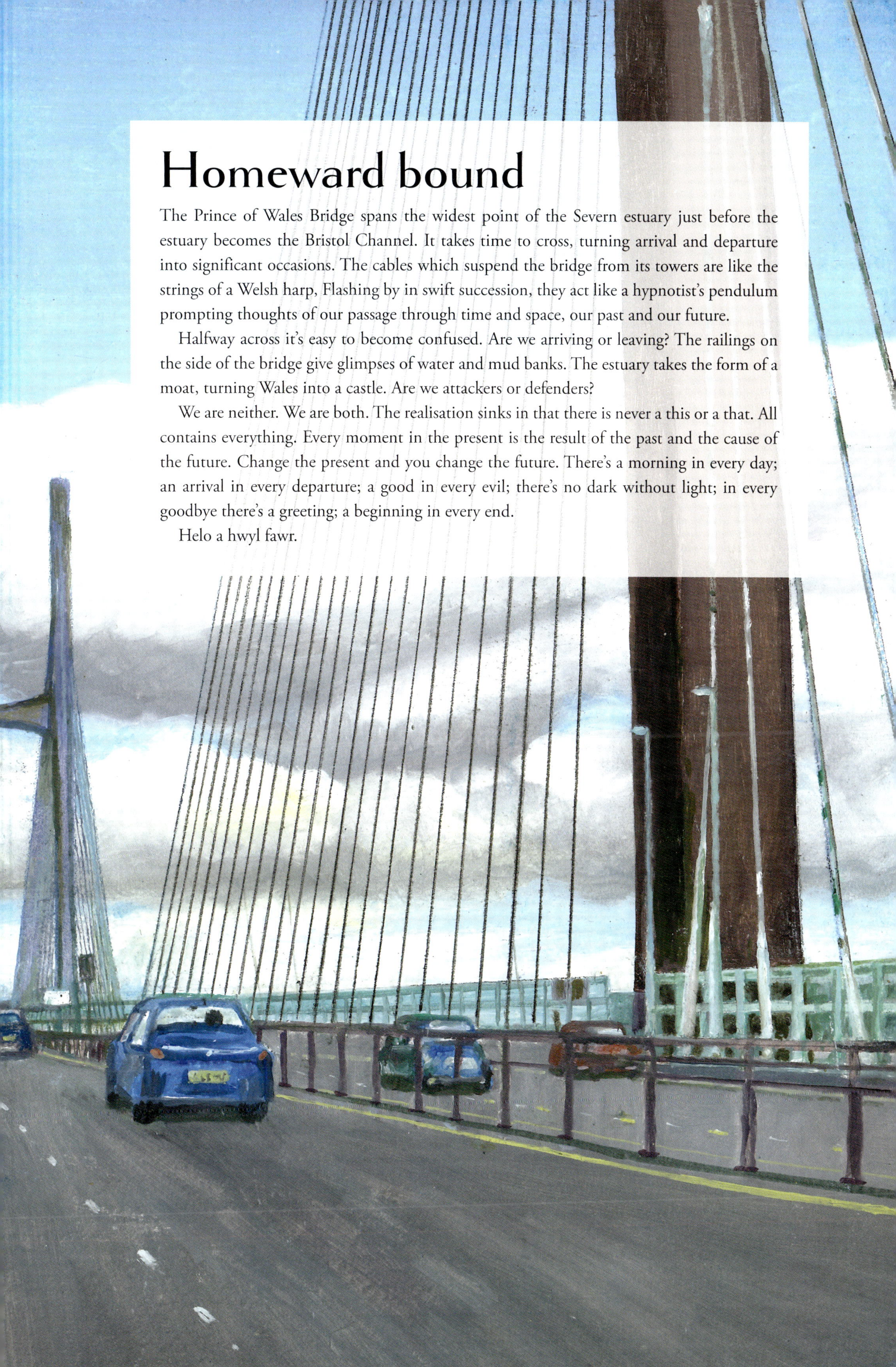

Homeward bound

The Prince of Wales Bridge spans the widest point of the Severn estuary just before the estuary becomes the Bristol Channel. It takes time to cross, turning arrival and departure into significant occasions. The cables which suspend the bridge from its towers are like the strings of a Welsh harp, Flashing by in swift succession, they act like a hypnotist's pendulum prompting thoughts of our passage through time and space, our past and our future.

Halfway across it's easy to become confused. Are we arriving or leaving? The railings on the side of the bridge give glimpses of water and mud banks. The estuary takes the form of a moat, turning Wales into a castle. Are we attackers or defenders?

We are neither. We are both. The realisation sinks in that there is never a this or a that. All contains everything. Every moment in the present is the result of the past and the cause of the future. Change the present and you change the future. There's a morning in every day; an arrival in every departure; a good in every evil; there's no dark without light; in every goodbye there's a greeting; a beginning in every end.

Helo a hwyl fawr.

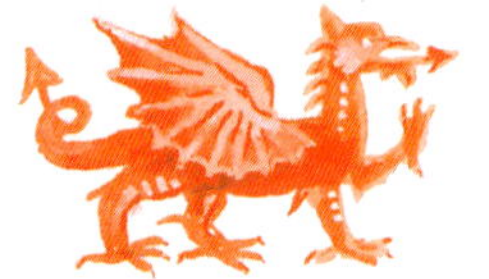